Marriage and Holy Orders

Marriage and Holy Orders

Your Call to Love and Serve

Michael Amodei

foreword by Fr. Joseph M. Champlin

ave maria press  notre dame, indiana

The Subcommittee on the Catechism, United States Conference of Catholic Bishops, has found that this catechetical high school text, copyright 2007, is in conformity with the *Catechism of the Catholic Church* and that it fulfills the requirements of Elective Course D of the *Doctrinal Elements of a Curriculum Framework for the Development of Catechetical Materials for Young People of High School Age.*

Nihil Obstat: The Reverend Michael Heintz
　　　　　　　Censor Liborum

Imprimatur: Most Reverend John M. D'Arcy
　　　　　　　Bishop of Fort Wayne-South Bend
Given at Fort Wayne, Indiana on 5 April 2006.

The *Imprimatur* is an official declaration that a book or pamphlet is free of doctrinal or moral error. No implication is contained therein that those who have granted the Imprimatur agree with its contents, opinions, or statements expressed.

Michael Amodei, author of the Student Text, is Senior Editor of adolescent catechetical materials at Ave Maria Press. He is the project editor on several high school textbooks and the author of *Send Out Your Spirit* (Ave Maria Press, 2003), a Confirmation program for teenagers. He has been a high school theology teacher, parish director of religious education, and youth minister.

Father Joseph Champlin, author of the foreword, is the former rector at the Cathedral of the Immaculate Conception in his home diocese of Syracuse. He has traveled more than two million miles lecturing in the United States and abroad on pastoral subjects. Father Champlin has written more than fifty books, including the best-selling marriage preparation program *Together for Life.*

Scripture texts in this work are taken from the *New American Bible with Revised New Testament and Revised Psalms.*
©1991, 1986, 1970 confraternity of Christian Doctrine, Washington, D.C., and are used by permission of the copyright owner. All rights reserved. No part of the *New American Bible* may be reproduced without permission of the copyright owner.

English translation of the *Catechism of the Catholic Church* for the United States of America copyright © 1994, United States Catholic Conference, Inc.— Libreria Editrice Vaticana. Used with permission.

Founded in 1865, Ave Maria Press is a ministry of the United States Province of Holy Cross.

www.avemariapress.com

ISBN-10 1-59471-041-4　　ISBN-13 978-1-59471-041-4

Project Editor: Robert Hamma

Cover and text design: Katherine Robinson Coleman

Cover Photos: top row from left: Thinkstock (3 images); middle row from left: Corbis, Holy Cross Archives; bottom row from left: Bill Wittman, Thinkstock, Superstock.

Illustrations: Julie Lonneman 46, 50, 80, 108, 125, 158, 210, 214, 265, 290.

Photo credits: *Agnus Images* 120, 121. *Associated Press* 232, 236 (2 photos), 237. 247, 248, 257, 258, 260, 263, 270, 272, 275, 315, 332. *Art Resource* 58 Victoria & Albert Museum, London / Art Resource, NY. *Corbis* 50, 51, 54, 56, 111, 156, 203, 238, 241-243, 283, 315. *Lighthouse Imaging* 42, 106, 216. Holy Cross Archives 240, 267. *Northwind Picture Archives* 208, 211, 219, 221, 298. *Superstock* 26, 34, 35, 78, 90, 94, 97, 109, 132, 160, 176 205, 284. *Veer* 19, 115, 126, 230, 231. Permission from the family of Catherine de Hueck Doherty 166-167, Kathy Coleman 169, Permission from the family of Gigi McMillan 65, Annie Pollard 168, Bill Wittman 57, 61, 62, 122, 128, 157, 207, 233, 266.

Printed and bound in the United States of America.

Engaging Minds, Hearts, and Hands

In this text, you will find:

 research activities and reading assignment to promote further knowledge about what each Christian vocation entails.

 Scripture readings and prayer reflections to help discern a particular vocation.

 service applications that encourage you to begin to practice the mission of the Christian vocation.

contents

fore**word**

On that terrible 9/11 day, when terrorists controlled airplanes, brought down the Twin Towers, smashed into the Pentagon, and were forced to a crash landing in Pennsylvania, most Americans reacted in identical fashion. They immediately sought to connect with the persons closest to them—spouses, children, parents, relatives, and friends. For at least a short period of time, people in the United States placed a higher priority on relationships than usual.

This textbook, *Marriage and Holy Orders: Your Call to Love and Service*, following the example and words of Jesus, centers upon that topic—relationships with God, others, and the world around us.

Christ's teachings guide us along the path to perfection in these relationships with a reminder of the two great commandments, love of God and love of neighbor, but he also calls us to even greater heights in his teachings of the Beatitudes, the necessity for forgiveness, and the importance of responding to any person in need.

The challenge of perfection is given to every person, regardless of his or her age or state in life. Some of you will, for various reasons, never marry. Single persons are free to be either self-giving or self-seeking. Still, as Pope John Paul II often stated, the human heart will not be content unless it is self-giving.

Most of you will marry, ministering to your spouse in the Sacrament of Matrimony, thus receiving special graces from God to develop a rich relationship with one another and to become model parents.

Over the past dozen years, I have celebrated hundreds of weddings. During their preparation, I asked the engaged couples why they wished to marry. Their universal response was friendship:

"He is my best friend." "And she is mine." That great start to a marriage relationship will, with God's help, grow through mutual giving, open communication, and ready forgiveness.

Recently I visited three couples, each married for about five years, and each with two children under three years of age. The joy that the little ones—the fruit of the love of husband and wife—have brought these couples was obvious. As parents, they can likewise count on God's grace to assist them in becoming the first and best teachers of their children in the ways of faith.

More than a half-century ago, I received the Sacrament of Holy Orders at my ordination to the Roman Catholic priesthood. It has been an incredibly rich and rewarding life—preaching and teaching, celebrating Mass and the other sacraments, leading and caring for God's people.

When my treatable, but incurable, rare form of cancer recently became public, I soon received more than 2,500 letters and cards of love, prayers, and support. Many of the people specifically mentioned ways in which I had helped them in the past as a priest—some citing incidents which took place more than three decades earlier! Few persons in other professions have their life's work so uniquely remembered and affirmed.

As you work through this text and course, keep in mind that God's call to love and serve others is essentially the same for all, whether you are a single person, religious, married, or ordained. My prayers and best wishes for success go out to you.

FATHER JOSEPH CHAMPLIN
Priest of the Diocese of Syracuse
Author of *Together for Life*,
which has been used by over nine million couples
to prepare for their Catholic wedding

✦ Look Back, Look Ahead

Since you probably don't remember, imagine yourself at nine months old.

Wearing only a diaper, you are sitting in a high chair waiting for your dinner. Here it comes! Mom puts on the bib to cover your tummy and offers you a spoonful of carrots, then a spoonful of ham. Both of these delicacies come from a jar. Yum!

Your meal nearly finished, you keep smacking your lips. You want some more. Mom thinks that's enough, but Dad comes through for you. He always does. He returns from the freezer with a container of chocolate ice cream. In spite of Mom's protests, he gives you a few tastes. Now you don't just smack your lips. You literally squeal with pleasure.

Dad and Mom both are enthralled with your excitement. They are enthralled with you, period. The love they have for you, and you for them, just oozes from this little scene in the kitchen.

Most parents would do just about anything for their children. You probably already know and experience that on a regular basis. Nowadays, it's not spoonfuls of baby food your parents are offering, but rather support at your games or activities, advice on your academics, and rules for your social life. Not to mention continuing to provide you with food, clothing, shelter—and school tuition.

If you ask parents why they love their children in such a boundless way and what they expect from the years of ongoing care for their children, most are able to articulate in some way that they "only want what's best for them." Delving further, you might find that what a parent means by "what's best" is very similar to the designs that God, too, has for each person—that he or she achieve lasting peace, joy, happiness, and love.

Wanting "what is best" for another is the essence of being a husband, wife, mother, or father. Not that an individual's dreams, goals, and personal happiness are completely overlooked, but the real pleasure of a marriage and family life comes when each member is at the service of the others.

The relationship between a man who receives Holy Orders and the entire People of God is similar. A bishop's, priest's, and deacon's work is to "feed the Church by the word and grace of God." His spouse is the Church. He wants "what is best" for everyone: our salvation in Jesus Christ.

This text and course are intended to explore how your personal life's calling, or vocation, is linked with marriage, Holy Orders, and service. These vocations are celebrated with individual sacraments—Matrimony and Holy Orders—called "Sacraments at the Service of Communion" because the focus for those who receive them is on the salvation of others, not of themselves. Salvation is "what is best" for all of us.

You may wonder why it is important to focus so much attention on Marriage and Holy Orders. Approaching the milestone of high school graduation and the start of college is a key time to consider your future life. If you have recently applied, or are about to apply, to college, or are debating an academic major or career, you have experience with the type of discernment that will be necessary as you consider a deeper life's calling.

There is a good chance that you will eventually marry. As the time for marriage moves from remote to proximate, it is important to consider the history, expectations, and blessings of Catholic marriage.

Likewise, the ministerial priesthood is essential to the Church. Bishops, and by extension, priests, extend the line of succession in the Church that is traced to the Apostles. Besides providing governance, bishops and priests minister the sacraments, especially the Eucharist.

Deacons likewise assist at liturgy and serve the needs of the Church in many other ministries. Vocations to Holy Orders are also fostered in Christian families. You may know someone your own age who would make a good priest. If you are male, you may explore this vocation in more depth in the years ahead.

Everyone is called to holiness and happiness. The sacraments of initiation—Baptism, Confirmation, and Eucharist—consecrate us to share the good news of Jesus Christ with everyone. The Sacraments of Matrimony and Holy Orders consecrate in unique ways those who receive them to work toward the salvation of others—spouse, children, or the Church herself.

May God's grace be with you in these exciting but anxious final semesters of high school. May the Holy Spirit guide you along the way of the Lord so that you may forever achieve all that is best for you.

✦ finding the Way

"What are your plans?"

Get used to the question. As the days before high school graduation approach, you will be asked more and more often what you plan to do next.

Do you have an answer in mind? Which of these responses is closest to describing how you might respond:

- "I am choosing between Harvard, Yale, and Princeton."

- "I am going to take a year off school and go to work."

- "I am going to the state college and have already decided on my field of study."

- "I am planning to take a few courses at the community college."

- "I have no clue."

There is little doubt that this time in your life is one of the most anxious and exciting that you will ever experience. Whatever you decide to do after high school graduation, your life will be different than it is now. Your school days won't be governed by homeroom, ringing bells, or horns to separate school periods and daily assignments. Your social life will be different, too. Even if you are not going away to college, some of your friends probably are. Your relationship with your parents is likely to change as well. If you do move away, you will communicate with your mom and dad differently: primarily by phone, e-mail, or instant message. When you come home for holidays and the summer, it may take

some time to re-establish yourself in the rhythm of the family.

Now, back up a bit. What if in answering the question "What are your plans?" you said, "I am going to be a good Catholic." Or, "I am going to be a better disciple of Jesus Christ." If these are goals you have for your life, why not answer these ways? It would surely make for a unique response.

Thomas Merton, a Catholic priest, Trappist monk, and one of the great spiritual writers of the twentieth century, was constantly trying to answer what he would do next with his life. Thomas had lived a Bohemian lifestyle around Europe and the United States as a child. Orphaned at age fifteen, he eventually settled in New York City, where he studied and taught English at Columbia University. With images of Catholicism from his earlier days spent in France, Merton began instruction and was then baptized into the Catholic Church at a parish near Columbia. Even before his Baptism, he felt he had a vocation to the religious life.

Merton decided to make a retreat to the Trappist Abbey of Gethsemani in rural Kentucky. One of his friends warned him as he was leaving, "Don't let them change you." Thomas answered, "It would be a good thing if they changed me."

In 1941, Merton entered the Abbey for good. When he was allowed by his superior to write, Merton was prolific. His autobiography of his spiritual journey, *The Seven Storey Mountain,* with the many twists and turns that led him to Catholicism and the monastery, became a best-seller and brought him lasting renown.

Unit 1 reminds you of your own baptismal call to holiness and happiness. It offers you a plan to discern your life's calling as you are introduced to the vocations of marriage, Holy Orders, consecrated

God Is **Calling You**

religious life, and committed single life. As you approach this new stage in your life, it is important to remember that God is with you. Don't forget this! As you begin your study, pray the words of Thomas Merton's famous prayer:

The Road Ahead

My Lord God,
I have no idea where I am going.
I do not see the road ahead of me.

I cannot know for certain where it will end.
Nor do I really know myself,
and the fact that I think that I am following
your will does not mean that I am actually
    doing so.

But I believe that the desire to please you does in fact please you.
And I hope I have that desire in all that I am doing.
I hope that I will never do anything apart from that desire.
And I know that if I do this, you will lead me by the right road
though I may know nothing about it.

Therefore will I trust you always though I may seem to be lost
and in the shadow of death. I will not fear, for you are ever with me,
and you will never leave me to face my perils alone.

Amen.

chapter**outline**

✦ Be Perfect

Living perfect in a Christian sense *means seeking an intimate, closer relationship with Jesus.*

✦ We Are Created in God's Image

We are unique in all earthly creation, *created to know and love God.*

✦ The Mystery of God's Love

The mystery of our own lives can bring us *peace if situated in the mystery of God's love.*

✦ Our Desire for God

We are made for God, by God *and will not be satisfied until we rest in him.*

✦ Sharing the Divine Life

To share in the divine life *is to participate in the life of the Holy Trinity.*

chapter one

Called to Holiness

"You have heard that it was said, 'You shall love your neighbor and hate your enemy.' But I say to you, love your enemies, and pray for those who persecute you, that you may be children of your heavenly Father, for he makes his sun rise on the bad and the good, and causes rain to fall on the just and unjust."

Matthew 5:43–45

✦ Be Perfect

"What do you mean you 'forgot to take out the trash'?"

"You should never strike out. You should hit the ball every time."

"An A-minus isn't good enough."

Can you imagine a parent, coach, or teacher talking to a kid in these ways? Our sensibilities would be challenged. Maybe because many of us have grown up in the friendlier world of youth sports where everyone's efforts—good or bad—are met with words like "Nice try. Good game. You'll get 'em next time." Or, in a school where everyone is rewarded publicly (or no one is rewarded) in order not to hurt anyone's feelings.

While the words at the top of the page may seem extreme and we may feel the need to reprimand the adult who would speak them to a child, one thing can be said about these state-ments: they do demand perfection. Unfortunately, perfection is some-thing few of us ever achieve in challenges like hitting a baseball or getting a straight-A report card. But there is one area where perfection is really the only acceptable goal and result. This is the area of Christian holiness.

Jesus himself said as much. In his Sermon on the Mount, Jesus spoke about the requirements for Christian charity, or love. He preached that love for neighbor was not enough. He challenged his disciples to "love your enemies, and pray for those who per-secute you." He further challenged: "So be perfect, just as your heavenly Father is perfect" (Mt 5:44, 48).

"Being holy" can be described as liv-ing a Christ-like life of charity and perfection. Another word for holi-ness is **sanctification**, from which the word "saint" evolved. This type of perfection is different from hitting the ball every time up to bat or wash-ing every spot on the kitchen win-dow or acing every test. Being "perfect" in the Christian sense means seeking a closer, more inti-mate union with Christ. This is accomplished through the **grace** of the sacraments and through service to our neighbor and to our enemy. The way of perfection also involves sharing the cross of Christ.

No Christian is given a free pass to avoid this challenge of perfection and the call to holiness. The challenge isn't reserved for the official saints of the Church, nor is it only for priests or nuns. Older, grandparent-types don't hold exclusive rights to this challenge either. All Christians, no matter their state or walk in life, are called to holiness, called to be saints. The good news is that we don't take up this challenge alone. Jesus said, "I

---

sanctification

A word that means holiness or blessing. To sanctify means to consecrate or set apart for sacred use.

grace

The supernatural gift of God's friendship and life. Grace allows us to respond to God and share in his nature and eternal life.

am the vine, you are the branches. He who abides in me, and I in him, he it is that bears much fruit, for apart from me you can do nothing" (Jn 15:5). Anything that God asks of us he makes possible by his grace.

Chapter 1 traces the origins of the call to holiness and the mystery of God's love that calls humans to share in his life and to pick up and share the cross of Christ. It will help you to learn that, no matter which course you choose for your life in the areas of career and vocation, you have an overarching vocation to Christian holiness or beatitude. It is a call to seek out and ultimately discover a reward of eternal joy lived in the presence of God.

- Recount a time when someone asked you to be perfect. Explain what happened.

✦ We Are Created in God's Image

Holiness is not something that is foreign to human nature. Of all visible creatures (that is, excluding angels), only we are "able to know and love our creator."[1] Not only that, our first parents, Adam and Eve, were created in a state of original holiness and justice in which they were meant to share in the life of God (see *CCC*, 375). God created *everything* for mankind, intending only that we would serve and love God and offer all of creation back to him. God wanted us to use all of his gifts according to his will as a means for reaching eternal destiny.

Needless to say, the gift of original holiness and justice was lost by the sin of Adam. This **Original Sin** was an abuse of the freedom God gave created persons. Freedom is God's precious gift that makes us "capable of loving him and loving one another" (*CCC*, 387). Tempted by the devil, Adam sinned by preferring himself to God. He went against his status as *creature*, trying instead to take on the role of creator. In the original state of holiness, man was destined to be **divinized** by God in glory. After the Original Sin, man would want to be like God, but often lived, in the words of Saint Maximus the Confessor, "without God, before God, and not in accordance with God."

The effect of Original Sin was devastating for Adam and Eve and for all

of humanity. Their disobedience alienated Adam and Eve from God, from each other, from themselves, and from all of God's creation. The effects of Original Sin have harmed all of their descendants through the ages. Original Sin deprives us of the original holiness and justice that God

Original Sin

The first sin of Adam and Eve, in which they disobeyed the Commandment of God, choosing to follow their own will rather than God's will. The effects of Original Sin are shared among humanity ever since.

divinized

In the Christian sense, sharing or partaking in the nature of God.

Augustine Answers Pelagius

In the fifth century, Pelagius, a monk from the British Isles, taught against the doctrine of Original Sin. While he upheld the freedom of the human will—that man was born with the ability to choose or not choose a life of sin—he also taught that human beings could reach God on their own merits.

Saint Augustine had already lived a remarkable life by the time he answered Pelagius. He had resisted his mother Saint Monica's prayers and prodding to be baptized until he was well into adulthood, and he had already spent years studying rhetoric which was opposed to Church teaching. Additionally, he had fathered a child out of wedlock. By the time of his conversion, he was well convinced about the power of divine grace that had allowed him to overcome his sins.

Augustine stressed to Pelagius the absolute necessity of God's grace to free a person from Original Sin and to enable him to reach God. Since the Church believes that grace is first given at Baptism, the corollary, as Augustine taught, was that Baptism was essential for salvation. It was at this time that infant Baptisms became the norm, since parents feared the dangers of a newborn dying while still in Original Sin.

intended for us. Instead, we are born with a human nature, though not fully corrupted, that is:

- wounded,
- ignorant,
- prone to suffering,
- subject to death, and
- inclined to sin.

The doctrine of Original Sin is closely related to the redemption offered by Christ. In Baptism, Original Sin is erased and we are turned back toward God. But the other effects of Original Sin remain. Life is a hard spiritual battle in which we work to choose God and avoid evil in all that we do.

It is helpful to understand the nuances of this battle between good and evil through exploring in more detail God's intentions for us humans, his most prized creations, and the eternal prize that awaits those who are faithful.

"Male and Female He Created Them"

If we are to appreciate the meaning of Christian vocation, it is important to understand the complementary but respective roles of man and woman. Man and woman have been created in perfect equality as human persons, yet in their particular beings as male and female. Both man

and woman are created with the same dignity and in the image of God, though God is neither man nor woman. (God is pure Spirit.) God created man and woman together and for each other. They are to be a community of persons and complementary as masculine and feminine who image God's power and tenderness in different ways.

In marriage, God unites man and woman so that they can celebrate their love and share the gift of life.

In God's plan, man and woman are intended to be stewards of God's resources on the earth. The first creation story of the Book of Genesis concludes:

> God blessed them, saying: "Be fertile and multiply; fill the earth and subdue it. Have dominion over the fish of the sea, the birds of the air, and all the living things that move on the earth." (Gn 1:28)

The state of original holiness and justice was one of intimacy. Adam and Eve each possessed an inner harmony and shared a beautiful harmony with one another, with creation, and with God. This was all lost by the Original Sin.

The *Catechism of the Catholic Church* teaches that where sin abounded, grace abounded all the more: "We must know Christ as the source of grace in order to know Adam as the source of sin" (*CCC*, 388).

Today, one of the ways God's grace is offered to us is in the Sacrament of Matrimony, the loving community of a man and a woman. This love is witnessed concretely in the love between a husband and a wife and likewise experienced by children raised in a Christian family.

Nature Haiku

World like a dewdrop
though it's only a dewdrop
even so, even so.

ISSA

The word haiku refers to a traditional Japanese lyric verse that references an aspect of nature or the four seasons. Use the following rules to write your own haiku focusing on God's creation of the world or an aspect of nature that helps you to meet and know God:

- Choose a topic related to the assignment above.

- The first line of the haiku has exactly five syllables.
  The second line of the haiku has exactly seven syllables.
  The third and final line of the haiku has exactly five syllables.

- Haiku have no rhyming words.

- It doesn't matter how many words are in each line, just how many syllables.

The Unity of Body and Soul

The second creation story says that "the Lord God formed man out of the clay of the ground and blew into his nostrils the breath of life, and so man became a living being" (Gn 2:7). This passage tells us that human beings are created with a body and a soul. The soul is the innermost part of man that makes us spiritual people in the image of God. The spiritual soul is not produced by our human parents. It is created immediately by God and is immortal.

However, the body shares in the dignity and image of God, as well. The body is intended to be a temple of the Holy Spirit. God created the body and it will rise on the last day. For these reasons, we are to regard our bodies as good and honor them.

"Sexuality affects all aspects of the human person in the unity of his body and soul" (*CCC*, 2332). Sexuality does not just mean the sex act. Being sexual means appreciating our identity as either male or female and living our lives as such. Obviously, sexuality is linked to our bodies because we show affection with gestures like handshakes, smiles, hugs, or kisses.

Our sexuality is more than just a series of bodily responses. It is also deeply connected to our passions and emotions. Specifically, it involves our capacity to love and to procreate. In a more general way, it affects our skill at forming friendships and bonds with many other people.

Every person is called to acknowledge his or her sexual identity—remembering that God gives both males and females equal personal dignity. In this acknowledgement of our sexual identity as male or female, we are better able to align our lives toward a good and productive marriage and family life. Even if you personally will never ultimately be married and raise a family, the acknowledgment of the importance of marriage and family life is crucial, because this is where humans are born and all vocations are cultivated.

One of the ways you support marriage and family life at your current age is through the practice of **chastity**. Chastity comes under the virtue of temperance, a cardinal virtue that regulates our attraction to pleasure and helps us use God's created goods in a balanced way.

Chastity helps us control our sexual desires and use them appropriately according to our state in life. It means a successful integration of sexuality within a person that brings about an inner unity of body and soul.

In the Sermon on the Mount, Jesus spoke out against duplicity. He said, "Let your 'Yes' mean 'Yes,' and your 'No' mean 'No'" (Mt 5:37). The type of integrity that Jesus directs us to unifies the powers of our body with those of our soul. Chastity helps us to master our passions and find peace. The alternative is letting ourselves be ruled by our passions and being unhappy.

This outlook contrasts with one that is often practiced today. Today, sex outside of marriage is touted as routine and acceptable. Among teenagers, random and impersonal sexual acts are boasted about, but later regretted. Certainly the popular media—especially in television programming geared to teens and young adults—promotes sex outside of marriage as normal.

Chapter 3 will develop the benefits of the virtue of chastity in more detail. For now, be clear about the teaching of the Church that calls all the baptized to chastity. The basic principle for sexual morality is that God intends sexual intercourse and all actions leading up to it to be shared exclusively by a man and woman in the union of marriage. This union in marriage is a way for a man and woman to imitate in the flesh God's generosity and fruitfulness.

In Union with Christ

Christ calls you to be "perfect as your heavenly Father is perfect." The flip side of this charge is that only in

chastity

The virtue by which a person integrates his or her sexuality into his or her whole self, body, and spirit, according to the vocation or state in life.

union with Jesus can the disciple attain the perfection of charity, or love, which is holiness. There is no way to be holy apart from Jesus Christ.

Union with Christ takes the form of **discipleship**. The word disciple means "follower." As disciples of Christ, our goal is to follow and learn

from Jesus. This relationship is deepened through prayer, participation in the sacraments, and practicing the Christian virtues. Practicing the cardinal virtues of prudence, justice, fortitude, and temperance and the theological virtues faith, hope, and charity deepen our discipleship.

Entering the final years of high school and transitioning to college, career, and vocation is a crucial time for Christian discipleship. You may have occasionally become blasé or inattentive in your relationship with Jesus. To this point, your relationship with Jesus has been mostly rote. For example, you may be in the concluding courses after years of religious formation and education and at a stage where you have tuned out much of the information that is being presented, maybe because you tell yourself "I've learned this many times before."

It is in Christ that our highest calling or most exalted vocation is brought to light. When we believe in Christ we become children of God the Father. This adoption makes us capable of acting rightly and doing good. As the *Catechism* teaches:

> In union with his Savior, the disciple attains the perfection of charity which is holiness. Having matured in grace, the moral life blossoms into eternal life in the glory of heaven. (*CCC*, 1709)

Before examining several Christian vocations in later chapters, this chapter is intended to remind you of and situate you in the mystery of God's love. Hopefully it will awaken a built-in desire to truly know God and share in his divine life. It is in this grace that you can then seek out the Christian beatitude or happiness, which is the goal of eternal life in God's kingdom.

discipleship
From the word "learner," the undertaking of learning and following Jesus Christ.

Running for Christ

Spend some time working out and getting in shape to run a 5K race (3.1 miles). As you train, offer the physical exertion to God. Remember the call of Jesus to "pick up your cross and follow" him. When you feel you can complete the course, check the local newspaper and sign up for a 5K race in your area. Ask family and friends to contribute some money based on your finish time. For example, $5 (thirty-five minutes and above), $10 (twenty-five to thirty-five minutes), $15 (twenty to twenty-five minutes), $20 (below twenty minutes). Collect all of the donations and contribute them to your local parish or a charity that helps those in need.

Would You Be A Saint If You Could?

If you had asked Aloysius Gonzaga the question above, no doubt he would have answered "yes." Born in 1568 to a wealthy family in Italy, Aloysius resisted his father's wishes that he be a great soldier. Growing up, he spent most of his time praying and reading books about the lives of saints. On his summer holidays, he spent his time instructing poor boys in the Catholic catechism. During the winter months, Aloysius began to practice the habits of a monk: he fasted three times a week on bread and water, whipped himself with a dog chain, and rose at midnight to pray on his knees on a stone floor in a room without heat.

Aloysius' father eventually permitted him to enter the Society of Jesus, the Jesuits. It wasn't long before he had a vision in which he knew he would die at a young age. A plague struck Rome in 1591, and Aloysius fell victim to its fever while ministering to the suffering. Eventually, the plague would claim Aloysius. On his death bed, he occasionally whispered the words "Into thy hands," in imitation of Christ. He died between June 20 and 21, 1591. This young man who died at the age of twenty-three was canonized a saint in 1726.

How would you describe the desire of Aloysius Gonzaga? Worthy? Courageous? Strange? Difficult? Impossible? The Church has canonized teenage and young adult saints in every era. What would it take for you to be a saint?

martyrdom

Giving one's life for one's faith. A martyr is willing to die in support of the Christian faith and doctrine.

Certainly, there are many places in the world today where a young Christian may be called to die for his or her faith. **Martyrdom** is a clear path to sainthood. But what if you were to construct a plan to be a saint around the life you are leading now in this time and place. Consider how you might apply the following "ways to become a saint":

1. *Know Jesus*. Yes, really know him. Not the perfunctory kind of relationship that may have crept in since the time of your First Communion. Make an effort to learn about Christ through reading Scripture, reading the lives of saints, and through prayer. Spend some time alone before the Blessed Sacrament.

2. *Forgive Your Enemy*. Don't prolong a grudge. Don't live in hate (or even dislike) over a trivial matter. Seek out a person with whom you have been at odds. Share a gesture of goodwill as a first effort at reconciliation. Eventually, tell the person you are sorry.

3. *Love Others*. You no doubt love your family members and friends. Make an effort to love others. Who are some "others" in your sphere: homeless people in your community, special education students in your school, classmates experiencing family problems, hungry children in another land? Think of some ways you can reach out to these people. Act on these ways.

4. *Show Courage*. Don't always "go with the flow." Assert your independence when it comes to moral living. Avoid promiscuity. Treat your body with respect. Speak about and pray to God in public.

5. *Serve*. There are many opportunities for service at your school or parish. Participate, for sure. Better yet, direct your own service project. For example, get together with some friends and work on a song or skit you can share at a local retirement home or hospital. Call the social director and arrange a date on which you can perform for the guests.

6. *Go to Mass*. Do you know someone who is a "daily Mass-goer," that is, a person who tries to go to Mass on the weekdays besides Sundays? Could this person be you? In addition, participate in a liturgical ministry. Train to be a lector, extraordinary minister of the Eucharist, or altar server. In addition to Mass, celebrate the Sacrament of Penance often.

Finally, pray to a saint to intercede for you on your behalf. Begin with Saint Aloysius Gonzaga, the patron of youth. Pray this prayer of Saint Aloysius to the Blessed Mother:

My Mother

Holy Mary, my Queen,
I recommend myself
to your blessed protection and
special keeping,
and to the bosom of your mercy,
today and every day and
at the hour of my death.
My soul and my body I recommend to you.
I entrust to you my hope
and consolation,
my distress and my misery,
my life and its termination.
Through your most holy intercession
and through your merits
may all my actions
be directed according to your will
and that of your Son.
Amen.

studyquestions

1. What were God's first intentions for man?

2. Name the effects of Original Sin.

3. Explain the respective roles God intends for man and woman.

4. How do we share in the dignity and image of God in body and soul?

5. In what ways can practicing chastity now help you to support marriage and family life?

6. How is the experience of Christian discipleship practiced?

journaldiscussion

- What does God love about you?

- Write a profile of yourself telling how you think God intends for you to be "perfect."

✦ The Mystery of God's Love

Christ's whole life is mystery, the *Catechism* teaches. This includes not only the mysteries of Christ's Incarnation and the Paschal Mystery covered in the creed, but the mysteries of his hidden life in Nazareth and a great deal of his public life that is not covered in the Gospels.

The term **mystery** refers first of all to the infinite incomprehensibility of God. God is not just unknown, he is unknowable. Our knowledge of God is entirely dependent on how much he wishes to reveal.

mystery

In a religious sense, a truth that is incomprehensible to reason and knowable only through God's Revelation.

Our own lives are also filled with mystery. An old joke goes like this: "Do you want to make God laugh? Just tell him your plans." Not only is the future unknown to us, but in God's providence, our lives, too, are filled with infinite, often surprising, possibilities.

Consider these true stories about what happened to these college students when they were just slightly older than you are now:

- Marc grew up just outside of Milwaukee. He went to Marquette University High School. He applied to a few colleges but easily had Georgetown University and Boston College at the top of his list. "I wanted to get away from Milwaukee," Marc recalled.

Marc's mother had different ideas. She wanted her oldest son to stay near to home. Reluctantly, Marc applied and registered at Marquette University, just blocks from his high school. Several surprises were in store for Marc in his four years at Marquette.

"First, I loved Marquette U," Marc said. "The family atmosphere was great. Second, I met my wife at Marquette. We wouldn't be together if I had gone off to school."

Marc's career plans changed, as well. An English major, he hoped to go to law school upon graduation. Instead, a mission trip to Central America sparked an interest in social justice ministry. Today, Marc is a parish youth minister near Milwaukee. He has led teenagers on several mission trips around the United States and to Mexico.

- In July, after graduating from high school in Southern California, Kara was working on a landscaping crew in local city parks with the intention of saving some spending money before starting college in the fall. Wearing work boots, she developed a sore between two of the toes on her right foot. For a couple of weeks, Kara ignored the pain and continued to work through the days, cutting shrubbery and picking up litter.

  Finally, Kara went to a foot doctor. He lanced the sore and bandaged it up. Kara went back to work. A few weeks later the "sore" came back, bigger and more painful than before.

  This time Kara went to see her regular doctor. The diagnosis was devastating. She had stage 2 melanoma, a dangerous form of cancer. Months of treatment followed, and Kara was forced to miss the entire fall semester. College had to wait, but Kara was so thankful to be on the road to recovery.

- Andy was on the sidelines on the athletic fields at the University of Notre Dame watching a pick-up football game. He was surprised to see one of his dorm mates running across the field telling him, "Come quick! Your mom has been taken to

  the hospital. Your parish priest wants to meet you by the library."

  Several thoughts raced through Andy's head. His mom had never been seriously ill. Certainly everything had to be okay. When he met up with his pastor at the designated place, Father Bernard motioned him to get inside the car. Andy could tell then that the priest wanted to tell him the news in the quiet of the car.

  The priest put his hand on Andy's shoulder. "It's serious. Your mom may not make it."

  Andy recalled the experience later, months after his mother's death. "I still can't believe he took the time to drive to Notre Dame to be with me. His comfort and compassion at that moment was beyond belief."

  After graduation and a series of unfulfilling jobs, Andy entered his local diocesan seminary to study for the priesthood. He looked back at this experience with of his pastor as the moment when he first consciously made a decision that he wanted to be a priest.

Everyone's life is filled with surprises and many unexpected twists and turns. Will you be the parent of a large family? Will you be successful in your career and be able to travel the world and own a vacation home? Will you grow in awareness of worldwide poverty and work tirelessly to help the poor? Will your parents be chronically sick and require you to be their caretaker? Will you get sick? What direction will your life take?

These questions, while part of the mystery of our own lives, can bring us peace when they are situated in the mystery of God's love. God has revealed himself as a God of love, who himself is "an eternal exchange of love, Father, Son, and Holy Spirit" (*CCC*, 221). God's love is everlasting. A firm plan for our lives is that we have been destined to share in this love of God.

God Gradually Reveals His Mystery

God's mystery is gradually revealed through history. God reveals himself and the mystery of his will over time in order to make us "capable of responding to him, and of knowing him, and of loving him far beyond [our] own natural capacity" (*CCC*, 52). God's revelation began to Adam and Eve, and he did not withdraw from doing so even when they sinned. God later made a covenant with Noah, and then a covenant with Abraham promising that his descendants would be a chosen people, the people of Israel.

An essential revelation came when God revealed his name to Moses in the burning bush:

> "I am the God of your father," he continued, "the God of Abraham, the God of Isaac, the God of Jacob. . . . I will be with you; and this shall be your proof that it is I who have sent you: when you bring my people out of Egypt, you will worship God on this very mountain." (Ex 3:6, 12)

This revelation of God's mysterious name—Yahweh, "I am who I am"—shares the news that God's faithfulness is everlasting: Yahweh is the God of the past (Abraham), the present (Moses), and the future ("I will be with you").

God *fully* revealed himself by sending his son, Jesus Christ:

In times past, God spoke in partial and various ways to our ancestors thorough the prophets; in these last days, he spoke to us through a son, whom he made heir of all things and through whom he created the universe. (Heb 1:1–2)

There is no further Revelation after Christ. God's Revelation is entrusted to the Church through two distinct modes: the Apostolic Tradition and Sacred Scripture. From the earliest days of the Church, Apostolic Tradition is the sharing of the message of Christ through preaching, witness, institutions, worship, and inspired writings. The Apostles shared all they received from Christ and learned from the Holy Spirit to their successors, the bishops. Apostolic Tradition includes the living transmission of the entire Word of God found in Tradition and Sacred Scripture. Tradition and Sacred Scripture are bound closely together and communicate with one another. Together they make up one "Sacred Deposit of Faith." The Apostles entrusted this Sacred Deposit (Tradition and Sacred Scripture) to the whole Church while the task of authentically interpreting Tradition and Sacred Scripture is entrusted to the Church's

Magisterium, the living, teaching office of the Church. Scripture, Tradition, and the Magisterium are so closely linked that one of them cannot stand without the other.

It is up to us as Christians to continue to grasp the full significance of God's Revelation in Jesus Christ. This is truly a life's work as we look for ways our personal life is intertwined with the life of our Savior.

The Holy Trinity: Central Mystery of Faith

Christians are baptized in the *name* of the Father and of the Son and of the Holy Spirit—not in their *names*. There is only one God but in three Persons: the almighty Father, his only Son, and the Holy Spirit. This is the Most Holy Trinity, the central mystery of our faith. The Trinity is a mystery in the strict sense because it is impossible for humans to figure out or reason on our own. This mystery was inaccessible even to the Chosen People of the Old Covenant.

The mystery of the Holy Trinity was only revealed at the coming of Christ. Jesus called God "Father" and revealed himself as being eternally begotten of the Father. Jesus revealed two great mysteries about the Holy Spirit: that the Holy Spirit is a distinct Person in relation to the Father and the Son and that he is sent to the Apostles and the Church by both the Father and the Son.

The mystery of the Trinity is a very difficult one to explain and understand. Some of the Church's **dogmas** about the Trinity can help. For example:

- *The Trinity is one.* The Trinity does not mean there are three Gods, but one God in three Persons. The three Persons do not share their divinity among themselves, but each one of them—Father, Son, and Holy Spirit—is God whole and entire. There are not three separate consciousnesses, intelligences, or wills in God. There is one God.

- *The three Persons are distinct from one another.* This means that the Father is not the Son, nor is the Son the Holy Spirit. Rather, the Father is eternally in relation to the Son, the Son is begotten of the Father, and the Holy Spirit proceeds from the Father and Son.

- *The divine Persons are related to one another.* The Father is wholly in the Son and wholly in the Holy Spirit; the Son is wholly in the Father and wholly in the Holy Spirit; the Holy Spirit is wholly in the Father and wholly in the Son. Because they are intimately related to one another, the three Persons have one nature or substance.

The relationship of community among the three Persons of the Holy Trinity helps to model the love we are to have for ourselves, for others, and for God. The divine economy, or economy of salvation, is the work of the Holy Trinity. The ultimate goal of this economy, of our lives, is entry into the perfect unity of the Blessed Trinity. As Jesus said, "Whoever loves me will keep my word, and my Father will love him, and we will come to him and

Magisterium
The teaching office of the Church. It was given by Jesus to Peter and the other Apostles and it extends to the Pope and the bishops.

dogmas
Central truths of Revelation that Catholics are obliged to believe.

make our dwelling with him" (Jn 14:23). As humans, we are built to seek out God and share the divine life. In the liturgy, the blessings of the Trinity are fully revealed and communicated. The Father is the source of all blessings of creation and salvation. In Christ he fills us with his blessings in order to pour into our hearts the gift of the Holy Spirit. From God's blessings at liturgy, our discipleship is ultimately modeled in our words and our actions.

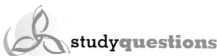

study questions

1. What does the term mystery mean in reference to God?

2. Name and explain the two ways that God's Revelation is entrusted to the Church.

3. How is the Holy Trinity a mystery in the strictest sense?

4. Name three of the Church's dogmas about the Trinity.

journal discussion

- In what ways has your life been surprising and full of mystery so far?

- Explain your own way of understanding the Holy Trinity.

✦ Our Desire for God

Imagine that in a few years—maybe just as you are about to graduate from college—you begin a serious dating relationship. You have very strong romantic feelings for this person and you definitely share a close bond of friendship. It is looking more and more like this person may turn out to be your future spouse.

A few question marks remain. You haven't met the parents of this special friend. Finally, a meeting is arranged. You will visit with them on Easter Sunday and share a meal with the family.

It turns out to be a delicious meal. But after dinner you share a private talk with the parents. In the course of the conversation you discover that these people are not religious at all. Though they had been raised Catholic, they haven't been to Church in years. They didn't go to Mass on this Easter Sunday. Your eyes wander around the house. You now notice that there are plenty of bunny rabbits and flowers and candies—but no crucifixes or other religious articles.

To top it off, the father tells, you: "While we support our children if they want to believe in a 'higher power,' my wife and I really have moved well beyond that stage in our lives. We believe humans have the power to create their own destiny. We really have no use for any superstitious rituals that involve worship in a God we don't believe in."

How would you feel if you heard this kind of talk? How would it effect your opinion of your beloved's parents? Of your beloved? You may know plenty of people who do not practice religion for reasons that range from laziness to feelings of unworthiness over a past sin. But how would you react to adults who have consciously made a decision *not to believe in God*?

Contrast this story of people who have seemingly turned their backs on God to the experience of the late Cardinal Joseph Bernardin of Chicago. He observed:

> My many years of ministry have convinced me that in the heart of every

human being there wells up an irrepressible desire to be united with God. I do not mean to imply that every person is able to *identify* this phenomenon as a longing for God. Some may seek fulfillment of it in some other way or may simply be aware of a kind of human emptiness. God has put this desire in our hearts, and not even sin cancels it.[2]

Saint Augustine, writing in the late fourth century, famously expressed the human desire for God:

> Despite everything, man, though but a small part of your creation, wants to praise you. You yourself encourage him to delight in your praise, for you have made us for yourself, and our heart is restless until it rests in you.[3]

Additionally, the *Catechism of the Catholic Church* adds:

> The desire for God is written in the human heart, because man is created by God and for God; and God never ceases to draw man to himself. (*CCC*, 27)

The experience described by Cardinal Bernardin and Saint Augustine is more typical of human behavior than of the parents who have made a conscious choice to ignore God. What does your personal experience tell you about a "longing for God"? Often, a person may not put stock in this longing until a personal need for God arises. For example, a person faced with a serious illness is often more inclined to seek out God in prayer. Or, maybe you have called on God when challenged by a relationship, worried about a test, or even thankful for a special favor. Can you think of a recent time when you called out to God?

Ways to Know God

God's self-revelation is pure gift. God has fully revealed himself and his divine plan by sending us his Son, Jesus Christ, and the Holy Spirit. However, even with natural reason man can know God with certainty based on his works. This is the inborn desire and longing human beings have for God of which Saint Augustine wrote.

These ways of approaching God are also called proofs for God's existence. Primarily, we can know God through examining the gift of creation, using two points of departure: the physical world and the human person. Consider some of the following ways which are contained in both categories:

Nature Imagine yourself on a mostly empty ocean beach at dusk. The salt air wisps through your lungs as you breathe slowly in and out. The rhythm of the crashing waves keeps a steady cadence. Sea gulls dive into the surf looking for an evening meal. Past the breakers the ocean looks like tinted blue glass for miles out to sea. The horizon and ocean meet at a splash of orange and blue. The setting sun is gone but its reflection remains as a fiery tunnel that appears to pass out into the other side of the world, to eternity, really.

Passion Your gaze to the horizon is interrupted. A man comes to the shore with a young child, probably not more than a year old. She is barefoot and wearing only a T-shirt and a diaper. Her father swings her by her arms and her toes glide atop the white foam. She giggles merrily and you can tell how much her dad enjoys being with her. Unassumingly, a man and woman walk across your view. They look to be in their late twenties. The man has his arm around the woman's shoulders. They are oblivious to you and the frolicking father and daughter. They are in love.

Reflection The light is completely gone now. The father has dried his daughter's toes and headed for the car. The twilit sky reveals its first stars. The moon is out casting its beam in a straight line right at you. You adjust your iPod to a sample of your favorite songs, close your eyes, and begin to think. You remember your mother who first exposed you to music and all of the arts. Naturally, your thoughts take you to your father who passed away suddenly only months before. You wonder about yourself and what direction your life will take. You feel peace about your chosen profession. But you are still hoping to find a special someone to share your life with. A flash of lightning dots the horizon and you can faintly hear the sound of thunder over the beautiful music. You brush the sand from your clothes, get up, and head home.

How does this scenario resonate with your experience of coming to know God? Are there particular natural scenes that awaken thoughts of God? Or do you feel God's presence enthralled in a relationship? How much time do you spend in prayer and reflection on God's presence in your life? Do you realize that the Sacred Scripture, the liturgy, and the practice of the virtues of faith, hope, and charity are sources of prayer? In addition, how aware are you of God's providence in every event of your life? As you reach for these goals,

more and more of God's mystery will be revealed to you.

Remember, Christ is God himself in human flesh. Exploring his life and words in detail is the fullest way to uncover God's presence. Coming to Christ will lead you to love more deeply and fully. Saint Thérèse of Lisieux wrote that "love is surely the best path leading to God. . . . Love appeared to be the hinge for my vocation."[4]

What It Means to Believe

The Catholic creeds (see page 306 of the Catholic Handbook for Faith) begin with the words "I believe" or "We believe." Saying that we believe in something relates to the theological virtue of **faith**. The virtue of faith enables us to believe in God and all that he has said and revealed to us. Faith is a gift of the Holy Spirit that enables us to commit ourselves to God totally, both our intellects and our wills. Faith has been described as our "lifeline" to God.

The *Catechism of the Catholic Church* reminds us that "believing in God, the only One, and loving him with all our being has enormous consequences for our whole life" (*CCC*, 222). The *Catechism* goes on to list several implications for a person with faith:

> *A faithful person comes to know God's greatness and majesty.* In the book of Job, Elihu was angry at Job for considering himself to be right over God. Elihu said:
>
> Behold, God is sublime in his power. What teacher is there like him?

faith

One of the theological virtues. Faith is an acknowledgment of and allegiance to God.

Who prescribes for him his conduct, or
who can say, "You have done
wrong?"

Remember, you should extol his work,
which men have praised in song.

All men contemplate it;
man beholds it from afar.

Lo, God is great beyond our knowledge;
the number of his years is past
searching out. (Jb 36:22–26)

A faithful person is thankful to God. Our
life and everything we receive each day—
for example, our breath, food, health,
friendships, talents—are all gifts from
the one God in whom we profess our
belief.

*A faithful person knows the unity of the
human community and the dignity of
every individual.* As the first creation
story in the book of Genesis proclaims,
we are all made in the image and likeness
of God. This is the reason we are to love
and respect every person as a son or
daughter of our loving Father.

*A faithful person makes good use of created
things.* When we have faith in God, we
detach ourselves from things that separate us from him and only use what can
bring us closer to him. We are also good
stewards of creation, protecting the environment both for our generation and
those to come.

*A faithful person trusts God in every cir-
cumstance, including hardship and adver-
sity.* When we pray in the Lord's Prayer
for "our daily bread," we count on the
Father to give us all the appropriate
goods and blessings, both material and
spiritual, that we will need.

Though we can discover God on our own, our
life of holiness as children of God is done in communion with others, in imitation of the community of the Persons of the Blessed Trinity.

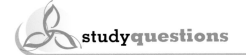

study questions

1. What did Saint Augustine say about man's inner desire for God?

2. Name and explain three ways man can discover God with natural reason?

3. Define faith.

4. Name and explain two implications for a person with faith.

journal discussion

● When do you long for God in your life? Be specific.

● Tell about a time when you experienced God's presence.

✦ Sharing the Divine Life

God is holy, eternal, and true. What does it mean to share the life of God? God in the Persons of the Trinity—Father, Son, and Holy Spirit—freely wills to communicate the way to holiness to all. This plan of God's "loving kindness" was conceived by the Father before the foundation of the world in his Son. It continues on through the gift of the Holy Spirit in the mission of the Church. To share in the life of God is to participate in the life of the Trinity. The *Catechism* teaches:

> The whole Christian life is a communion with each of the divine persons, without in any way separating them. Everyone who glorifies the Father does so through the Son in the Holy Spirit; everyone who follows Christ does so because the Father draws him and the Spirit moves him. (*CCC*, 259)

Since there is a certain resemblance between the unity of the divine persons and the unity we are to establish with others, the way we should go about loving God and growing in his holiness is very clear: "Love of neighbor is inseparable from love for God" (*CCC*, 1878). In the Sermon on the Mount, Jesus acknowledges the Ten Commandments as the source for loving God and loving neighbor, but adds an admonition to avoid anger and work toward reconciliation with our neighbor as a way to show love. He said:

> "I say to you whoever is angry with his brother will be liable to judgment, and whoever says to his brother, 'Raqa,' will be answerable to the Sanhedrin, and whoever says, 'You fool,' will be liable to fiery Gehenna. Therefore, if you bring your gift to the altar, and there recall that your brother has anything against you, leave your gift there at the altar, go first and be reconciled with your brother, and then come and offer your gift." (Mt 5:22–24)

The Aramaic word Jesus used, *Raqa*, is equated with a term like "blockhead" or "imbecile." The message is clear: We are not to name-call. We are not to slander or gossip. We are to live in harmony with other people. We are not to lash out in any way. We are to settle our differences with other people. The fruits of reconciliation are immense. Achieving peace, harmony, and love with others is the way we achieve this same kind of relationship with God.

The People of God

We share God's life by our participation in the **Church**. At creation, God intended for the world to be in communion with his divine life. This communion brought about the Church, a gathering of all people in Christ. From the time of the Original Sin, God, in his providence, ordained a plan of salvation through Christ and the Church as the way to restore holiness and to bring us salvation. The importance of the Church is that God wants "to make men holy and save them not merely as individuals without any mutual bonds, but making them into a single people, a people which acknowledges him in truth and serves him in holiness."[5] We share God's life in our relationships with one another.

Christ loves the Church. He gave up his life for the Church, and he has remained present in the Church in all the days since. The Church is the sign of Christ's loyalty to us, his people. Like Christ, the Church is a sacrament, a sign of our inner union with

Church

The Church is the community of people who profess faith in Jesus Christ and who are guided by the Holy Spirit. The Roman Catholic Church is guided by the Pope and his bishops. The Nicene Creed describes the Church as one, holy, catholic, and apostolic.

Choosing to Be Catholic

The Catholic Church has two rites for initiation. The most common is the baptism of children. The Rite of Baptism for Children provides for the **catechesis** of parents and godparents and includes the rite for baptizing children. Later, as the children grow, they, too, are taught the lessons of faith. Eventually they receive the other two sacraments of initiation: Confirmation and Eucharist.

The other is the Rite of Christian Initiation for Adults (RCIA) for anyone who wants to be Catholic and has reached the age of reason (approximately seven years old). In this rite, the person is catechized before receiving all three sacraments of initiation—Baptism, Confirmation, and Eucharist—during the Easter vigil liturgy. Many times a parish celebration of the vigil will include the initiation of people from childhood to adulthood.

A few years ago at Saint Clement of Rome Church in New Orleans, a group of teenagers participated in the RCIA process through the parish's Life Teen program, a Eucharist-based youth ministry program. They learned more about the faith from and with other teens their own age. Nicholas, one of the teen sponsors, said "We thought they would relate to teens better. Especially when they see other teens living out their baptismal promises."

Some of the stories of teens seeking initiation into the Church were dramatic. One girl said, "I was struggling with my mom. I like the Eucharist and confession, the fact that sins are wiped away."

Another boy, Blake, was a junior in high school when he decided to become Catholic. He recalled that his life had been "in a slump" and that a turning point came when he stole his grandmother's car when he was in ninth grade.

"That was the first time I ever saw my grandma cry over something I did," he said. "I felt terrible. I was depressed and I couldn't do anything." It was his grandmother who first suggested that Blake attend a Life Teen Mass at Saint Clement's. He liked the homilies that were geared to teenagers. After two months of attending Mass, he went on a retreat where he experienced a conversion.

"I was on a Jesus high for a week," he said. "I started going to church every weekend. I went from doing nothing but bad stuff to going to church and not hanging out with my old friends."

Blake's grades improved and his aunt and uncle asked him to be the godfather for their yet-to-be-born baby. Because he wasn't yet Catholic he couldn't be the child's godfather. But that situation would change when Blake and the others came into the Church at the Easter vigil.

catechesis
The process of religious instruction and formation in the Christian faith.

God. The Church is an *efficacious symbol*. This means that the Church is a symbol that not only points to a reality—in this case, our salvation—but she also causes it. We come to know God through the Church.

The Seven Sacraments are one way Catholics share in the divine life of Christ. This is why the Church affirms that the sacraments are necessary for salvation. The sacraments renew the mystery of God's love. They pour out the blessings of the Father in his Son and through the Holy Spirit and communicate the fruits of Christ's **Paschal Mystery**. They help us share in eternal life even now while we live on earth and await the second coming of Christ. The Second Vatican Council document *The Constitution on the Sacred Liturgy* (*Sacrosanctum concilium*) explains the purpose of the sacraments:

> The purpose of the sacraments is to sanctify men, to build up the Body of Christ, and finally to give worship to God. Because they are signs

Paschal Mystery
The way our salvation is made known through the Life, Death, Resurrection, and Ascension of Jesus Christ. The Paschal Mystery is made present in the sacraments, especially the Eucharist.

they also instruct. They not only presuppose faith, but by words and objects they also nourish, strengthen, and express it. That is why they are called "sacraments of faith." They do, indeed, confer grace, but in addition, the very act of celebrating them most effectively disposes the faithful to receive this grace to their profit, to worship God duly, and to practice charity. (59)

Baptism, Confirmation, and Eucharist are the sacraments of initiation. They ground us in our common vocation to holiness and in the mission of sharing the Gospel with others. Baptism is the sacrament of regeneration and renewal by the Holy Spirit: "Through Baptism we are freed from sin and reborn as sons of God; we become members of Christ, and are incorporated into the Church and made sharers in her mission" (*CCC*, 1213). Two other sacraments, Holy Orders and Matrimony—which are the primary subject of this text—are directed to the salvation of others; if they contribute to the salvation of those who receive them, it is because of their service to others.

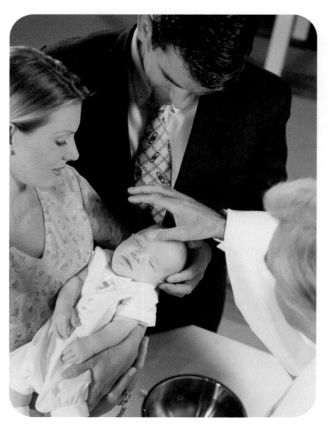

Our Vocation to Beatitude

If you randomly asked ten of your classmates to name just one thing they want out of life, there is a good chance that more than a few would say "To be happy." God has made us with a natural desire for happiness. As Saint Augustine put it,

> We all want to live happily; in the whole human race there is no one who does not assent to this proposition, even before it is fully articulated.[6]

Jesus offered a formula for happiness at the beginning of the Sermon on the Mount (Mt 5:3–12; also in the Sermon on the Plain in Lk 6:20–26). These are the Beatitudes, the heart of Jesus' preaching. The word *beatitude* means happiness, though if you read the Beatitudes you may wonder how so. The Beatitudes explain clearly how we should love God and love our neighbor in a Christ-like way. This is often a difficult thing to do and not what the world might associate with happiness—for example, the accumulation of goods, popularity, and sensory pleasures of all kinds. Rather, the Beatitudes teach us how we should live in order to reach our eternal destiny.

Supreme happiness is described in several ways in the New Testament, but most typically as "the coming of the Kingdom (or reign) of God." Other expressions to characterize the beatitude to which we are called are:

- the vision of God,
- entering into the joy of the Lord,
- entering into God's rest.

This desire for happiness comes from God and is placed in our hearts in order to draw us to God, the only one who can ever fulfill this desire. The Beatitudes make us like God and able to share eternal life. The Second Letter of Peter explains:

> His divine power has bestowed on us everything that makes for life and devotion, through the knowledge of him who called us by his own glory and power. Through these, he has bestowed on us the precious and very great promises, so

that through them you may come to share in the divine nature, after escaping from the corruption that is in the world because of evil desire. (2 Pt 1:3–4)

The Beatitudes teach us to be dependent on God alone for our happiness and contentment. In the first Beatitude, "Blessed are the poor in spirit, for theirs is the kingdom of heaven," the poor are associated with their Hebrew name, *anawim* (ah-nah-weem). These were people without material possessions who nevertheless kept a positive attitude, realized their helplessness, and sought God for all their needs, material and spiritual. Most importantly, they trusted that God would take care of all their needs.

The Beatitudes form the core of our Christian vocation to holiness. They teach us that true happiness is not connected with monetary riches, human fame, or any human achievement, for that matter. The Beatitudes ask us to "purify our hearts of bad instincts and seek the love of God above all else" (*CCC*, 1723).

No matter which directions our particular vocations (marriage, religious life, holy orders, dedicated single life) and careers lead us, our common Christian vocation, begun at Baptism, is to the love of God.

Chapter 2—Discerning God's Will—offers a plan to seek out particular ways to follow God's providence and to determine which state of life God intends for you. A plan for discerning life choices is offered as well as ways to apply the evangelical counsels of poverty, chastity, and obedience to your personal Christian vocation.

Saint Josephine Bakhita: Modeling Beatitudes

Born to a wealthy Sudanese family in 1868, Bakhita was kidnapped at a young age and eventually taken to Italy. She worked for a rich family as a nanny and grew to love the country and Catholicism. She converted in 1893 and joined the Institute of Canossian Daughters of Charity, taking the name Josephine and serving as a sister for more than fifty years. She performed any menial task that was asked of her, and she was especially a comfort to the poor and suffering who came to the convent.

Pope John Paul II canonized Saint Josephine on October 1, 2000. He said of her:

"In our time, in which the unbridled race for power, money, and pleasure is the cause of so much distrust, violence, and loneliness, Sister Bakhita has been given to us once more by the Lord as a universal sister, so that she can reveal to us the secret of true happiness: the Beatitudes. Here is a message of heroic goodness modeled on the goodness of the Heavenly Father."

- Write a short report on the life of Saint Josephine Bakhita. See her biography at the Vatican website: www.vatican.va.

- Choose a second saint who models one or more of the Beatitudes. Explain how. Include some of the saint's own words or words spoken about him or her in your report.

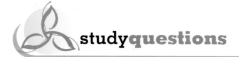

studyquestions

1. Why is our participation in the Church necessary for sharing in God's life?

2. How do the sacraments help us to share in the divine life?

3. What are the ways that supreme happiness is described in the Old Testament?

4. What do the Beatitudes teach us about happiness?

journaldiscussion

- Name the things that make you happy.
- Write a profile of a holy person.

summarypoints

Be Perfect

- We are called to holiness, that is, living "perfect" in a Christian sense by seeking a closer, more intimate union with Jesus Christ.

We Are Created in God's Image

- Our first parents were created in a state of original holiness and justice in which they were meant to share the life of God. Original Sin caused a loss of this gift and permanently affected humanity.

- Jesus Christ is the source of grace and redemption, opposite from Adam and Eve, who were the source of sin and the fall of mankind.

- God created man and woman in perfect equality, each in the image of God, and for each other. In marriage, man and woman are united to celebrate their love and share the gift of life.

- The soul is the innermost part of man that makes us spiritual people in the image of God.

- Our body likewise shares in the dignity and image of God.

- Sexuality affects every aspect of the human person in the unity of body and soul.

- The virtue of chastity helps us to integrate our sexuality and bring unity to body and soul.

- Being a disciple of Christ is our highest calling and most exalted vocation.

The Mystery of God's Love

- God has revealed himself as a God of love—in community with a Trinity of Persons, Father, Son, and Holy Spirit. Nevertheless, God remains an incomprehensible mystery of faith.

- God's mystery is gradually revealed through history.

- In the Old Testament, he revealed himself in covenants with Noah, Abraham, and Moses. To Moses, God revealed his name: Yahweh.

- God fully revealed himself in his Son, Jesus Christ. There is no further revelation after Christ.

- Christ revealed the mystery of the Holy Trinity, the central mystery of the Christian faith. The mystery of the Holy Trinity does reveal that there is only one God but in three Persons—Father, Son, and Holy Spirit.

Our Desire for God

- Human beings are created with a deep-felt desire to know God.

- While God's Revelation is pure gift, humans are created with a natural reason that allows us to know God with certainty based on his works.

- We can know God through our experience of nature, our feelings or passions, and through personal reflection.

- The virtue of faith enables us to believe in God and all that he has said and revealed to us.

- Believing in God has enormous consequences for our whole life.

✦ Sharing the Divine Life

✦ Our relationships with other people resemble the unity of the divine Persons, Father, Son, and Holy Spirit.

✦ We share in the divine life by loving God and loving our neighbor.

✦ We share in God's life through the Church. We also share in God's life in our relationships with others.

✦ Participating in the sacraments and receiving their graces is another way we share in the divine life.

✦ Our primary Christian vocation is to beatitude, that is, "supreme happiness."

✦ Supreme happiness is most often described in the New Testament as "the coming of the Kingdom of God."

assignments applications

1. Research and report on the human understanding of perfection. For example, make a list of consumer products and businesses that advertise and promote perfection. What is the difference between these human understandings of perfection and the Christian understanding of perfection?

2. Read and compare the first story of Creation (Gn 1:1–31) and the second story of Creation (2:4–25).

3. Listen to Haydn's *The Creation* or Beethoven's Symphony no. 9. Write a short essay or poem describing the images that came to mind from these pieces.

4. Attend a workshop, retreat, symposium, or lecture having to do with Scripture, faith, or religion. Report on what it taught you about Christian discipleship.

5. Read and report on the main sections of chapter 1, using "The Dignity of the Human Person" from the Second Vatican II document *Gaudium et Spes*. The document can be accessed at the Vatican website (www.vatican.va).

6. Write a profile of someone you know who, in the twists and turns of life, has come to know God.

7. Look up and define *immanent Trinity* and *salvific* or *economic Trinity*.

8. Make a list of twenty-five ways a person can come to know God.

9. "The Church is necessary for salvation." Use the *Catechism of the Catholic Church* to explain and defend this statement. Use the search function at: www.scborromeo.org/ccc.htm.

10. Make a collage or notebook with photos that express each of the Beatitudes.

Notes

1. Quoted from *Gaudium et spes*, 12.

2. From the program "Jesus: The Way, the Truth, and the Life," 1984.

3. Quoted from the *Confessions of Saint Augustine*, 1, 1, 1: PL: 32, 659–661.

4. Quoted from *The Storey of A Soul* by Thomas Merton.

5. Quoted from *Lumen Gentium*, 9.

6. Quoted from *De moribus ecc.* 1, 3, 4: PL 32, 1312.

chapter**outline**

✦ ## Finding a Calling

Finding a calling is much more than determining a career or profession. It involves determining a God-given vocation.

✦ ## Journeying to Perfection

God's providence directs us to perfection that will not be reached until the fullness of the kingdom is revealed.

✦ ## Discernment through the Ways of Prayer

A discernment process helps us to prayerfully consider the many available vocational options in life.

✦ ## Exploring Christian Vocations

The sacraments of initiation and the sacraments at the service of communion frame an understanding of the Christian vocations.

✦ ## Christian Discipleship: Serve One Another

We must put aside our personal desires to follow God's will.

God's Plan for Your Life: Single Life, Consecrated Life, Marriage, and Holy Orders

You open wide your hand and satisfy the desire of every living thing.

You, Lord, are just in all your ways, faithful in all your works.

You, Lord, are near to all who call upon you, to all who call upon you in truth.

Psalm 145:16–18

✦ Finding a Calling

Perhaps on the far reaches of your life's radar screen you have begun to think about what profession you might like to work in when you are older and

None of the reasons above is better than another. Certainly, personal interest and aptitude will have a major influence on which area you eventually choose as a college major. Likewise, selecting a major to help prepare you for a profession or graduate school is a very typical practice.

finished with school. More likely, you probably haven't even gotten that far in the midst of keeping up with your high school classes, an after school job, athletics, and your social life. As far as future planning, you may have only just begun exploring college choices and filling out college applications. If so, when you get to the section that asks you to list a college major, what will you do? Which one of the following statements best represents how you will respond?

- I will list a major based on a subject I like in high school.

- I will list a major that will prepare me for a future profession.

- I will list a major with the expectation that I am likely to change it.

- I will not list any major, as I have no idea at this time what I want to focus on.

Equally common are students who begin college as "undeclared majors" and others who quickly determine their original major is not suited for them.

Choosing a college major that leads to a profession is an important decision that you may face shortly. However, it is really just one piece of the life puzzle that involves finding your calling.

"Finding a calling" is much different from "finding a profession." A profession is associated with a **career**. A career builds on the kinds of work you have aptitude for and like to do. Careers are different than *jobs*; whereas you may have several jobs in your lifetime, you may change careers a lot less frequently.

Today, many students enter college with the thought of preparing for a career. Decisions are made based on a

career
A chosen occupation that is more likely to express one's talents than a job.

professional approach; for example, making a list of advantages and disadvantages for a particular career. Their survey is a very rational one based on the probability for achieving success in areas like social importance, personal satisfaction, and income potential. The decision is also based on personal aptitude and skills as well as personal likes and dislikes. This means that you are unlikely to choose a career in medicine if you are doing poorly in sciences like biology and chemistry. Or, even if you do well in science, medicine might be a poor career choice if the sight of blood makes you squirm.

As we make these important decisions about our future professions, there is another decision process we should be involved in. It involves choosing a course for life based on vocation. Recall that the word vocation is taken from the Latin word *vocare*, which translates "to call."

In Chapter 1, you learned that we all have a primary Christian vocation to love and serve God by loving and serving other people. The fulfillment of this vocation leads to Christian beatitude, or eternal happiness. There are some more specific ways Christians accomplish this vocation. The **laity** seek the Kingdom of God by engaging in daily, worldly tasks and directing these to God's will. For married people, this includes sharing love for each other and raising a Christian family. Priestly and religious vocations are dedicated to the service of the Church. Bishops and their helper priests are entrusted with teaching, sanctifying, and governing the Church in the name of Christ. Religious sisters, brothers, and priests live out their promises of chastity, poverty, and obedience and of engaging in missionary work as directed by their communities.

Chapter 2 introduces these particular Christian vocations and offers some more suggestions for discerning your own vocation. Part of the formula for determining your life's calling is easy to decipher: your "caller" remains the same God of the Old and New Testaments. Other parts of the formula may not be as clear. What is your special gift? Are you able to make a lifelong commitment to your special gift? How will sacrifice be a part of this vocation?

Remember: your vocation is much different than "having a job" or "choosing a career." The risks are greater. But so are the rewards.

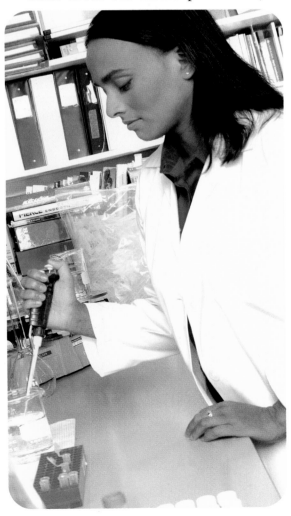

laity
All of the baptized faithful except those who have received the Sacrament of Holy Orders.

Life Strategies

James VanOosting, author and dean of the College of Arts and Sciences at Seton Hall University, traces the two biblical calls of Moses (Ex 3:1–4:17) and Mary (Lk 1:26–38) to explain four characteristics common to any vocation. He writes:

> First, a person is called *for a special purpose*: Moses to lead his people from captivity to the Promised Land, Mary to give birth to God's son. Accepting a call means making a commitment to its fulfillment.
>
> Second, the person who is called has a *special gift*. This should not be confused with aptitude, skill, or talent. The gift associated with vocation must be revealed to the individual.

Third, implicit in vocation is the presence of a *caller*. In biblical narratives, the caller has a name—Yahweh, God, Jesus. The caller's voice is heard as something outside the person being called.

Fourth, accepting a vocation leads to a *life of sacrifice, faith and often darkness*. Neither Moses nor Mary could have predicted what answering the call would mean. Each had to sacrifice other life possibilities in order to say yes to the caller. Each had to exercise faith in order to accept the unknown, to walk into darkness in order to find the light.[1]

CHOOSING A MAJOR

Former Notre Dame football coach Lou Holtz likes to describe an age-old formula for a direction for life. It goes like this:

> *First*, think about what it is you like to do.
>
> *Second*, determine something you like to do that you are also good at.
>
> *Finally*, find someone to pay you for it.

There may be a few other ways to state the final part of the formula. Maybe, "Does what you like to do have value for yourself or others?" Or, "Does anyone need you to do it?"

Use this approach to determine an area of study (major) you might like to pursue in college with the thought that it may lead to a career. Next, analyze: What are the strengths of this process? What are its weaknesses? How would this process work for determining a vocation?

journal**discussion**

● As of right now, what would you name as your college major? What is the basis of that decision?

✦ Journeying to Perfection

You are at an age when some major life decisions are on the horizon. Besides choosing a college and an academic major, you will face broader life decisions involving a particular Christian vocation. For example,

Will you be married?

● Marriage is the most "popular" vocation in numbers. Nearly 55 percent of adults over the age of fifteen years old are married.

Will you be a lifelong single person?

● The percentage of never-married persons aged twenty-five to thirty-five has increased by 20 percent in the past thirty years, suggesting more lifelong singlehood.

Will you choose a religious vocation as a sister or brother?

● Religious vocations have risen in some developing countries recently. However, in the forty years from 1965–2005, the number of religious sisters decreased in the United States from 179,954 to 68,634, and the number of religious brothers from 12,271 to 5,451. Opportunities for a life of radical service, discipleship, and excitement remain available for those men and women willing to take the plunge into religious life.

If you are a male, will you pursue a calling to the ordained priesthood?

● The total number of priests in the United States has also decreased since 1965. By 1998, 24 percent of diocesan priests were over seventy years old, the retirement age for priests. There is certainly a need for men to prayerfully consider a vocation to the priesthood.

Devoting a life to any of these Christian vocations requires many choices—both prior to the initial commitment and through the challenges of living out the vocation. Think about some of the questions that are likely to arise for the various vocations:

● Whom will I marry?

● What type of parent will I be?

● Who will take care of my parents when they are older?

● How will I get along with others in a religious community?

● Will I be able to keep a vow of celibacy?

● Will I be accepted into a seminary to study for priesthood?

Though the median age is getting older for commitment to each of these vocations (e.g., twenty-seven for males and twenty-five for females getting married for the first time), the likelihood is that in the next ten years you will have made a commitment to *pursue* one of the particular Christian vocations described above. There is also a chance you could already be married, a parent, a professed religious, or a priest before the age of thirty.

Charting any of these life courses can bring feelings of anxiousness, anticipation, excitement, and more. But any undue concern about your future should be eliminated when you come to an understanding that God is in control of your life and that God only wants the best for you.

As the *Catechism* teaches, "Creation has its own goodness and proper perfection, but it did not spring forth complete from the hands of the Creator" (*CCC*, 302). Instead, the universe, including each person, is created by God "in a state of journeying" toward an ultimate perfection that hasn't yet been reached. The ways that God guides his creation toward perfection is known as **divine providence**.

It is comforting to know that God loves and cares for us so much that he has a special plan for our lives and guides us to it. As the book of Proverbs teaches:

> Many are the plans in a man's heart, but it is the decision of the Lord that endures. (Prv 19:21)

divine providence
God's interest and action in guiding his creation to perfection.

Seek First the Kingdom

Jesus spoke to his disciples about their anxiousness for their lives on earth. He said:

> So do not worry and say, "What are we to eat?" or "What are we to drink?" or "What are we to wear?" All these things the pagans seek. Your heavenly Father knows that you need them all. But seek first the kingdom [of God] and his righteousness, and all these things will be given you besides. (Mt 6:31–33)

Jesus seems to be telling us that we should not worry about our futures. But what else is he saying? What does this mean for you practically as you get ready to make some key vocational choices for your life?

Essentially, Jesus tells us to put our trust in divine providence, the will of God. We should trust that our heavenly Father will take care of not only our "bigger" needs, like whom we might marry or whether or not we should seek out a religious calling, but also our smaller day-to-day needs. In fact, trusting God means that we depend on him for every detail of our lives.

God is the master of his plan of creation. He is also the master of our individual lives. But to carry out his plan he makes use of our cooperation. The *Catechism* explains:

> God is the first cause who operates in and through secondary causes: "For God is at work in you, both to will and to work for his good pleasure." (*CCC*, 308 quoting Phil 2:13)

God will always work in us and with us as "unconscious collaborators" of his will. However, we can enter even more completely into the divine plan when we consciously align our actions, prayers, and sufferings with him.

Applying this to your immediate and long-term future, it is wise to create a life that first of all involves God in every facet and in every motivation. For example, if your primary motivation for being a lawyer or a doctor is to make money, not to help those who are in need of legal assistance or to heal the sick, your motivation is skewed in terms of following God's will. Remember the story of King Solomon from the Old Testament. When God said to Solomon, "Ask something of me and I will give it to you" (1 Kgs 3:5), Solomon first chose the gift of God's wisdom, and God was pleased, saying to him:

> "Because you have asked for this—not for a long life for yourself, not for riches, nor for the life of your enemies, but for understanding so that you may know what is right—I do as you requested . . . In addition, I give you what you have not asked for, such riches and glory that among kings there is not your like." (1 Kgs 3:11–12a, 13)

Following God's will for our lives brings us blessings and holiness. Observe the way the rest of natural creation allows God to guide them.

Imagine if the climatic seasons, the animals of land and sea, and day and night itself resisted following God's will rather than being guided by it. Rather, nature proceeds in harmony and with regular motion. Yet often people do resist the will of God for their lives:

- Mary, a high school junior, has never felt closer to the Lord than after a school retreat. However, when Sister Catherine invites her and some other girls to a day of prayer led by her community's vocation director, Mary declines. "Me, a nun?" She does not accept the invitation.

- Patrick has been told often by his teachers that he would "make a good priest." Patrick has always been drawn to private prayer before the Blessed Sacrament. But he is careful never to let his mind wander to thoughts of the priesthood. "What would my parents and friends think if I told them I wanted to be a priest?" he wonders. But he never asks them.

- Kendra, a high school senior, is the youngest of five children. Her parents are older now, and her father's health has been poor. All but one of her siblings live some distance away. Kendra is not sure about her college choice. All her friends are leaving home for college. She really would prefer going to the local college and staying near her parents. But everyone seems to be encouraging her to move away. "Maybe I should try it. It might be fun," she thinks.

How should the teenagers mentioned above handle their dilemmas? What do Jesus' words—"seek first the kingdom [of God] and his righteousness, and all these things will be given you besides"—have to do with these situations? What does it mean to you to determine God's will for your life? The next section explains some of the ways to connect with divine providence.

Thy Will Be Done

We pray to follow the will of God each time we pray the Lord's Prayer: "Thy kingdom come; thy will be done on earth as it is in heaven." God's

Kingdom will reach its fullness only at the end of time, but we are to live, experience, and work for it right now. We do this by following the plan God has intended for us.

The more we seek God's plan for us, the more we advance toward perfection. When we resist God's plan for our own desires, we go backward. Saint Frances de Sales suggested that "for my part I know no other perfection than loving God with all one's

Saint Francis de Sales

heart. Without this love the virtues are only a heap of stones." Also, we can recognize God's will through the experiences of our daily lives. Remember, "God is the sovereign master of his plan. But to carry it out he also makes use of his creatures' cooperation" (*CCC*, 306).

Also, to know God's will for our lives, we can pray. Saint Claude de la Columbière reminded us that Christ promised that he would give us *everything* we need, even the smallest

free will
God's gift that allows us to shape our own lives and direct ourselves to the goodness God intends.

things. He shared these other reflections on how to pray for God's will for our lives:

- *We can pray to obtain what we want.* We are not prohibited from praying for money and position in life, but, like Solomon, we must pray for things in their proper order.

- *We can pray to be delivered from evil; however, we are reminded that God is even able to derive good from evil and sin.* For example, poverty of materials or of the spirit can increase our dependence on God. If we suffered these things, would we seek out God much more than we do? What benefit would that be for our sanctification?

- *We can pray to accept all of God's gifts as blessing.* For example, we can pray, "either give me so much money that my heart will be satisfied, or inspire me with such contempt for it that I no longer want it."

When we cooperate with God we are exercising his great gift of **free will**. With the angels, people journey to the ultimate destination of perfection by free choice and by loving God and others. Because this choice is free, the possibility of going astray and committing moral evil exists. God is not the cause of moral evil but he does permit it because he respects our freedom and, mysteriously, knows how to derive good from evil.

As the *Catechism* explains:

Only at the end, when our partial knowledge ceases, when we see God "face to face," will we fully know the ways by which—even through the dramas of evil and sin—God has guided his creation to that definitive sabbath rest for which he created heaven and earth. (*CCC*, 314)

In the meantime, we continue to delve deeper in prayer to discover more about ourselves and about God. Discernment is a process that helps us to make good choices in line with God's will.

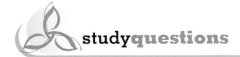

studyquestions

1. What does it mean to say that we are created by God "in a state of journeying"?

2. Define *divine providence*.

3. How can we become conscious collaborators with God?

4. What did King Solomon first ask for in prayer? What was he given?

5. How do we advance toward perfection?

6. What did Saint Frances de Sales say about perfection?

7. Define *free will*.

8. Why does God permit moral evil?

journaldiscussion

● How have you resisted God's will for your life? What was the result? How have you accepted God's will? What happened then?

● If you could have any prayer answered, how would you answer it? How might your answer be different than God's to your prayer?

✦ Discernment through the Ways of Prayer

As God gradually reveals himself to us and leads us to know more about our own selves, the way we reciprocate to him is through prayer. Saint John Damascus described prayer as "the raising of one's mind and heart to God." When we pray we consciously pay attention to God. We direct our thoughts to the loving God who first calls us.

There are many different ways to pray. Jesus modeled several of the ways of prayer. For example, he *praised* the Father for revealing God's will to the humble and lowly (see Lk 10:21). He *thanked* God when he raised Lazarus from the dead (see Jn 11:41–42). He prayed prayers of *petition* (see Lk 22:31–32) and *intercession* (see Jn 17). And when his disciples asked him to teach them to pray, he taught the Lord's Prayer in the Sermon on the Mount (see Mt 5–7). Jesus is the perfect model of prayer. He prayed before

all of the important decisions of his life; for example, in the desert before beginning his public ministry, before choosing his Apostles, before performing miracles, and on the mountain at the time of his Transfiguration. His final words were a prayer of trust: "Father, into your hands I commend my spirit" (Lk 23:46).

Constant and consistent prayer is a way to determine what God intends for us, especially when we are faced with an important decision. We can express our prayer in different ways: in *vocal prayer* (mentally or aloud) as Jesus did when he taught the Our Father; in *meditation* in which you actively use your thoughts, imaginations, and desires to think about God's presence in the world and in your life; and in *contemplative prayer*, a form of silent, wordless prayer in which you simply rest in the presence of the all-loving God.

Discernment is the name for a process of prayer that incorporates many of the types of prayer and expressions of prayer described above.

Discernment calls us to look at all sides of a decision, considering many alternatives. Discernment involves praying over a decision, asking for the guidance of the Holy Spirit, and, finally, actually making a decision, acting on it, and evaluating it.

Discernment is not only for big decisions. It also involves reflecting on the ordinary, everyday actions of our lives. It is not really the events themselves that are the focus, but rather the feelings the events evoke in us when we reflect on them—for example, joy, sorrow, anxiety, contentment. It is through these feelings that we can begin to understand more about how God is calling us each day.

Beginning any discernment process means you have a sensitivity to your innermost thoughts and desires and that you can reflect on what you experience. This is harder to do than it might seem, as it means taking time to remove yourself from a world filled with noises and distractions to find a place and time to be *quiet*. Is there ever a time around your home when it is quiet and you can be alone? In most households, these times (and places) are rare. A first step for discernment is to determine when and where you can devote at least ten minutes to a **centering prayer**, with the purpose of finding God in the depths of yourself. Follow a process like the one described in the following section to help you begin deciphering how to stake out on the best course for your life.

Listening to God

Making a decision about what you are going to do with your life and what you are going to be in accor-

dance with God's will cannot be accomplished without making a habit of prayer. Discerning your vocation really means finding out how you will personally respond to God's love. It means continuing to develop and deepen your relationship with God. This is accomplished through perseverance in prayer.

centering prayer
A method of prayer that readies us to receive the gift of God's presence by quieting our spirit to allow God to rest within.

You might have been taught as a child that prayer is "talking with God." More accurately, prayer is a dialogue with God in which the greater half is spent *listening* to what God has to say to you. There are many ways to pray, but in any of them, there can be no greater objective than simply being tuned in to God's presence in your life and the ways God speaks to you constantly through the experiences of your day. The Sacred Scripture, the liturgy of the Church, and the practice of virtues are other sources of prayer. A

centering prayer is an effective way to quiet down and place yourself in the presence of the Lord. Follow these steps to take on this process:

Step One: Find a quiet place to pray. Ideally, you should have a place in your home where you can be without noise and distraction. Relax by slowly inhaling and exhaling. Assume a comfortable position with your spine in a straight line. Close your eyes. Now move to the very center of your being. Become aware of God's presence. Express your faith in words like these:

"Lord, I believe you are with me."

"Still my thoughts."

"Thank you for keeping me alive in your love."

"Be with me now, Lord."

"Help me to experience your presence."

Step Two: After a minute or so, select a special word that makes you think of God and his love. Recite this word over and over. The repetition will help you to keep distractions away. Choose a name, quality, or title that carries some deep meaning for you. For example:

- Jesus
- Father
- Spirit
- Love
- Lord
- Truth
- Savior
- Life
- Way

After a short time you can stop reciting the word as you become aware of the Lord at the center of your being. If distractions come your way—and they often do—return to the word to refocus on God and his loving presence.

Step Three: At the end of your time in prayer, thank the Father for his presence. Tell Jesus of your love for him. Ask the Holy Spirit to remain with you always. Slowly and meditatively recite an Our Father.

If you make this type of prayer a habit, you will be better able to think about your life and describe how you feel about a variety of your experiences. It is these insights that will help you determine a vocation. This process is very similar to the one undertaken by Saint Ignatius Loyola in the sixteenth century.

Saint Ignatius's story is well known. He was a Basque soldier who was wounded in battle. During his convalescence from an injury, he asked the nuns who were caring for him to bring him some romantic novels to help him pass the time. The only books the nuns were able to provide were of the life of Christ and the lives of the saints. Ignatius pored through these books, pausing from time to time to think about what he would do when he was fully recovered. Sometimes he would picture himself as a knight who was pledged in service to a rich lady. Other times, due to what he was reading, he would imagine himself doing heroic service in God's name.

The imagining wasn't the key to the experience for Ignatius, however. He began to notice that even though thoughts of being a knight were exciting and helped him to pass the day, ultimately they made him sad and left him feeling empty. Yet the thoughts of imitating the saints, Ignatius realized, left him with a feeling of lasting joy and satisfaction, even long after he stopped imagining them. Ignatius thought about these two different feelings. One day he had an insight: the imaginings that left him at peace had their origin in God, whereas the others did not. Ignatius sensed that both the spirit of God and the spirit of evil were at work in him. More importantly, Ignatius understood more about how God communicates: not typically in dramatic events, but through his own feelings about the ordinary events of his life. This was the root of the Ignatian model of discernment, still practiced today.

Saint Ignatius

Overcoming Distractions

Even when you choose a quiet time and place for prayer, distractions will inevitably interfere with your prayer. Perhaps you find yourself simply reviewing the events of your day. Or you can't let go of some tension caused by an argument with a parent or friend. The first cure for distractions while praying is to make sure the place and time you have chosen is really as secure as you hoped and that you are able to be isolated from as many outside noises and interruptions as possible. Beyond that, remember these points to help you deal with distractions:

- Call on the Holy Spirit to be with you and to guide your prayer time.

- Focus on a religious picture, icon, crucifix, or lighted candle to help keep your attention on prayer.

- Don't try to resist distracting thoughts. Let them happen. Observe them and then imagine them evaporating into the air or flowing down a river out to sea. When your mind is cleared, return to the focus of prayer.

- Be patient. Don't try to "feel" something when you pray. God will answer your prayer in his due time.

- Remember that prayer is happening no matter the distractions. Wanting to pray is itself a prayer. Keep reminding yourself that God is always present to you.

God's Plan for Your Life: Single Life. Consecrated Life. Marriage. and Holy Orders

51

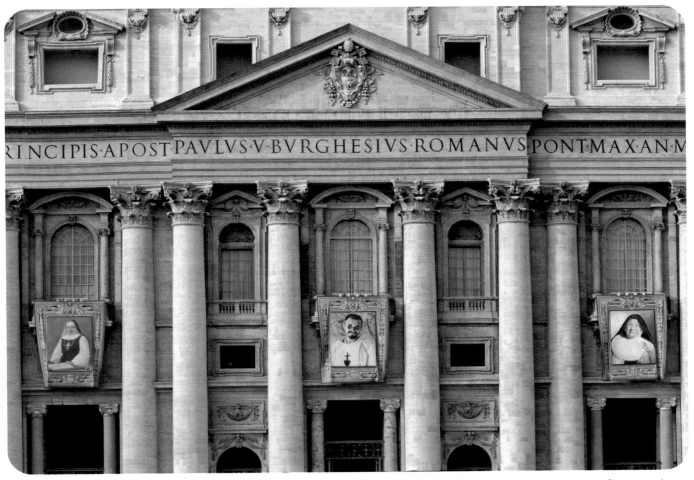

Pope Benedict XVI beatified (from left to right) Maria Pia Mastena, Charles de Foucauld, and Maria Crocifissa Curcio at St Peter's Cathedral on November 13, 2005.

Abandonment to God's Will

Father,

I abandon myself into your hands: do with me
    what you will.
Whatever you may do I thank you:
I am ready for all, I accept all.
Let only your will be done in me, and in all your
    creatures—
I wish no more than this, O Lord.
Into your hands I commend my soul;
I offer it to you with all the love of my heart,
for I love you, Lord, and so need to give myself,
to surrender myself into your hands
without reserve,
and with boundless confidence,
for you are my Father.

—Charles de Foucauld

Charles de Foucauld (see pages 196–197), who lived as a hermit after a religious conversion, wrote this prayer as a statement of his abandonment to the will of God. Research and print three other prayers that speak of surrendering to God's will. Then write your own heartfelt prayer surrendering your own will to the will of God.

Beginning to Plan for a Vocation

At your age and stage in life, the intention in discerning your lifelong vocation is only to consider prayerfully some first steps that may eventually lead to priesthood, religious life, marriage, or the committed single life. A discernment process is not intended to predict what may end up being your ultimate vocation, only to begin the journey to a particular vocation while allowing God to direct you and guide you.

Any one of these particular Christian vocations will involve many other smaller choices and decisions along the way. Once you have begun a regular practice of prayer, you can continue along a discernment process that will help you find the right course for your life. *Don't forget: praying is the most essential element of this process.* Consider how the following steps, based in the Ignatian model, can help you on the way to a Christian vocation.

1. *Dream and Imagine.* To dream and imagine the future is one of the privileges of freedom that God provides. Picture yourself in each type of particular Christian vocation, along with possible careers that might go along with each. For example, you might imagine yourself married with a family with a career as a high school history teacher. On the other hand, you might imagine the same teaching career paired with the vocation of a priest, religious, or single person. Remember how Saint Ignatius got in touch with and then described his feelings as he imagined two very different kinds of futures. Take some time to reflect on how you feel when you think about different types of vocations. Name some of the feelings. Is there one vocational choice that seems to make your heart skip a beat while also bringing a feeling of commitment?

2. *Gather Information.* Think back to your decision of what college major to pursue that was presented at the opening of the chapter. Can you imagine making this type of choice without gathering as much information as possible? Once you are drawn to a certain

major, you would want to learn as much as possible about the requirements and job possibilities associated with the major, not to mention the accompanying social life and setting of the particular colleges who offer the major. You would probably do plenty of research on the Internet, talking with representatives of the college and with students who are enrolled in that major. You would also be wise to speak with professionals who are employed in the fields associated with that major to help with your decision. Now, think about how you might gather information about a particular Christian vocation. If you are considering a religious vocation, you might follow the same procedure: check the Internet and read about religious communities, research requirements for the seminary and Holy Orders (for priesthood), speak to priests, sisters, or brothers, **seminarians**, and **religious novices**. If you are thinking about marriage, the gathering of information about married life is perhaps more informal, but still necessary. Observe the way that a variety of married couples get along and speak to them about the rewards and challenges of married life. If you are debating between two or more options (for example, between religious life and dedicated single life), make a list of all the reasons for choosing and not choosing each. Pay attention to all of the things you find attractive about the particular lifestyle or vocation along with obstacles that may have to do with your age, education, or health.

3. *Pray Over the Options.* Whereas your initial prayer was a centering prayer to help you to find God in the depth of your person and feelings, Saint Ignatius also taught the value of repetitive prayer to gauge your feelings with respect to the options you have both imagined and researched.

Discernment is really a prayerful pondering or deliberation of the many options available to you in life. At your age, you are just beginning this process. As you weigh the advantages and disadvantages of each option, your goal should be to try and understand them as God might understand them for your life. The more you pray and mull over the options, the more likely a sense of direction may emerge or some of the options may drop off as possibilities. Eventually you should be at a point where you will be able to make an informed decision about an important vocational choice.

In order to help begin this process, the following section introduces the particular Christian vocations discussed in this book. More information on two vocations connected with sacraments—marriage and priesthood—will also be covered in more detail in separate units.

study questions

1. What is meant by discernment in a religious sense?

2. How is a centering prayer an important first step in a discernment process?

3. How is personal prayer more than "talking with God"?

4. What was the insight Saint Ignatius had about his imaginings?

5. Name and explain the three steps of discernment described on pages 52–53.

journal discussion

● Describe a quiet place where you can pray.

● Which time of the day or night do you prefer for prayer?

● Tell how you have adapted a centering prayer to begin a discernment process.

seminarians
Men who attend a seminary or school focusing on theology in training and formation for the life of a priest.

religious novices
Women or men who have entered a religious order but have yet to take their final vows.

✦ Exploring Christian Vocations

The sacraments of initiation—Baptism, Confirmation, and Eucharist—are mainly intended for our holiness and salvation. These sacraments provide us with the graces we need to live a life in Christ and evangelize the world with our words and actions.

Two other sacraments—Holy Orders and Matrimony—are mainly directed to the holiness and salvation of others. Those who are ordained are appointed to nourish others by sharing God's word and grace with the whole Church in Christ's name. Those who are married help one another attain holiness and they pass on the faith to their children, thereby extending the People of God well into the future. Because of their focus on others, the Sacraments of Holy Orders and Matrimony are called **Sacraments at the Service of Communion**.

Both the sacraments of initiation and the Sacraments at the Service of Communion provide a framework for understanding Christian vocations. In Baptism and Confirmation, we receive a share in the common priesthood of Christ. We have great freedom to live out Christ's mission as priest, prophet, and king according to our own particular life choices. Lay people share in Christ's priestly office by uniting their lives to Christ's sacrifice on the cross and by their participation in the Sacrifice of the Mass. Lay people share in the prophetic office by teaching and evangelizing, spreading the Gospel of Christ. Sometimes this is done formally through tasks like catechizing in parish programs or using the media to share the good news. Most often we are prophetic when we share our faith in Christ through our daily conversations and actions with our friends, fellow students, co-workers, and all those with whom we come in contact. Lay people participate in Christ's kingly office by helping to remove sinfulness in secular institutions overrun with corruption.

Callings involving the many different charisms of religious life, the committed single life, as well as priesthood and marriage, flow from the graces of Christian Baptism. The Sacrament of Matrimony provides an additional source of consecration for the duties of marriage and parenthood. The

Sacraments at the Service of Communion

The Sacraments of Holy Orders and Matrimony, which, unlike the sacraments of initiation, are directed toward the salvation of others. "They confer a particular mission in the Church and serve to build up the People of God" (CCC, 1534).

ministerial priesthood of bishops and priests likewise has its own sacrament of consecration. The ministerial priesthood serves the common priesthood. The ministerial priesthood is "a *means* by which Christ unceasingly builds up and leads his Church" (*CCC*, 1547).

Though there is exemplary value in taking vows of poverty, chastity, and obedience for the sake of God's Kingdom, God calls us to holiness in many different ways. As Saint Paul wrote to the Corinthians:

> There are different kinds of spiritual gifts but the same Spirit; there are different forms of service but the same Lord; there are different workings but the same God who produces all of them in everyone. (1 Cor 12:4–6)

This is the time of life when you should take the time to consider prayerfully the way to holiness to which God is calling you. Learn about several specific Christian vocations, including ones described in this text.

Committed Single Life

Probably the main reason that the single life is not often thought to be a permanent Christian vocation like marriage, priesthood, or the religious life is that there is no ritual to mark a commitment to the single life due to the fact that everyone transitions through the single life on his or her way to other permanent vocations. However, the single life is an authentic and valuable vocation that more and more Catholics are freely choosing. Some singles may desire marriage or religious life, but circumstances have kept them from these vocations. Widows and widowers also find themselves returning to the single life and, in many cases, embracing it as a new calling. The *Catechism of the Catholic Church* explains some of the reasons a person might choose to remain single:

> Some forgo marriage in order to care for their parents or brothers and sisters, to give themselves more completely to a profession, or to serve other honorable

ends. They can contribute greatly to the good of the human family. (*CCC*, 2231)

There are many benefits of a vocation to the single life, both for the single person and for the Church. Without the responsibilities of marriage or religious life, single people can have a dedicated devotion to their career. Tim, age fifty, has spent most of his career as a drug and substance abuse counselor living in residential treatment facilities. "I love my work. The rewards are great," Tim shared. "Early on I realized that to continue in the exact type of work I am doing, I would have to give up the idea of being married. Living at the residential home five days a week precludes for me, at least, being an effective husband and father."

Single persons have a greater opportunity for silence and solitude that is often translated to a deep prayer life. Amy, thirty-three, spends the first hour every morning before work in quiet prayer. "My prayer time is the fuel for my day. I can't imagine my life without it." Single people also have the time to develop talents in creative areas like writing, poetry, and art that improve the quality of life in the world for all.

Single persons also provide support to those who are married, ordained, or religious. Because they are not committed to any one person, single persons are free to love all. They can have deep friendships with men and women of a wide range of ages and vocations. They remind married couples of the spiritual love that is a vital component of their relationship—one that outlasts their earthly life.

Of the challenges faced by single persons, loneliness is probably the greatest. A single person has no immediate family member to offer consolation and support when he or she experiences a rough day on the job, or to share the joy of a rewarding day at work. For this reason, it is important for single people to cultivate close and lasting friendships with other Catholics committed to the same lifestyle. Also, living a chaste life is difficult in this day and age for single adults. Society and culture promote promiscuity and uncommitted sexual relationships. Friendships help in this area as well. As the *Catechism* teaches, "The virtue of chastity blossoms in friendship" (*CCC*, 2347). The challenge to remain chaste while acknowledging that sex is to be reserved for a committed marriage partnership is likewise a powerful witness to the sanctity of sexual love.

A vocation to the single life must be compatible with a person's temperament and gifts. A person who decides to accept the challenges and reap the rewards of a vocation to the single life should have some or all of the following characteristics: self-confidence, self-reliance, self-motivation, resourcefulness, compassion, and hospitality. To succeed in this vocation single persons need a great dependence on God. Living in this dependence, single people are a dramatic witness to all the Church of a life in Christ.

Consecrated Life

Under the umbrella of the consecrated life are many particular and traditional Christian vocations. Consecrated life is defined as a life dedicated to living by the **evangelical counsels** of poverty, chastity, and obedience. All Christians are called to live these counsels based on their state in life. However, professing these counsels within a permanent state of life recognized by the Church is what characterizes a life consecrated to God. Those who follow the call to the consecrated life have made a commitment to follow Christ more completely, to give themselves to God above all things, and to seek out the perfection that comes with loving God and loving other people. The example of those

living a consecrated life shows that there is more to life than what we experience on earth. The consecrated life proclaims the glory of the world to come.

Religious who make public profession of the evangelical counsels have been with the Church since its earliest days. Religious are both men and women. In fact, they are both lay people and ordained, as many ordained men live in community with other religious

and take public vows to follow the counsels. Bishops have the role of discerning new forms of living the consecrated life and submitting those grounded in the Holy Spirit to the Pope for approval. Traditional ways the consecrated life is practiced in the Church include living in community with others (sisters or brothers). This is the type of consecrated life that we commonly describe as "religious life." Other styles of consecrated life include an eremitic lifestyle as a hermit, taking a vow as a consecrated virgin or widow, or participating in a secular institute of consecrated life or a society of apostolic life. In all of these models, the evangelical counsels are embraced.

Characteristics of Religious Life

You are probably most familiar with religious life as lived by sisters or brothers, some of whom may be or have been your teachers. Teaching and the operation of Catholic elementary and high schools has been one of the primary ministries of religious in the United States throughout the nation's history. Generations of American Catholics owe their education to religious women and men who founded and then supported countless schools. More commonly, since the Second Vatican Council in the 1960s, religious, women and men have taken the opportunity to choose many other ministries besides teaching. Today's religious, responding to new needs, are involved in many types of service to the Church; some work as pastoral associates and pastoral ministers in parishes, others as chancellors of dioceses. The other ministries in which religious participate are even more varied: they might do anything from running homes for battered women and children to working in the media to produce and direct programming for Christian evangelization.

While it is true that there has been a decrease in vocations to the religious life in recent years, some religious communities around the world are flourishing. For example, the Missionaries of Charity, founded by Mother Teresa, has eight branches, all of which are growing: active sisters, contemplative sisters, active brothers, contemplative brothers, missionary fathers, lay missionaries, volunteers, and sick and suffering coworkers.

The most common characteristic of religious life is belonging to a community. This lifestyle has roots in the Gospel and in God himself: Jesus ministered to others in community, with both men and women followers. When Jesus sent out his disciples, he sent them out in pairs. God, too, is a relationship of Persons: Father, Son, and Holy Spirit. Religious communities often mirror the lifestyle and purpose of their founder who established the community's charism. Religious women traditionally have lived in convents. Religious men have lived in monasteries or rectories. However, today, because of a variety of different ministries that may require a religious to live separated from the community, some religious live alone though they remain in communication with their sisters or brothers.

Two other characteristics of religious life are the *active* and *contemplative* forms. Contemplative religious spend the majority of their days in solitude and silence, praying, studying, and doing penance. Female religious contemplatives are known as nuns. Male religious contemplatives are known as monks. Their lives center around praying the complete Liturgy of the Hours, or Divine Office, the Church's official prayer. Some contemplatives live an **eremitic life** as hermits, people who seek God while living alone. Hermits most often live on the grounds of a monastery or hermitage. The monks or nuns bring the hermits

eremitic life
The life of a hermit; a person who chooses the eremitic life most often lives alone and devotes himself or herself to developing a deep intimacy with Christ through silence, prayer, and penance.

food or drink. By devoting their lives to contemplative prayer, these religious remind the world of the time when everyone will be caught up in contemplation of God.

Active religious also pray and do penance and live in community. However, these sisters and brothers are out in the world participating in some of the active ministries described above. Many religious are missionaries, meaning they evangelize either in foreign missions in other countries or in home missions in their own countries.

Other Types of the Consecrated Life

There are some consecrated lifestyles that do not require a person to be a fully professed member of a religious community.

One example is *consecrated virgins*. These are women who live a life of perpetual virginity but remain lay women and support themselves. They are consecrated by their local bishop to their diocese. Consecrated virgins support the clergy through prayer and sacrifice. Traditionally, the Church has consecrated women to a life of virginity. Saint Agnes, Saint Cecilia, Saint Lucy, and Saint Agatha are well-known virgin martyrs. This tradition died out before being restored in 1970. There are approximately two hundred consecrated virgins

living in the United States working as accountants, university professors, doctors, fire-fighters, and in many other professions.

Secular institutes are forms of consecrated life for single lay people and diocesan priests. They profess the evangelical counsels but do not take public vows and do not live in community. Secular institutes usually take on a special focus; for example, the Mission of Our Lady of Bethany, founded in 1948 in France, works and prays to bring God's love to the most rejected of society, including prostitutes and prisoners. There are over thirty recognized secular institutes in the United States. Some are for men only or women only. Others have members who are lay men, lay women, and priests.

Also standing alongside the consecrated life are *societies of apostolic life,* whose members do not take public vows but engage in many good works for the Church. One familiar example is the Knights of Columbus, a lay organization with over 1.5 million members worldwide. Founded in New Haven, Connecticut, in 1882 by Father Michael J. McGivney, the Knights of Columbus was intended to provide a structure to make sure Catholics could receive insurance benefits not afforded to them in the workplace due to bigotry. The Knights of Columbus continue to provide this benefit along with serving many charitable causes within the Church.

Saint Agnes

Formation for the Consecrated Life

There are really two steps to choosing the consecrated life: discernment followed by acceptance into a religious community. Under these two steps are several other stages in the process.

A discernment process may take shape like the one described on pages 49–50. Two additional things can help you when personally discerning a vocation to the consecrated life. First, choose a person to be your spiritual director. This person may be found with the help of your parish priest or through a religious community. A spiritual director can provide more perspective on religious life and help you to gauge whether or not you might flourish in such a situation. Second, research several different religious communities to find out their charism or gift. Talk with some of the members and prayerfully determine which community most attracts you.

The second major step of formation is acceptance into a religious community. This takes place through an application process followed by a series of interviews with the **vocation director** and other members of the community. Once accepted, these stages of formation typically follow:

Postulancy. The first stage is one in which the candidate lives with the community in one of its houses and participates in one of the ministries the community is involved in. The person is called a postulant, that is, one who is beginning formation.

Novitiate. After a period of about one year, the candidate progresses to a more intensive time of study, both of theology and of the community's history and life. A novice begins to live the life of the vows of the community. He or she may study the community's charism. This period typically lasts for two years, with the last year set aside for solitude so that the novice can concentrate more on personal prayer.

Temporary Profession. At the end of the novitiate, the novice requests entrance into the community. She or he makes temporary vows which are renewed annually for up to nine years. During this time the person may be known as "junior professed."

Perpetual Vows. After several years, if the religious continues to have a total desire to remain consecrated to God, he or she is invited to make a public, perpetual profession of religious consecration.

Formation programs vary from congregation to congregation, and often depend on whether or not the community is an active or contemplative community. Also, formation does not end with final vows. Throughout their lives, religious continue to form their lives to live more completely the counsels of poverty, chastity, and obedience.

vocation director
A contact person for a religious order or for a diocesan office dedicated to answering questions of inquirers and encouraging vocations.

Marriage

Marriage is a vocation founded by God with the intention of furthering the human race and of offering the means that contribute to the eternal destiny of both the husband and wife and their children. Christ himself blessed marriage in his ministry. Marriage is modeled on Christ's union with the Church.

The vocation of marriage is one that springs from God's love. A man and woman work in their marriage to duplicate for each other the committed and eternal love that God has shown to them. The love between a man and woman often develops slowly and is cultivated by a growing friendship that leads to intimate sharing. At the time of the celebration of the Sacrament of Matrimony, the husband and wife exchange and bestow the marriage vows with and on each other. In fact, the man and woman are the ministers of this sacrament; the priest or deacon only serves as a witness and a representative of the Church.

Living in a Christian family helps us to imagine and prepare for marriage. Witnessing the loving example of parents, grandparents, and neighbors in marriage is a way to begin to plot out a style for married life that you might eventually choose as a husband or wife, and as a parent. Besides just observing and thinking about what it would like to be married, there are several practical things you can do now to prepare for a possible vocation to marriage. For example, you can work on:

- *Respect and Honor.* Both of these qualities demand giving other people their due and acknowledging their worth and goodness. You can practice these skills now in the way you treat your family members and friends of both sexes.

- *Listening.* Successful married couples are adept at good conversation. Good conversation involves excellent listening skills as one person concentrates on what the other is saying rather than just thinking up what to say next. How good a listener are you? Work in your current relationships to practice good listening skills that involve give and take and learn to make reasonable compromises when experience conflicts with family and friends.

- *Commitment.* Marriage demands faithful and unbroken commitment. Remember, the intimate bond between a husband and wife is intended to represent the same bond that Jesus shares with the Church. It is an unbreakable bond; this is the reason that the Church does not recognize divorce. You can practice commitment in your schoolwork, an after-school job, in your participation on a team or other extracurricular activity, and to your family and friends.

- *Chastity.* In marriage a husband and wife are faithful to each other physically. This is how they observe the counsel of chastity for their state in life. For you, chastity means refraining from sex until marriage. Remaining chaste until marriage is the best gift you can give your future spouse on your wedding night and beyond.

- *Love.* Married people have a particular, exclusive love for one another. They also have an all-encompassing love for all persons. It is difficult to imagine the exclusive love that will one day be yours if you marry, but you can prepare for it by cultivating an exclusive and deep love for God through prayer, works of charity, and love for your neighbor, including your enemies.

Much more on the preparation for marriage, the rite of Matrimony, and the challenges and rewards of marriage will be covered in Unit 2.

Priesthood

Like the call to consecrated life, a call to the vocation of priesthood may not take place in typically

logical or sequential steps. It is likely that each priest has a unique story about how his vocation was first awakened. Some of the signs that a man is being called to priesthood may include:

- other people telling him he would make a good priest;

- a desire to pray;

- going to Mass more than usual and imagining himself as presider;

- trying out some of the ministries associated with priesthood (e.g., teaching, caring for the sick, counseling others).

The Sacrament of Holy Orders confers a sacred power on the priest for the service of the faithful. The sacrament is conferred only on baptized men, following the example of Jesus and the early Church, who only called men to be Apostles and bishops. In the Roman Catholic Church, priests live celibate lives and promise to remain celibate as a witness to the kingdom of heaven. The sacrament is received in three degrees—bishop, priest, and deacon. These ordained ministers serve the Church by teaching, by leading worship, and by their governance.

Priests can also be members of religious communities, for example, the Jesuits or the Franciscans. A religious-order priest takes the same vows of poverty, chastity, and obedience as the other members of the community (i.e., the brothers). The difference is that the religious priest is ordained and a brother is not. Diocesan priests are not members of religious communities. They are ordained to serve in a particular diocese, giving obedience to the local bishop. The diocesan priest makes promises of celibacy along with the promise of obedience. However, he does not typically take a vow of poverty. Most often a diocesan priest is assigned to work in a parish.

Unit 3 offers more information on each degree of ordained ministry on the preparation men typically undergo on the road to priesthood, and on their life and ministry as priests.

Vocation Week

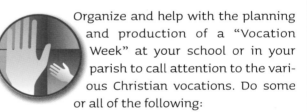

Organize and help with the planning and production of a "Vocation Week" at your school or in your parish to call attention to the various Christian vocations. Do some or all of the following:

- Make several posters and collages that emphasize words like call, prayer, vocation, discernment as well as the particular Christian vocations and display them around your school or parish.

- Arrange for a panel of speakers to address teens on the specific preparation and practices of vocations like marriage, religious life, ordination, and the committed single life.

- Plan a prayer service or Mass with the theme of vocation awareness.

- Organize a standing committee that will continue with vocation-themed events throughout the year.

studyquestions

1. Why are Holy Orders and Matrimony known as "sacraments at the service of communion"?

2. How can a lay person live out Christ's mission of priest, prophet, and king?

3. What are some reasons a person might choose a vocation to the committed single life?

4. Name two challenges of the single life.

5. What characterizes a life consecrated to God?

6. What are the roots of religious life shared in a community?

7. How are the active and contemplative forms of religious life different? How are they similar?

8. Briefly explain the following forms of religious life: consecrated virginity, secular institutes, societies of apostolic life.

9. What is the purpose of marriage?

10. Who are the ministers of the Sacrament of Matrimony?

11. Explain the difference between a religious-order priest and a diocesan priest.

 **journal**discussion

- Of all the types of religious life described in this section, which is the most attractive to you? Explain why.

- Name and explain three Specific things you can do right now to prepare for marriage.

messianic secret
A motif in the Gospel of Mark in which the recognition of the identity of Jesus as the Son of God is suppressed.

- What do you think are some signs (besides those listed on page 61) that a man is called to the priesthood?

✦ Christian Discipleship: Serve One Another

A great secret unfolds in the Gospel of Mark known as the **messianic secret**. As the secret is gradually revealed, the readers learn the answers to the questions,

- Who is Jesus?

- What is his mission?

Perhaps equally important, they also have a clearer understanding of what Christian discipleship really entails.

The mystery or secret first begins to be brought to light as Jesus and his disciples set out for Jerusalem by way of the region of Caesarea Philippi. Along the way, Jesus asks them,

"Who do people say that I am?" When Peter finally and correctly answers, "You are the Messiah," Jesus tells him and the others not to tell anyone else about that. Jesus then predicts the events of his Passion and Death. He also addresses the crowd with information about the conditions of being a disciple:

> "Whoever wishes to come after me must deny himself, take up his cross, and follow me." (Mk 8:34)

The disciples find the entire message about a suffering messiah and suffering disciples harsh and confusing.

A similar conversation plays out again in Mark 9:30–32 before this Gospel intrigue reaches its climax as Jesus addresses the question from the Apostles James and John about whether they will be able to sit at his right and left hand after he comes in glory. Jesus tells them that there is another path to glory and greatness, the path of discipleship:

> "You know that those who are recognized as rulers over the Gentiles lord it over them, and their great ones make their authority over them felt. But it shall not be so among you. Rather, whoever wishes to be great among you will be your servant; whoever wishes to be first among you will be the slave of all. For the Son of Man did not come to be served but to serve and to give his life as a ransom for many."(Mk 10:42–45)

During this journey to Jerusalem, Jesus teaches us what it means to be a disciple:

- A disciple must put personal desires aside to follow the Father's will.

- A disciple must accept suffering, even to the point of death.

- A disciple must serve others.

This was the life Christ lived for us. This was the life that brought us salvation. All Christians, at every age or state in life, are called to do the same if they are to be counted among the disciples. Consider the way the people described below have lived the challenge of discipleship.

Matt Talbot: Putting Aside Personal Desires

By age twelve, Matt Talbot was already drinking in the Dublin pubs nearly every evening. Like many poor Irish, Talbot came to the pubs to socialize and escape his overcrowded one-room tenement, which he shared with his parents and his surviving eight brothers and sisters. The pub was a place of some joy, plenty of stories, and of course alcohol.

Eventually Matt went to work as a day laborer, spending ten-hour days as a hod carrier, the person who carried a heavy load of bricks or mortar alongside a bricklayer as building after building

was constructed in Dublin. After work, it was off to the pub where Matt refrained from dancing, playing cards, and meeting women. "He was only interested in one thing," a friend from those days remembered, "and that was drinking."

Matt was a generous person with a good disposition, and he would often buy rounds of drinks for his coworkers and friends. Then at the age of twenty-eight, something happened to Matt that changed his life. One Saturday at the racetrack, Matt won a big bet that gave him enough money to skip a week of work. He spent each of those days in the pub just drinking. He timed it so that his gambling money ran out on payday at the brickyard where he worked. Matt stood on the road between the brickyard and the pub as his fellow workers finished their work and headed for the pub waiting for someone to buy him a few drinks as he had for them.

Some of the workers greeted Matt, but didn't invite him along.

Others pretended they didn't even see him as they went inside the pub.

Matt later recalled that something died inside of him that day. He went home sober and told his mother that he would make a pledge: no drinking for three months. He was afraid to promise any longer. His mother told him not to make that kind of pledge unless he really thought he could keep it.

Matt replaced his time in the pub with time in church. He began his day with Mass, then went to church again at the end of the day for more prayer, frequent confession, and conversation with a spiritual director. He became a **third-order Franciscan**. After the deaths of his father and oldest brother, he returned home to live with his mother.

At night Matt's mother would awake to see him praying with his arms extended in the form of a cross. He began to sleep only about three hours a day, and even then he used a board plank with a wooden block for a pillow. Eventually he would leave the

tenement for church where he would kneel on stones until the doors opened for the earliest Mass.

In 1925 Matt collapsed on the streets of Dublin and died. When onlookers came to his body they found heavy, penitential chains wrapped around his arms and legs. This discovery and a reflection of his coworkers and friends that this man had managed to conquer alcoholism through prayer, study, almsgiving, fasting, and penance led many people to take a deeper look at his life. His spiritual director, who had preceded him in death, had already told people that Matt deserved to be called a saint.

The Church called him "venerable" in 1973, and it continues to examine his cause for beatification and sainthood.

third-order Franciscan
Founded by Saint Francis of Assisi, the third order is comprised of people who are committed to living the Franciscan rule while out in the world.

Father Timothy Vakoc: Accepting Suffering, Even to the Point of Death

In May 2004, the weekend of the twelfth anniversary of his ordination to the priesthood, Father Timothy Vakoc, an Army Chaplain from Minnesota, was critically injured when a bomb exploded near his Humvee in Iraq.

"Tim took the brunt of the blast," said his brother, Jeff. "The soldiers did first aid on him and deciding that they couldn't wait for the medics or they would lose him; they drove him back to the base on two flat tires, and he was flown to Baghdad from there."

Father Vakoc lost his left eye, sustained brain damage, and remains permanently paralyzed on his right side from the attack. His recovery, first at Walter Reed Army Hospital in Washington, D.C., has been slow. An Army nurse who cared for him said, "He was seen to finger a rosary placed in his hand, and to make a slight pedal motion with his foot. At that point, he began to joke and tease family and medical attendants, hiding items placed in his hand intended for physical therapy."

A special visitor, Archbishop Edwin O'Brien, told Fr. Tim: "You are still a priest and this bed is now your altar."

Father Vakoc had been in the Army for eight years and in Iraq for nine months before the attack. What was he doing there? "I think he felt that God had put him there and that was what he was supposed to be doing," said his brother.

The explanation from Father Vakoc on why he put himself in harm's way was even more to the point: "The safest place for me to be is in the center of God's will, and if that is in the line of fire, that's where I'll be."[2]

As of December 2006, Fr. Tim is now speaking, sings along to familiar songs, shakes hands at Mass, and blesses everyone who comes to see him. He is truly still ministering as a priest.

Gigi McMillan: Serving Others

In 1995, Gigi and Dan McMillan's son Ben was diagnosed with a brain tumor. "Within forty-eight hours, our son went from being a normal kid to a kid with a life-threatening disease going into brain surgery," recalled Gigi.

The McMillans needed immediate and very specific information about brain cancer, which affects approximately three thousand children annually in the United States. The McMillans spoke with another mother whose child had faced the same situation. In just one conversation, each mother knew twice as much as they knew before. "Just imagine if there were fifty parents talking," Gigi remembered thinking. "We'd all know fifty times as much."

Gigi McMillan partnered with another friend, Kathy Riley, to create the We Can Pediatric Brain Tumor Network (www.wecan.cc), which has grown from a small group of parents at one hospital to an independent, nonprofit organization that provides support groups in seven cities, a sibling program, a bereavement program for families of children who die, and a family camp in Idyllwild, California.

A Group of "We Can" kids. Ben McMillian is on the lower right. Two of these children have since died.

"The first few years, it was hard for me," Gigi admits. "But after three or four years, it wasn't about me anymore, it was about the three hundred families in our network. It was about giving back. The ultimate healing is to help someone else so the network grows as parents pass on what they received."

Today, Ben is doing well. The McMillans' daughter Julie sits on the board of We Can. The McMillans also have two other children, Patrick and Sharon. Gigi McMillan believes that the best thing she can pass on to her children is a sense of community so they will grow to see that giving to and serving others is "not a duty, but a joy."[3]

Your Call to Discipleship

In Baptism, you were initiated to a life in Christ. As you mature in faith, you, too, are challenged to put aside your own desires to follow God's will, to accept your suffering as a way to share in the suffering of Christ, and to serve others.

In Baptism, you were also initiated into the Church, a community of people who travel the road of discipleship with you. Your Christian vocation to holiness and whatever particular vocation you ultimately accept is intimately bound up with others. The *Catechism of the Catholic Church* highlights the communal character of the human vocation:

> The human person needs to live in society. Society is not for him an extraneous addition but a requirement of his nature. Through the exchange with others, mutual service and dialogue with his brethren, man develops his potential; he thus responds to his vocation. (*CCC*, 1879)

Whereas your last years of high school are the time to *begin* to discern in more detail the particular Christian vocations like marriage, Holy Orders, religious life, and the committed single life, there is no time like the present to deepen your commitment to Christian discipleship. Try out these suggestions for growing in your relationship with Jesus Christ:

- Spend more time in prayer. "Pray constantly . . . always and for everything giving thanks in the name of our Lord Jesus Christ to God the Father" (1 Thes 5:17; Eph 5:20). Model

your prayer in Christ and make him the primary focus of your prayer. His humanity is the way that the Holy Spirit teaches us to pray to God the Father. Like Christ, pray, "not mine, but your will be done." Prayer while participating at Mass and Eucharistic adoration are two ways to be in Christ's presence when you pray.

- Don't seek out suffering, but accept disappointments, setbacks, and pain that do come your way as an opportunity to share in the cross of Christ.

- Do something helpful for another person. Keep this act of service off your college application! Rather, take it back to God in prayer.

In God's due time, his plan for the rest of your life will be known to you. While the challenges of Christian discipleship will never be diminished, you will be at peace in your God-given vocation.

 study questions

1. What is the messianic secret?

2. What does it mean to be a disciple of Christ?

3. What is the role of society in helping persons determine their vocation?

- Describe a time that you put aside a personal desire. What was the result?

- Name a cause for which would be willing to die. Explain why.

- How do you feel about serving others: is it more of a duty or more of a joy? Explain.

✦ Finding a Calling

✦ Choosing a vocation is different from choosing a career or having a job.

✦ A particular Christian vocation like marriage, religious life, or priesthood is a call from God that helps us to love and serve God by loving and serving other people.

✦ Journeying to Perfection

✦ The teenage to young adult years are the time to begin seriously considering a life's vocation.

✦ God providentially has a plan for each of our lives.

✦ The first step to determining a vocation is to involve God in every facet and every motivation of our lives.

✦ Jesus reminds us to "seek first the kingdom of God and his righteousness" and everything else will be given to us besides.

✦ Prayer is the way we can come to know God's will for our lives.

✦ We have the gift of free will that allows us to make our own choice about loving God and others.

✦ At the end of time we will see how God has guided us to perfection.

✦ Discernment

✦ Discernment is a process that involves looking and praying over all sides of an issue.

✦ The central action of discernment is to reflect on the ordinary events and actions of our lives.

✦ The first step of the discernment process involves centering prayer, a form of prayer designed to help us find God in our depths.

✦ Prayer involves more listening to God than talking to God.

✦ Saint Ignatius taught that God communicates with us through how we feel when we imagine and reflect on the ordinary events of our lives.

✦ An Ignatian model for discerning a vocation involves dreaming and imagining, gathering information, and praying over options.

✦ Exploring Christian Vocations

✦ The sacraments provide a framework for understanding Christian vocations.

✦ In Baptism and Confirmation, we receive a share in the common priesthood of Christ, which we are able to live out by participating in his priestly, prophetic, and kingly offices.

✦ Two sacraments—Holy Orders and Matrimony—are called sacraments at the service of communion because they are mainly directed to the holiness and salvation of others.

✦ While there is no liturgical ritual to mark the single life as a permanent vocation, it is a valuable and authentic vocation that many Catholics are freely choosing.

✦ Many choose the committed single life in order to care for aging parents, to devote themselves to a demanding career, or to serve other worthwhile causes.

✦ The consecrated life is a life dedicated to living the evangelical counsels and one marked by public vows.

✦ The most typical way we understand the consecrated life is life lived in community by religious sisters and brothers.

◆ Other types of the consecrated life include consecrated virginity, secular institutes for single lay people and diocesan priests, and societies of apostolic life whose members do not take public vows.

◆ Marriage is a vocation modeled on Christ's union with the Church.

◆ The purpose of Christian marriage is to further the human race and to contribute to the eternal destiny of husband, wife, and children.

◆ The Sacrament of Holy Orders confers a sacred power on priests for the service of the faithful.

◆ Priests can be members of religious communities or committed to serve in a specific diocese under the direction of the local bishop.

◆ Christian Discipleship: Serve One Another

◆ In the messianic secret revealed in the Gospel of Mark, we come to a clearer understanding about the meaning of discipleship.

◆ A Christian disciple is called to put aside personal desires to follow the Father's will, accept suffering to the point of death, and serve others.

◆ Matt Talbot overcame dependence on alcohol through prayer, fasting, and penance.

◆ Father Timothy Vakoc faced the dangers of war because he felt that was the place to which God had called him.

◆ Gigi McMillan was a wife and mother who found that serving others is a joy, not a duty.

◆ Whatever our ultimate and particular Christian vocation, we must understand that it is cultivated and practiced in communion with the rest of society.

assignments applications

1. Determine three possible college majors based on your skills and interests. First, assess your existing skills. In what subjects do you perform well at school? What are some other tasks you do well at home or work? What are some

talents that others have told you that you possess? Second, identify your personal interests. What is something that inspires you? What do you enjoy doing? What do you want to achieve?

Third, think about some life goals. What are your main motivations for a career? Do you want to work for a large organization or on your own? Write up an assessment of your skills and interests. Then, work through one or more college websites (search: determining a college major) to attempt to match your profile with a college major. Write a report of your findings.

2. Read the call of Moses (Ex 3:1–4:17) and the call of Mary (Lk 1:26–38) and identify VanOosting's four characteristics common to any vocation in these biblical examples:

    ✦ called for a special purpose

    ✦ the presence of a special gift

    ✦ the name of the caller

    ✦ the life of sacrifice, faith, and often darkness that follows.

    Optional: Apply these characteristics to a career or vocation that you are considering for yourself.

3. Prepare a PowerPoint presentation using charts and graphs to detail current statistics on the Catholic vocations (marriage, single life, consecrated life, priesthood). See for example: The Center for Applied Research in the Apostolate (CARA) (http://cara.georgetown.edu/index.htm).

4. Prioritize a list of five things you want in life. Write them in a journal. Pray a Novena (see page 334 of this book, the Catholic Handbook for Faith) with the hope that Mary or another saint will intercede for you and your prayers will be answered.

5. Read a biography of Saint Ignatius Loyola. Write a report focusing on five interesting facts about his life.

6. Visit a local seminary, diocesan office, convent, or monastery. Speak with a vocation director about the requirements for priesthood or religious life. Write a report summarizing any new insights that you gleaned from your visit.

7. Report on one of the following Catholic single persons: Saint Benedict Joseph Labre, Saint Praxedes, Saint Joseph Moscati, Dag Hammarskjöld, Flannery O'Connor, or Jean Donovan. Explain how their vocation to the committed single life allowed them the freedom to work for humanity.

8. Write an essay explaining how you can incorporate the Gospel counsels—poverty, chastity, and obedience—into your current lifestyle.

9. Recall the two purposes of marriage: to contribute to the holiness and salvation of the spouse and to help propagate the human race. Interview at least five married people. Ask: "What is the main purpose of marriage?" Record their responses. Note ways the interviewees expressed one or both of the purposes of marriage in their own words.

10. Write profiles of three people you know (or know of) who best represent each of the following requirements of discipleship:

    ✦ puts personal desires aside to follow the Father's will;

    ✦ accepts suffering, even to the point of death;

    ✦ serves others.

Notes

1. From "Vocation Education," *America*, July 1, 2002.

2. Adapted from the article "Catholic chaplain from Minnesota critically wounded in Iraq" Catholic News Service, June, 2004.

3. From the article "Giving Back" by Erika Ross. *Vistas* (Loyola Marymount University), Fall 2005: vol. 8, no. 4.

Prayer
for the Transition from High School

The last semesters of high school are filled with planning for the next stage in life. Which college will you attend? Which career will you prepare for? What will it be like to leave family and friends at home? How will you grow in a personal and adult faith? These are only some of the questions to consider on a regular basis. Pray often for a smooth transition from high school. Keep Christ close to your heart as you make these important decisions. On several occasions, pray using the following format.

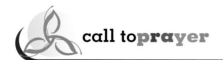 **call to prayer**

Pray the following words or choose some similar words of your own. Construct your prayer around some specific situations arising in your final months, weeks, and days in high school.

Come, Holy Spirit.
Be with me today in my studies.
Improve my work habits.
Help me to learn to relax when taking exams so that I am able to test to my potential.
When I apply to colleges, allow me the chance to show the "real me" to those who make decisions.

Come, Holy Spirit.
Allow me to appreciate my friends.
Give me a moment to see their goodness.
Help me to be always faithful to these dear people I have grown up with since childhood.
Always give me the opportunity to stay close to my friends,
whether we are physically near or far apart.

Come, Holy Spirit.
Continue to inspire my teachers, counselors, and coaches who have inspired me.

In these last days of high school, give me the courage to truly follow their lessons.
Allow me the inspiration to thank them for their gifts with sincere appreciation.

Come, Holy Spirit.
Bless my parents and family.
They are everything to me.
They have modeled for me your life and love.
Keep them healthy and happy for many more years.

Come, Holy Spirit.
Help me find my way to my loving Father through his Son.
Share with me a sign of my calling.
Give me good ears to listen to your voice.
Give me the strength to follow your lead.

Amen.

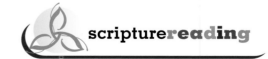 **scripture reading**

Slowly and prayerfully read the following Gospel passage from John 14:15–21. How is God with you now? How will you stay close to God after you graduate from high school? Listen carefully to Jesus' words.

A reading from the Gospel of John.

"If you love me, you will keep my commandments. And I will ask the Father, and he will give you another Advocate to be with you always, the Spirit of truth, which the world cannot accept, because it neither sees nor knows it. But you know it, because it remains with you, and will be in you. I will not leave you orphans; I will come to you. In a little while the world will no longer see me, but you will see me, because I live and you will live. On that day you will realize that I am in my Father and you are in me and I in you. Whoever has my commandments and observes them is the one who loves me. And whoever loves me will be loved by my Father, and I will love him and reveal myself to him."

The Gospel of the Lord.

Praise to you, Lord Jesus Christ.

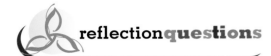

reflection questions

Read through the entire list of questions. Then go back and choose one question to spend time with in greater detail. Listen to what God is saying to you. Take notes in a notebook or prayer journal. Choose another question on a different occasion. Form your own questions having to do with your transition from high school. As your answers change, write your new answers.

+ What are my goals for my senior year in high school?

+ How can I better express my true self to my family and friends?

+ To whom do I need to say I am sorry?

+ Where do I see myself in five years?

+ What are my God-given talents?

+ How might I use my talents in a career?

+ How can I show my family I appreciate their love and care?

+ What do I need to do to learn to be more independent?

+ How can I improve my faith-life?

+ What can I do to be more active in the Church?

+ What kind of Catholic will I be when I get out of high school?

+ Who do I want to become?

+ Act of Hope

Pray an Act of Hope for your future life using these traditional words.

O God,
I hope with complete trust that you will give me,
through the merits of Jesus Christ, all necessary graces in this world
and everlasting life in the world to come,
for this is what you have promised
and you always keep your promises.
Amen.

unit**two**

Called to Holiness
through Marriage

✦ The Gift of Love

There is an oft-told story about a young married couple called Jim and Della, who are too poor to give each other a Christmas gift that will truly express their love for one another.[1] On Christmas Eve, Della decides what she would really like to do is to give her husband a watch chain to go with the gold watch Jim had inherited from his grandfather. The only problem is that the chain costs $21 and she only has $1.87. Della decides to sell her beautiful brown hair, which reaches to her knees, to the local wigmaker so that she can buy Jim the platinum watch chain.

Della's heart is pounding with excitement as she waits for Jim to come home so that she can give him her present. But when Jim sees his wife without her long locks of hair he is surprised and bewildered. The present Jim has bought his wife is a set of beautiful tortoiseshell combs.

"Dell, let's put our Christmas presents away and keep them awhile," Jim says while collapsing on the couch. "They are too nice to use just now. Besides, I sold my watch to get the money to buy your combs."

The story illustrates the totality of mutual self-giving without any reservation, the most remarkable quality of the marriage covenant between a husband and a wife. This is a remarkable quality because there is a natural desire in each person to "find himself or herself" and then guard and protect this person that we discover without any inclination at all to give ourselves away.

It is this special kind of self-giving love for another that forms the heart of Christian marriage and leads a husband and wife to gift each other with the entire reality of their being: mind, heart, spirit, will, body, weakness, and strength. This self-giving is rooted in Jesus' example of obedience to his Father and a man's and woman's own call to discipleship, knowing that in losing one's own life, he or she will really find it (see Mk 8:34–38).

In marriage, two people pledge themselves to one another—"for better, for worse, for richer, for poorer, in sickness and in health, until death do us part"—permanently. This total self-giving surrender that endures until death mirrors God the Father's eternal love for his creatures and Christ's love for his Church. It is the kind of love that allows a person to recognize and understand who he or she is in God's eyes and then be willing to hand that person over to his or her beloved.

Think some more of Della from the story. Her long hair defined much more about her than physical appearance. The beauty of her hair was truly a glimpse inside of herself and defined her in many ways.

Likewise Jim's watch was a gift of his legacy, a connection with a beloved ancestor that he might someday pass on to his own child as a gift of himself.

Nevertheless, the love these spouses shared for one another was greater than any love they had for their possessions or for themselves. This was the love they gave to each other in their special Christmas gifts.

1. Adapted from "Gift of the Magi" by O. Henry.

chapter**outline**

✦ Benefits and Purpose of Married Life

The purpose of marriage—having and raising children and giving oneself to another—go hand in hand with its many benefits.

✦ Marriage in the Bible

Some of the Church's teachings on marriage are present in the Old Testament. In the New Testament, Christ validates the goodness of marriage and elevates it to a sacrament.

✦ Love and Other Elements of Relationships

Four elements—love, infatuation, friendship, and exploitation—in combination impact all human relationships, including marriage.

✦ Vocation to Chastity

Chastity integrates a person's sexuality with his or her whole being, strengthening the unity of body and soul.

✦ Choices Leading to Marriage

Many choices and experiences you are making and having now could have an impact on your future marriage.

chapter three

Preparing for Marriage in God's Plan: Friendship, Chastity, Dating

So the Lord God cast a deep sleep on the man, and while he was asleep, he took out one of his ribs and closed up its place with flesh. The Lord God then built up into a woman the rib that he had taken from the man.

Genesis 2:21–22

✦ Benefits and Purpose of Married Life

God's plan for his creation included marriage from the very beginning. It will include marriage until the very end of time as well. Marriage is always necessary as a means for the procreation of the human race *and*

various benefits and purposes" (*Gaudium et Spes*, 48). Jesus Christ raised marriage to the dignity of a sacrament, participating in the life of the couple as they grow together, deepening their unity and growing in perfection. A primary purpose of marriage is the procreation and raising of children. Another is the willingness of the spouses to give themselves to the other, a way they work to their own and each other's salvation.

the wholesome and proper raising of children. That will never change, in spite of the various ways marriage has been lived out by couples through the ages and in the differences in the ways couples experience marriage today.

When we speak about God as the author of marriage, we first have to acknowledge that God made marriage good because he created the world and everything in it to be good. The first man and woman were drawn immediately to this goodness: the man "clings to his wife, and the two of them become one body" (Gn 2:24). God didn't stop there. He continues to gift this intimacy between a husband and wife "with

The benefits of marriage go hand in hand with the purposes of marriage. Raising children and sharing family life has great rewards. Companionship, friendship, commitment, and sexual intimacy are some of the benefits. As you begin to explore married life as a possible vocation for yourself, collect a list of reasons why you think marriage would be good for you.

In this chapter, you will trace the origins of marriage in God's plan, especially as expressed in Sacred Scripture. You will also look at the root of the vocation of marriage as it applies to your own life, from relationships you are developing now with friends of the opposite gender, to the responsibilities of chastity, to the ever-evolving progression of relationship that leads to marriage: typically understood as moving from friendship, to dating, to courtship (exclusive dating), to engagement.

As these issues are explored, it is important to keep in mind that the bond between a husband and wife never depends solely on their own human decisions. That is because God is the author of Matrimony. The benefits and purposes of marriage are key to the continuation of the human race and the personal development and eternal destiny of the husband, wife, their children, and society at large. These are larger-than-human tasks and rewards. To make marriage fruitful, Jesus Christ blesses this union and remains with the couple as their lives unfold.

journal**discussion**

- What does it mean to "give yourself to another?"
- Rank what you think would be the five greatest benefits of married life.

A Top Ten List

Author Maggie Gallagher (*The Case for Marriage*) spent time reviewing the scientific evidence on the benefits of marriage for adults and then had fun putting together a list—David Letterman style—of the top ten reasons marriage can make a difference in your life. While the list does not include religious graces of marriage (e.g., the benefit of getting to Heaven is not mentioned!), it is fun to consider the items she collected[1]:

10. It's Safer. Marriage lowers the risk that both women and men will be victims of violence, including domestic violence. For example, two-thirds of violent acts against women committed by intimate partners were committed by boyfriends, former boyfriends, or former husbands—not by husbands.

9. It Can Save Your Life. Married people live longer and healthier lives. For example, nine out of ten men who are married at age forty-eight will live to at least age sixty-five but only six in ten unmarried men will live that long. For women, marriage reduces a middle-aged wife's risk of dying before she's a senior citizen from two in ten to just one in ten.

8. It Can Save Your Kid's Life. Children lead healthier, longer lives if parents get and stay married. One study showed that a parent's divorce knocked four years off the adult child's life expectancy.

7. You Will Earn More Money. Married men make as much as 40 percent more money than single men, even after considering education and job history. Married women also achieve a salary boost; however, it declines once they become mothers.

6. In Fact, Married People Get Much Richer. Married people not only make more money, they manage money better and build more wealth together than they would alone.

5. There Is Less Risk of Cheating. Marriage increases **sexual fidelity**. Men who live with their girlfriends are four times more likely to cheat on them than husbands are on their wives. Cohabiting women are eight times more likely to cheat than wives.

sexual fidelity
The faithfulness of a husband and wife to each other and their marriage vows.

4. You Won't Go Bonkers. Marriage is good for mental health. Married men and women are less depressed, less anxious, and less psychologically stressed than single, divorced, or widowed Americans.

3. Marriage Will Make You Happy. Overall, 40 percent of married people, compared with 25 percent of singles or cohabitors, count themselves as happy.

2. Your Kids Will Love You More. Adult children of divorced parents describe their relationships with their mothers and fathers less positively than adults with parents of intact marriages.

1. Your Sex Life Will Be Better. Married people are more likely to report a satisfying sexual life than are singles or cohabitors.

✦ Marriage in the Bible

As the *Catechism* teaches: "God created man and woman *together* and willed each *for* the other" (*CCC*, 371). The two creation stories in the book of Genesis illustrate this teaching in several ways. For example:

- Man and woman are made "for each other." "The Lord God said: 'It is not good for the man to be alone. I will make a suitable partner for him'" (Gn 2:18). None of the animals were a suitable partner for man (Gn 2:19–20).

- Man and woman are created as a communion of persons, equal to one another, and complementary as masculine and feminine. "That is why a man leaves his father and mother and clings to his wife, and the two of them become one body" (Gn 2:24). By forming them as "one body," God unites them in a way in which they can transmit human life and, hence, cooperate in a unique way in the work of God the Creator.

- Man and woman are to be stewards of God, caring for the earth's resources. They carry out this role according to God's will, not arbitrarily or destructively. After blessing them, God said: "Be fertile and multiply; fill the earth and subdue it. Have dominion over the fish of the sea, the birds of the air, and all the living things that move on the earth" (Gn 1:28).

Scripture consistently speaks of the "mystery" of marriage: its God-given meaning, its origin and its end, the various ways it has been lived out, its difficulties resulting from sin, and its new meaning expressed in the New Testament by Christ. Recall that Matrimony is one of the "sacraments at the service of communion." This means that the sacrament directs the husband and wife to focus on the other in self-giving love that brings them their holiness and salvation. Through their service to each other and their intimate union, a husband and wife "experience the meaning of their oneness and attain to it with growing perfection day by day" (*Gaudium et Spes*, 48).

Tracing some of the examples and teachings of marriage through Scripture reminds us of its mystery and its constant care and partnership with God.

The Influence of Sin and the Introduction of the Law

As a result of the first sin, the original communion between man and woman that God intended was broken. The struggles that married couples

face today—including discord, a spirit of domination, infidelity, jealousy, and conflicts—are all a result of sin. The beautiful and idyllic life God had intended for man and woman was damaged by sin. For women, the pain of childbirth was one of the effects of sin, as the desires for sexual relations remained (see Gn 3:16). No longer simply a steward of the earth's resources, the effects of sin for man were the toil of work. The Lord said:

> By the sweat of your face
> shall you get bread to eat,
> Until you return to the ground,
> from which you were taken;
> For you are dirt,
> and to dirt you shall return. (Gn 3:19)

In spite of sin, the human race was extended, though seriously flawed with Original Sin. To heal the wounds of sin, a man and woman rely on the help of God's grace, which in his infinite mercy he extends to them: "For the man and his wife the Lord God made leather garments, with which he clothed them" (Gn 3:21). Since the fall of man and the first sin, marriage has helped couples overcome self-absorption, egoism, and pursuit of one's own pleasure and choose instead to be open to others, to care for one another, and to be self-giving.

Some of the moral teachings about marriage held by the Church today were present in the Old Testament. For example, specific laws about who could be married were spelled out in Leviticus 18. The law of Moses was also clear in protecting the wife from cruelty and domination by the husband. Teaching about the indissolubility of marriage was also introduced, though the Mosaic law permitted a decree of divorce. Jesus later explained that it was the "hardness of heart," a residue of sin, that allowed this decree because "from the beginning it was not so" (Mt 19:8).

The practice of the Israelites was to marry within their local tribe and, if not possible, then within the larger tribal confederation (see, for example, Numbers 36:1–12). There was no wedding or religious rite that marked the marriage. A betrothed (engaged) woman was considered legally married. When the marriage was consummated, the husband received the wife, and the family of the wife was given a **dowry**, considered to be compensation for the loss of the daughter's value as a laborer. Though there was not an official rite to mark these occasions, a week-long party was celebrated in honor of the new union.

Examples of polygamy can be cited in the Old Testament among the patriarchs and kings, but the understanding and practice of marriage under Mosaic law and the teachings of the Prophets evolved to examples of exclusive and faithful married love that was far beyond what was being practiced by the Canaanites and other pagan religions of the time. The Books of Ruth and Tobit describe the faithful and tender relationships between a husband and wife. The Song of Songs illustrates an unbreakable human love that is as "strong as death":

> Set me as a seal on your
>   heart,
> as a seal on your arm;
> For stern as death is love,
> relentless as the nether world
>   is devotion,
> its flames are a blazing fire.
> Deep waters cannot quench
>   love,
> nor floods sweep it away.
> (Sg 8:6–7)

dowry

Money or property brought to the bride's family by her husband at their marriage, or money or property given by the bride's family to the husband.

Lessons from Ruth

The book of Ruth is named after a Moabite woman who was joined to the Israelites through marriage and who became the great-grandmother of King David and an ancestor of Jesus. The story tells a timeless tale of loyalty, fidelity, and tenderness between spouses, and it shows how God rewards these virtues.

The story begins in Moab, a hostile land to Israel, where Naomi, a Jew, and her Israelite husband and children have settled to avoid famine. After Naomi's husband and two sons die, she decides to go back to Israel because the famine has ended. Her two daughters-in law, Orpah and Ruth, are accompanying her. But Naomi encourages them to stay in Moab with their families.

However, Ruth tells her mother-in-law: "Do not ask me to abandon or forsake you! for wherever you go I will go, wherever you lodge I will lodge, your people shall be my people, and your God my God" (Ru 1:16). Ruth does accompany Naomi to Israel, where a rich landowner and distant relative of her husband, Boaz, notices her and eventually marries her. Their son, Obed, was the father of Jesse, who in turn fathered David, the great king from whose line Jesus was born.

Read the book of Ruth. Then do the following:

- List three qualities that describe Ruth's character. Cite verses that support your descriptions.

- Write about a time when you were loyal to a friend or a friend was loyal to you.

- Why is loyalty important in a marriage? How can husbands and wives express to their loyalty to one another?

---

efficacious
Something that embodies the reality it represents.

The New Covenant and Marriage

The term "marriage in the Lord" (*CCC*, 1612) refers to marriage as a symbol of Christ's unfailing love of his spouse, the Church. In the New Covenant between God and mankind, Christ restored marriage to its original state before the first sin.

The New Testament documents Christ's validation of the goodness of marriage. As he began his public life, Jesus performed his first miracle—at his mother's request—at a wedding. Christ's presence at the wedding at Cana is not only a statement of the goodness of marriage, but a statement that from then on marriage will be an **efficacious** sign of his presence.

In his preaching, Christ taught clearly the original meaning of marriage as it was intended from the beginning: marriage was to be indissoluble to death. He said: "What God has joined together, no human being must separate" (Mt 19:6). This is a hard command to keep to this day.

Even the first listeners were struck by the difficulty of Jesus' words and of the permanence of marriage. Yet Jesus himself helps married couples to keep this command. He is the source of grace in marriage. As the *Catechism* teaches:

> It is by following Christ, renouncing themselves, and taking up their crosses that spouses will be able to "receive" the original meaning of marriage and live it with the help of Christ. This grace of Christian marriage is a fruit of Christ's cross, the source of all Christian life. (*CCC*, 1615)

Jesus comes into the life of married baptized Christians through the Sacrament of Matrimony. The fruits of the sacrament remain; Jesus remains present with the couple through their entire marriage. In the same way he loves the Church and handed himself over to the Church in his life, Death, and Resurrection, husbands and wives love each other with faithfulness that does not end until death, through the daily giving of themselves to the other.

Because of Christ's love for them and the grace of his presence in their marriage, the words of Saint Paul to the Ephesians are made clear:

> Husbands, love your wives, even as Christ loved the church and handed himself over for her to sanctify her, cleansing her by the bath of water with the word, that he might present himself the church in splendor, without spot or wrinkle or any such thing, that she might be holy and without blemish. (Eph 5:25–27)

Christian marriage, in Saint Paul's eyes, takes on a new meaning, which is the same as the intimate relationship Christ has with the Church. The wife should serve her husband in the same way the Church is of service to Christ. The husband should love his wife with the same depth of love that Christ has for the Church.

Love, an essential ingredient in the relationship between husband and wife, is explored in more depth in the next section, along with three other elements that factor into human relationships.

study questions

1. How does the book of Genesis illustrate the Church's teaching that God created man and woman together and for each other?

2. What are some ways that sin has affected marriage?

3. How has marriage helped spouses overcome some of the effects of sin?

4. What are some moral teachings about marriage that were foreshadowed in the Old Testament?

5. Describe the practice of marriage in the Old Testament.

6. What does the term "marriage in the Lord" refer to?

7. What does the Church believe about Christ's presence at the wedding at Cana?

8. How is marriage an efficacious sign of Christ's presence?

9. According to Saint Paul, what is the meaning of Christian marriage?

journal discussion

- Tell about how a relationship of yours helped you to overcome self-absorption, egoism, or pursuit of your own pleasure.

- Write your own poem or verse describing the depths of love.

- What is your reaction to Christ's teaching: marriage is to be indissoluble to death?

✦ Love and Other Elements of Relationships

"How will I know the right person to marry?"

"What's the secret to a happy marriage?"

"When is it right to have sex?"

In reality each of these questions demands multi-faceted answers. But if you asked them of your peers and many young adults, you would likely hear a common thread running through their responses, the words "in love."

Using the words "in love" to describe feelings for another can be accurate or not. Certainly you *love* your parents, grandparents, and some of your friends. But you would never say that you are "in love" with them. Or, you might say you are "in love" with a boyfriend or girlfriend, someone you have been dating regularly for a significant amount of time. In a different situation yet, you may say you are "in love" with someone you barely know (a cute guy or girl you have barely spoken to) or the latest "hot-looking" movie star, musician, or athlete.

To be honest, many of the ways people use the description "in love" would be more aptly described as being *infatuated* with another. Infatuation, while often used as a synonym for love, is more accurately defined as a "foolish or extravagant attraction." Infatuations are typically short in duration, while true love lasts. Think about some other elements of true love:

> Love is patient, love is kind.
> It is not jealous, [love] is not pompous, it
>   is not inflated,
> it is not rude,
> it does not seek its own interests,
> it is not quick-tempered,
> it does not brood over injury,
> it does not rejoice over wrongdoing but
>   rejoices with the truth.
> It bears all things, believes all things,
>   hopes all things, endures all things.
> Love never fails. (1 Cor 13:4–8b)

Certainly the questions that began this section can only be answered in a sentence that includes the word *love*. You would certainly need to love your future spouse. A relationship without love has little chance to be a happy one. And it would never be right to separate sex from love, just as it would be wrong to have sex outside of the commitment of marriage.

However, love is just one element of a relationship between a man and a woman. Certainly, infatuation is another. Having sexual feelings and attractions for someone, while often foolish or extravagant, can be the springboard for moving the relationship along to something deeper.

Two other elements make up a part of human relationships. One of these is an element you are already very familiar with: friendship. This is a relationship where two people like each other, trust each other, and want to spend time together. Another element in human relationships is

exploitation. Before you tune out here to the negative connotations of exploitation, understand that because of the ongoing human struggle with sin, you will always have to fight the urge to put yourself and your own needs over what is best for your friend, or even someone you will marry. The self-giving aspect of marriage requires spouses to work with God's grace to do what is best for the other, not themselves.

This section helps to define these four elements—love, infatuation, friendship, and exploitation: LIFE—that in combination impact all human relationships, including the relationship between a man and woman leading up to marriage and being married.[2]

More About Love

There are many types of love. However, in the English language there is only one word for love. Often, love is used as a synonym for *like*. We say things like "I love that song" or "I love pepperoni pizza." Using the word love this way is quite different from saying "I love you, Mom" or "I love you, Jeffrey." Of course, it's also different from saying "I love God."

Love encompasses the entire Christian vocation. Chapter 1 shared some of the mystery of God's love, and Christ's call to love self, love God, and love others, the greatest Commandment. Putting this Commandment into practice now is a practical way to prepare for a future marriage.

For example, healthy self-love is the first requirement of any other type of love. Healthy self-love is different from

the conceited love often associated with *narcissism*, which is the excessive concern for one's appearance, comfort, importance, or abilities. Healthy self-love, on the other hand, translates outward: the person who is comfortable with himself or herself is able to live for the sake of others.

At Baptism, we receive the virtue of charity, or love, which enables us to love God. God has loved us first. The first Commandment requires us to love God above everything—in heart, soul, and mind—and "all creatures for him and because of him" (*CCC*, 2093).

Jesus equates this love for God with love for others. We experience love for others in varying ways depending on the kinds of relationships we share. We love parents, siblings, relatives, and friends in different ways. Married people have a particular, exclusive love for a spouse. We also have an encompassing love for all human beings and are called by Jesus to love even our enemies.

exploitation
Using another person or group for selfish purposes, including for sexual gratification.

A relationship of love is both the most rewarding and most challenging of all relationships. Much of your happiness in life will depend on the depth and constancy of your love relationships. It takes a great deal of practice to learn how to give and receive love.

A love relationship is characterized by several related qualities, including the following:

- *Commitment.* Love weathers the ups and downs of disagreements, tragedies, and other challenges to persevere. Also, because it takes patience to forge bonds of understanding and trust, commitment to the long-term is essential.

- *Forgiveness.* Love accepts the other person as-is, though not perfect, and will forgive the other in order to strengthen the relationship. Also, someone who loves is always ready to say, "I am sorry. Please forgive me."

- *Respect.* Love respects the personal gifts the other person brings to the relationship, helps to nurture those gifts, and encourages the other person to reach his or her full potential.

Love is different from other relationships like friendship because it can exist even when it is mostly one-sided. You can love someone who might never return your love, or even completely rejects it. A parent's love for a wayward child is sometimes like that. No matter how indifferent or rebellious or selfish their children are, parents continue to love them.

Ultimately, love is the greatest virtue and the core of our lives because God himself is love (1 Jn 4:8). Within the communion of the Holy Trinity God expresses this love: "God himself is an eternal exchange of love, Father, Son, and Holy Spirit, and he has destined us to share in that exchange" (*CCC*, 221). God created everyone out of love and calls us to love. The love between a husband and wife is an intimate expression of God's love:

> Since God created him man and woman, their mutual love becomes an image of the absolute and unfailing love with which God loves man. It is good, very good, in the Creator's eyes. (*CCC*, 1604)

Infatuation and Friendship

Two other elements of human relationships that play a part in the development of romance between a man and woman are infatuation and friendship.

You've known the skills for making and keeping friends since the time you were young. Basically, friends are people who like to spend time together. They usually find activities and pursuits that interest both of them and begin to build a relationship around those things. Or, friendships begin simply through the practice of good communication skills, talking and listening to one another.

Friendship is often comfortable and easy, enriching and fun. It is based on mutual trust, understanding, acceptance, and enjoyment of one another. Friendship is not exclusive or possessive; it allows the other person freedom to do things on his or her own and to make other friends. Some friendships last for a short while and end due to one person moving away or a disagreement between the friends that was never reconciled. Other friendships last for a lifetime. Fifty-year class reunions of high-school classmates are dotted with stories of friends who have known and maintained contact with one another their entire lives. Also, you can have friends of many different ages, backgrounds, religions, and ideas. You can have friends of either gender, male or female. The best friendships grow into a love. Love between friends is rooted in loyalty and affection. This type of love is known as **filial love**, a connection that can last a lifetime, but that is not romantic.

The dynamic of friendship between boys and girls is an interesting study. Until about second grade, boys and girls have friends of both genders. Around that time, both boys and girls separate into single-gender friendships. Boys and girls may have little contact with each other outside of participation in certain classroom activities until adolescence. During the junior high school years and the start of high school, friendships between the two genders take hold again. A senior at a Coral Springs, Florida, high school explained why she appreciates being friends with guys: "With girls, there is a lot of competition. With guys, you can just be yourself, and you don't have to worry about comparing yourself."[3]

However, the element of romantic infatuation brings another dynamic to the relationship between males and females. A romantic infatuation is any relationship that involves sexual attraction or sexual feelings. While a normal response to someone who is attractive, romantic infatuation is usually based on impressions rather than knowledge of the person in question. Infatuation is also a very emotional feeling that can also be irrational. Some become obsessed with their infatuations and allow them to control their lives. You may know someone whose life has been turned upside down over an infatuation—maybe an infatuation with someone they have never even talked to or never will. This may have even happened to you.

While romantic infatuations are normal and exciting, they can be dangerous if a person decides to become sexually intimate with someone based only on an infatuation. Unlike friendships, infatuations are typically short-lived. A person who acts out sexually with someone he or she is infatuated with is on the course to heartbreak and hurt.

Most teen romances are partly infatuation and partly friendship. A male high school senior said, "Friendships can exist between boys and girls, but it isn't the main purpose I want to get to know them for."[4] It is better for teen couples to concentrate on deepening the friendship aspect of their relationships—learning to communicate, to share, to compromise, to trust one another's friends and families—than to focus on sexual attractions. If

the primary focus of a relationship is on sexual feelings and their physical expression, the couple could very easily begin to use one another just to get emotional and sexual satisfaction. When that happens, the relationship will almost certainly degenerate into exploitation.

filial love
Typically, this is the type of love that children have for their parents or siblings or friends have for each other.

Exploitation in Relationships

Exploitation refers to any relationship that is based in selfishness. Exploitation takes what it can get without showing any respect or concern for the other person. If you are exploited by someone, you feel used. By the same token, no one likes to admit that he or she is using someone else.

However, the human condition of sinfulness causes everyone to deal with exploitation as both givers and receivers. Friends take each other for granted, sometimes playing one against the other. Students "kiss up" to teachers for better grades. Weaker or unpopular teens get picked on or teased because someone else wants to look stronger or more popular.

Exploitation in a relationship charged with sexual attractions and feelings often takes place as well. Consider this list of some ways teens have been exploitative involving sex:

- saying "I love you" with the intention of convincing someone to have sex,
- getting someone drunk to be able to make easier advances toward sex,
- "hooking up" with someone casually in order to fulfill sexual desires,
- cheating on a boyfriend or girlfriend who is committed to remaining chaste,
- ruining someone's reputation by telling others what they did sexually.

The best way to avoid exploitation in a romantic relationships is to keep the focus on friendship, not on feelings associated with infatuation. If a teenage couple are friends as well as having romantic feelings for one another, the respect and mutual trust that are basic to friendship help to control the sexual element in their relationship. Because they are friends, they will have many common interests and goals, they will like and respect one another's families, and will have friends in common, as well. They will do constructive things when they spend time together.

Is It Love or Infatuation?

Compare the characteristics of love and infatuation. Then in your journal write at least five other characteristics for each.

Infatuation . . .
- comes and goes quickly.
- is insecure and jealous.
- is emotional and dependent.
- feels pressure to act quickly.
- is centered around physical attraction, sex, and pleasure.
- may lead you to things you regret.
- harms your other relationships.
- makes it difficult to work.
- is confining.
- is self-centered.

Love . . .
- grows slowly.
- is confident and peaceful.
- is balanced and independent.
- can wait for the right time.
- is attracted to the whole person.
- brings out the best in you.
- enhances all of your relationships.
- helps you organize and work well.
- is freeing.
- is self-giving.

Relationships that focus on friendship first are growing toward true love. Those charged mainly with the emotional feelings of infatuation are in greater risk of slipping toward exploitation. This is where the gift of chastity helps.

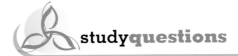

study questions

1. Define *infatuation*.

2. What are some elements of true love?

3. How is healthy self-love different from narcissism?

4. Explain how commitment, forgiveness, and respect are part of a love relationship.

5. Why is love the greatest virtue?

6. What does it mean to say that friendships are not "exclusive or possessive"?

7. Explain the difference between a healthy and unhealthy infatuation.

8. What are some ways romantic relationships can be exploitative?

journal discussion

- What does the phrase "in love" mean in your peer group?

- When you are in new situations, what skills do you use to make friends?

- Who is the friend you have had the longest? Who is a new friend? How are those relationships different? the same?

- Do you believe it is possible for teenage boys and girls to be "just friends"? Explain.

- What does it feel like to be exploited in a relationship?

On the other hand, teen romances that are predominantly based on infatuation are more dangerous. The couple spends their time professing their love for one another, is jealous of time not spent together (particularly when that time is spent with other friends or family), and may have a diminishing list of interests outside of their relationship. The sexual aspect of the relationship gets more involved, often leading to the dangers and sinfulness of sex outside of marriage.

✦ Vocation to Chastity

Every person needs to have a healthy self-understanding that includes an understanding of human sexuality. You are called to accept and acknowledge your sexual identity, male or female. One's sexual identity includes the physical, moral, and spiritual dimensions and the complementarity that is intended for the unity of the couple in marriage and the flourishing of family life.

Human sexuality means much more than sexual intercourse. Also, human sexuality is quite different from the sex drive of animals, governed by sheer instinct. Human sexuality is under the dominion of both our body *and* soul. A *facet* of human sexuality is the ability to have sexual intercourse.

"Sexuality affects all aspects of the human person in the unity of his body and soul" (*CCC*, 2332). Human sexuality especially affects the capacity to love and to procreate, and in a more general way, the ability to relate with others.

Marriage involves the total self-giving of a husband and wife to each other, both emotionally and physically. Healthy sexual relations in marriage are expressions of mutual love, not selfish pleasure. Sex has two important purposes in marriage:

- It is unitive: it is intended to communicate love, and to unify a husband and wife in the most intimate of ways.

- It is procreative: it allows the possibility of having children and extending the human race.

Chastity is the moral virtue under the cardinal virtue of **temperance** that helps us, from our earliest years, to moderate our desires for sexual pleasure. The virtue of chastity integrates a person's sexuality with his or her whole being, strengthening the unity between body and soul that encourages healthy personal development.

Why It's Good to be Chaste

The choice to be chaste or not is a clear one: we either learn to govern our passions and find peace, or we let ourselves be ruled by our passions and become unhappy. The stories of teenagers who have made both choices support those results. On the negative side:

> He would tell me that he loved me and wanted to marry me. But it was after we had sex that made me detest him. He would never look me in the eyes, and we wouldn't have anything to talk about. I felt dirty and cheap. We began to have fights about things that never bothered us before. There was name-calling, tearful conversations, and him ignoring me in front of people. . . . My self-esteem was extremely low around him. I was diagnosed with depression after three years of the relationship and one attempt at suicide.
>
> —Margaret, age 17

When I was young I played blues and rock. We toured, we had girls in every town. As soon as you talked to a girl your mind was already planning sex. This destroyed something very important in

---

temperance

The cardinal moral virtue that moderates the attraction of pleasure and provides balance in the use of created goods.

my life. I can truly say that it took many years to heal this wound. My wonderful wife, my children, the Catholic Church, and much praying made the healing possible. I will perhaps never be completely healed. I lost something important.

—Staffan[5]

Oppositely, those who have made a conscious and often public choice to practice chastity tell of many advantages. A twenty-year-old woman offered this reflection:

My high school and college years were the best years of my life. I learned that "no" to sex meant "yes" to fun. My reputation as a virgin got out fast. I had more dates, better grades, and good quality friendships. Guys knew they didn't have to perform (sexually) for me, so we could concentrate on getting to know each other and having a great time.[6]

Many of the advantages of chastity have to do with freedom—freedom from a negative lifestyle and freedom for a positive lifestyle. For example, chastity gives you the freedom *from*:

- guilt, doubt, worry, and regret;
- having to wonder, "How far will I have to go with this person?";
- being used by others and using other people;
- sexually transmitted diseases and (for girls) the possibility of not being able to bear a child because of an STD;

- pregnancy;
- having to choose between raising a child you aren't ready for and giving your baby up for adoption;
- the trauma of abortion;
- loss of reputation;
- pressure to marry early or to marry the wrong person;
- the ghosts of past sexual relationships invading your marriage.

Also, chastity gives you the freedom *to*:

- exercise control over your life;
- develop real friendships based on mutual respect, shared thoughts, and feelings;
- develop skills, talents, and interests;
- have many relationships;
- develop self-respect and self-control;
- finish your education and achieve financial stability before having to marry;
- find a potential mate who values you for the person you are;
- enjoy greater trust in marriage (because you don't have to worry, "Is he/she going to fool around with someone else, the way we fooled around before we were married?");
- stay out of sexual sin and grow in your relationship with God.[7]

The person who practices chastity witnesses God's faithfulness and loving kindness to

others. Chastity also bears fruit in the gift of friendship. You are free to make friends with people of both genders, leading to much more than the casual relationships typical between acquaintances, but rather a deep spiritual communion that can last to eternity.

Staying Chaste

It is good to be chaste. It is also difficult to be chaste. The practice of chastity begins early on in family life and is witnessed by parents to their children. Pope John Paul II taught that:

> [Early childhood] is the period when esteem for all authentic human values is instilled, both in interpersonal and in social relationships, with all that this signifies for the formation of character, for the control and right use of one's inclinations, for the manner of regarding and meeting people of the opposite sex, and so on. (*Familiaris Consortio*, 66)

Practicing chastity is not only for teenagers, no matter what you might think. All the baptized are called to lead a chaste life. As introduced in Chapter 2, some profess virginity or consecrated celibacy, which allows them to dedicate their lives more completely to God. Those engaged to be married are to live chastely, using the time to grow in mutual respect, practice their fidelity to one another, and live in the anticipation of receiving one another from God. Married people have a vocation to conjugal chastity. This obligation involves both being faithful to one another (marital fidelity) and remaining open to the gift of life during sexual sharing. (See chapter 5 for more information.)

One way to practice chastity is to avoid offenses that are against the moral norms of chastity taught by the Church. These include:

- *Lust*, the disordered desire for sexual pleasure. Sexual pleasure is disordered when it is only sought for itself.

- *Masturbation*, the deliberate stimulation of one's genitals in order to receive sexual pleasure. Masturbation is contrary to the purpose of sex, which is intended for an interpersonal, committed, loving relationship in marriage that includes the possibility of procreation. It is "an intrinsically and gravely disordered action" (*CCC*, 2352). The degree of sinfulness of this act depends on a person's immaturity, force of acquired habit, anxiety, or other psychological or social factors.

- *Fornication*, that is, sex between an unmarried man and unmarried woman. "It is gravely contrary to the dignity of persons and of human sexuality which is naturally ordered to the good of spouses and the generation and education of children" (*CCC*, 2353).

- *Pornography*, the display of real or simulated sexual acts, is a grave offense against chastity because it perverts the conjugal act intended only for marriage. It also does grave injury to the actors, those who sell it, and those who watch it.

- *Prostitution*, paying for sex, is a social scourge. It is gravely sinful for those who pay for sex. The guilt of those who engage in prostitution (mainly women) can be reduced depending on their destitution, whether or not they have been blackmailed, or social pressure.

- *Rape* is the violation of another person through sex imposed by force or deception. This also includes the so-called "date rape" in which a person on a date is forced against her (or his) wishes to have sex. Rape causes deep wounds that last a lifetime. It is always an intrinsically evil act.

Of course there is more to being chase than avoiding the sinful and often illegal offenses listed above. Chastity requires day to day focus if one is to achieve its graces. At your stage of life, you can perfect the virtue of chastity through the following means (see *CCC*, 2340):

- *Self-knowledge.* It is important to take stock of your own personality traits in order to be able to access your strengths and weaknesses for facing any challenges, including the area of chastity. For example, you can determine some situations in which you are vulnerable (e.g., gossiping, telling off-color jokes) and determine ways to avoid these difficult areas.

- *Asceticism.* This traditional word refers to a life of self-discipline and self-denial. This virtue-filled way of living can be practiced at your age through deliberately learning to give up certain pleasures, much the way you may have done so in a Lenten season. Christian asceticism can lead you to growth in patience, self-acceptance, humility, and the desire to live Gospel values.

- *Following the Commandments, especially the Sixth Commandment, "You shall not commit adultery."* Recall that Jesus expanded on this commandment, explaining: "You have heard that it was said, 'You shall not commit adultery.' But I say to you, everyone who looks at a woman with lust has already committed adultery with her in his heart" (Mt 5:27–28).

- *Practicing the other moral virtues.* Chastity is a moral virtue under the cardinal virtue of temperance, but the other moral virtues can help you to keep a promise to be chaste. They are *prudence* ("helps to recognize good in life and the correct way to achieve good"), *justice* ("guides us to give God and others what is their due"), and *fortitude* ("helps us to resist fears, even the fear of death").

- *Prayer.* God wants you to be happy and to lead a good life. Refraining from sex until marriage is the right choice in God's eyes. Pray constantly for the grace to accept the gift of chastity, a grace from God. The Holy Spirit helps Christians to imitate the purity of Christ.

Chastity, like human sexuality, is not something that you can just put on or call up in certain occasions, like when you are at a party or out with someone you like of the opposite sex. Rather, chastity is something that is with you daily, communicating itself to others through your words and actions. Modesty, or moderation, is a very helpful tool to communicate your chastity to others. Outwardly, modesty involves managing your behavior, watching your speech, wearing non-suggestive clothing; in general, not calling undue attention to oneself. As with most other areas of life, living chastely comes down to backing up your verbal promise and commitment with your actions.

Homosexuality and Chastity

Some people—both men and women—experience an exclusive or predominant sexual attraction to persons of the same sex. While there are a number of people who have these objectively disordered homosexual tendencies, recent studies have shown that the number is not as high as often portrayed. For example, you may have heard that "one in ten people is gay or lesbian." A study by the Alan Guttmacher Institute reported that only two percent of the 3,321 American men in their twenties and thirties that were studied reported any homosexual contacts in the past ten years.[8]

No matter the number of homosexual persons, most who have these tendencies find them to be a trial. The *Catechism of the Catholic Church* reminds us that:

> They must be accepted with respect, compassion, and sensitivity. Every sign of unjust discrimination in their regard should be avoided. These persons are called to fulfill God's will in their lives and, if they are Christians, to unite to the sacrifice of the Lord's Cross the difficulties they may encounter from their condition. (CCC, 2358)

Like the inclination itself, the homosexual sex act is intrinsically disordered. Sexual intercourse is intended both to be life giving and to bring together a union of body and spirit of male and female in marriage. Because of this, homosexual persons are called to live a chaste life. Like unmarried heterosexuals, homosexual persons must control their desires and resist the temptation to have sex. Obviously this presents a different and often greater challenge for homosexual persons. Whereas single heterosexuals at least can look forward to a future marriage, homosexuals cannot marry one another.

By refraining from being active and not taking on a gay lifestyle, by seeking proper help and advice, by remaining discreet with those in whom they confide, by maintaining heterosexual friendships, and through regular prayer and participation in the sacraments—especially Reconciliation and Eucharist—persons with homosexual tendencies can lead a life of intellectual, emotional, and spiritual intimacy that can, as with any person, approach Christian perfection.

study**questions**

1. How is human sexuality different from sex?

2. What are the two purposes of sex in marriage?

3. Define *chastity*.

4. Name five advantages for teenagers to be chaste.

5. Who is called to chastity?

6. Why is masturbation sinful? How might a person's culpability be reduced?

7. Define *fornication*.

8. Name and explain five ways the gift of chastity can be perfected.

9. Why is chastity a different and often greater challenge for homosexuals?

journal**discussion**

- What is your best reason for practicing chastity?

- How would you communicate to others that you have made the decision to be chaste and to refrain from sex until marriage?

- How would your peers react to a teen who chooses chastity?

- Write your own prayer for chastity.

Chastity Testimonials

Research statistics on how many teenagers have made a commitment to chastity. Cite several benefits of chastity shared by teens you read about in your research.

✦ Choices Leading to Marriage

As cited in Chapter 2, most people do marry. There is a very good chance that within five to fifteen years, you will be on the verge of marriage or already married. It is also true that decisions you are making today and your current experiences are contributing to a future marriage. The previous section pointed to an obvious example: persons who make the decision to live chastely or not are affecting their future marriage. People who are sexually active before marriage may incur many consequences that will affect a future marriage: sexually transmitted disease, pregnancy, and the emotional fall-out that results from a bad break-up are just a few.

Also, think about your friends: what you like about them, why you get along, what you enjoy doing together, and how you make up after an argument. Friendship is a key part of marriage. In the best cases, husbands and wives begin their relationship as friends first, and friendship remains a key part of their marriage. The interpersonal skills you are practicing now are likely to be the same you will take into a marital relationship. Your personal interests and aptitudes may also factor into a future marriage. The saying "opposites attract" may sometimes be true, but consider also what happens when people with little in common do marry. When two spouses have much in common in areas like academics, career goals, social circles, and hobbies, this can help get their marriage off to a good start and help them stay the course for the long term.

Ideally, a married couple should share the same religion. The Catholic Church does not view a mixed marriage (marriage between a baptized Catholic and a baptized non-Catholic) as an

When You Do Fall in Love

Finding a person to love who loves you is something to look forward to. When this happens you want to make sure that the person knows the real you. To be able to do that, you should feel comfortable to be open and honest with the other person so that you can share who you really are. Hopefully the person with whom you fall in love will share your moral and ethical standards—and practice your religion along with you. Here are some other issues of compatibility a serious couple should think about and ask one another:

- What do you believe are the roles of a husband and wife in a marriage?
- What is the way that you solve problems?
- How important is a career to you?

- How many children do you want to have?
- What kind of parent do you think you will be?
- How important is God in your life?
- What are ways that you practice your faith?
- How well do you get along with my family? with your own?
- How do you see your life in five years? Ten years? Twenty years?
- How would you describe your ultimate goal for life in one sentence?

insurmountable obstacle for marriage, "but the difficulties of mixed marriages must not be underestimated" (*CCC*, 1634). A marriage between a Catholic and a non-baptized person requires even more caution. Couples who brand themselves "in love" often believe that their love will conquer all. But if practice of their religion has not been central in their teen and young adult years, they may not understand how disunity of denomination may become a true challenge to their family in the years ahead.

This is the time to consider how the many choices, experiences, and beliefs that you are making, having, and holding today will impact your future, in this case regarding your possible marriage.

Family Life

Preparation for marriage begins even in infancy and continues through childhood and adolescence—primarily in the family, but also in school and friendship groups. In the family, children are taught two

fundamental truths: that we are called to live in truth and love and that "everyone finds fulfillment through the sincere gift of self" (*Gratissimam Sane*, 16).

Parents are responsible not only for sexual education of their children, but also for reminding their children that the world's attitudes toward sex and marriage are often in conflict with Christian ideals. This is why it is the parents' responsibility to make judgments about what is appropriate for children to watch on television, see in the movies, and view on the Internet. In doing so, parents work to form in their children a critical conscience that will allow them to be discerning of the messages of popular culture versus the truth of the Christian Gospel, Church teaching, and their own family values. A letter written to a prominent pagan from a Christian in the second century spoke of the courage that is necessary to live in the world without belonging to it:

> Christians are not distinguished from the rest of mankind by either country, speech, or customs . . . the whole tenor of their way of living stamps it as worthy of admiration and admittedly extraordinary. . . . They marry like all others and beget children; but they do not expose their offspring. Their table they spread for all, but not their bed. They find themselves *in the flesh*, but do not live *according to the flesh*.[9]

The *Catechism* teaches that the "family is the community in which, from childhood, one can learn moral values, begin to honor God, and make use of freedom. Family life is an initiation into life in society" (*CCC*, 2207). In a healthy family, there is openness of communication among family members. They listen to one another. They care for one another through compassion, courtesy, forgiveness, and humor. Parents catechize their children in the life of faith and in participation in the life of the Church, especially the sacraments.

Young people your age can really test the parenting skills of their moms and dads. All of the foundational work of parenting in teaching what is right and wrong in areas of religious practice, chastity, consumerism, and many other ethical and moral areas is reaching a critical point. You are at a time of crucial decision-making now. You are growing to adulthood and nearing the time when you will make important decisions that will start you on career and vocation. Parents continue to offer suggestions, critiques, and discipline at this stage of your life with the intention of communicating some final principles they have valued and taught for years—all the while understanding that very soon you will be making choices in these key areas on your own, for better or worse.

Opposite from healthy families are troubled families in which communication has been lacking or is absent altogether. In the worst cases, physical abuse or emotional abuse takes place between spouses or is inflicted on children.

Today, several online dating services take pains to identify a person's attributes, interests, and traits in the hope of matching the person with someone a computer or staff deems compatible. Some common categories include areas like emotional temperament, social style, physicality, and values and beliefs. Most surveys question how a person's family background contributed to how the person responds in each of these areas. A recent study of over 5,000 married couples revealed that a well-adjusted marriage was more typically one in which the husband and wife:

- came from similar family backgrounds,
- had parents with a long and successful marriage,
- did not experience conflict with in-laws,
- both went to college,
- knew each other long before marriage,
- had many friends of both sexes,
- did not live together before marriage,
- agreed on parenting styles,
- both practiced a common religious faith.

Being aware of these factors can help you plan for a successful marriage. You have control over some of these factors. For example, you can develop friendships with both sexes regardless of your current family situation. You can practice your religion, even if your parents are not active participants themselves. Most importantly, you

can begin to develop yourself into a person who will be suitable and compatible with another. It's a lot like developing a background that makes for a good résumé. Any possible future marriage partner would hope that you would have as little emotional trauma to overcome as possible.

Making New Friends

To this point in your life, making friends may have come naturally to you. You have been brought together socially with friends, maybe through a team or an activity. You like the same things. But what comes next? If you do not work to cultivate the friendship, the people you hang out with are merely acquaintances, not friends. Friends are fewer than acquaintances because of some qualities that they possess. For example,

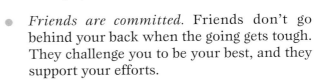

- *Friends are committed.* Friends don't go behind your back when the going gets tough. They challenge you to be your best, and they support your efforts.

- *Friends are forgiving.* Any close relationship will have conflicts. Friends are able to ask for and offer forgiveness.

- *Friends are dependable.* Friends keep promises. They agree to spend time together and then do it. They don't repeatedly stand each other up.

- *Friends are compassionate.* When one friend is going through tough times—an illness or death in the family, the rejection for college admissions—the other friend is there to listen and simply be present. Also, a friend is able to share the joy of a friend's success. Jealousy does not get in the way.

What about making new friends? You will probably need to strike a balance between letting friendships develop naturally with people you are acquainted with versus taking the initiative to go out and meet new people and work to form a relationship. In either case, you must be a social person, that is, someone who is around other people. A recluse will have a difficult time making friends.

Your friendship skills will serve you well later on when you meet and deepen a relationship with a possible future spouse. The word *friend* is derived from a word that means love. True friendship has all the earmarks of love. It is caring, accepting, honest, open, nurturing, and giving. Friendship is a relationship of mutual give and take between two persons who have chosen this special way of relating. Friendship is also a precursor to a dating relationship. It would be rare for a person to want to go out with someone who is not a friend. Taking it a step further: most married couples would name their spouse as their best friend. However, guys and girls are often more hesitant and not as honest around friends of the opposite sex because they don't want to ruin the chance for a possible relationship.

Here are some basic suggestions for making and being friends with those of the opposite sex:

- *Seize opportunities for interaction.* For example, join with your current friends when they do things with others of the opposite sex: eat lunch, go to the movies, sit at football games, study.

- *Be yourself.* Don't change because you are around both boys and girls. Treat everyone with the same respect you'd like to receive in return. Be open and honest, but go slowly in what you reveal about yourself. Don't come on too strong. You know the appropriate time to talk about personal issues. Don't reveal something personal just to impress someone.

- *Communicate well.* When you are around people you have just met, practice good listening skills. Give the other person full attention when he or she is speaking. Try to understand what they are truly saying. Think before you speak, but don't worry if what you say doesn't come out just right. No

one is critiquing everything that comes out of your mouth (and if they are, that is *their* issue). Ask a clarifying question. For example, if someone tells you about a movie they just watched, you might say, "I heard this movie wasn't as good as the original. What do you think?"

- *Don't gossip.* Gossip is the bad habit of talking about other people. Gossiping also includes listening to rumors or stories about others. One sure way to ruin a friendship with someone of the opposite sex—maybe before it even has the chance to begin—is to talk about the person with some of your other friends, especially if the talk is filled with rumors and half-truths.

By the end of high school, some of your friends may be pairing off into couples. Everyone grows emotionally at their own pace. Try not to let this ruin your friendship with your friends of either sex. Continue to be available to offer your support and compassion and to spend time together. If it turns out your friend goes a different direction than you, that's okay. You are responsible for your own life and for making right decisions for you. You may be apart from a friend for the time being. There's nothing to say that some day you might not renew your friendship.

Dating

Just using the word "dating" as a heading for this section may have caused you to wonder how this material could possibly relate to your life either now or when as you get closer to the time that you may consider marriage. In the past, dating was

associated with the view of exclusively going out with someone with the idea that it might be leading to finding a marriage partner. Today, however, most high school students are readying for college, and most college students are primarily planning for a career and do not have plans to be married so soon after graduation.

Today it often seems that teens and young adults move directly into an exclusive relationship. If they do go on a traditional date, it is a signal that they are a "couple" and now "boyfriend and girlfriend." More recently, various new jargon describes how guys and girls get together. One of the most shocking and dangerous is described by

In previous generations, dating referred to a male asking a female to go out for a "date," which usually involved sharing a meal, taking in a movie, or going to a dance. Nothing more was expected of the occasion, and the two were free to go out with someone else any time afterward. Today, a survey of one thousand college women revealed that only 50 percent had been asked out on more than six traditional dates during their four years in college. And one-third in the survey said they had been asked on no more than two dates. Recent facts seem to bear out that the ritual of dating with the thought of it leading to marriage has nearly died out among teenagers and young adults. Author Leon Kass wrote, "Today there are no socially prescribed forms of conduct that help guide young men and women in the direction of matrimony."[10]

the term "hooking up," which allows sexual interaction ranging from kissing to having sex between people without commitment or even affection. Another term to describe this behavior is "friends with benefits," which means having an agreement with someone to engage in sexual behavior any time the two of them decide to. People who choose this behavior say that it is their way of releasing sexual tension without having to invest time in developing a relationship. The emotional fallout of regret over this type of sinful behavior among males and females was significant:

> The New York-based Institute, a nonprofit group that promotes the importance of family and fatherhood, conducted the report for the women's forum by surveying 1,000 women enrolled at secular four-year colleges.

With 100 women on college campuses for every seventy-nine men, women are more apt to initiate relationships with men and are more willing to experiment with casual relationships, even when they know such liaisons leave them emotionally empty, the survey found.[11]

While this type of behavior has been a reality on many if not most college campuses and in several high schools in the past decade or more, there is no mincing words to define any form of behavior that treats the sacredness of sex in such a casual and perverse way: it is gravely sinful. This means that as you progress through relationships with those of the opposite sex from acquaintances to friendship and possibly on to a serious relationship that can lead to marriage, you need structure that allows for meaningful interaction and a chance to get to know someone without the pressure and temptations to follow along and behave in the ways described above.

Back to the term dating. Or perhaps a more up-to-date term: "hanging out." This can describe a relatively safe way to get to know others and to develop friendships. This may first involve several people—both males and females—getting together for activities like a meal, movie, or game. Perhaps some in the group come as established couples, but more come together as friends. This group dating allows people to be less shy, to learn how to converse and behave around the opposite sex, and is freer of opportunities to act on sexual temptation.

From group dating, single or personal dating may come next. Single dating would mean a male and a female going out together as a couple. They may go to a school dance or out for dinner. An advantage of single dating is that the couple can get to know each other better by having some time to talk and share about themselves. A negative part of single dating is that sometimes the expectations are not clear. For example, one of the persons may misjudge that the single date equals a permanent relationship. Or, one or both may feel that because they are alone, they must be sexually intimate. Single dating may have the potential to lead to a long-term relationship. Or, the couple may just remain friends, acquaintances, or go their own ways.

Eventually you may find someone you want to date on an exclusive basis. This would be a person you would call a boyfriend or girlfriend. In days gone by, this kind of dating has also been known as "going steady" and is often the first step leading to marriage. Today teens who date one person exclusively do not necessarily have expectations that the relationship is heading to marriage. Instead of "going steady," they may describe their relationship as "going out." In either case, there are positive aspects to this form of dating. One is that the two people can let their guard down a bit and be more honest and trusting of each other. In this way the two people really have a chance to get to know each other.

A negative aspect of dating exclusively—especially if it occurs at too young of age—is that the person will be deprived of the chance to meet and socialize with a larger and more diverse group of people that he or she is bound to encounter in college and beyond. And, a couple involved in an exclusive relationship must be honest about their moral convictions so the two of them can work together to avoid situations when they might act contrary to them.

Needless to say, there are many choices a person makes from the time they are young to the time they are engaged to be married and celebrate the Sacrament of Matrimony that will have long-term effects on the health of their marriage. Some of the most important choices a person makes in the area of chastity, commitment, and interpersonal relationships are happening for you right now.

Ideas for "Hanging Out"

There are many things teenagers can do in groups with both girls and boys, or on personal dates. Of course the big three of popular dates are a movie, a nice dinner, and a dance. Other traditional but fun dating ideas include:

- bowling
- going to a water park
- taking a nature hike
- shopping together
- miniature golfing
- touring a museum
- going to the movies
- going to an amusement park
- attending a concert
- skiing
- visiting a park
- watching a game
- playing tennis
- going to Mass together

Meet with a group of two or three of your closest friends and plan a group activity that can involve up to ten other teens. Add a service dimension to the activity. For example, arrange for a group of teens to participate in a charitable walk, run, or bike ride. Or, hold a pizza party at someone's house where everyone helps make his or her own pizza and brings money or a canned food donation to help a local food pantry.

Send out invitations to your event. Invite a few people that you know and other people whom you don't know well, but would like to get to know better.

Share a report on your event with the rest of the class.

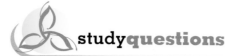

studyquestions

1. When does marriage preparation first take place?

2. How is a child initiated into "life in society" in a family?

3. Name at least three qualities of a well-adjusted marriage.

4. Name and describe at least three qualities of friendship.

5. What are some ways to make friends with someone of the opposite sex?

6. What was the term "dating" associated with in the past?

7. What are the advantages and disadvantages of single or personal dating?

journaldiscussion

- What are some difficulties that could arise for a married couple that practices two different religions?

- What are some things you can control right now to give you a greater chance for a happy and healthy marriage?

- Describe the emotional fallout you can imagine from practices like "hooking up."

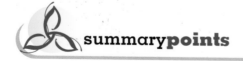

summarypoints

✦ Benefits and Purpose of Married Life

✦ God planned that people should be married from the very beginning of creation.

✦ God created marriage to be good because he created the world to be good.

✦ Jesus Christ raised marriage to the dignity of a sacrament.

✦ A primary purpose of marriage is the procreation and raising of children.

✦ Another purpose of marriage is the willingness of spouses to give themselves to one another to aid in their salvation.

✦ Marriage in the Bible

✦ The book of Genesis teaches that God created man and woman together and willed each for the other.

✦ Scripture speaks of the mystery of marriage, its God-given origin and end, the way it has been lived out, and its meaning in the New Testament.

✦ Original Sin broke the original communion between man and woman.

✦ The teaching on the indissolubility of marriage is present in the Old Testament.

✦ Christ restored marriage to its original state before Original Sin.

✦ Jesus comes to the life of the married couple through the Sacrament of Matrimony.

Love and Other Elements of Relationships

- True love is the essential element of a relationship between a husband and wife.

- A love relationship is characterized by commitment, forgiveness, and respect.

- The love of a husband and wife is an intimate expression of God's love.

- Most teenage romances are part infatuation and part friendship.

- The best friendships grow into a love that is rooted in loyalty and affection.

- Exploitation refers to any relationship that is based in selfishness.

- The best way to avoid exploitation in a relationship is to keep it based on friendship, not infatuation.

Vocation to Chastity

- Human sexuality affects all aspects of the human person, body and soul.

- Chastity is the moral virtue of temperance that helps us moderate our desires for sexual pleasure.

- Advantages of chastity are related to being free from a negative lifestyle and free for a positive lifestyle.

- Practicing chastity is for everyone based on his or her state in life.

- Avoiding offenses against chastity—lust, masturbation, fornication, pornography, prostitution, and rape—are ways to remain chaste.

- Means for perfecting chastity include self-knowledge, asceticism, following the Commandments, practicing moral virtues, and prayer.

✦ Choices Leading to Marriage

✦ Choices you make now can affect a future marriage.

✦ Ideally a married couple should share the same religion.

✦ Preparation for marriage takes place from infancy on, beginning through the example of the family.

✦ Friendship should be a precursor to a dating relationship.

✦ Getting to know people of the opposite sex as friends first is a good way to begin the process that will eventually lead to dating.

✦ The old term dating can be described today as "hanging out."

✦ It is best to begin dating in larger social groups of friends.

✦ Personal dating has the advantage of allowing the opportunity to get to know the other person better.

✦ Exclusive dating should be reserved for a time closer to marriage.

assignments
applications

1. Interview five married couples you know well. Present the following written questions to each spouse individually:

   ✦ Why do you like being married?

   ✦ What is the secret to a good marriage?

   Also, make sure to find out some more information from each couple: how long they have been married, whether or not they share the same religion, and how many children they have. Write your own report on the findings, not only listing each response, but tallying them and forming some hypothesis based on the gender of the person responding, the length of the marriage, etc.

2. Read the entire book of Ruth. Then read and compare the two genealogies of Jesus Christ from Matthew 1:1–17 and Luke 3:23–38. How do they differ? Read study notes on each passage and write a short report explaining what you found out about the differences between the two.

3. Create a collage, song lyrics, poem, or other creative application using a favorite verse describing love from the Song of Songs.

4. Read the Gospel story of the Wedding at Cana (Jn 2:1–12). Write a dialogue script of the incident, including the main characters Jesus, Mary, and the head waiter, but also adding some lines from others who may have witnessed this miracle: some of Jesus' disciples, some of his enemies, the bride and groom, and other wedding guests. Choose a group of classmates to practice this vignette. Act it out before the entire class.

5. Collect and copy photos of a married couple that you know (e.g., parents, grandparents, aunts and uncles) tracing their relationship through the various stages of infatuation, friendship, dating, engagement, and marriage. Arrange the photos in a scrapbook. Ask the husband and wife to share remembrances about each photo. Record their comments as photo captions. Share the book with your classmates.

6. The friendship of King David and Jonathan, the son of Israel's first king, Saul, is well-known. Read part of their story from 1 Samuel 18:1–5; 20:1–42. Write a report that notes some of the qualities that made up their friendship.

7. Write a letter to your possible future husband or wife that tells what you are doing right now to keep yourself chaste and pure while awaiting the time of your marriage.

8. Search on the Internet and read the article "Practicing Chastity in an Unchaste Age" by Bishop Joseph F. Martino, Bishop of Scranton. Write a report summarizing the benefits of chastity and the risks of being unchaste using evidence from the article.

9. Read and summarize the section on chastity and homosexuality in the *Catechism of the Catholic Church*, 2357–2359. Include in your

paper a statement of what you would want and dream for your child if he or she had a homosexual orientation.

10. Work in a small group with a mixture of boys and girls. Discuss and write several ideas for making school dances and proms less expensive. Meet with the class and come to a consensus on the issue. Consider sending a representative to the school's student council or administration team to present the class's ideas.

Notes

1. The list is summarized from the article "Why Marriage Is Good for You," by Maggie Gallagher, *City Journal* (Autumn, 2000).

2. Much of the material described on the relationships between love, infatuation, friendship, and exploitation is credited to Sister Kieran Sawyer, SSND, and her programs *Learning to Love: A Family-Based Program of Relationships and Abuse Prevention* (Ave Maria Press, 2006) and *Sex and the Teenager: Choices and Decisions* by Sister Kieran Sawyer, SSND (Ave Maria Press, 1999).

3. Quoted from "High School: When Boys and Girls Become Just Plain Friends at Long Last," *Sun-Sentinel* (November 16, 2005).

4. Ibid.

5. Both of the testimonies were taken from the purelove.com website.

6. Coleen Kelly Mast, *op. cit.*

7. Both lists of advantages are taken from *Sex, Love, and You: Making the Right Decision* by Tom and Judy Lickona with William Boudreau, M.D. (Ave Maria Press, 2003).

8. Reported in *Family Planning Perspectives* (March/April, 1993).

9. Quoted from *Letter to Diognetus*, V 1, 4, 6, 7, 8.

10. Quoted from "The End of Courtship" by Leon R. Kass, *The Public Interest* (Winter, 1997).

11. Quoted from "Campus Romance, Unrequited: Dating Scene Fails Women, Study Says" by Michael A. Fletcher, *The Washington Post* (July 26, 2001).

chapter**outline**

✦ Caught Up into Divine Love

Notre Dame's Moose Krause shared a life of love and fidelity with his wife, Elise.

✦ Preparing for Marriage

Preparation for marriage is a life-long task that begins with lessons learned in the home and extends to parish-sponsored programs for immediate preparation in the months before the wedding.

✦ The Celebration of Marriage

In a nuptial Mass, the Liturgy of the Word, the couple's consent, the nuptial blessing, and Holy Communion are emphasized.

✦ The Effects of the Sacrament of Matrimony

Marriage between two baptized Christians can never be dissolved. To live this covenant of love, God shares with the couple a lifetime of grace.

chapter four

The Sacrament of Matrimony

"The kingdom of heaven is like a mustard seed that a person took and sowed in a field. It is the smallest of all the seeds, yet when full-grown it is the largest of plants. It becomes a large bush, and the 'birds of the sky come and dwell in its branches.'"

Matthew 13:31–32

✦ Caught Up into Divine Love

Across the street on the east side of Notre Dame Stadium, the home of the famous Fighting Irish football team, there is a bench with a statue of a man chomping on a rather large cigar. This man is Edward Walter Krauciunas, born in 1913 to a poor but devoted Catholic family in Chicago. When he came to Notre Dame as a student in 1930 to play football and basketball, one of his teammates shortened

brought in twenty local Moro scouts. The American soldiers expected the usual preparation talk explaining how to rely on the scouts in case of danger. Instead, Krause turned it over to the Moros who began to sing the Notre Dame Victory March in their native language. The soldiers laughed and cheered and then went out and completed a successful raid.

But Moose was, first of all, a family man. On August 29, 1938, he married Elizabeth Linden of Chicago. Moose and Elise had three children,

Moose Krause

his last name to "Krause" and gave him the nickname "Moose." Over the next sixty-two years of his life, Moose Krause not only played for Notre Dame, he coached both football and basketball and was the school's athletic director.

Besides his athletic success, Moose Krause was a Marine aviation officer who flew many reconnaissance missions in the Solomon Islands during World War II. Once, prepping his soldiers before a raid of a Japanese garrison, Moose

Edward Jr., Mary Elise, and Philip. In 1967, Edward Jr. was ordained a Holy Cross priest in Rome. It was shortly after this joyous time that the Krauses lives were forever changed. Elise was traveling in a taxicab that was struck from behind by a drunk driver. Elise was not expected to live, though Moose was sure that she would survive.

Survive she did, until her death in 1990. However, Elise's injuries from the accident were permanent and debilitating. She suffered severe damage to two parts of her brain, one that affected her memory and the other her emotions. Elise was in intensive care following the accident for many months, then spent years at home with special care, and finally spent the last eight years of her life at the Cardinal Nursing Home in South Bend, Indiana.

Moose was devoted to Elise throughout the years following the accident. He called the situation "a veritable crucifixion for both of us," but that didn't stop him from giving Elise his constant care and devotion. Moose passed up chances for many social outings befitting the Notre Dame athletic director to stay near his wife. He explained to his son, "There is nowhere I would rather be than in the room with your mother." The situation did contribute to Moose's turning to alcohol, but after a heart attack and at the advice of his children, he stopped drinking and attended Alcoholics Anonymous meetings for the rest of his life.

The years Elise spent at the Cardinal Nursing Home became a greater achievement for Moose than his years in athletics. He visited his wife at least twice a day, spoon-fed her meals when she could no longer feed herself, and sang her songs when she was unable to speak. On their fiftieth wedding anniversary, Moose came to the nursing home in a white tuxedo and the couple renewed their marriage vows. The Notre Dame president, Father Theodore Hesburgh, C.S.C, later told Edward Jr., "Your father has had many public successes in life, but nothing is more important in God's eyes than how he cared for your mother in those years."

Author Donald DeMarco defines fidelity as "the virtue that allows us to persevere in living out an unswerving commitment." This may be taken on three different levels: commitment to a task, to an ideal, or to another person, as in marriage. Moose Krause's fidelity to his wife modeled in the flesh the unwavering love that Jesus Christ has for his Church. The Second Vatican Council taught on married love that:

Christ the Lord abundantly blessed this many-faced love, welling up as it does from the fountain of divine love and structured as it is on the model of His union with the Church. For as God of old made Himself present to His people through a covenant of love and fidelity, so now the Savior of men and the Spouse of the Church comes into the lives of married Christians through the sacrament of matrimony. He abides with them thereafter so that, just as He loved the Church and handed Himself over on her behalf, the spouses may love each other with perpetual fidelity through mutual self-bestowal. (*Gaudium et Spes*, 48)

When Christ established the New Covenant, marriage was raised to a sacrament of service of one spouse to the other that contributes to their salvation in Christ. The history of Christian marriage in every era emphasizes the fidelity of one spouse for the other and the permanence of marriage that Jesus proclaimed. This chapter notes the historical development of the sacrament and explores the immediate preparation couples undertake for the marriage, the celebration of the wedding, and the effects of the sacrament on their lives.

The history of the Church is filled with examples of married love like that of the Krauses. Former Notre Dame football coach Ara Parseghian said in testimony of Moose Krause after Moose's death in 1992: "I call him 'Saint Edward.' If every person had that kind of compassion and respect for his spouse, this would be a lot better world."

- Write or tell about a married couple with as much devotion to one another as Moose and Elise Krause.

- Name the commitment to which you have been most faithful. Explain.

Tracing the Development of the Sacrament of Matrimony

Marriage is an institution established by God from the time of creation. Jesus blessed the relationship between a husband and wife and restored the ideal of marriage, which God intended from the beginning: "So they are no longer two, but one flesh. Therefore, what God has joined together, no human being must separate" (Mt 19:6). Christian marriage was modeled on the relationship between Christ and the Church; hence it became a divine institution, not a secular one.

From its earliest days, the Church presided over marriage between Christians and contracted the marriage within the Church. In the second century, Saint Ignatius of Antioch wrote of the necessity of the Church's role in a marriage:

> It is right for men and women who marry to be united with the consent of the bishop,

Saint Ignatius of Antioch

that the marriage be according to the Lord and not according to lust.[1]

In the early Church, marriages were celebrated in much the same way that local cultures had for centuries: the father of the bride handing his daughter over to the groom; the bride wearing a ceremonial gown with a veil; their joining of right hands; the exchange of rings; a procession of family and friends to the husband's house, where a marriage feast would take place; the groom carrying the wife over the threshold of the house and into married life. These customs were mostly unopposed by the Church, though Saint John Chrysostom commented negatively in the fourth century on dancing at weddings:

> Is the wedding then a theater? It is a sacrament, a mystery, and a model of the Church of Christ. . . . But why is there any need of dancing at all? They dance at pagan ceremonies; but at ours, silence and decorum should prevail, respect and modesty.[2]

Saint John Chrysostom wrote more extensively on marriage than any other Church father to that point. In *On Marriage and Family Life*, he shared three main ideas on marriage. First, he taught that marriage is not an obstacle to salvation; otherwise God would not have initiated it. Second, God established marriage for the procreation of children. Third, Chrysostom taught that marriage was a means of salvation for the couple, as it had the capacity to replace evil desires and promiscuity with service to the spouse and to family life.

In the fifth century, Saint Augustine wrote some of the most definitive work of the Church fathers on marriage, emphasizing that marriage is good because God creates it and that it offers three good things:

- the procreation of children by the conjugal act,
- the chastity of the spouses and their fidelity to one another,
- the indissoluble union of the marriage.

From the seventh century on, the Church became more involved in the wedding ceremony. The bishop or priest would give a **nuptial blessing**. Eventually the wedding ceremony developed into a liturgical rite performed at church rather than in a home. Civil laws came to require that a priest officiate at weddings.

By the Middle Ages, the wedding ceremony was very formal and required an exchange of vows by the couple before a priest, in front of witnesses, and in a church. The legislation of these changes helped to counteract the abuses of secret marriages in which the consent was often questionable.

By the twelfth century, the Church made it explicit that marriage is one of the Seven Sacraments. This understanding was later affirmed and taught as doctrine at both the Council of Florence (1439) and the Council of Trent (1563). The Church also taught that marriage was to be a sacrament lasting until the death of a spouse and prohibited divorce and remarriage. This teaching remains to this day.

The Second Vatican Council continued to emphasize the mutual consent of the couple as the essential element of the sacrament. The Council also taught that the couple's love:

> merging with divine love leads the spouses to a free and mutual gift of themselves, a gift proving itself by gentle affection and by deed. Such love pervades the whole of their lives. Indeed, by its generous activity it grows better and grows greater.[3]

Through the couple's mutual consent, they enter a lifelong covenant of love. They accept each other in permanent and exclusive union that is open to the procreation and education of children.

Do one of the following:

- Saint Augustine is famously quoted on marriage: "The procreation of children is the first, natural, and legitimate purpose of marriage." Read more about this teaching (e.g., *Gaudium et Spes*, 50, and the *Catechism of the Catholic Church*, 1652–1654) and write an analysis of its meaning.

- Read and outline the main teachings from the *Doctrine on Marriage* from the Council of Trent documents (twenty-fourth session).

- Read chapter 1, "Fostering the Nobility of Marriage and the Family" from *Gaudium et Spes* (47–52). Answer: What is the significance of the Second Vatican Council's using the word "covenant" rather than "contract" regarding marriage?

nuptial blessing
Nuptial is a Latin-derived word that means wedding. The nuptial blessing is intended for the bride and the marriage covenant. It takes place after the couple gives their consent to be married.

✦ Preparing for Marriage

The remote preparation for marriage begins in the family during infancy and extends through childhood and adolescence. The Second Vatican Council teaches:

> It is imperative to give suitable and timely instruction to young people, above all in the heart of their own families, about the dignity of married love, its role and its exercise, so that, having learned the value of chastity, they will be able at a suitable age to engage in honorable courtship and enter upon a marriage of their own.[4]

It is in the family that we learn how to give generously of ourselves. We also learn that:

- every person should have a healthy understanding of himself or herself, including the aspect of sexuality;

- sexuality is a part of a person's being; we relate to each other through our personalities, which include our sexuality;

- from creation, God made man and woman for each other and complementary as masculine and feminine;

- God decreed that sexual intimacy is between a man and woman and is reserved for marriage;

- marriage involves a total self-giving of the husband and wife to each other, emotionally and physically;

- healthy sexual relations in marriage are expressions of mutual love, not selfish pleasure.

Hopefully, with these and other lessons of family life learned and engrained, a man and woman set out to "find each other" and begin a more proximate time of getting to know each other leading to marriage. Note that the quotation above referred to this time as "courtship."

However, before considering more about exclusive dating, courtship, or whatever other term precedes a formal marriage engagement, consider how many young men and young women have typically gone about finding a partner for marriage.

One of the ways two people have been brought together for marriage in the past or in other cultures is through arranged marriages. One family made an agreement that promised their daughter to the son of another family. The couple may not

even have met each other until shortly before the wedding. In these cultures, love was understood to follow and grow out of marriage. Arranged marriages are still prevalent today in places like India. Growing up in a Western society, this method for meeting a future spouse likely seems limiting, impractical, or even scary to you.

The more common method for finding a partner in our culture begins—for better or worse—with a feeling of infatuation as described in Chapter 3. After meeting, the couple makes the crucial choice to determine if the feelings of infatuation can lead to a friendship and allow them to get to know each other on a deeper level. On the other hand, true friendships between men and women can and do progress to a romantic relationship. Also, sometimes people do take a more pragmatic approach to searching out a potential spouse, determining qualifications based on categories like a person's educational background and financial stability.

Recall that the first two predictors of a successful marriage have to do explicitly with family life (see page 95): that the spouses came from similar family backgrounds (especially religion) and that they had parents with a long and successful marriage. Don't waste this knowledge! A wise piece of advice in searching out a possible future spouse is to look for someone with a family background similar to yours. Again, one of the easiest ways to determine something about a person in this area is to find out if he or she is a practicing Catholic. More information will follow as you learn more about each other, but at least you've started out on an important area of common ground.

Nowadays, certain Catholic Internet dating services can help to accomplish the same objective, allowing young adults to "match up" with others of similar beliefs, values, and family backgrounds. At your age, however, it is wise and practical to socialize with friends who hold and practice the same faith and values that you do and who come from families that support the commitment of married life.

The traditional dating process does offer several benefits. By dating, a man and woman get to

know each other by sharing a wide spectrum of activities and experiences together. They discover whether they are compatible. Remember, a man and woman stand a better chance of having a good relationship if they have similar interests, come from the same social group, have the same or similar values, and practice the same religion. Major differences sorely try a marriage, especially when they involve the important values that shape most major decisions of our lives. Being "in love" is usually not enough to bridge major gaps. The many people who cite "irreconcilable differences" as the reason for their divorce prove this.

Sometimes love is blind to the flaws in a person or in the relationship that would seriously affect a marriage. Those who are in love may even think they can change the other person after the marriage. They usually end up regretting their choice. The person still smokes or drinks, spends too much time with other friends, is messy, or overspends. Rather, a person who is getting serious about a dating partner should ask himself or herself questions like these:

- How does my partner treat me?

- How does my partner treat others?

- Is this person someone I will be proud to marry in front of my family and friends?

- Is this person someone with whom I want to have and raise children?

If the person you are dating comes up short in any of these areas, it is better to forget the relationship altogether and move on. With God's help, the right person will eventually come your way. You shouldn't have to settle for anything but the best.

Pray While You Pound Pavement

Constantly, in whatever method of dating and courtship you use to work toward a wholesome preparation for marriage, it is wise always to pray to God to help you choose the right spouse. However, as chastity educator Mary Beth Bonacci explains:

My original thinking on the subject, which still informs *part* of my thinking, was that we wouldn't take the "sit back and let God do all the work" approach in anything else in our lives. If you needed a job, you wouldn't just pray to God to drop that perfect job into your lap while you sat at home watching "Jerry Springer." You'd pray, but you'd also be out there pounding the pavement. So . . . we should "act like everything depended on us, and pray as if everything depended on God."[5]

- Make a list of five different ways you could meet someone of the opposite sex who is likely to share your same values and practice your same religion.

- Write a prayer in which you ask God to bless you and a possible future spouse.

Proposing Marriage

Doug was two years older than his girlfriend, Linette, whom he had first met attending Saint Monica Catholic High School in California. The father of their mutual friend was Ed Farmer, the play-by-play announcer for the Chicago White Sox.

After dating a few years, Doug decided to propose marriage to Linette, and he had a creative plan for doing that. He arranged with Ed Farmer to "share" Doug's proposal on the radio during a spring training game in Arizona while Doug, Linette, their parents, and friends sat with them in the stadium. While Linette and Doug had talked about marriage several times before, the proposal was a secret. In the fifth inning, Ed Farmer told his listening audience that one of the fans at the game, Doug, had something special to ask Linette. His audio was beamed to everyone in the stadium. Doug got down on one knee in the midst of peanut shells and hot dog wrappers on the aisle steps and asked Linette to be married.

She said, "Yes!" (Thank goodness!)

Everyone in the immediate family and group of friends hugged and wished them well. The rest of the fans at the game stood and cheered. It was truly a remarkable marriage proposal that turned out just as planned.

Of course, not every couple has a proposal story as dramatic as this. But every couple certainly remembers the time when one of them, traditionally the man, asked the other to be married and the proposal was accepted. This is certainly a different beginning to engagement than an arranged agreement. Typically nowadays it is only after the couple has decided to marry that they will tell parents, family members, and friends of their decision.

One difference in the pattern is that often a man will ask the woman's parents (especially her father) for permission to marry their daughter. Asking permission in this way shows the parents that the man respects their feelings and their daughter. Occasionally the parents may express some reservations about the impending engagement, but in the large majority of cases this is a genuine way to build respect and trust in the family and will be well-appreciated by the parents.

At the time of the marriage proposal or shortly afterward, the man usually gives a single-banded diamond ring to his **fiancée**. At the wedding a second gold band may be added. After all of these signs of the engagement are made public, the couple is able to

announce their engagement formally to the rest of their family and friends. An engagement announcement may be sent to the newspaper.

A meaning of the word *engage* is "to attach or bring together." An engagement period is intended to bring the man and woman closer together before they are married, and also to bring their families into closer contact with one another.

Usually the engagement period lasts for at least six to eight months and up

fiancée
Meaning "to trust," a fiancée is a woman to whom a man is engaged to be married. The man engaged to the woman is called a fiancé.

to one year, though it may be longer or shorter depending on events in a couple's life. For example, the couple may have recently graduated from

college and decided to attend grad school in a different part of the country. In that case, they may choose to be married right away so that their family and friends from home can share in their wedding.

In most cases the year-long engagement is necessary to prepare for the tasks of the wedding—where it will be, the music that will be played, and the guests who will be invited.

Much more importantly, especially for a Catholic wedding, engagement is a special time for prayer and further spiritual preparation for the Sacrament of Marriage. The engagement time is necessary to discuss with a priest how well the couple meets the requirements for marriage and

allows for sufficient time to complete a parish or diocesan-sponsored marriage preparation program.

Requirements for a Catholic Wedding

One of the first things a couple seeking a Catholic wedding will do is contact their Catholic parish and meet with a priest or deacon. Usually this is done at least six months prior to

the wedding date. Marriages are typically permitted in the parish where one of the persons lives or has established at least a month-long residence. The Church prefers the couple to participate or plan to participate actively in the parish where they live.

Part of the initial preparation for marriage involves understanding both Church and state requirements for a valid marriage. Civil laws determine the legality of marriage. For example,

age requirements for the legality of marriage vary from state to state. Church laws set the conditions for the Sacrament. Before marriage preparation, the couple will be asked if they meet some of the basic requirements to receive the Sacrament of Matrimony. Basically, the couple must be of mature age, unmarried, not closely related by blood or marriage, willing to have children if they are of child-bearing age, and they must be freely giving consent to marry. The matrimonial consent is the most important element, since it is the quality of that consent that determines the validity of the marriage. **Impediments** are obstacles to a valid and licit celebration of a sacrament. A priest interviews the couple separately to find out if impediments exist. Each person will be asked to testify to the truth of their statements with an oath.

Related to consent, a person cannot be pressured to marry. For a valid Catholic marriage to take place, the couple must understand what they are undertaking, that a marriage is a permanent covenant of love. Here are some other major impediments to a valid Catholic marriage (the referenced number is to the *Code of Canon Law*):

- A man under age sixteen years and a woman under fourteen years cannot validly enter marriage (c. 1083).

- If either the man or woman is physically incapable of sexual intercourse, the marriage is not valid. If there is doubt about this impediment, the marriage should not be impeded or declared null as long as the doubt exists (c. 1804).

- A person who is legally married to another may not be married until the invalidity of the prior marriage has been legitimately and certainly established (c. 1085).

- A priest may not be validly married; neither may a publicly professed religious who has taken lifetime vows of chastity (c. 1087, 1088).

- A person may not marry descendants or ancestors in a direct line (e.g., parent, grandparent, son, grandson, etc.), whether or not the relationship is by blood or by marriage. Neither may a person marry siblings or first cousins.

- Relationships by marriage (e.g., a man and his second wife's daughter) or adoption (e.g., siblings) are not valid.

Also, when one of the partners is not Catholic, permission for the marriage must come from the local bishop. In the case of a Catholic marrying a baptized non-Catholic, the bishop may also make an exception allowing the minister of the non-Catholic partner

impediments
External circumstances or facts that prevent a sacramental or legal marriage from taking place.

to participate at the wedding along with the priest or deacon. The minister might read from Scripture or bless the couple; however, the priest would receive the couple's vows. With permission of the bishop, the marriage may be celebrated in the church of the non-Catholic partner. In that case, the priest would be allowed to participate but the minister of that church would preside, and receive the couple's vows. Also, when a Catholic marries a non-baptized person, the wedding may not take place during a Mass. The following are necessary conditions for a mixed marriage:

- The Catholic partner must declare that he or she is prepared to remove dangers from falling away from the faith and promise to do all in his or her power to have the children baptized and raised in the Catholic Church.

- The non-Catholic partner is informed of the promises made by the Catholic party.

- Both the Catholic and non-Catholic are instructed in the essential requirements and Church teachings on the Sacrament of Matrimony and family life.

Special mention must be given to couples who approach the Church and who are living together without being married. The Church does not permit such "trial marriages"; they are one of the offenses against the dignity of marriage (see *CCC*, 2391). However, only the local bishop, and only for a serious cause, can prohibit a reception of the Sacrament to those who are properly disposed and not prohibited from Church law from receiving them.

More likely is that early in the engagement period, the couple would be taught about the Church's understanding of marriage and would make an adjustment in their living situation. For example, the couple may be encouraged to live apart for a few months before they are married. Other pastoral solutions might have the couple marrying, but in a smaller, private ceremony. A point to remember is that persons who dream of a large Catholic wedding should think twice before entering into a live-in arrangement prior to marriage.

Parish Preparations

The Church puts a great deal of emphasis on suitable marriage preparation, not only of the variety that takes place in families and

through catechetical programs (e.g., like the course you are enrolled in now), but through required participation by the couple in a parish- or diocesan-sponsored conference, retreat, or workshop during the months of engagement.

Besides interviewing the couple to determine if any impediments to the marriage exist, the priest helps the couple understand what the Sacrament of Matrimony entails. He may direct the couple to take a "pre-marriage inventory" that helps the couple gauge the effectiveness of their communication with one another as well as ways to improve on it. The FOCCUS (Facilitating Open Couple Communication, Understanding, and Study) is one of the most widely used inventories. It is a nearly two hundred question inventory, adapted for Catholics, with questions on things like communication issues, finances, sexuality, religion, and consequences of living together. A sample question might be arranged like this:

> My future spouse and I agree that our marriage commitment means we intend to pledge love under all circumstances.
>
> ❏ Agree
>
> ❏ Disagree
>
> ❏ Unsure

The survey is sent to a company where it is analyzed and returned to the parish for the pastor or a designated minister to go over the results with the couple and to talk about some of the information the survey revealed.

After the inventory, a second component of marriage preparation would be participation in a program of some kind such as Engaged Encounter or Pre-Cana. These may be diocesan-sponsored, which usually take the shape of either a weekend retreat or a series of classes. Or it may be a parish-based program that takes place in homes or the parish center. In either, the program is facilitated by one or more married couples and a variety of issues is covered. The Engaged Encounter weekend also includes the participation of a priest. The couples attend presentations that address issues like sexuality, vocation, sacrament, unity, and communication. Each person then has time to record personal responses in a journal before meeting one-on-one with the future spouse to discuss the presentation and their responses. The Pre-Cana program is similar to Engaged Encounter except that it is usually held at the parish. Married couples facilitate conversation with engaged couples over the course of several weekly meetings.

Another important topic covered in Church-sponsored marriage preparation programs is **Natural Family Planning (NFP)**. This method of self-observation of the fertile and infertile periods of a woman's menstrual cycle is morally approved by the Church and is a safe method for regulating the birth of children. An orientation on NFP and the Church's teaching on birth control is begun prior to the wedding. The couple may also be encouraged to take a more detailed course in NFP sponsored by the diocese or local hospital some time early in their marriage.

All of these forms of preparation are directed explicitly at the marriage—not simply the day of the wedding. Often couples get wrapped up in the peripheral tasks for the wedding day and do not focus on the really important elements that are necessary for a long and successful marriage. Brooke and Steve Sullivan, part of the Pre-Cana team at the Cathedral of Saint Mary of the Immaculate Conception parish in Lafayette, Indiana; concur:

Natural Family Planning

NFP is the Church-approved method for planning and spacing the birth of children in marriage.

Marriage preparation is a chance to reflect on the marriage. Who is the person you will be spending your life with? Are your values, morals, family history, hopes, dreams, and life experiences going to be compatible when the going gets tough? These questions must be discussed openly and honestly before the vows are said in order to ensure this will be a lifelong sacrament.[6]

When one of the persons getting married is not Catholic, adjustments to the preparation may be warranted. For a marriage between two baptized Catholics, the Church also strongly recommends that they have each received the Sacrament of Confirmation or plan to be confirmed before the wedding. The Sacrament of Penance is usually celebrated by the couple near to the wedding date, often along with the wedding rehearsal a day or two before.

Historically, on three consecutive Sundays before the wedding the marriage is announced in the parish bulletin. These announcements are called **marriage banns**. They were originally intended to allow anyone who knew of a reason why the couple should not be married to make the reason known to them and the Church. Now this function is handled as part of the interview with the priest. Though no longer required by Church law, the tradition of marriage banns remains as a way to inform the parish of the impending wedding.

Planning the Wedding

Vince and Lani attended to all the details of planning their wedding. Both had invitation lists of over one hundred family members and friends and each wanted to make the day special, not only for themselves, but for all who shared it with them. They reserved the banquet hall at a local country club. Vince had a buddy who played in a music trio who would donate the music for the reception. The food menu would incorporate both Vince's Italian and Lani's Filipino family backgrounds. Vince paid the rental cost of the tuxedos for his groomsmen. Lani arranged for manicures as a gift to her bridesmaids.

Flowers. Photos. Videos. The special four-tiered cake. The wonderful day seemed to come off without a hitch.

Upon returning from their honeymoon, the couple invited some of their family and the wedding party to join them at their apartment while they opened their presents. It was then Lani and Vince first began to hear the compliments about how nice

marriage banns
Announcements of a couple's intention to be married printed in a parish bulletin for the three weekends preceding the marriage.

their wedding turned out. This didn't surprise them. What did surprise them was what people seemed to find most memorable about the wedding day: the wedding liturgy. Some of the comments from their friends:

- *From Lani's best friend, Kari:* "I really paid attention to the Gospel. I've known you guys for so long. I kept thinking about how your relationship has grown and will continue to grow now that you are married." (The couple had chosen the parable of the mustard seed: "It is the smallest of seeds, yet when it is full-grown it is the largest of plants" from Matthew 13:31–32.)

- *From Vince's mother, Lucy:* "The entire Mass was so moving. I was really choked up when Donnie [Vince's brother] prayed the intercessory prayer for my mom and dad. I could feel their presence watching down on this day from Heaven."

- *From Vince's coworker Jon:* "As far as I remember, your wedding was the first time I had been to a Catholic Mass. It seemed so solemn, yet happy. I was surprised and impressed that you and Lani were on your knees for so long. You both seemed so prayerful and content."

Even for all the planning and worrying, about the peripheries of the wedding day, the constant stream of comments that Vince and Lani heard about the wedding were that so many people were moved by the liturgy. For a good while, Vince and Lani's wedding was remembered as the one with "the good Mass."

The wedding is the culmination of preparation during which a couple has explored their relationship in more depth and prayed for God's grace to make a lifetime commitment to each other. Some weddings are lavish and expensive. But they do not have to be. The most important part of the wedding is the celebration of the Sacrament that brings two people and two families into one.

The Church allows couples to personalize the nuptial ceremony while following the pattern that is standard for all Catholic weddings. The

couple takes an active role in planning the marriage liturgy while being careful to keep the wedding simple and not burdened by excessive display. Liturgy planning usually takes place in the final visit with the priest. Special focus is placed on the choice of Scripture readings. The Liturgy of the Word may contain three biblical readings, the first of them from the Old Testament, which tell the story of marriage in the history of salvation and speak about the couple's responsibility for welcoming and raising children. After the Gospel, a homily is given. The couple may also assist—indirectly, at least—in helping the celebrating priest or deacon with his homily preparation by sharing with him something of their lives—for example, their hopes and dreams—prior to the wedding. He can then use this information to help him personalize the homily while drawing from the meaning of the Scripture.

Also, the couple may choose various prayers and blessings, as well as select the music for the wedding with the help of a liturgical musician. Most dioceses and parishes have rules (or at least strong suggestions) for appropriate music for weddings. Some of the questions a couple may be asked to consider regarding music: Are the music and lyrics liturgical in nature? Is it a well-written piece of music? Can the assembly sing it? Does it correspond to the rite of marriage or to a particular part of the liturgy? The parish liturgical musician is a valuable source to help answer such questions.

The couple can also compose the specific intercessory prayers that are a part of the Liturgy of the Word. The exchange of the vows, or marital consent, is an essential part of the Sacrament of Matrimony. There are two standard vows approved for use in the United States. The couple may choose between the traditional and revised versions.

There is also opportunity for family members and friends to participate in some of the special liturgical ministries like lectors, extraordinary ministers of communion, altar servers, gift bearers, musicians, and more.

According to cultural or family traditions, there are some other special adaptations to the liturgy. For example, at some point in the ceremony the parents of the couple may offer them a special blessing. In the United States, the lighting of a unity candle—the light from two smaller candles merges into one light of a central, larger candle—has become a popular tradition. Another tradition from Mexico that is now popular throughout North America is the bride's offering of a flower bouquet before the statue of the Blessed Mother, usually accompanied by the playing of "*Ave Maria.*" Devotion to Mary, the Mother of the Church and Queen of the Family, is something that should guide not only a couple's marriage preparation and wedding, but also their years together as husband and wife, father and mother. These traditions are always subject to the norms of the liturgy as determined by the Church.

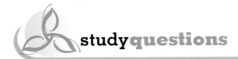
study questions

1. Name three things we learn about marriage from our participation in family life.

2. Typically, what are ways men and women find a partner for marriage in today's Western society?

3. What are some advantages of the traditional dating process?

4. What is the main purpose of the engagement period?

5. How long does the engagement period usually last?

6. Where do Catholic weddings typically take place?

7. What are the basic requirements for the Sacrament of Matrimony?

8. What is an impediment to marriage? Name two impediments.

9. What are the necessary conditions for marriage between a Catholic and non-Catholic partner?

10. Explain some possible resolutions for a couple living together before marriage who want to have a Catholic wedding.

11. Name three requirements of marriage preparation.

12. Define *marriage banns*.

13. What are some ways the couple can help to plan their wedding liturgy?

How Would You Plan a Wedding Liturgy?

Working with a priest, a couple can individualize their wedding with Scripture readings, prayers, blessings, music, and other traditions as long as these are not in excess and do not detract from the essential rites, especially the matrimonial consent.

Use the following suggestions or decide on some of your own to plan the Scripture readings for your wedding. Choose one reading from each category. Look for a unifying theme between the readings. After you've finished, write a short homily connecting the theme of the readings to the Sacrament of Matrimony.

Liturgy of the Word

Old Testament Readings (choose one)	Responsorial Psalms (choose one)	New Testament Reading (choose one)	Gospels (choose one)
✦ Genesis 1:26–28, 31a	✦ Psalm 33:12, 18, 20–21, 22	✦ Romans 8:31b–35, 37–39	✦ Matthew 5:1–12
✦ Genesis 2:18–24	✦ Psalm 34:2–3, 4, 6–7, 8–9	✦ Romans 12:1–2, 9–18	✦ Matthew 5:13–16
✦ Genesis 24:48–51, 58–67	✦ Psalm 103:1–2, 8, 13, 17–18a	✦ Ephesians 5:1–2a, 21–28	✦ Matthew 7:12, 24–29
✦ Tobit 7:9–10, 11–15,	✦ Psalm 112:1–2, 3–4, 5–7a, 7b–8, 9	✦ Colossians 3:12–17	✦ Matthew 19:3–6
✦ Tobit 8:5–10	✦ Psalm 128:1–2, 3, 4–5	✦ 1 Peter 3:1–9	✦ Matthew 22:35–40
✦ Song of Songs 2:8–10, 14, 16a; 8:6–7a	✦ Psalm 145:8–9, 10, 15, 17–18	✦ 1 John 3:18–24	✦ Mark 10:6–9
✦ Jeremiah 31:31–32a, 33–34a	✦ Psalm 148:1–2, 3–4, 9–10, 11–12ab, 12c–14a	✦ 1 John 4:7–12	✦ John 2:1–11
		✦ Revelation 19:1, 5–9	

journaldiscussion

- What do you perceive are disadvantages of an arranged marriage? Advantages?

- What are some strategies for finding a marriage partner that has Catholic values and who grew up in a Catholic family?

- What would be your ideal wedding proposal experience?

✦ The Celebration of Marriage

For Catholics, marriage is a sacred **covenant**, that is, an agreement or pact between the couple themselves *and* the couple and God. A civil law marriage is a legal contract regulated by the government. A contract is an agreement initiated by people that can be terminated by people. In a contract, each party's responsibilities are spelled out, and the contract is good for a certain period of time. A covenant is an agreement that is initiated by God. In a marriage covenant, the couple agrees to love each other until death.

covenant
A sacred and unbreakable agreement between human beings or between God and a human being that involves mutual commitments. The New Covenant is made in the name of Jesus Christ, and it brings salvation to the world.

The marriage covenant is modeled on the faithfulness Yahweh exhibited in his covenant with the Israelites in the Old Testament. More, it reflects the New Covenant first established by Christ at the Last Supper and with his Death on a cross. This lasting covenant is sealed in the blood of Christ. In the Roman Catholic Church, the celebration of marriage between two Catholics normally takes place during Mass. For it is in the Eucharist that:

the memorial of the New Covenant is realized, the New Covenant in which Christ has united himself for ever to the Church, his beloved bride for whom he gave himself up. It is therefore fitting that the spouses should seal their consent to give themselves to each other through the offering of their own lives by uniting it to the offering of Christ for his

Church made present in the Eucharistic sacrifice, and by receiving the Eucharist so that, communicating in the same Body and the same Blood of Christ, they may form but "one body" in Christ. (*CCC*, 1621)

In the celebration of marriage, certain elements of the wedding Mass are emphasized, especially:

- the Liturgy of the Word, which shows the importance of Christian marriage in the history of salvation;

- the consent of the spouses to marry, which the couple gives to each other;

- the special nuptial blessing; and

- the reception of Holy Communion by the groom and bride, and by all present.

Liturgy of the Word

The choice of Scripture readings has previously been discussed. The couple, with the help of the priest or other pastoral ministers, can choose Scripture from both the Old Testament and New Testament, including the Gospels, that remind them of God's institution of marriage from the beginning of time and Christ's presence in their own marriage, beginning with his presence in the liturgy and continuing on as he shares his life with them throughout their marriage.

Remember, Jesus himself attended a wedding. The village of Cana was about eight miles north of Nazareth, at least a three-hour walk for the guests traveling by foot. The wedding feast could last for a number of days, as there was eating, drinking, and dancing to celebrate the union of the man and woman. *And Jesus was there in person.* When a disaster struck the party—they ran out of wine— Jesus' mother asked him to help. *Jesus listened to Mary's request.* The miracle of the changing of water to wine alleviated the first problem in the couple's marriage. *Jesus was the solution to the problem.* After the guests drank the new wine and realized what Jesus had done, they began to believe in him. *Jesus' presence in the marriage was an occasion to come to believe in him.*

The Liturgy of the Word reminds a man and woman being married today that Jesus is with them, not only on their wedding day, but throughout their marriage. Through the intercession of Mary, Jesus will bless their marriage and bring grace to their family. When problems and difficulties arise in the marriage, Jesus is the answer. Finally, the longevity and model of the couple's marriage will be a sign of Christ to all who come in contact with them.

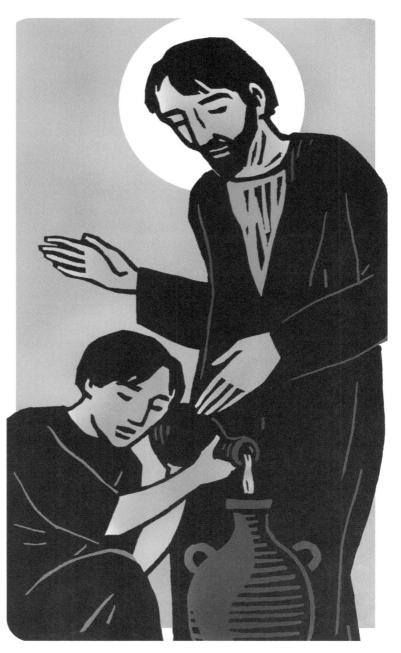

The Wedding at Cana

Matrimonial Consent

The essential rite of the Sacrament of Matrimony takes place directly after the Liturgy of the Word. It is when the couple literally gives themselves to each other by consenting to enter marriage:

"I take you to be my wife."

"I take you to be my husband."

These are the words that bind the couple to each other, making them as God intended from the beginning of creation "one flesh" (Gn 2:24). The woman and man also promise to one another to be true "in good times and in bad, in sickness and in health" and to "love and honor you all the days of my life." The mutual consent of the couple brings the marriage into being. Their sharing sexual intercourse after marriage consummates their union and makes the marriage indissoluble.

For the words of consent to be valid, they must be given freely. No one can coerce or force someone into marriage. The person may be pressured into speaking the words of consent, but if the words are not freely expressed, the marriage is invalid. Also, to be valid, there can be no impediment according to natural or Church law. The Church can annul a marriage, that is, determine it null and void, if any of these situations are found to be invalid.

The spouses themselves are the ministers of the Sacrament of Matrimony. They mutually confer upon each other the graces of the Sacrament by expressing their consent in public before the Church. Catholics must marry in the presence of a priest or deacon and in the presence of two witnesses. Typically the maid of honor and best man serve in the role of witnesses.

The consent of the couple is usually expressed through a series of questions by the priest by asking them to state their desires. He begins by asking them about their freedom to make the choice to be married, their faithfulness to each other, and their willingness to accept and raise children. For example, he will say:

N. and N., have you come here freely and without reservation to give yourselves to each other in marriage?

Will you honor each other as man and wife for the rest of your lives?

Will you accept children lovingly from God, and bring them up according to the law of Christ and his Church?

The couple takes turns answering each question separately. Then the priest invites them to declare their consent. Joining right hands, the groom says:

I, N., take you, N., to be my wife. I promise to be true to you in good times and in bad, in sickness and in health. I will love you and honor you all the days of my life.

The bride states her desires:

I, N., take you, N., to be my husband. I promise to be true to you in good times and in bad, in sickness and in health. I will love you and honor you all the days of my life.

The presence of the priest, the Church's minister, the official witnesses, and the other guests visibly and publicly expresses that the marriage is a reality. The place where the marriage takes place—the parish church—is another important sign. Sometimes couples wish to celebrate their wedding in a place other than a church—for example, outdoors or in a home. While a local bishop may approve such a change of venue, it is only in extraordinary circumstances. The wedding takes place in a church because the marriage is a sacrament of the Church. Some other reasons a Catholic marriage must follow Church form include:

- The marriage leads the couple to certain rights and responsibilities within the Church, both toward each other and to their children.

- The public and official nature of the couple's consent "protects the 'I do' once given and helps the spouses remain faithful to it" (*CCC*, 1632).

- The consent requires the certification of witnesses. As soon as the wedding concludes, the pastor of the parish records in the marriage register the name of the spouses, the name of the priest or deacon, the names of the witnesses, and the date and place of the wedding.

Typically in the United States and in many other places, after the couple gives their consent to marriage and it is received and accepted by the priest in the name of the Church, the priest blesses the rings of the bride and groom and they exchange them. The circular ring is a sign of the eternal love of the couple and of the marriage that will last until death.

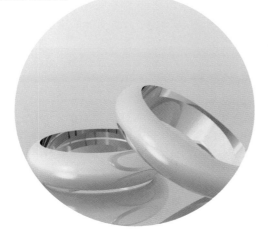

Pastoral Care for High Risk Marriage

Out of pastoral concern, the Church will take special care before permitting the marriage of couples that fall in several "high risk" categories. Because of a higher-than-average divorce rate within these marriages, intense preparation must be undertaken. Some of these high-risk categories are:

- *Mixed Marriages.* In marriages between couples of different faiths, situations like the religious formation of the children, the practice of faith, and the feelings of other family members can create difficulties.

- *Inactive Catholics.* Sometimes a wedding is the time a couple will choose to return to the Church after not practicing their religion. The causes of this inactivity must be explored. Often the couple will be asked to participate in catechetical formation prior to the wedding, including preparation for the Sacrament of Confirmation if it has not yet been received.

- *Premarital Pregnancy.* The Church desires to support the couple and their child. However, because of concern about duress and questions about freedom of consent, the typical types of marriage preparation (inventory, retreats, consultation) will not be waived.

- *Youthful Marriages.* When one or both partners are under twenty-one, the Church will take care to point out the seriousness of the commitment. If one or both partners are under nineteen, the Church may discourage the marriage until one or both have reached that age. If the couple persists in wanting to be married, permission from the local bishop may be needed.

- *Divorce and Remarriage.* If one or both partners have been previously married and divorced, the Church requires the previous marriage be annulled, or declared void. More information on annulments will be presented in chapter 6.

Nuptial Blessing

After the Our Father, the priest faces the couple, who have joined their hands, and gives them a nuptial or wedding blessing. This blessing is intended to bring the love of God and all of his graces on the couple throughout their marriage. The priest extends his hands in blessing over the couple. The following words are part of one of the four Nuptial Blessings in the *Rite of Marriage*:

Father, stretch out your hand,
    and bless N. and N.

Lord, grant that as they begin to live this
    sacrament
they may share with each other
    the gifts of your love
and become one heart and mind
as witnesses to your presence in their marriage.
Help them to create a home together
and give them children to be
    formed by the Gospel
and to have a place in your family.
Give your blessings to N., your daughter,
so that she may be a good wife and mother,
caring for the home,
faithful in love for her husband,
generous and kind.
Give your blessings to N., your son,
so that he may be a faithful husband
and good father.
Father, grant that as they come together to your
    table on earth,
so they may one day have the joy of sharing
    your feast in Heaven.

We ask this through Christ our Lord.
Amen.

Holy Communion

Prior to the wedding, the bride and groom make themselves disposed for the celebration of their marriage and for the reception of Holy Communion by receiving the Sacrament of Penance. During the wedding liturgy, they are the first to receive Holy Communion under both species, bread and wine. It is appropriate for the man and woman, who have just been joined as one, to drink from a common cup. It is the Holy Eucharist that communicates and nourishes their love and is to be the center of their entire married life.

It is also appropriate for all of the guests to share in Holy Communion, as they are able according

to Church law. Priests take care to show special consideration to those who only take part in the Eucharist at special occasions like weddings or may have abandoned their faith altogether. A wedding is a great opportunity for the guests to learn about the Church's teaching on Eucharistic sharing and what is necessary for worthy reception of Communion. It is also a chance for all the guests to share in the many graces of t¹ Eucharistic banquet, even if some are una; receive Holy Communion.

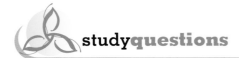

study questions

1. How is a covenant different from a contract?

2. Why is it appropriate to celebrate a Catholic wedding at Mass?

3. What is the essential part of the marriage rite?

4. How can a couple's consent to marry be considered null and void?

5. What is the role of the priest or deacon at marriage?

6. What are some reasons a Catholic marriage must follow the form prescribed by the Church?

7. When does the nuptial blessing take place?

8. What is symbolic of the husband and wife sharing from a common cup at Holy Communion?

journal discussion

● In Jesus' voice, tell the couple at Cana why you are at their wedding and why you are willing to help them solve the problem of having no wine.

● Whom do you imagine for your best man or maid of honor at your wedding? How is this person representative of the faithfulness and love present in marriage?

✦ The Effects of the Sacrament of Matrimony

The Sacrament of Matrimony is a sign of life and love. The matrimonial bond is one established by God himself. In this bond, couples are assured a lifetime of God's grace. Marriage and family life becomes the place and means where the husband and wife grow together to perfection and holiness while jointly contributing to the glory of God. As the *Catechism of the Catholic Church* teaches:

> The covenant between spouses is integrated into God's covenant with man: "Authentic married love is caught up in divine love." (*CCC*, 1639 quoting *Gaudium et Spes*, 48)

Partnered with Christ, the couple works toward their own salvation. Assuredly this life will have many ups and downs, tragedies and joys. At one

Night Out

Offer your services (free of charge) as a babysitter to a married couple with young children. Instead of accepting money for your services, tell the couple you wish them to share three things about their relationship/marriage for a school project. Here are the three things:

1. Share the story about how you met. Also, tell about the first time you had the feeling that you would marry your spouse.

2. If you could change anything about your wedding day what would it be?

3. What did you find to be the greatest adjustment to married life? How did you learn to make this adjustment.

Write a summary of what you found out from the husband and wife. Share it with your classmates.

Don't forget to babysit the children. Have fun!

moment there is the joy of welcoming children and nurturing them in life and faith. Later, the same children can be the cause of pain to parents either of their own decision (e.g., abuse of drugs, abandoning the faith) or, in a worse case, their suffering serious illness or death.

The key trait of the marriage covenant is that it is caught up in the New Covenant of God's love—when Jesus Christ came to give his life for all of humanity. By giving us his Son, the Father showed his faithful love and fidelity. Jesus draws all people into one body, loves us personally and unconditionally, and calls on us to grow in love by serving others. The Sacrament of Matrimony helps couples to live these values of Jesus. Hence, there are two main effects of the sacrament:

- The couple is united in a permanent bond. Human authority can never dissolve a consummated marriage between two baptized

persons. The Church does not have the power to dissolve a bond that has been established by God.

- The husband and wife are promised a lifetime of God's grace, by which their love is perfected and their unity strengthened.

Human beings are predestined to reproduce the image of God's Son. Through the witness of their married life, the couple brings the presence of Christ to the world. Some of the graces of the Sacrament are examined in more detail in the following section.

Graces of Married Life

The Sacrament of Matrimony offers a husband and wife the gift of unconditional love, which freely binds them for life. In sickness or health, in poverty or wealth, in good times and in bad times, the couple promises to be faithful. The graces of married life that spring from the Sacrament can be witnessed in several ways, for example:

The man and woman are given the grace to love each other unselfishly, as Christ has loved us. Would it ever be possible for true love to be shared selfishly, for one person to put his or her needs before the other's? In marriage, the couple always places the other first. This is manifested in major life decisions. Imagine the wife who orchestrates several family moves from place to place to support her husband's career. Or, the husband and father who passes up a new job because it would leave no time for his family.

Unselfish love is also part of the sexual sharing between a married couple. Whereas a person's selfish lovemaking is only concerned with his or her own "needs" or pleasures, unselfishly, a married couple does not separate the unitive dimension of sexual intercourse from the procreative, while respecting the wishes and feelings of the other. "The truly human performance of these acts fosters the self-giving they signify and, enriches the spouses in joy and gratitude" (*Gaudium et Spes*, 49). Conjugal love always seeks the happiness of the beloved and has concern for the spiritual perfection and eternal salvation of the other.

The man and woman are given the grace to remain faithful in their union to death. Remember that God is the author of marriage and established the permanence of marriage from the beginning of creation. Marriage, therefore, is a natural reality. The Church confirms this reality in the Sacrament of Matrimony, building on a reality that already exists.

The wedding ring is a sign of this permanence. During the blessing and exchange of rings, the man and woman place the rings on each other's fingers, praying that they will be a sign of their love and fidelity for one another. This commitment to permanence is deepened by the couple's common faith, celebration of the Eucharist, and through meaningful and daily communication.

The man and woman are given a grace that strengthens them for eternal life. Each year the newspapers tell the stories of a husband and wife who, after years of marriage, die within weeks or days of each other. Usually, one of the spouses had been ill, while the caretaker spouse was in good health. Nevertheless, the surviving spouse withers of a broken heart. The powerful love they shared as a couple seems to will them into eternity.

A vision in the Book of Revelation describes God's eternal reign as the "wedding day of the Lamb." Throughout Scripture, marriage is one of the ways to describe the everlasting covenant between God and his people. The ever-growing love between a wife and a husband and the love they share for their children allow them to witness and persevere in their desire for God's reign in eternity.

The man and woman are blessed with children and are given the grace to raise them in faith and love. The blessings of conjugal love that spouses share extend to the "fruits of the moral, spiritual, and supernatural life that parents hand on to their children by education" (*CCC*, 1653). Children are like a sacrament because they point to God's love living in their parents. They are also a result of God's love lived in their parents.

Besides the graces the Sacrament of Matrimony bestows directly on the couple, the witness of Christian marriage is a grace to society that is able to witness the success of married life. Imagine the testimony received by a husband and wife on the occasion of their fiftieth wedding anniversary. The praise would not be centered on accomplishments like how much money

Model of Unselfish Love

One of the most remarkable examples of unselfish love was that of recently canonized Saint Gianna Molla. A wife, mother, and doctor, she understood full well the risks to her own life when a tumor was discovered on her uterine wall early in her pregnancy with her fourth child in 1961. Gianna asked her husband to promise that if it were necessary he would choose to save the life of their child, rather than to save her own life. Their daughter, Gianna Emanuela, was born on Good Friday, April 21, 1962. While the baby was born healthy, Gianna developed a fatal infection and died a week later. Almost immediately after her death, devotion to Gianna developed among those who knew her and were touched by her faith and love. On May 16, 2004, Pope John Paul II canonized her.

domestic church
The "domestic church" is a name for the family, the Church in miniature.

they earned, the job promotions they received, or the vacations they shared, but rather on

- their love and care for each other;

- the fruitful lives of their children;

- their gifts of time, talent, and money to others;

- their faithfulness and participation in the life of the Church.

In today's secular society, a married couple's authentic love and their commitment to the permanence of their marriage is a bold example to the world. Likewise, the importance they attach to raising their children is also paramount. The Second Vatican Council retrieved an ancient term to call the family the **domestic church**. The prayer and service undertaken by individual families are the foundation of life in the Church.

study**questions**

1. What are the two main effects of the Sacrament of Matrimony?

2. How is unselfish love a part of sexual sharing in marriage?

3. Why is marriage a "natural reality"?

4. How does a married couple keep its commitment to permanence?

5. What is meant in Scripture by the "wedding day of the Lamb"?

6. What are the blessings of conjugal love?

journal**discussion**

- What does this statement mean to you: "Authentic married love is caught up in divine love"?

- Imagine you and your spouse have celebrated your fiftieth wedding anniversary. Name some things you would want to be commended for on your marriage.

summary**points**

Caught Up into Divine Love

- Moose and Elise Krause modeled the virtue of fidelity in their marriage.

- Fidelity is the virtue that allows us to persevere in living out our commitments.

- Marital fidelity is modeled on the fidelity Christ has for his Church.

Tracing the Development of the Sacrament of Matrimony

- Christian marriages were originally celebrated as they had been by local cultures for centuries. From the earliest days, the marriage between Christians was contracted within the Church.

- Saint John Chrysostom taught that marriage is not an obstacle to salvation, that God established marriage for the procreation of children, and that marriage was a means of salvation for the couple.

- In the fifth century, Saint Augustine taught that marriage is good because of the procreation of children by the conjugal act, the chastity of the spouses, their fidelity to one another, and the indissoluble union of the marriage.

- From the seventh century on, the Church became more involved in weddings. Eventually the ceremony developed into a liturgical rite performed at church.

- The Council of Florence (1439) and the Council of Trent (1563) each affirmed that marriage is a sacrament and that marriage was indissoluble.

- The Second Vatican Council continues to emphasize that the mutual consent of the couple to marry is the essential element of the Sacrament.

Preparing for Marriage

- The remote preparation for marriage begins early in life within the family.

- In the custom of arranged marriages, one family promises their daughter to the son of another family.

- Coming from similar family backgrounds and having parents with a long and successful marriage are two predictors for a good marriage.

- Benefits of traditional dating include allowing a man and woman to get to know each other by sharing many activities and experiences together.

- It is important to ask questions about a dating partner's behavior and values prior to developing a serious relationship.

- Typically today it is only after a couple themselves decide to marry that they will tell the news to family and friends.

- An engagement period is intended to bring the man and woman, and their families, closer to one another prior to marriage.

- Preparation for Catholic weddings begins with couples first contacting a parish and speaking with a priest.

- Civil laws set the conditions for the legality of a marriage. Church laws set the conditions for the Sacrament.

- Impediments are obstacles to a valid and licit celebration of marriage.

- Permission for marriages between a Catholic and non-Catholic must come from the local bishop.

- Engaged couples may be directed to participate in a pre-marriage inventory, a program or retreat like Engaged Encounter or Pre Cana, and a class in Natural Family Planning.

✦ In a marriage between two baptized Catholics, the Church strongly recommends they have each been confirmed.

✦ The Sacrament of Penance is celebrated by the couple prior to marriage.

✦ The wedding liturgy is more important than the peripheries of the day (e.g., the food, flowers, or music).

✦ The Church allows the couple to personalize the nuptial ceremony while following the standard Catholic form for weddings.

✦ The Celebration of Marriage

✦ Marriage is a sacred covenant between the couple themselves and between the couple and God.

✦ The marriage between two Catholics normally takes place during Mass.

✦ In a Catholic wedding the Liturgy of the Word, the marital consent, the nuptial blessing, and the reception of Holy Communion are elements that are emphasized.

✦ The words of consent bind the couple to one another. They must be given freely. The couple themselves are the ministers of the Sacrament of Matrimony.

✦ A Catholic wedding is witnessed by a priest or deacon and two official witnesses, usually the maid of honor and best man.

✦ The Church takes special care in permitting "high risk" marriages (e.g., mixed marriage, of inactive Catholics, pregnant before marriage, youthful marriages, previously married and divorced).

✦ The nuptial blessing is intended to share God's love and bring his graces on the married couple.

✦ The married couple is the first to receive Holy Communion. They share the Blood of Christ from a common cup to express their unity.

✦ The Effects of the Sacrament of Matrimony

✦ The marriage covenant is integrated into God's covenant with man.

✦ The married couple works toward their own salvation partnered with Jesus Christ.

✦ The two main effects of the Sacrament of Matrimony are that the marriage is indissoluble and that God shares with them a lifetime of grace.

✦ Several other graces are present in married life: unselfish love, fidelity, strength for eternal life, and children and the strength to raise them.

✦ Christian marriage witnesses God's grace to today's secular society.

assignments applications

1. Read *Mr. Notre Dame: The Life and Legend of Edward "Moose" Krause* (Diamond Communications, 2002). Write a report that focuses on how the virtue of fidelity was present in the life of Moose Krause.

2. Manichaeism was a philosophy that challenged the sacredness of marriage, teaching that the body was evil and that the soul alone was good. Read about this philosophy and report on how the Church responded to it.

3. Research and report on the marriage and wedding customs from at least three different periods in history and three different locations.

4. Rent and view the video/DVD of O. Henry's *The Gift of Love* (popular release). In it a woman struggles with accepting an arranged marriage while she feels love for a Swiss immigrant. After you watch the presentation, work with a group of friends to enact a few scenes from the presentation for your classmates. Provide the class with a synopsis of the entire story.

5. Make a list of five rules for dating. Ask your parents to make a separate list of rules. Share and discuss both lists. Write a summary of the rules and your discussion.

6. Do an Internet search for "Catholic dating services." Review five of the best websites. Report on the values the site requests for those who sign up for the service. Also, report on the method each site suggests for couples to meet for the first time. Rate each site with one to five stars. Explain your ratings.

7. Interview a married couple that mentors engaged Catholic couples. Ask them to share with you five important ways for Catholic couples to prepare for marriage. Report on what they said. If possible, ask them to speak with the class about their ministry.

8. Peruse a Catholic missal for a song that you believe would be appropriate for a Catholic wedding. Rehearse the song individually or with a group. Play and sing the song for your classmates.

9. Read about the gift of virginity offered for the sake of God's Kingdom from the *Catechism of the Catholic Church* (1618–1620). Search for information on "Consecrated virginity" and report on how this vocation is being practiced today.

10. Make a collage or poster that celebrates the witness of long and successful Christian marriages. *Optional*: Cut out stories from the newspaper that report on the wedding anniversaries (twenty-five years and above) of Catholic married couples and include them on the collage.

Notes

1. Quoted from *The Ecclesiology of Saint Ignatius of Antioch*, Polc: 5:2.

2. Quoted from *Hom.* 12:4 in *Col*; cf. *Inan. gl.* 88.

3. Quoted from *Gaudium et Spes*, 48.

4. Ibid., 49.

5. Quoted from "Singles: To Search or Not" by Mary Beth Bonacci, *Arlington Catholic Herald* 2004.

6. Quoted from "Beyond the Wedding: Romance and Reality" (*The Catholic Moment*, February 13, 2005)

chapter**outline**

✦ Her Story, His Story

Focusing on compatibility is a way to build a positive marital relationship.

✦ Adjusting to Married Life

The graces of the Sacrament of Matrimony help a couple to face the challenges of the first years of marriage.

✦ The Gift of a Child

A married couple is a steward of fertility, sharing in God's creative power as they accept the gift of a child.

✦ The Family in God's Plan

Christian marriage and the Christian family are the means for building up the Church.

✦ The Family Is the Domestic Church

The Church is present in the family.

chapter five

The Christian Family

Children, obey your parents [in the Lord], for this is right. "Honor your father and mother." This is the first commandment with a promise, "that it may go well with you and that you may have a long life on earth." Fathers, do not provoke your children to anger, but bring them up with the training and instruction of the Lord.

Ephesians 6:1–4

✦ Her Story, His Story

Leo and Lorraine, a real couple whose names were changed for this story, were married in a Pittsburgh-area Catholic church on December 4, 2004. Lorraine describes the first

six months of marriage as "a little bit like summer camp when I was a kid. You know, filled with all kinds of fun, but still, I was missing something from home." Lorraine went on to explain what she meant and more about how she remembers being newly married.

There are definitely certain things about my old life—the one before I became Mrs. Brier—which I do miss. Leo and I met in college, but after graduation I moved back home with my parents while Leo attended law school on the East Coast. Unlike a lot of people my age, I liked being back home with my mom and dad. My student teaching assignment (I

teach fourth grade) was at a school less than ten minutes away. In the evening Mom had dinner waiting for me.

After eating, I would grade papers and then wait for Leo to call. Usually I would crawl into bed with the phone and tell Leo everything that happened to me during the day. My last words each night before closing my eyes were to Leo: "I love you and miss you."

Finally Leo graduated from school in June, 2004. We finished our final wedding preparations all during that summer. We both were so excited and in love. One of the big things that attracted me to Leo during our sophomore year in college was that we both had made the same commitment to remain sexually pure until marriage. Now that the wedding was just a few months away, I couldn't wait for marriage so that we could finally give ourselves to each other, soul and body.

Our wedding was beautiful. I cried all the way through the Mass. I guess tears run in my family because I could hear my dad crying, too, from his first pew in the church.

Leo and I had planned a honeymoon that included something we both liked: downhill snow skiing. We stayed at a resort in the Poconos. One mistake that we made was that we traveled on the day of the wedding all the way to our hotel, a four-hour drive. We were both wiped out from the long and emotional day. And here it was our wedding night.

Leo was so patient with me, and I with him. We didn't need any manuals or instructions to tell us how to love each other. Sex came naturally as God intended from the beginning of creation. It was worth waiting for. Married sex was great!

We had a wonderful time on our honeymoon. But around the second to last day I started getting homesick. This is where that old summer camp thing comes in, I guess. I couldn't get over the feeling that I just wanted to get home. And I have to admit a part of me was thinking of my parents' home, not Leo's apartment that was to become "our apartment" once we got back to town.

Those first few weeks and months living there were exciting but difficult. I started my first teaching job in January and I had to wake up early and get to bed early each night. Leo was studying for the bar exam, but he did most of his best work very late at night after I was already asleep. It was hard to find quality time alone together.

There were some other more ordinary things that bugged me. For one, Leo had to be reminded constantly to make the bed. I had made my bed at home every day from the time I was about four years old. I would have still made it after I got married. Except my husband woke up later than me and then left the bed unmade!

In general Leo was messier than me— coffee ground stains left in the kitchen sink (I don't drink coffee), dirty clothes left in random places around the apartment. Sometimes I just felt like spending one night back in my old childhood room surrounded by my childhood dolls and my teenage posters on the wall. I also missed my dad and mom.

I don't mean to be so dramatic. There were so many things I liked about being married from day one that all of these things paled by comparison. Mainly I liked living with my best friend. Even through all of our work we laughed a lot, went out when we could, prayed and worshipped together, and continued to bring more and more of our individual "I"s into our collective "we"s.

Leo remembers the first days of his marriage to Lorraine as "something like an extended vacation." After nearly nineteen years of being in school, Leo was "off" for the first time, home studying while Lorraine went to work. "Our different schedules bothered Lorraine more than me, but I have to admit I wish we could have gone out more together during those times." With some prodding, Leo told about one thing in the transition to marriage that did bother him.

Well, one thing was Lorraine's student loans that really became our student loans once we were married. Lorraine comes from a big family with three other younger siblings still to go through college, so I can understand why her parents need each child to help pay for their schooling. Meanwhile, with only one brother, it was easier for my mom and dad to pay off my tuition, though my academic scholarship did help.

I had found our apartment when I got back from law school and deliberately chose a less-than-upscale neighborhood with the thought that the money we were saving on rent could go right in the bank to help us build up money for a down payment on our own place. Lorraine's—I mean our—student loan payments thwarted that plan

from the beginning. Now that I have hooked on at a law firm and am getting paid a regular salary, we are saving plenty of money and are planning to move into

our new house just in time for the birth of our first child. Lorraine's school loan is almost history; it seems kind of dumb to have even given it a second thought way back then.

I guess another difference that Lorraine and I have is that I like to socialize with a large group of friends whenever I can. An ideal night for me would be to play a game of co-ed softball (with Lorraine, of course!) and then go out for some pizza with all of our teammates/friends. Lorraine, to her credit, did try the softball experience but found that a weeknight out was not conducive to having to teach a bunch of nine-year-olds the next day. Shortly afterward, I came to the conclusion that it was time for me to be more of a homebody as well—at least on the nights my wife wasn't able to come out with me.

While I have always been a Catholic and practiced by going to Sunday Mass, Lorraine has taught me the meaning of being involved at the parish. We just finished working on the parish festival committee. Now she has us signed up to help

with high school youth ministry. I've been a little intimidated by these kinds of experiences, but I have enjoyed them, too. And I've met a great group of new friends around the parish—some younger people like ourselves—and some older married couples (my mom and dad's age!) who have really counseled us through these first two years of married life.

All in all, I am very happy to be married.

The first days, weeks, months, and even years of married life are a time of adjustment for both the wife and the husband. Even if the couple is from similar family backgrounds, has known each other for a good while, and has truly developed a relationship of love that is based in deep friendship, the graces of the Sacrament of Matrimony that are visible in the success of fifty-year marriages do take some time to blossom. Good advice for the newly married couple is to stay the course and work slowly and lovingly to give themselves over to their spouse.

Over a five-year period, from 1979 to 1984, Pope John Paul II gave a series of 129 short talks mainly on the meaning of human sexuality, marital love, and erotic desires. These talks have been grouped together under the title *Theology of the Body*. One of the constant themes that arises in these talks is the compatibility or "mutuality" of a man and woman in marriage. So often today we hear of the differences between males and females (see: *Men Are from Mars, Women Are from Venus* and books like it), that there lingers an animosity between the two genders. Pope John Paul II oppositely wrote that masculinity and femininity represent the dual aspect of the one human constitution. Quoting Genesis 2:23—" bone of my bone, flesh of my flesh"—the Pope pointed out how the unity of a husband and wife in marriage is a way to help understand the communion of love between the three persons of the Trinity.

Understanding the meaning of compatibility—not focusing on disunity and differences—from the earliest days of marriage onward is a way for the couple to work through the natural adjustments of married life. In the spirit of unity and compatibility, some of the transitions of marriage leading to having children and raising a family will be examined in this chapter.

journal**discussion**

- What are some issues that you believe would be difficult to compromise on in a marriage (e.g., differences in political beliefs, financial planning, social habits, religion)? Explain.

✦ Adjusting to Married Life

A prominent billboard at the edge of town revealed a message from God. It read: "Loved the wedding—invite Me to the marriage," with the point being that to make a marriage work, the

"Loved the wedding— invite Me to the Marriage."

couple must remember that the grace of the Sacrament of Matrimony is the promise that Christ will remain present in married life. It's up to the couple not to forget that.

Another truth is that a marriage doesn't come pre-assembled. The love between a man and a woman in marriage is a great mystery and is always evolving. Part of the mystery of married love is that it mirrors God's infinite love. How are the man and woman able to commit themselves to a lifetime together? Why do they make great sacrifices in order to make the other happy? The love of the Persons of the Trinity sheds more light on this mystery of love.

The Trinity is a communion of Persons so closely bonded together that they are one. One way to understand

this is that the Father and Son, beholding the goodness in each other, respond with love. Their love is another Person, the Holy Spirit. The Holy Spirit is the love between the Father and the Son. When a man and woman are married, their union is likewise a community of love. Their unitive and fruitful love and their total self-giving reflect and reveal to others, especially to their children, the divine love of the Trinity.

The adjustment to married life and the gift of compatibility is made easier by the ongoing grace offered by the Father through the presence of Jesus Christ in the marriage. The love that the Father lavished on humanity through the **Incarnation** in Jesus and the redemption that Christ brings to the world is unconditional and everlasting. A husband and wife

Incarnation
The taking on of human nature by God's Son.

share this kind of love with one another. They mutually say and live this promise: "I will never reject you. I will love you until death." Through their unconditional and everlasting love for one another, a husband and wife reproduce in their children the very image of Christ so as to create a unity of the human race with Christ, their Savior. The man and woman and their children come to a clearer understanding of God and his love for the world.

Saint Paul's Letter to the Ephesians has a famous passage that is addressed to wives and husbands (Eph 5:21–22) that teaches us that the relationship between a married couple is modeled on the love of Christ for the Church. The passage begins:

> Be subordinate to one another out of reverence for Christ. Wives should be subordinate to their husbands as to the Lord. (21–22)

The passage is often misinterpreted to mean that husbands are the "lords" over their wives. Rather, the husband is not the lord over the wife, but Christ is the Lord of both the man and the woman and their marriage. "The husband and wife are in fact 'subject to another,' and are mutually subordinated to one another," writes Pope John Paul II.[1] Mutual respect and love for one another is the basis of this relationship.

The graces of the Sacrament of Matrimony are necessary to ease the transition to the day-to-day challenges of married life. New social habits, financial issues, fitting into a new family that includes in-laws on both sides, all while continuing to nurture the romance of the relationship, merit specific attention in the early days, months, and years of married life.

Problems and Solutions

As the statements of Leo and Lorraine attested, the first years of married life can have their ups and downs. The United States Census Bureau reports that approximately 10 percent of all marriages end in divorce between the fourth and fifth year. Another 10 percent end in divorce by the tenth year. The statement that the "first two years of married life are the most difficult" has some truth to it. Consider the dilemmas that arise from the following issues:

In-law Issues

- Both his parents and her parents insist that Christmas be celebrated in their homes.
- His mother criticizes his wife's cooking and housecleaning.
- Her father is always dropping over unannounced and lets himself in without knocking.
- Her parents insist on helping out with the rent.

Social Issues

- He meets a close female friend for lunch and conversation every few weeks.
- She confides personal information about the marriage to her best friend.
- His buddies hang out at the house on weekends, drinking beer and watching sports on television.
- She likes to go out to dinner on weekends. He wants to stay at home.

Financial Issues

- He has maxed out the limit on two credit cards.
- She makes more money than he does.
- He wants to keep separate checking accounts.
- She has to work full-time while he finishes school.

Communication Issues

- She tries to settle arguments with yelling.
- He clams up and doesn't speak if something is bothering him.
- She acts bored while listening to him tell about his day.
- He never admits blame and rarely says "I'm sorry" for anything.

Sexual Issues

- He thinks that sex can be used to settle problems and ease conflicts.
- She withholds sex as a way to exert control.
- He tries to negotiate the couple's commitment to natural family planning.
- She thinks romance needs to be planned and is not as spontaneous about it.

The areas of issues above and the problems they present are real to life and occur in one form or another in many new marriages. And this is not to mention some more adjustments of the everyday variety a couple must make. Lorraine's complaint that Leo doesn't make the bed can be a real concern when one spouse values neatness more than the other. A recently married man complained so often to his wife that she couldn't keep house as well as his mother that she went out and hired a maid service to help her with the housework. In that case, housework led to problems in at least three of the common categories: in-law issues (comparing his wife to his mother), finance issues (hiring a maid service taxed the couple's budget), and communication issues (he started arguments over the housekeeping; she didn't even tell him when she hired the maid).

Yes, the first years of marriage are filled with some obstacles that must be handled constructively for the foundation of married life to take hold in a positive way. Keeping an open mind to differences in personalities, keeping the channels of communication open, loving one another, and praying both together and individually are some ways to handle the challenges. Think about these solutions in more detail, focusing on these suggestions:

Love Yourself. Healthy love for self is necessary to appreciate the differences and uniqueness of a spouse. Everyone is different. By loving oneself, a spouse will be more open and content to let her or his partner bring an individual style and personality to the marriage. A sense of humor also helps. Laughing at one's own mistakes and learning not to take oneself so seriously is a key component of appreciating the other and settling differences.

Talk It Over. Communication is central to a good marriage. It is never wise to stew over something a spouse did to cause hurt. Rather, it is better to talk it over with a partner and let him or her know if boundaries were crossed and if pain was caused. Communication doesn't only involve pain and anger issues. Couples who communicate well share the events of their day, the dreams and thoughts they have, and news they've heard from friends old and new. This type of productive communication also involves good listening skills. This translates to paying attention to what a spouse is saying—and learning to read cues to the importance of what is being said. Also, "talk it over" does not mean venting personal issues about marriage with a friend, co-worker, or family member. Couples learn which issues in a marriage are sacred and should be kept between the two of them.

Love Your Spouse. A common thread shared by married couples in the first years of marriage is that romance is alive and well. As they did during the dating and courtship years, the couple still makes time to go out for dinner or a movie, write each other love notes, call each other by

endearing names, and remember even the smallest of anniversaries (e.g., "the day I first noticed you in the library"). These efforts at romance should not be lost; in fact, they should be increased in marriage as a couple now has the chance to interact with one another on a daily basis under the same roof. Also, romance and thoughtfulness is part of a married couple's lovemaking that culminates in the self-giving of one another in sexual intercourse.

Worship and Pray. Think about the billboard message again. God wants to know if the couple will

invite him into their marriage. As a married couple forms its new family, prayer and worship must be central. Couples who attend Sunday Mass together, participate regularly in the Sacrament of Penance, and attend retreats and workshops foster a grounding in the life of the Church that will also be essential as they become parents. Household traditions like shared Scripture reading, prayer before meals, and prayers to begin the morning and end the day can strengthen their current relationship as well as build new and lasting family traditions.

In the Gospels, Jesus outlined the conditions of discipleship:

> "Whoever wishes to come after me must deny himself, take up his cross, and follow me. For whoever wishes to save his life will lose it, but whoever loses his life for my sake and that of the gospel will save it." (Mk 8:34–35)

Christian married couples live out Jesus' call to discipleship *in marriage*. There is no escaping the fact that for a marriage to work, each spouse will have to give up something of his or her previous self—perhaps giving up spending every holiday with Mom and Dad, regular nights out at ballgames with friends, confiding secrets to a best friend, control over a bank account—and many other things besides. It is in the "giving up" of one's own desires for the other that the marriage finds success and each spouse finds satisfaction and life.

A Prayer for Newly Married Couples

For a Passionate, Creative Love
Lord, send out your Spirit
and renew the face of the earth.
Father, Jesus gave his life
because he loved deeply and
    completely.
May our love for one another
be all encompassing and all
    consuming.
Make our love be pleasurable.
Make it be creative as it is stable,
passionate as it is respectful,
gentle as it is strong,
so that all who know us will see in our
love the hand of our Creator God.
And when you bless us with children
may they grow in the knowledge of the
passionate and energizing love
that has its beginning in the love
    you have
for the world and all its peoples.
We ask this through Jesus, our Lord
    and brother.
Amen.[2]

Write two prayers for a newlywed couple you know or for a newlywed couple at your parish. Choose prayer titles/subjects from among the following:

- A Prayer to Bless Our First Home
- A Prayer for Better Communication
- A Prayer to End a Conflict
- A Prayer to Celebrate an Anniversary
- A Prayer to Welcome a First Child
- A Prayer of Thankfulness for Each Other

The Love of Husband and Wife

The love between a husband and wife is expressed through their **conjugal love**. As the *Catechism of the Catholic Church* teaches: "In marriage the physical intimacy of the spouses becomes a pledge of spiritual communion" (*CCC*, 2360). As Lorraine expressed in the opening story, sexual sharing in marriage is something to look forward to.

The two purposes of sex in marriage—unitive and procreative—help achieve the twofold end of the marriage: the joy and pleasure of the couple and the transmission of life. Sex helps to sustain a marriage. It fosters intimacy, provides a sense of emotional security, and reduces stress and anxiety. Pope Pius XII taught that sex allows the spouses to "experience pleasure and enjoyment of body and spirit."[3]

Sexual sharing in marriage helps the couple point to and participate in a deep love that hints at the love between God and all of humanity and that is the destiny of God's creation.

As with other aspects of their relationship, a married couple must work at sexual sharing. They need to learn how to make sex pleasurable and a satisfying experience for both. Never should sexual intercourse be used to control the other person or to avoid problems. Sexual intercourse is only one aspect of the couple's giving themselves to each other. Their love is also evident in other concrete ways: through the sharing of their deepest dreams and desires, in hugs and kisses, in affectionate words, and through understanding and forgiveness.

conjugal love
The total love between a husband and wife that encompasses their entire being, body and soul.

Rate Yourself as a Listener

Listening is a skill that comes with practice and effort. For married couples, being a good listener is an essential skill. Give yourself points for each of the following listening skills using the scale below:

- I do this most of the time (3 points)
- I do this some of the time (2 points)
- I rarely do this (1 point)
- I never do this (0 points)

1. When someone is talking to me, I am usually thinking of what I can say in response.
2. I try to pick out what is "right" or "wrong" about what the person is saying.
3. I offer the person advice.
4. I tend to daydream when someone is talking to me.
5. I do not look the person right in the eye.
6. I do several things while carrying on a conversation.
7. I assume I understand what the person is saying and feeling.
8. I change the subject when it is my turn to speak.
9. I do not pay attention to any non-verbal signs (e.g., crossing of arms or legs, tears, facial expressions).
10. I listen and talk at the same time.

Write your scores for each item on a piece of scrap paper. Add up the points. Then look below to see how you rate as a listener.

0 to 10 points: You would make a good friend (or spouse). You are a good listener.

11 to 18 points: You are a pretty good listener but need some improvement on the areas of weakness. Work to improve in those categories.

19 to 24 points: In some areas you listen very well, in others poorly. Use the areas where you are a good listener to help you improve your weaker listening skills.

25 to 30 points: Take some time to sit in silence and reflect on your listening skills. Look at some of your relationships and analyze how poor listening may have affected how you get along with others.

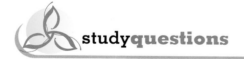

study questions

1. How does the relationship of the persons of the Trinity shed light on the mystery of love in marriage?
2. What is the meaning of the passage in Ephesians 5:21–22?
3. Name one example to illustrate a possible dilemma in married life from each of the following issues: in-laws, social, financial, communication, and sexual.
4. Share an example of how a disagreement between a married couple might involve more than one of the issues mentioned above.
5. Why is self-love necessary for both a man and woman in marriage?
6. What is the condition of discipleship that Jesus outlines in Mark 8:34–35? How does this requirement impact a person who is married?
7. Besides sexual intercourse, what are some other ways a married couple shares their love with one another?

journal discussion

- What issues do you believe cause the most lasting difficulties and hurts in a marriage? Explain.

- Imagine you married a person with mostly different interests, talents, and personality than you. Describe what that person would be like. What would it be like for you to be married to that person?

✦ The Gift of a Child

The decision of a married couple to be open to the gift of a child is a courageous and loving one. The Church teaches that "it is necessary that each and every marriage act remain ordered *per se* to the procreation of human life."4 Catholic married couples who observe this teaching and do not break the dual purpose of sexual intercourse as being both unitive and procreative truly stand out today as Christian witnesses. Why so? A scan of the media—movies, television shows pitched at teenagers, advertisements, and the like—reveals that most of popular culture and society today associate sex only with pleasure and with the *avoiding* of pregnancy and birth typically through the use of **contraception**. (See chapter 6 for more information on practices which are anti-life.) Sex is falsely thought of as something that is casual, requires little or no commitment, and is available with many partners. Often, people who choose to view and practice sex in those ways look for ways to make sure that sex does not result in pregnancy.

Even in modern married life, the commitment and openness to the possibility of a pregnancy resulting from sexual intercourse is often limited:

"We need time to adjust to marriage."

"Once we have enough money saved for a down payment on a house we will think about starting a family."

"My twenties are a time to establish myself in a career. The thirties will be for having children."

"We have one of each, a boy and a girl. We don't need any more children."

"How can we ever afford to have another child? Have you seen the cost of college these days?"

God intended for sex to be both an expression of love between husband and wife *and* for the procreation of children. "A child does not come from outside as something added on to the mutual love of the spouses, but springs from the very heart of that mutual giving, as its fruit and fulfillment" (*CCC*, 2366). When Catholic couples marry, they are asked if they "will accept children lovingly from God, and bring them up according to the law of Christ and the Church." When a couple answers affirmatively to this question, they have promised to be open to the possibility that their sexual sharing will result in pregnancy and the gift of a child.

A child is not something that is owed to a couple at a specific, predetermined time of marriage. A child is

contraception
A method of preventing pregnancy that is intended to alter or avoid the body's natural state of fertility. Examples include condoms, the pill, and the intra-uterine device. The Church condemns the use of any artificial contraception.

coitus

A term for sexual intercourse between a man and a woman.

certainly not to be considered a piece of property, or simply an heir to a human family tree. Rather, a child is "the supreme gift of marriage." One of the reasons this is so is because in having a child the couple cooperates with the creative power of God, who from the very beginning blessed the first man and woman and said "Be fertile and multiply" (Gn 1:28).

Regulation of Procreation

A particular aspect of responsible parenthood (other aspects will be covered on pages 152–153) is the regulation of procreation. This issue is

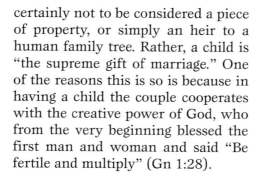

typically misinterpreted by many Catholics and non-Catholics alike. One misunderstanding is that Catholic couples are to have as many children as possible. This is not a Church teaching. Rather, for just reasons, married couples may plan and space the birth of their children. Just reasons may include issues like the parents' physical or emotional health, the inability of one or both parents to care for a child, the needs of other family members, or, in some cases, the lack of income and resources to care for a child properly.

The wide spectrum of responsible parenting means a willingness to

accept children if a pregnancy does unexpectedly occur. And it means taking a hard and prayerful look at reasons why a couple might wish to delay pregnancy or limit the number of children. Responsible parenting means putting the raising of children before things like convenience, career advancement, or material possessions. It means thinking of children as a blessing, a gift from God—and being willing to raise all the children with whom God blesses the marriage.

The regulation of procreation is only morally acceptable when practiced using natural means. Only through the use of natural means is the couple able to preserve the essential aspects—the unitive and procreative—of the conjugal act. The Church teaches that it is "morally permissible to take into account the natural rhythms of human fertility and to have **coitus** only during the infertile times in order to regulate conception."[5] With both the wife and husband monitoring her fertile and infertile periods, they become "cooperators or almost interpreters" of God's plan.[6] The husband and wife become stewards of their fertility, while participating with God in the decisions that can result in the birth of a new person, in God's image, who is destined to live with God for all of eternity.

Participating in this way with God in determining the timing of children demands that married couples practice the virtue of conjugal chastity. The wife and husband will have to abstain from sexual intercourse during the wife's fertile periods if they are trying to avoid a pregnancy. Usually couples will have only about a week of **continence** in every fertile cycle. When a wife has a less regular cycle, the period of continence may be closer to twelve to fourteen days. Refraining from sex

continence

Partial or complete abstinence from sexual activity.

in marriage can be difficult for couples, but again the graces of the Sacrament of Matrimony can help them control their passions rather than being enslaved by them. In general, couples who share in decisions of procreation based on the woman's natural fertility cycle cite several benefits for doing so including improved communication, the absence of feelings of being used, development of non-genital aspects of love and affection, peace of conscience, and the lack of worry of being exposed to health risks that are a side effect of unnatural methods of preventing procreation. The practice of natural methods of regulating procreation strengthens the fidelity of the spouses for one another and promotes a life-long marriage.

Finally, the Church continues its traditional practice of commending the generosity of married couples who choose to have large families. As each child is truly a blessing of God, large families have multiple blessings.

Options When a Couple Cannot Conceive a Child

Marriage is not solely for the procreation of children. As the Second Vatican Council fathers explained:

> Therefore, marriage persists as a whole manner and communion of life, and maintains its value and indissolubility, even when offspring are lacking—despite, rather often, the very intense desire of the couple. (*Gaudium et spes*, 50)

Couples who discover that they are unable to have children suffer greatly. The Church encourages scientific research to reduce human sterility; however, it demands that the methods respect the rights and goodness of the human person and do not involve the dissociation of the husband and wife from the act of procreation.

Specifically, the Church opposes heterologous artificial insemination and fertilization that involves a third person other than the mother or father by the gift of sperm or ovum or the use of the **surrogate mother**. These practices are wrong because they violate the child's right to be born to a mother and father, and the couple's right to become parents only through each other.

Techniques that involve only the married couple (homologous artificial insemination and fertilization) are perhaps less reprehensible, yet still morally unacceptable. The reason is that they separate the act of sexual intercourse between the married couple from the act of procreation. The conception and birth of the child are no longer a result of the union of the couple, but of other persons like doctors and biologists. Procreation is deprived of its proper meaning when it is not the product of the conjugal act of the husband and wife's union.

One option for couples who face challenges involving physical sterility is to devote themselves to the demanding tasks of service for those in need. They can also offer support to other children in the family (e.g., nieces and nephews) as well as other children in the community who have special needs. For example, they may offer their service as parish catechists, coaches of youth sports, or scouting leaders. Another option is for a married couple to adopt children and raise them as their own.

surrogate mother
A woman who carries another woman's child by pre-arrangement or by legal contract.

Some children available for adoption may have been abandoned, others are willingly—and courageously—offered for adoption by birth mothers who, for a variety of reasons, are unable to raise them. Unfortunately, the loving decision to offer a baby for adoption is more and more a rare one. In a recent year among unwed pregnant teenagers, only 3 percent chose to allow the baby to be adopted by a married couple who was able to provide a loving home. Sadly, 37 percent chose to have their baby aborted.

In all cases, married couples who suffer from infertility should unite themselves with the cross of Jesus Christ, the source of all spiritual fruitfulness.

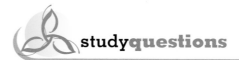

study questions

1. What is meant by "artificial contraception"?

2. What are some less-than-moral reasons married couples might give for not being open to the possibility of pregnancy?

3. What are some just reasons Catholic couples may plan and space the birth of children?

4. How is conjugal chastity involved in planning and spacing pregnancies?

5. What is the Church's attitude toward large families?

Natural Family Planning

Today's modern methods of Natural Family Planning (NFP) are the sympto-thermal method and the ovulation method. These methods respect the bodies of the spouses, encourage tenderness between the couple, and foster freedom. NFP methods are in contrast to contraception that deliberately interferes with marital intercourse to prevent pregnancy and thus prohibit one of the essential aspects of sexual sharing in marriage, openness to procreation, and is contrary to the inner truth of conjugal love, which is total and self-giving.

The sympto-thermal method is based in the woman's basal body temperature. Due to hormonal activity, a woman's resting temperature changes during the menstrual cycle. A lower temperature is an indication that **ovulation** has not yet occurred. Higher temperatures indicated a rise in progesterone which is known to signal the end of the fertile time. The sympto-thermal method also observes changes in the texture and shape of the woman's cervix and the color and thickness of the cervical mucus.

The ovulation method likewise observes the mucus pattern of the cervix. Through daily examination of the color and thickness of the woman's

> **ovulation**
> The time in a woman's fertile cycle when an egg is released from her ovary.

cervical mucus, she can determine the days of the fertility cycle when she is likely to get pregnant.

Most couples who practice NFP combine both methods to help increase the accuracy of the forecasts between periods of fertility and infertility. They usually keep a chart that displays the cycle. If a couple was trying to have a baby, they would want to make sure to have sexual intercourse during the fertile cycle. If they were trying—for good reasons—to avoid a pregnancy, then they would abstain from intercourse during the woman's fertile period.

Sometimes NFP is called the "rhythm" or "calendar" method. This was a method developed in the 1930s that attempted to predict the time of ovulation based only on the previous menstrual cycles of the woman. This method was inaccurate because some women have very irregular menstrual cycles and almost all women have menstrual cycles that vary in length from time to time.

Rather, modern natural family methods are more accurate. In a recent year, only 1 to 3 percent of couples who carefully followed the rules for avoiding pregnancy all the time became pregnant. Catholic couples usually receive an introduction to NFP during their marriage preparation programs. It is then strongly suggested that they take a more detailed course in NFP at a local parish or hospital, or through their diocesan Marriage and Family Life office after they are married.

6. Why does the Church find heterologous artificial insemination and fertilization morally reprehensible?

7. What are some options for a couple who face the challenges of physical sterility?

8. Explain the two modern methods of Natural Family Planning.

- How would the modern perception of pregnancy change if every child was considered to be a "blessing"?

- How many children do you think you would like to have after you are married? Why did you choose this number?

✦ The Family in God's Plan

The love shared between a husband and wife begets children. "A man and woman united in marriage, together with their children, form a family" (*CCC*, 2202). The Christian family is a communion of persons, imaging the relationship between the persons of the Holy Trinity—Father, Son, and Holy Spirit. For example:

- The procreation and education of children is modeled in the Father's work of creation.

- The family shares in the prayer and sacrifice of Christ.

- And, in company with the Holy Spirit, by its very example of day-to-day living, the family witnesses the Gospel to the world.

The marriage bond formed between the man and woman in the Sacrament of Matrimony is the beginning of family life. Later, the couple welcomes children. The competing message of society (besides the contraceptive message that discourages children altogether) is that men and women have children for reasons like "having something to love," "answering a

'biological clock,'" or "finally giving in to the pressure of family and friends." To be fair, even non-religious parents do list a very good reason to have a child: "We have a love for children and want to raise a child."

For Catholics, child rearing extends the grace of the Sacrament of Matrimony to touch new lives. Remember that Matrimony is a "sacrament in the service of communion." This refers to a man and woman conferring holiness on each other and helping each other on the path to salvation. This same blessing extends to the children of a Christian family. A baby is a unique reflection of the love between a husband and a wife. No other combination of parents could create this child. Through the years, a child will offer the family

deep satisfaction and opportunities for intimacy and love. Ask most parents and they will tell you that there has been nothing else that they have ever experienced that has brought as much satisfaction as begetting new life and raising their children.

Christian marriage and the Christian family are also the means for building up the Church: "The Church thus finds in the family, born from the sacrament, the cradle and the setting in which she can enter the human generations and where these in turn can enter the Church."[7]

It is in the context of the Fourth Commandment—"honor your father and your mother"—that the *Catechism of the Catholic Church* addresses the scope of family life. This Commandment begins the second part of the Ten Commandments, focusing on love for others. Children learn to honor and love God from their parents. They then extend this same charity to their parents, other family members, and everyone else who is their neighbor.

Being a Responsible Parent

Obviously, responsible parenthood extends beyond making the correct and moral decisions on family planning and birth spacing. Once the child is born, the real work begins! To put it succinctly, it is the responsibility of the parents to educate their children both morally and spiritually. Always before anyone else—relatives, teachers, peers, media—parents have the *first responsibility* to educate their children.

The moral and spiritual education of a child begins when the parents *create a home* where "tenderness, forgiveness, respect, fidelity, and disinterested service are the rule" (*CCC*, 2223). A loving home is one in which the children feel safe and secure, both physically and emotionally.

Parents first and foremost create a loving home by modeling the virtues in their own relationship. "Actions speak louder than words" never applied more than to the task of parenting. Think about the difficulty in teaching a child a lesson in loyalty to a friend if the parents have been unfaithful to one another. More positively, parents who show respect for one another—for example, Mom allows Dad to choose the evening's entertainment or Dad puts the children to bed when Mom is tired—are more likely to have the lesson of respect resonate among their children. Also, husbands and wives who say "please" and "thank you" to each other and to their children are more likely to hear the same respect in return.

One of the most essential ways parents work to create a loving atmosphere at home is their insistence on the family sharing a meal together, usually dinner. A recent national study reported a link between regular family meals, academic success, and positive psychological adjustment. In addition, rates of alcohol and drug use and inappropriate sexual behavior among teenagers are lower when they have grown up sharing regular meals with their families.

Establishing family traditions early on, even before the birth of the first child, is another important task. The traditions do not need to be elaborate. Rather, they should be memorable and unique to the family and the individual family members. For example, birthdays can be celebrated by always allowing the person to choose whatever dinner he or she would like. Traditions around the seasons of the Church year might include attending a parish reconciliation service at Lent, holding an Easter egg hunt for all the neighborhood children, collecting clothes and sponsoring a Thanksgiving meal for a needy family, and baking and sharing Christmas cookies.

You may not imagine yourself ever having to **discipline** a child, but if you are a parent, this, too, is a necessary task. Parents who do this well are also able to acknowledge their own failings to their children. Discipline equates with the structure necessary to teach children how to live together in solidarity with others and to accept personal responsibilities that help to make the family function better. Clearly established consequences for both good and bad behaviors help children to develop skills that will serve them well as they mature, often by being able to discern between the virtues learned in the family with the opposing and often degrading influences of society.

Parents also have the responsibility and privilege of sharing the mysteries of the Catholic faith and facilitating their participation in the Church from an early age. These responsibilities are discussed further on pages 157–161.

The Duties of Children

Under the requirements of the Fourth Commandment, children are subject to duties in their participation in a family just as their parents are. Children are to obey their parents in everything that concerns the family's physical and spiritual wellbeing. The respect of children for their parents derives from the gratitude they have for those who gave them the gift of life, care for them, and allow them to grow. The book of Sirach teaches:

> With your whole heart honor your father; your mother's birthpangs forget not.

discipline
A process of training that is expected to produce an acceptable pattern of behavior as well as improved mental and social character.

Remember, of these parents you were born; what can you give them for all they gave you? (Sir 7:27–28)

There are many examples of the specific kinds of duties children are responsible for in family life. From the time they are very young, children are given specific household chores, from picking up their own clothes to setting the dinner table to doing yard work. In the same way, children are to obey the requests of their teachers and other adults to whom their parents have entrusted them. However, children who are convinced in conscience that the request of any adult, including a parent, is morally wrong, are not obliged to obey it.

Mutual respect is also required among children for their brothers and sisters to help promote harmony in all of family life. Special gratitude is also due from children to those who have helped pass on the gift of faith: grandparents, godparents, pastors, catechists, and other teachers and friends.

Obedience to parents extends for as long a child lives at home. When a child is of legal age and no longer living at home, obedience to parents is no longer required. However, respect for one's parents never ceases. Adult children should continue to seek out their parents for advice and take the advice to heart with a willingness to accept it. The Fourth Commandment also requires adult children to give their parents "material and moral support in old age and in times of illness, loneliness, or distress" (*CCC*, 2218).

Learn'n Care

Arrange to babysit for a young child (under age seven). Write a report summarizing what you did to care for the child's physical and emotional needs while you were in charge. Also, write three new things you learned from the child and the experience.

The Family in Society

The family is called the "original cell of social life." Family life, where children learn moral values, begin to honor God, and make good use of freedom, is really an initiation into life in society at large. Because of this, it is the responsibility of society to defend family life. And, when individual families cannot fulfill their responsibilities like those described above (e.g., the physical and emotional needs of the children), it is up to other agencies in society to help fill in and meet these tasks.

More proactively, society is responsible for supporting and strengthening family life so that more and more individual families can fulfill their own needs. Pope John Paul II, in his apostolic exhortation *Familiaris Consortio*, addressed the ideal of mutual support between family and society by recounting a "charter of family rights." Emphasized were the rights to:

- establish a family, have children, and bring them up in keeping with the family's own moral and religious convictions;

- protection of the stability of the marriage bond and the institution of the family;

- profess one's faith, to hand it on, and raise one's children in it, with the necessary means and institutions;

- private property, to free enterprise, to obtain work and housing, and to be able to emigrate;

- in keeping with the country's institutions, medical care, assistance for the aged, and family benefits;

- protection against threats to security and health, especially with respect to dangers like drugs, pornography, alcoholism, and the like;

- form associations with other families and so to have representation before civil authority.[8]

Our participation in individual families helps provide us with a Christian perspective on the larger human family. We begin to understand that every person, living and dead, is somehow related to us by origin or descent. This means that everyone we encounter is due our respect. People near or far are not numbers, statistics, or units, they are "someones" who also deserve our particular attention.

Intentional families

Today, in many families, both parents work and the children participate is multiple activities besides school. All of these are factors in preventing families from sitting down and sharing a regular meal together. To counteract these factors, steps must be taken to form "intentional families," that is, families that intentionally make time to be together and to establish rituals that will last. Whereas most families celebrate birthdays and anniversaries, there are many other events that can be intentionally celebrated, including the start of school, a teen getting a driver's license for the first time, or the feast day of patron saints of family members. Other ways to form intentional families include:

- *Family Meetings.* These are regularly scheduled gatherings during which family members are free to express themselves honestly without facing judgment in an effort to air problems and reach solutions.

- *Family Nights.* A family night might mean something as simple as playing board games together or having a cookout. It could also include watching and discussing a movie, going miniature golfing or bowling, or attending a sporting event or play. The objective of a family night is to be together and have fun.

- *Faith-Sharing.* Besides practicing their faith by attending Mass and parish functions together, families can share a weekly prayer service where Scripture is read and discussed and special intentions of petition and thanksgiving are prayed for.

- *Service and Outreach.* Individual families serve the wider human community. Scheduling a service event like preparing a meal for and serving the homeless is beneficial to the family members who spend time together as well as those they serve.

Among other benefits, these scheduled events can be used to express feelings, to heal, to have fun, and to generate good memories.

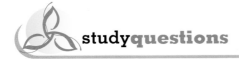

studyquestions

1. How does the Christian family image the relationship between the Persons of the Holy Trinity?

2. Name some elements that make up a loving home.

3. Which Commandment sets the context of family life?

4. Why is disciplining their children a necessary task for parents?

5. What is the relationship adult children are required to have with their parents under the Fourth Commandment?

6. What is the primary responsibility of the family in society?

7. Highlight three main rights in the "charter of family rights."

journaldiscussion

- What are good reasons for a married couple's choosing to have a child?

- What are some traditions and practices from your family life that you can imagine using to help you create a loving home in the future?

- Write "ten rules" for family life.

✦ The Family Is the Domestic Church

The Church is present in the family; this is the way that it was from the very beginning, not only in creation when man and woman came together as one, but from the earliest days of the Church itself when the Eucharist was celebrated in family homes and presbyters and other ministers received their vocation from family life. The Second Vatican Council reemphasized the ancient teaching of the family as *domestic church* and its task as such:

> For from the wedlock of Christians there comes the family, in which new citizens of human society are born. By the grace of the Holy Spirit received in baptism these are made children of God, thus perpetuating the People of God through the centuries. The family is, so to speak, the domestic Church. In it parents should, by their word and example, be the first preachers of the faith to their children. They should encourage them in the vocation which is proper to each of them, fostering with special care any religious vocation. (*Lumen Gentium*, 11)

If you interview a priest or religious, there is little doubt that they would list their own families as sources of their religious vocation. The encouragement children receive from parents to be open to religious life or ordination is certainly one help to cultivate a vocation. Also, the daily examples of faith, hope, and love lived in family life keep open those possibilities.

The domestic church was never better represented than in Nazareth by the **Holy Family**. Jesus observed the Fourth Commandment in his obedience to Joseph and Mary while also obeying the will of God the Father. Jesus' handing over his will to the will of the Father beginning in these early years at home previewed the ultimate sacrifice he would eventually offer on the night of his arrest in the garden of Gethsemane. "Not what I will but what you will" (Mk 14:36), Jesus prayed. It was in the Holy Family, this special domestic Church, that Jesus shared the same type of life—family life—as a majority of human beings do. It was in his family that he "advanced in wisdom and age and favor before God and man" (Lk 2:51–52).

Holy Family
The family of Joseph, Mary, and Jesus in which Jesus was raised and lived until he began his public ministry.

Growing in Faith in the Christian Family

The Christian family is a child's first experience of Church and the primary environment for growth in faith.[9] It is the parents' responsibility to be the first and prime educators of the faith. All the other members of the family—grandparents, aunts and uncles, siblings, and cousins— contribute to the environment where God's loving presence is easily experienced and witnessed and faith in Jesus Christ is proudly professed.

At an early age, it is the parents' responsibility to teach their children the basic Christian prayers and to begin to form their consciences in light of the teachings of Christ and the Church. These lessons are not usually deliberate; rather, they are

How Families Encourage Religious Vocations

When Catholic families typically had more children on average than they do today, it was common for mothers and fathers to encourage and pray for one or more of their sons to become a priest. Vocations to the consecrated religious life were also supported by Catholic families. There are many Church leaders today who believe that the lower number of vocations to the priesthood and religious life will only be turned around when families once again take the lead role and positively affirm the value of these vocations and allow their children the openness to explore them. There are several things parents and families can do to encourage religious vocations, including:

- Practice a life of devotion to prayer, the Eucharist, sacred Scripture, the Rosary, the Sacrament of Penance. Children raised in a family where the parents celebrate in these ways will naturally understand the importance of faith-life in relation to other competing interests and tasks.

- Parents should tell how they view their marriage and their roles as mother and father as a God-given vocation.

- Befriend priests, sisters, and brothers. Invite them to your home for dinner. Listen to the stories of their calling, vocation, and ministry.

- Share stories of saints, especially those who founded religious orders.

- Paint a picture of priesthood and religious life that is exciting, dramatic, and freeing—a radical acceptance of Jesus' call to discipleship.

- Invite some teenagers to your house and have an open discussion about their plans for the future, including college, career, and vocational plans. Commend the uniqueness of each of the ideas.

- Visit a seminary or religious house. Arrange for a tour or participate in a sponsored retreat there.

- Cultivate the habit of service to the poor and needy. Learn to share material possessions and the gift of self.

Assignment

Write a three- to five-page report on the life of a saint who was a priest or who founded a religious order. Include as many of the following details in the report as possible:

- The name of the saint and the religious order he or she founded (if applicable)

- The years of the saint's life

- The place where the saint lived

- The family's influence on the saint's vocation

- Some influential words or deeds of the saint

- The charisms of the saint's religious community or his view on priesthood

- The year the saint was canonized.

shared through the routine of daily family life and the examples of the parents and other family members. Also, grandparents and other older family members are able to share the wisdom and experience of many years lived in the faith. These stories often leave an indelible mark on the lives of young children.

Children also contribute to the growth in holiness of their parents. There are countless stories of how the birth of a child and parenthood awakens in mothers and fathers a sense of the holy and divine that may have been dormant. A child reminds parents of the miraculous cycle of life and love. And, in the security of their parents, children experience God's love. Mother Teresa of Calcutta once told the story of a little girl—six or seven—whom she picked up off the street and took to Shishu Bhavin (a children's home). Mother Teresa gave the girl a bath, some nice clothes, and some food. The same evening the girl ran away. The little girl was brought to Shishu Bhavin a second time and a third time. Each time, she ran away. Finally, Mother Teresa sent another sister to follow her. The sister found the girl with her mother and her own sister sitting under a tree. The mother was cooking a meal from food scraps she found in the street. Explained Mother Teresa:

> And then we understood why the child ran away. The mother just loved that child. And the child loved the mother. They were so beautiful to each other. The child said "bari jabo"—it was her home. Her mother was her home.[10]

Faith experienced and shared in a Christian family cannot be duplicated in any other setting. Father Theodore Hesburgh, C.S.C., the President of the University of Notre Dame from 1953 to 1987, recalls that he always wanted to be a priest. When he was in eighth grade, a priest from Notre Dame visited his school in Syracuse,

New York, and asked him and his mother if he would enter the high school seminary at Notre Dame, Indiana, the following semester. "If he doesn't come and go to high school at Notre Dame, he may lose his vocation," the priest told Mrs. Hesburgh.

Father Ted said that his mother was opposed to him going that far away from home at a young age. "My mother looked the priest in the eye and said, 'It can't be much of a vocation if he is going to lose it by living in a Christian family.'" After high school Ted Hesburgh entered the college seminary at Notre Dame. He has been a priest for over sixty years.

As children grow, parents have the responsibility to choose a school for their children that corresponds to their religious convictions. Most often the integration of religious truth and values is best served in Catholic schools. The United States Catholic Bishops teach that "Catholic schools afford the fullest and best opportunity to realize the threefold purpose of Christian education among children and young people."[11] Catholic schools can forge a deeper relationship between school and family. They can easily facilitate the student's participation in the liturgy and the sacraments. And they can provide a more favorable environment for teaching the Catholic faith. The right to choose a school for their children is a fundamental one for parents.

Children themselves, as they grow, have the right to choose their own profession and state in life; for example, married, single, religious, or priesthood. While parents should advise and counsel their children in these areas, they should not exert pressure in the choice of a profession or in that of a spouse. But they should offer good counsel when their children plan to start their own families.

Finally, regarding the meaning of domestic church and the Christian family, it is important to know that no one in this world is without a family. Childless couples and others without a natural family due to poverty and other reasons all belong to the great family, which is the Church. Pope John Paul II taught: "No one is without a family in this world: the Church is a home and family for everyone, especially those who 'labor and are heavy laden.'"[12]

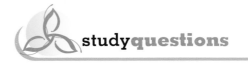

study questions

1. What is meant by the term *domestic church*?

2. How was the Holy Family representative of the meaning of domestic church?

3. What are two early tasks of parents regarding their children's religious formation?

4. Why are Catholic schools an appropriate place to educate children?

5. How should parents support their children in their choice of a profession and vocation?

journal discussion

● How has your family life been a model of the domestic church?

● What is your earliest memory of a religious lesson imparted by a parent, grandparent, or other relative?

summary points

✦ Her Story, His Story

✦ The first days, weeks, and months of married life are a time of adjustment for the husband and wife.

✦ Focusing on unity and compatibility is a way to ease the transition from single life to married life.

✦ Adjusting to Married Life

✦ The relationship of the Persons of the Holy Trinity helps to shed light on the mystery of love present in marriage.

- The graces of the Sacrament of Matrimony—offered by the Father through the presence of Jesus Christ—are present in a marriage from its very beginning.
- The first years of married life are filled with obstacles that can be aided by self-love, communication, love of spouse, and shared worship and prayer.
- Christian couples give up something of their individual selves when they enter marriage, as they practice the conditions of discipleship taught by Jesus.
- Sexual sharing in marriage is the sign of a husband and wife's total love for one another and helps them to participate in the love God has for all of humanity.

The Gift of a Child

- Catholic married couples consent to welcoming and raising children according to the laws of Christ and the Church.
- A child is a "supreme gift of marriage."
- Contraception is prohibited by the Church.
- The wide spectrum of responsible parenting means a willingness to accept children if an unexpected pregnancy does occur.

- The regulation of procreation is only moral by natural means.
- Using natural means, the married couple become stewards of their fertility and share in God's creative power.
- Marriage is not solely for the procreation of children. It has its value even when a couple is unable to bear children.
- Couples who are unable to have children are encouraged to serve other needy children in the community or to adopt and raise a child as their own.
- Infertility solutions that separate the conjugal unity of the husband and wife are not approved by the Church.

The Family in God's Plan

- The Christian family is a unity of persons, imaging the relationship of the persons in the Holy Trinity.
- A married couple confers God's blessings and holiness on a child as they do on each other.
- One of the first responsibilities of parenting is to create a loving home while caring for the child's physical and emotional needs.
- In the context of the Fourth Commandment, children are subject in their family duties to parents and other adults designated by their parents.
- The family is the "original cell of social life." Society is responsible for supporting and strengthening family life.
- Participation in family life helps provide us with the perspective that everyone we encounter is related to us by origin or descent.

The Family Is the Domestic Church

- The Church is present in the family.
- The domestic church was best represented by the model of the Holy Family.
- The Christian family is the child's first experience of Church and the place where his or her faith is cultivated.
- Parents are responsible for the initial Christian education of their children. Later, parents have responsibility to choose schools for their children that correspond to their religious convictions.

✦ Children have the right to choose their own profession and vocation with the help of the counsel, not pressure, of their parents.

assignments applications

1. Choose and read at least five articles from Pope John Paul II's *Theology of the Body*. (Do an Internet search: "Theology of the Body.") Write three-sentence summaries of each article.

2. Over the next seven days, choose one of the following Gospel passages per day and read and reflect on its meaning in light of marriage and family life:

Matthew 5:1–12	Matthew 5:13–16
Matthew 7:21, 24–25	Matthew 19:3–6
Matthew 22:35–40	John 2:1–11
John 15:9–12	John 15:12–16
John 17:20–23	

3. Interview two newly married couples (three years or less of marriage). Ask them the following questions. Record and share their answers:

● How does God play a part in your relationship?
● What is the most difficult part of marriage?
● What is the most joyful part of marriage?
● How does your marriage reflect your family upbringing?

4. Work with a group of classmates to come up with ten "billboard slogans" designed to remind married couples of some essential truths about married life.

5. Share a three-minute home video that depicts some positive characteristics of family life. The video can be of ritual celebrations like birthdays, holidays, sacraments, or reunions. Play the video for the class with the sound down. While it is playing, offer an explanation of the event taking place and tell why it is important to your family.

6. Read and outline *Humanae Vitae*, Pope Paul VI's 1968 encyclical on the regulation of birth.

7. Send for information on Natural Family Planning from the Couple to Couple League (www.ccli.org). Arrange a display or notebook that highlights the material you received. List some positive benefits of Natural Family Planning not mentioned in this chapter.

8. Develop a PowerPoint presentation that represents up-to-date statistics on marriage and family life. Include statistics for both the general population and specifically for Catholics including the following areas:

● average age for first marriage
● average number of children per marriage
● divorce statistics.

9. Research and report on the mission and functions of the Christian Family Movement (www.cfm.org).

10. Plan and give a witness talk that expresses your faith in Jesus Christ to a group of younger children (e.g., at a religious education class).

Notes

1. Quoted from "*Reverence for Christ the Basis of Relationship Between Spouses,*" General Audience of Pope John Paul II, 11 August 1982.

2. The prayer "*For Passionate, Creative Love*" is taken from *Before I Do: Preparing for the Sacrament of Marriage* by Anthony Garascia (Notre Dame, IN: Ave Maria Press, 1999).

3. Pius XII, *Discourse*, October 29, 1951 quoted in CCC, 146.

4. Quoted from *Humanae Vitae*, 11.

5. Ibid., 16.

6. Ibid., 10.

7. Quoted from *Familiaris Consortio*, no. 15.

8. *Familiaris Consortio*, 46, quoted in CCC, 2211.

9. *National Catechetical Directory* 29, D.

10. Quoted from *Words to Love by* Mother Teresa (Notre Dame, IN: Ave Maria Press, 1983).

11. Quoted from *To Teach As Jesus Did*, 1010 U.S. Conference of Catholic Bishops (1972).

12. *Familiaris Consortio*, 8.

chapter**outline**

✦ **Twists and Turns**

Catherine de Hueck Doherty overcame poverty and a failed marriage to found an apostolate for the poor with the help of her second husband, Eddie Doherty.

✦ **Marriage Is a Lifelong Commitment**

A Christian marriage, by its very nature, can never be dissolved.

✦ **Challenges to Marriage in American Culture**

Several anti-life practices have arisen in America, due in part to individualism couched in moral relativism.

✦ **The Question of Divorce and Remarriage**

The gravity of divorce is serious; however, there are variables in each situation that affect one's culpability.

✦ **Sacramental Grace in Marriage**

The grace of the Sacrament of Matrimony perfects the couple's love and strengthens their indissoluble unity.

chapter six

Transitions, Challenges, and Rewards of Marriage and Family Life

If God is for us, who can be against us? He who did not spare his own Son but handed him over for us all, how will he not also give us everything else along with him?

Romans 8:31b–32

✦ Twists and Turns

Imagine a young Russian girl, born to wealthy aristocrats at the turn of the twentieth century. Her family was devoutly Christian, members of the Russian Orthodox Church. The girl's name was Catherine Kolyschkine, and her life at first took the course that one would expect for someone of her social class. When she was fifteen, she married her cousin, Boris de Hueck.

World War I and the Russian Revolution changed the world Catherine knew. Most of Catherine's family was killed, and Catherine and her husband barely escaped death at the hands of the Bolsheviks. Catherine and Boris escaped to England, and then, in 1921, to Canada, where their son, George, was born. Along the way, Catherine had become a Roman Catholic.

Though safe in Canada, Catherine and Boris were now at the lowest end of poverty. Boris was sick and unable to work. Catherine took whatever job she could find to support her family. In the meantime, Boris began a series of extra-marital affairs. The couple became estranged, and Catherine eventually had the marriage annulled.

One of Catherine's talents was as a lecturer. She was discovered by a Canadian lecture bureau, and she soon began to travel on its behalf around North America. Catherine became wealthy again and was able to support her son in the custom that she had known growing up.

But Catherine was restless. The Russian Revolution, the war, and the breakup of her marriage had left an indelible mark on her. She couldn't resign herself to simply returning to a life of comfort. Jesus' words to the rich, young disciple—"If you wish to be perfect, go, sell what you have and give to the poor, and you will have treasure in heaven" (Mt 19:21)—were never far from Catherine's thoughts.

In 1930, Catherine acted on those words. With the blessings of the archbishop in Toronto, Catherine sold all of her possessions, provided for her son, and then went to live in the worst slums of the city, desiring only to console the poor as a lay apostle. Eventually other men and women came to work with Catherine. They established a "Friendship House," where they lived simply modeling the life of Saint Francis of Assisi. They begged for food and clothing and shared everything they gained with the poor. They also began a newspaper, *The Social Forum*, which was based on the social teachings of the Church.

Catherine's work was misunderstood by many, and eventually the Friendship House in Toronto, and later in Harlem, ended in failure. But another

Eddie Doherty and Catherine de Hueck Doherty

part of Catherine's life was on the rebound. A famous American journalist, Eddie Doherty, was assigned to do a newspaper story on Catherine's **apostolate**. While reporting, he fell in love with Catherine. They were married in 1943. Four years later Catherine and Eddie moved to Combermere, a small village north of Toronto where the bishop had invited them to come and continue their work. Catherine and Eddie were not sure what direction their life would take in this out-of-the-way place. But on their arrival in Combermere, they planted a small apple orchard. Somehow they knew that this new place would be their home.

Indeed it was. A new community was founded—Madonna House. Eventually it was to grow to nearly two hundred members, including several priests. In 1954 the community established itself more formally with the Church, and its members took vows of poverty, chastity, and obedience. Catherine and Eddie even took vows of chastity and lived celibate lives from that time on. Eddie was ordained a priest in the Melkite Greek Catholic Church in 1969.

Eddie died in 1975. Catherine de Hueck Doherty died on December 14, 1985, after a long illness. She left behind a spiritual family of over two hundred members besides many foundations established around the world. Her devotion to the poor has led to the cause for her canonization to be opened by the Church.

Yes, life took many unexpected twists and turns for Catherine. It included two marriages, one broken and one of deep committed love: to Eddie Doherty, to the poor, and to God. Catherine once wrote on marriage and family life in an article titled "A Palace of Joy and Peace." The secret to a happy married and family life is not in wealth or material stability, but in the oneness of love between the man and woman, blessed in the Sacrament of Matrimony, and shared in union with Christ. In Catherine's words:

> So it is with a husband and wife. The two are to become one. They leave their parents, their maternal home, to cleave to one another, and eventually become "one flesh."

> This means a surrender, a giving of oneself . . . until, in truth, the two *are* one flesh, one mind, one heart, one soul!

> For those who understand the vocation of marriage (and alas, how few there are!) the veil of faith becomes gossamer thin. The depths of its mysteries are seen . . . as at Communion, when husband and wife are one in the heart of Christ.

apostolate
An association of men and women committed to discerning ways to apply the Gospel to everyday life.

Madonna House

Now *that* is where the oneness is felt most deeply by those who believe, and who, believing, *see*!

The oneness of the marital vocation . . . the oneness of love, in mind, heart, soul, and body . . . of a man and woman bound by the soft, yet unbreakable, bonds of an awesome sacrament: *this* is what will form a home.

It doesn't matter if this "home" is a palace or a hovel (or anything in between); or whether comfortable or uncomfortable (by our crazy modern standards)!

Home is not a dwelling built by hands. It is built by *love*! It is built by that unity, that oneness, which turns a veritable hovel into a palace of joy and peace. This transformation takes place because the tranquility of God's order reigns in the heart of it.

Such a home—and all that goes into making that home—will form strong, sound, mentally healthy parents . . . and children.[1]

The "oneness" of the relationship between a husband and wife in marriage is intended to last until death. Yet, as Catherine's own life attests, the commitment does not come without change and challenge. Today, in twenty-first century American culture, the challenges of married life include not only the typical personal changes that come with growing older, but also external threats of individualism and an anti-life mentality. In this chapter, these threats will be addressed along with the question of divorce and remarriage.

Finally, as Catherine discovered in her marriage to Eddie Doherty, the specific graces of the Sacrament of Matrimony will win out: tenderness, forgiveness, respect, fidelity, and service of others. Christ, the source of grace in married life, facilitates the growth in holiness of the married couple and their children.

journal**discussion**

- Has there been one event in your life that has led you to consider making a dramatic change in your life? Explain.

- What do you perceive to be the greatest challenges to marriage in today's American society?

✦ Marriage Is a Lifelong Commitment

The Church *Code of Canon Law* describes the effects of marriage in this way:

From a valid marriage arises *a bond* between the spouses that by its very nature is perpetual and exclusive; furthermore, in a Christian marriage the spouses are strengthened and, as it were, consecrated for their duties and dignity of their state *by a special sacrament*.[2]

Recall that the bond forged in the Sacrament of Matrimony is covenantal in nature; it is binding because it has been initiated by God. This type of bond is different from others we often encounter in everyday life. For example:

- A young child's connection with his teddy bear usually disappears before preschool.

- A product warranty agreement between a store and a customer runs out after a year.

- A "lifetime contract" between a coach and a team lasts only as long as the coach wins enough games.

The Christian marriage bond is different *and* unique. Because it is from God, it is *perpetual*. This means that it will continue without interruption and last until the death of one partner. It is also *exclusive*. The bond of unity is between these two married people. Their faithfulness and fidelity is to one another. No one else can come between them.

Of course we all know of people who were married—Catholic or not—whose marital bond did not prove perpetual or exclusive. Roughly 20–23 percent of Catholics who have been married have been divorced compared to a slightly larger percentage of Protestants. However, it is important to understand how the Church views the unity and indissolubility of marriage and how a couple is to face the changes and transitions that are inevitably a part of marriage and life in general as each grow in years.

In reality, marriage by its very nature *is* lifelong. It can never be dissolved. True love lasts. As the Song of Songs states about love: "Deep waters cannot quench love, or floods sweep it away" (8:7). Fidelity means faithfulness to duties or obligations. In marriage, fidelity refers to the faithfulness to the vows promised between husband and wife. Being faithful isn't always easy; it takes strength and determination to persevere and make marriage a lifelong commitment.

Personal Changes that Effect Marriage

The photo of the married couple on this page clearly shows that change is part of married life. Both the man and the woman will change physically: the man's thick, wavy hair from his twenties turns into just enough for a combover or less; the woman's shapely figure takes on a "new" shape, especially after bearing children.

Professor and Mrs. James E. Robinson on their wedding day, July 24, 1950, on their 50th wedding anniversary July 24, 2000.

When you marry someone for life, it's wise to be aware that the person across from you on your wedding day may look significantly different (not worse!) as the years progress.

More seriously, some people experience devastating physical changes, even when they are very young. One married woman in her early thirties with two young children was devastated by an undiagnosed neurological condition that caused her unspeakably painful migraine headaches. As this condition worsened and appeared more often, the side effects included vomiting and passing out to a state of semi-consciousness.

The husband and the young children had their lives put on hold. The children missed their mom more and more often as their grandmother came to care for them. The husband had to pass up a job promotion because he had increased responsibilities in caring for both his wife and children.

Yet, the man looked on the condition as positively as possible: "My wife is the one suffering. Not me or my children. We are learning first-hand about compassion and love." Still, it was not what either one expected when they were first married.

People change emotionally, too. In a marriage, the responsibilities associated with supporting a household, raising children, and cultivating a deeper love with a spouse require both the husband and wife to pay special attention to the changing emotional needs of their partner and themselves. Sometimes the sheer busyness of days keeps husbands and wives from connecting emotionally. If this goes on, the spouses may find that their relationship has grown cold, distant, and that one or both of them may feel depressed. To remain emotionally charged, a couple must make a commitment to do things like:

- make each other feel special
- listen to each other's needs
- do things to make the other happy
- appreciate the other's virtues
- appreciate their shared past and look forward to the future.

Spiritual changes also occur over the course of a marriage. Typically, at the time of parenthood, married couples began to reclaim the practice of faith they learned as children. Parents seek to have their children baptized and later enroll them in formal religious education. Personally, as the spouses mature they seek a deeper faith that discovers meaning in religious worship and symbols that previously may have been practiced only as rote. However, each spouse must recognize that the other person may be at a different place in life spiritually. Also, life events—both joyful and tragic—affect people in different ways. What is important is that neither the husband nor wife will let the other lag behind or remain alienated spiritually while he or she moves forward.

Lyrics of Love

Choose lyrics from a contemporary or classic song that express the following characteristics of married love:

- intimacy
- commitment
- openness to life
- fidelity
- indissolubility

Create an 8 1/2" x 11" poster that represents love in color and design and includes some or all of lyrics you have chosen.

you will

always be

in my heart

and in

my soul

friends

forever

Other Transitions in Married Life

Besides personal changes, there are several other external factors that affect married life. Imagine how the relationship between a husband and wife would be impacted by the following situations:

Career Change/Job Relocation. Today's economy is tenuous. Even once solid careers are now more fluid. In one case, John, age fifty-five, the CEO of a major hospital, was given a large buyout payment while being let go. With two teenagers still at home and a daughter planning a wedding, John was not able to consider retirement. Ultimately, John moved his family from a large eastern city to the Midwest countryside, where he purchased a bed and breakfast restaurant and inn. He counted on his family to pitch in and help with the new business while each of them adjusted to a new way of life.

- When are times that career choices must come first in married life? When are times when other family considerations should take precedence over career?

Conflicts with Children. When children reach adolescence and attempt to assert their own independence, each parent may have a different idea about how to address this issue. If the parents disagree, the teen may play one parent against another. This can cause a serious rift in the marital relationship. Teens who have had behavioral problems or have abused drugs or alcohol will have adverse effects on themselves, their families, and the relationship between parents. It is important to note that even if the child is the *subject* of the disagreement, how the parents handle disagreement is their own responsibility.

- Describe how conflicts with teenagers can negatively impact the relationship of a husband and wife.

Middle Years of Marriage. There are many events and issues that can lead to transition in the middle years of marriage. When children leave the house for college, career, and marriage, the couple experiences the "empty nest" syndrome. The husband and wife are alone with one another for the first time in many years. If they have not spent significant time cultivating their own relationship while instead focusing all of their energies on raising their children, they may have to take a step back and recommit to one another. Also, one or both partners may experience the so-called "mid-life crisis" in which the realization sets in that life is more than half over and some of the dreams of youth will not be fulfilled. This may lead to boredom, depression, or, oppositely, the tossing aside of routines for the allure of new adventures. Negatively, a spouse may give up on marriage and seek out a relationship with someone new and/or younger in an effort to "recapture youth." Physical changes in the middle years of marriage can also impact a relationship. Sexual sharing between a husband and wife is still appropriate after the childbearing years as sexual intercourse still fulfills the unitive, one-flesh dimension of married life. But the couple has to address the issue and communicate how sex will continue to be a part of their marriage.

- What are some ways a couple can keep their relationship focused on each other even during the child-rearing years? What would be some appropriate ways to handle a mid-life crisis?

Retirement. The retirement years are not as well defined as they once were. In years past, age sixty-five was the definite time of retirement. At that point, the couple may have raised the children, paid off their mortgage debt, and had enough pension and Social Security income to live a comfortable life through their remaining years, on average only to their early seventies. Today, many adult children return home to live with their parents. Also, more and more grandparents are being called on to provide part- or full-time childcare for their grandchildren. Many grandparents are guardians or adopted parents of their grandchildren. Also, with today's higher cost of living and variances in pension and Social Security plans, many people choose or are forced to work more years than ever before. Life expectancy is also at an all-time high: a baby born today is expected to live 78.2 years. Finally, couples who do have more traditional retirements also face traditional problems; for one, getting used to being around each other for a majority of the waking hours when for years one or both spouses went to work all day. On the positive side, this last stage of life should be one in which the couple can enjoy their children, grandchildren, and each other. They may have the time to do things together that they have always wanted to do: travel, take classes, volunteer, or develop interests in music and art.

- How can the retirement issues listed above cause stress on a marital relationship?

In all of these stages, the couple must understand and learn to be comfortable with the opposing forces that are normal in all relationships. There is tension between wanting to be autonomous and wanting to be connected. We all seek intimacy and sharing, yet we need our own space and independent identity. There is also a tension in wanting both novelty and predictability. We like routine, but we also like to experience new things. There is a tension between wanting to share our thoughts and experiences and needing privacy in some matters. All of these tensions are part of any relationship. In marriage, a couple learns how to work these tensions out together.

The Unity and Indissolubility of Marriage

In marriage, the man and woman grow continually in their life together through their daily fidelity to one another and through their mutual self-giving. The root of this relationship is the natural complementarity that exists between a man and woman. God made both man and woman for each other. But even more than this natural complementarity that keeps the couple together is the gift of the Holy Spirit given to them in the Sacrament of Matrimony. Pope John Paul II wrote of this gift:

> The gift of the Spirit is a commandment of life for Christian spouses and at the same time a stimulating impulse so that every day they may progress towards an even richer union with each other on all levels—of the body, of the character, of the heart, of the intelligence and will, of the soul—revealing in this way to the Church and to the world the new communion of love, given by the grace of Christ. (*Familiaris Consortio*, 19)

This unique relationship of spouses is characterized not only by unity but also by its indissolubility. A marriage demands absolute fidelity between spouses. As the *Catechism* teaches: "Love seeks to be definitive; it cannot be an arrangement 'until further notice'" (*CCC*, 1646). Fidelity is not just a matter of being physically faithful to one's spouse. Fidelity also requires

that one be faithful in one's heart, too. Indulging in daydreams about another person or about life without one's spouse is an occasion of unfaithfulness. Fidelity to one other person may seem impossible; there are, after all, many people in the world whom you can be attracted to and infatuated with, even after you are married. But that is why God instituted the Sacrament of Matrimony. The Sacrament allows a couple to do what is impossible:

> The gift of the sacrament is at the same time a vocation and a commandment for the Christian spouses, that they may remain faithful to each other forever, beyond every trial and difficulty, in generous obedience to the holy will of the Lord: "What therefore God has joined together, let man not put asunder." (*Familiarias Consortio*, 20, quoting Mt 19:6)

The graces of the Sacrament face strong and severe threats today against the unity and indissolubility of marriage. Some of these, specific especially to modern American culture, will be covered in the next section.

fighting fairly

Conflicts and arguments will inevitably arise in a marriage. Conflicts can be constructive if communication to solve them is handled well. Fighting fairly promotes self-knowledge, freedom, security, power, and intimacy. If the legitimate emotion of anger is expressed without harm to the other, it can be positive. Listed below are some suggestions for "fighting fairly" in marriage:

1. Set a time and place for the argument.

2. Avoid discussing a problem when you are speaking more from emotions than from reflective thought.

3. Define what the fight is about and what you want to see changed. Describe the benefits of the change.

4. State your feelings using "I" messages. For example, "I do not like that you spend two nights a week out with your friends." Not, "You are so inconsiderate to be out two nights a week with your friends." Don't attack or blame the other person.

5. Stay within defined limits. Don't pile on gripes from the past.

6. Paraphrase your spouse's arguments to be sure you understand them. Allow him or her the chance to do the same.

7. Focus on the other person's behavior and ideas.

8. Make sure you both have similar understandings of the problem area. Look for areas in which you both agree or disagree.

9. Call "time out" or agree to break whenever the discussion becomes too heated.

10. Decide how to resolve the issue in a way that satisfies your spouse also.

- Practice this method of solving conflicts with a peer or family member. Write a report summarizing the strengths and weaknesses of this method.

- With a classmate, enact an argument that illustrates how to use each of these steps for fighting fairly.

study**questions**

1. What does it mean to say that marriage is perpetual and exclusive?

2. What is the meaning of fidelity in marriage?

3. Name an example of a physical, emotional, and spiritual change in a person that can impact a marriage.

4. What help does a couple receive to keep their marriage from dissolving to modern temptations?

journal**discussion**

- How can the statement "Change is good" relate to married life in a positive way?

- How can a couple overcome the typical transitions of married life to keep a successful marriage?

◆ Challenges to Marriage in American Culture

Freedom—the freedom to choose a spouse and the freedom to raise a family according to a parent's own values and beliefs—is a right crucial to the success of marriage. Equality in marriage is also a God-given right. Each spouse merits the full dignity of a person created in God's image. America was founded on freedom and equality among its citizens, and these ideals continue to support married life. However, the accompanying **pluralism** that composes American society allows for many threats to marriage.

One of the direct effects of pluralism is the prevalence of mixed marriage, that is, a marriage between a Catholic and a person of another Christian denomination or someone who is non-Christian. While these differences are not insurmountable, they can diminish the unity between the husband and wife, between the spouses and in-laws, and cause tensions over the religious education and formation of the children.

Even more serious is the acceptance of individualism in many areas, especially in the area of permissive sexuality. Individualism has much in common with **moral relativism**, that is, the philosophy that dictates choices based on "whatever is best for me." At one level, individualism can mean putting off marriage for career. At a more serious level, individualism includes an attitude of sexual permissiveness that leads to several anti-life practices.

Many of these attitudes of modern American culture (in reality now pervasive worldwide), are offensive to women. Pope John Paul II pointed out that:

> the Christian message about the dignity of women is contradicted by that persistent mentality which considers

pluralism
A condition in which several distinct ethnic, religious, or cultural groups are present and tolerated within a society.

moral relativism
The belief that the standards of right and wrong are arbitrary or transitory, determined by the individual or culture.

the human being not as a person but as a thing, as an object of trade, at the service of selfish interest and mere pleasure: the first victims of this mentality are women.

This mentality produces very bitter fruits, such as contempt for men and for women, slavery, oppression of the weak, pornography, prostitution—especially in the organized form—and all those various forms of discrimination that exist in the fields of education, employment, wages, etc. (*Familiaris Consortio*, 24)

American culture, represented by popular media, can be called anti-life and degrading of women in many forms: music lyrics, television programs, movies, advertisements. You are probably able to fill in the blanks with media examples that contradict the Christian value of sexuality and the sacredness of marriage. For

example, _____ is a reality television show that promotes and validates promiscuous sex. In the song, _____ women are called by derogatory names. "Sex sells" certainly is the theme of the _____ advertising campaign.

The pervasive degrading of the meaning of sex has continued to lead to the acceptance of several anti-life practices including contraception, sterilization, in vitro fertilization, donor parenting, surrogate parenting, and the killing of infants through **direct abortion**. In addition, the anti-life material has contributed to other offenses against marriage: adultery, polygamy, incest, sexual abuse, free union, and the right to trial marriages. The abuses will be defined in this section. Divorce, another commonly accepted practice of American culture, will be discussed in the next section.

direct abortion
The deliberate and intentional killing of unborn human life by means of medical or surgical procedures.

Anti-Life Practices

The corollary to the Church's teaching that sexual intercourse in marriage must be procreative—that is, open to life—is that the Church prohibits any artificial means that prevents conception. Besides direct sterilization of either the man or the woman, the Church also prohibits "any action which either before, at the moment of, or after sexual intercourse, is specifically intended to prevent procreation—whether as an end or a means."[3] An explanation of some of these disallowed practices follows.

Direct abortion is the most serious and reprehensible anti-life practice. It refers to the deliberate termination of pregnancy by the killing of the unborn child and can take several forms. For example, a typical abortion procedure common during weeks seven to twelve of pregnancy is known as "suction and curettage." A hollow tube with a knife-like edge is inserted into a woman's womb. A powerful vacuum is attached to the tube, and the baby is then cut into small pieces and sucked into a jar. A saline abortion is typical in weeks sixteen to twenty-four. A needle is inserted through the woman's stomach and into the womb, injecting a high concentration of salt that is ingested by the baby. Over the course of an hour, the baby is poisoned. The woman delivers a dead baby within twenty-four hours. Other direct abortion methods used later in pregnancy include "dilation and extraction," commonly called "partial-birth abortion." In this method, the baby is twisted in the mother's womb so that it can be pulled out feet first. The baby's head stops at the narrow opening of the womb. A blunt scissors-like instrument is poked into the base of the baby's skull and the baby's brains are removed. The head collapses and the baby's body is removed from the mother. The non-surgical RU 486 pill injects an artificial steroid into the woman that blocks the necessary effects of a natural hormone called progesterone in early pregnancy. With the pregnancy-supporting effects cancelled out, the baby shrivels and detaches itself from the wall of the womb and is expelled.

There are physical dangers to the mother in each of the abortion methods. Also, there are psychological problems that typically occur in women who have had a direct abortion. These include symptoms like guilt, a sense of loss, bad dreams, and flashbacks. Participating in an abortion is a grave offense. Participants include not only the mother. They could also include the medical staff involved, the father who encouraged the abortion or refused help and support to the mother to keep the child, and other relatives or peers. So serious is this offense, that anyone who has an abortion or cooperates in one incurs automatic **excommunication**.

Direct sterilization refers to procedures taken by either the man or woman to destroy the normal functioning of healthy reproductive organs in order to prevent the future conception of children. For males, this is typically done with a surgical procedure called a *vasectomy*, the removal of all or part of the vas deferens, the main duct through which sperm are carried. For women, direct sterilization takes place through a *tubal ligation* in which the fallopian tubes are surgically tied to prevent pregnancy.

Other forms of artificial birth control (e.g., the "pill," intra-uterine device, condoms), though not usually permanent in nature, are also prohibited. All of these also include short- and long-term health risks for the woman. Serious health risks for the "pill" include abnormal blood clotting and heart attacks, cancer, and gall-bladder disease. Side effects include headaches, acne, weight gain, vaginal infections, and depression

As explained in chapter 5, techniques of procreation that disassociate the husband and wife from conception (e.g., donation of sperm or ovum, surrogate uterus) are also gravely immoral.

What Has Happened Since 1968?

The consequences of the "contraceptive mentality" have been far-reaching, especially since 1968 when Pope Paul VI released his encyclical *Humanae Vitae*, which reaffirmed the Church's teaching on married couples using only natural means to regulate and space the birth of children. In his writing, the Pope warned of what would happen if artificial birth control became widely practiced:

Responsible men can become more deeply convinced of the truth of the doctrine laid down by the Church on this issue if they reflect on the consequences and plans for artificial birth control. Let them first consider how easily this course of action could open wide the way for marital infidelity and a general lowering of moral standards. Not much experience is needed to be fully aware of human weakness and to understand that human beings—and especially the young, who are so exposed to temptation—need incentives to keep the moral law, and it is an evil thing to make it easy for them to break that law. Another effect that gives great cause for alarm is that a man who grows accustomed to the use of contraceptive methods may forget the reverence due to a woman, and, disregarding her physical and emotional equilibrium, reduce her to being a mere instrument for the satisfaction of his own desires, no longer considering her as his partner whom he should surround with care and affection.

Finally, careful consideration should be given to the danger of this power passing into the hands of those public authorities who care little for the precepts of the moral law. Who will blame a government which in its attempt to resolve the problems affecting an entire country resorts to the same measures as are regarded as lawful by married people in the solution of a particular family difficulty? Who will prevent public authorities from favoring those contraceptive methods which they consider more effective? Should they regard this as necessary, they may even impose their use on everyone. It could well happen, therefore, that when people, either individually or in family or social life, experience the inherent difficulties of the divine law and are determined to avoid them, they may give into the hands of public authorities the power to intervene in the most personal and intimate responsibility of husband and wife.

—*Humanae Vitae*, 17

What has happened since 1968? Unfortunately, Pope Paul VI's predictions about the results of a contraceptive mentality have come true in so many cases. Here are some of the results:

- The rates of abortion, venereal diseases, out-of-wedlock births, and divorce have risen dramatically.

- Sexual exploitation and sexual abuse of women occur at unprecedented levels.

- Population control policies are now a part of nearly every foreign aid discussion between developing and developed nations. The export of contraception, abortion, and sterilization tools to developing nations is now a requisite for reception of foreign aid.

- The defining element of a woman's identity—her potential for bearing new life—has been redefined as a liability. Her new identity is as a person with the freedom to choose to end life if she wishes while, ironically, the man bears no responsibility.[4]

Assignment

- Write a position paper on the "contraceptive mentality," explaining its adverse effects on women. In the paper, cite up-to-date statistics to support your claims. In addition, mention how the contraceptive mentality also adversely impacts men.

Other Offenses Against the Dignity of Marriage

The union of marriage is also being attacked in several other ways, not just in America, but worldwide. One of the great offenses is the dissolution of marriage itself through divorce. This issue will be taken up separately in the next section. Marriage is impacted negatively by several other offenses described below.

Adultery is not only associated with so-called "marital affairs" in which one partner has an ongoing sexual relationship with someone other than his or her spouse. Adultery refers to any marital infidelity and occurs when two people, of which at least one is married, have sexual relations. Even if these relations are one-time only, adultery has occurred. Jesus, of course, condemned merely the thought of adultery:

You have heard it said, "You shall not commit adultery." But I say to you, everyone who looks at a woman with lust has already committed adultery with her in his heart. (Mt 5:27–28)

Adultery is an injustice on several levels:

- It is a failure to keep the commitment of the marriage vows.

- It injures the marriage bond.

- It violates the rights of the other spouse.

- It undermines the institution of marriage.

- It compromises the life of the couple's children, who need the stable union of their parents.

Another particularly unjust offense against marriage is *polygamy*, which means having more than one wife. This practice contradicts the unique and exclusive nature of the marital bond.

A Christian who has previously lived in polygamy has the responsibility to honor legal and moral obligations to his former wives and children, including financial obligations.

Incest refers to sexual relations between relatives or in-laws within the degree that prohibits marriage between them. Incest corrupts family relationships and regresses those who inflict this on others from their human nature to an animal nature.

Sexual abuse is an attack on a child or adolescent by an adult who has been entrusted to care for them. This reprehensible behavior can cause a child emotional and physical scars for life.

A so-called *free union* is when a man and woman live together without being married. People do this for a variety of reasons: they may reject marriage or be unable to make a commitment. Some women remain concubines, that is, "kept women," who have few legal rights or social status. All of these reasons are immoral and contradict the dignity of marriage.

Trial marriages are those in which the couple claims that marriage is imminent, that they are living together to experiment what it will be like to be married. However, sexual relations are only intended for the full commitment of marriage. Marriage demands a total and definitive gift of one spouse to the other.

A more recent threat to marriage in America and in other developed nations is the issue of *gay marriage*, a proposal for a contractual union between two people with homosexual orientations. The term itself is oxymoronic in that marriage is intended as a complementary relationship between a man and woman, with one of its key purposes being procreative.

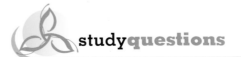

study questions

1. How does pluralism threaten married life?
2. How is individualism related to moral relativism?
3. What effect does individualism have on marriage?
4. Name some physical and psychological risks of abortion for a woman.
5. What are the typical means of direct sterilization for a man and woman?
6. What is meant by the "contraceptive mentality"?
7. Name at least two of Pope Paul VI's warnings regarding artificial birth control and its results.
8. In what ways is adultery unjust?
9. Define *polygamy*.
10. Explain the difference between free unions and trial marriages.

journal discussion

- Name several ways that popular American media and culture have affected your understanding of marriage.
- What would you do if a close friend told you she was considering having an abortion?
- How do you think the world can be converted from the "contraceptive mentality"?

The Question of Divorce and Remarriage

The Catholic Church upholds the teaching of Jesus that marriage is indissoluble. This teaching is true for marriages between baptized Christians (not only Catholics) who marry validly. A valid marriage between baptized Christians cannot be dissolved for any reason other than the death of a spouse. While divorces do occur among Christians, including Catholics, it's important to be aware of their significance. A divorce is a serious offense against God, the Church, and one's spouse for several reasons, including:

- *Divorce breaks the contract to which spouses freely consented, to live with each other until death.* The saying "you are only as good as your word" certainly applies in the case of the marriage consent. While people do go back on their word all the time, that does not mean that breaking a promise is right.

- *Divorce injures the covenant of salvation of which the Sacrament of Matrimony is a sign.* Recall that the relationship of a husband to a wife parallels that of Christ for his Church, the covenant that won for us our salvation.

Jesus' love for the Church is the model for the committed relationship between a husband and wife.

- *Divorce harms the family and society.* It is hurtful to the children who have to live through the separation of their parents. Because divorce perpetuates itself, it becomes a plague on society.

The gravity of divorce is made more serious when a person enters a new marriage outside of the Church: "the remarried spouse is then in a situation of public and permanent adultery" (*CCC*, 2384). This teaching has been consistently held from the time of the Church fathers. Even if the husband or wife did not originally seek the divorce, he or she is still held to the same standards:

> What then shall the husband do, if the wife continue in this disposition [adultery]? Let him divorce her, and let the husband remain single. But if he divorces his wife and marries another, he too commits adultery. (Hermas)[5]

> If a husband, separated from his wife, approaches another woman, he is an adulterer because he makes that woman commit adultery; and the woman who lives with him is an adulteress, because

she has drawn another's husband to herself. (Saint Basil)[6]

While this is a frank description of the results of divorce, it is important to remember there are many variables in each situation. There are many cases when one spouse is the innocent victim of a **civil divorce** pursued by the other. There is a great difference in culpability between a spouse who tried to keep the marriage together and the one who did not. In cases like this, the Church deems it permissible for a civil divorce to take place in order to ensure the rights and care of the children and the protection of the inheritance. Also, for reasons that may include adultery or danger to the spouse and the children, the Church allows for a husband and wife to separate. This means that the husband and wife live separately but do not obtain a civil divorce. They are still married.

A civil divorce does not end a sacramental marriage. Divorced Catholics remain members of the Church and should educate their children in the faith. They are encouraged to attend Mass and other Church activities and ministries in order to receive the graces of Church life and the support of other Catholics. Divorced Catholics who have not remarried remain in good standing with the Church and can receive the sacraments. Those who remarry solely on the basis of a civil divorce put themselves out of communion with the Church. Because

civil divorce
The dissolution of the marriage contract by the legal system.

Ongoing Support for Marriage

The Church does not abandon a couple to the challenges of marriage after the wedding day. Different Church-sponsored programs help to strengthen marriages and repair divisions between spouses.

Marriage Encounter was founded in the late 1950s by Father Gabriel Calvo, a Spanish priest, who developed a series of conferences intended to help married couples become more open and honest and to recapture or strengthen the romance in their marriage. The format for Marriage Encounter is a weekend spent together during which the couple works on their communication skills. A team of married couples and a priest share their experiences of marriage in several presentations. After the presentations, the participants are given time to reflect on how the material applies to their own married life. In the privacy of their own rooms, the couples openly and honestly share their feelings, hopes, disappointments, joys, and frustrations with one another.

Retrouvaille—a word meaning "to discover again"—is a program to help troubled marriages and is patterned after the Marriage Encounter weekend. Couples who are anxious about their relationships, alone or distant from their spouse, disillusioned or bored in their marriage, without the time or desire to communicate, frustrated, hurt, or angry with their partner, and unable to see how any of these situations can improve are encouraged to participate in this program.

Cana II is a program for couples preparing for remarriage in the Catholic Church following widowhood or the annulment process. It meets the needs of couples when one or both have been previously married. A team of married couples facilitates the workshop.

they are living contrary to the law of Christ and the Church, they are unable to receive Holy Communion or the other sacraments.

Declaring a Marriage Null

A Catholic whose marriage has ended in divorce or a Catholic who wishes to marry a divorced non-Catholic can only do so if the prior marriage is declared null. A valid marriage requires the proper intention at the time the matrimonial consent is given. The couple must promise and intend to be faithful to one another and to make their marriage both life-long and open to life. If either of these two meanings of marriage is excluded by either the man or woman on their wedding day, then no marriage has ever taken place.

A couple of points must be made here. First, this is a Church process and has nothing to do with the legal status of a prior marriage or the legitimacy and custody of a couple's children. Also, a ruling on the validity of the marriage only concerns the *intention* of one or both spouses on their wedding day. Behavior during the course of marriage is only taken into consideration when the behavior can serve as evidence of a lack of a full or correct intention.

For example, someone who marries but has no intention of being permanently faithful to his or her spouse violates the principles of fidelity and indissolubility. Evidence of this lack of intention will usually arise shortly after the wedding when the person is unfaithful to his or her partner. Or, a person of childbearing age could marry but not intend to have children. This, too, would render a marriage invalid.

A decree of nullity—commonly known as an **annulment**—is a finding by the Church that at the time vows were exchanged, at least some element of a valid marriage was lacking. Some common grounds for nullity besides the ones previously mentioned are:

- *Insufficient use of reason.* One or both parties did not know what was happening during the wedding because of insanity, mental illness, or a lack of consciousness.

- *Error about the quality of the person.* One or both parties intended to marry someone who either possessed or did not possess a certain quality, for example: marital status, religious conviction, freedom from disease, or arrest record.

- *Future conditions.* One or both parties attached conditions on the decision to marry. For example, "I will marry you if you complete your education."

annulment
The Church's declaration that a sacramental marriage was invalid, that it never existed in the first place.

- *Force.* One or both parties married because of an external physical or moral force that they could not resist.

- *Misunderstanding of marital sacramental dignity.* One or both parties believed that marriage is not a religious or sacred relationship but only a civil contract or arrangement.

Also, it's important to remember that the annulment process is not concerned with the behavior after the wedding day. If a valid marriage was made on the day of the wedding, then that marriage is an indissoluble bond, regardless of what happened later in the marriage. A husband may cheat on his wife, but if that was not his intention on the day of the wedding, that issue will not factor into a decree of nullity. Or, a woman may later decide not to have children. But if this was not her intention at the time she made her marriage vows, then this too is not considered grounds for annulment.

Anyone who is divorced or considering marriage to someone who is divorced must obtain a decree of nullity in order to be married in the Church. The process begins by submitting the facts of the marriage, with supporting witness statements to the diocesan **marriage tribunal**. In most dioceses the facts of the marriage are collected through an interview by an advocate who will ask the details of the marriage. This information is held in confidence. The report is turned in to the marriage tribunal. The former spouse will be contacted and a list of witnesses who can testify about the marriage will be asked to provide information. After the evaluation of the facts, a judgment on the validity of the marriage is made. A second court, usually from a neighboring

diocese, must verify the judgment. Whatever decision is reached, it may be appealed to the Holy See's court for matrimonial cases.

There are also different rulings for marriages and divorces that may involve one or both spouses who are not Christian or Catholic. Marriages between two unbaptized persons in which one of the spouses refuses to live with the other spouse who has decided later to convert to Christianity can be dissolved when the baptized person enters into a marriage with another baptized person. This is called the "Pauline Privilege" because it was originally allowed by Saint Paul according to 1 Corinthians 7:12–16. The "Petrine Privilege," named for Saint Peter, is sometimes used to dissolve a marriage. It occurs when one spouse is a baptized Christian and the other is unbaptized and the unbaptized

marriage tribunal
A staff of diocesan representatives of the bishop who have received special education and instruction to represent the Church in proceedings for marriage cases.

person refuses to live with his or her spouse after the spouse has converted to the Catholic Church.

An annulment is not a divorce. It is the Church's declaration that a sacramental marriage never existed in the first place. When a marriage is annulled, the man and woman may enter a marriage with another person as long as the grounds for nullity from the first marriage no longer exist.

Lending a Hand

Inquire at a parish about their pastoral programs to support divorced and remarried Catholics. If the group meets regularly, participate in or begin a child care service for the children of the parents who attend.

Pastoral Care of Divorced and Remarried Catholics

The Church does not abandon people who are divorced, including those who are divorced and remarried without having their marriage annulled. In *Familiaris Consortio*, Pope John Paul II wrote:

> I earnestly call upon pastors and the whole community of the faithful to help the divorced, and with solicitous care to make sure that they do not consider themselves as separated from the Church, for as baptized persons they can, and indeed must, share in her life.

Pope John Paul II suggested several ways for those who are divorced and remarried to re-enter the life of the Church, encouraging them to:

- listen to the Word of God,
- attend Mass,
- continue to pray,

- contribute to works of charity and community efforts in favor of justice,
- bring up their children in the Christian faith,
- cultivate the spirit and practice of penance as a way to seek God's grace.[7]

Of particular care and concern are the children born to the new marriages. The Church hopes that parents will seek the sacraments and religious education of their children. Doing so is one way for the parents to regain their own path to Christ through the Church.

Likewise, all Catholics are to exhibit the spirit of welcome to those who have suffered through the irregularities of divorce and remarriage by assisting them in the tasks outlined above. Many diocesan and parish programs to support those who are divorced provide pastoral care. For example, the Diocese of Oakland provides pastoral counseling and community resource referrals to divorced Catholics, and it encourages the formation of parish support groups, led by others who have been through the experience of separation and divorce. These groups offer presentations, a variety of social and recreational opportunities, and allow the participants to meet others who understand the struggle and can share coping skills, learn forgiveness, experience God's love, and find new friends to help them continue on their journey of faith.

In the midst of pastoral care, the Church affirms that divorced persons who have remarried without receiving the decree of nullity are unable to receive communion. Also, the absolution offered in the Sacrament of Penance can only be offered if the person is willing to live in a way that does not contradict the indissolubility of marriage. In some cases, this may mean the man and woman must separate or live celibately with their spouse. Besides reaching out to those who are divorced and remarried, Pope John Paul II consistently taught that:

> With firm confidence [the Church] believes that people who have rejected the Lord's command and are still living in this state will be able to obtain from God the grace of conversion and salvation, provided that they have persevered in prayer, penance, and charity.[8]

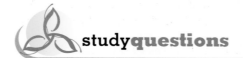

study questions

1. What is the only way that a valid marriage can be dissolved?

2. List three reasons a divorce is a serious offense.

3. What are some ways the culpability of divorce is diminished?

4. What is a *civil divorce*?

5. What is the status of divorced Catholics in the Church?

6. Name two grounds for nullity of marriage.

7. What is a decree of nullity?

8. Explain why a decree of nullity of marriage only concerns the *intentions* of one or both spouses on their wedding day.

9. Define *Pauline Privilege* and *Petrine Privilege*.

10. What is the Church's responsibility to divorced and remarried Catholics?

journal discussion

- How has divorce impacted your life or the life of a close friend?

- What are some positive lessons that you have learned from the Church's teaching on the indissolubility of marriage?

✦ Sacramental Grace in Marriage

Jeff and Clare were high school sweethearts who moved to California shortly after they were married. Jeff was an aspiring actor and Clare was determined to allow her husband to "reach for his dreams," even if it meant postponing having their first child.

Lo and behold, God had other plans. While the acting career was off to a slow start, Clare found out she was pregnant just weeks after they moved into their small studio apartment a few blocks from the beach in the South Bay. A beautiful son, Matthew, was born just weeks before Christmas.

Jeff decided to pursue an alternate dream: he studied for and became a police officer. Both he and Clare loved California and decided to stay. Central to their new life was their participation at their local parish. They volunteered as catechists for the high school Confirmation program. Jeff was a lector at Mass. And both made many new friends in the parish.

The months turned into years, and when Matthew was almost three, the couple had their second child, Michael. They had saved enough money to put a down payment on their own condominium right across the street from Clare and the boys' favorite park.

Eventually Matthew started kindergarten at the parish school. It was during that year that the family's life was turned upside down. For Matthew's sixth birthday, the parents took the boys to the dollar theatre at the mall to watch a recently released Disney film. After the movie, it was off to the food court for some pizza slices and soft drinks.

Jeff asked everyone to tell his or her "favorite parts" of the movie. Clare and young Michael had no trouble recounting several scenes they liked. But usually talkative Matthew inexplicably could not share a preference for any one scene. In fact, it seemed to Jeff and Clare that he really had no clue what the movie was about at all. On the way home, Clare guessed, "Maybe Matthew needs glasses. Maybe he had trouble even seeing what was on the screen."

Early the next week Clare took Matthew to the eye doctor. It was true that his eyesight had weakened, and the optometrist suggested the parents take Matthew to an ophthalmologist. The concern in the doctor's demeanor was noticeable immediately to Clare. What the further tests revealed devastated the young family. Matthew was nearly legally blind. He had a condition called Batten's Disease, a rare hereditary disease that includes blindness, seizures, loss of coordination, and finally death. A person who develops the disease in childhood may live only into his twenties.

If this news wasn't enough, the doctors were also concerned about Michael. Did he carry the gene for Batten's as well? The chances were about fifty-fifty. The first tests on Michael were negative. But then a few months later he began to complain of headaches and poor vision. Michael, too, is now confirmed to have Batten's Disease.

Jeff looked back at his and Clare's time together. Their high school prom was only eight years in the past, but it seemed a different lifetime. Jeff's dreams of landing the "big Hollywood part" evaporated overnight. His new plan, following the lead of his wife, was to find a cure for their children's condition. Even more, the priority was to appreciate and enjoy every single day they could spend with Matthew and Michael.

Meanwhile, Clare feared that not only would she lose her children, she would lose Jeff. After the disease was discovered, some friends from the parish decided to hold a yard sale to raise money for the couple at the couple's condominium. It was a good idea turned bad. A woman shopper slipped on the patio and fractured her arm. She started a lawsuit against Jeff and Clare. At that point, Jeff began to lose it. His depression was constant, twenty-four hours a day. He talked of moving back to Florida and spending time with his sister and her family. "I couldn't believe what was happening to us," Clare recalled.

Meanwhile, the entire parish was praying for the boys and the couple. "I could feel the power of their prayer," Clare said. With help, Jeff recovered dramatically and continued spending all of his free time either with the boys or on establishing a foundation for them to pay for their expenses and to research the disease. "It is our faith that saved us," Jeff said. "When we take the boys to Mass on Sunday, I can feel the sets of eyes on us. I can tell that people love and care for us. I also knew that our faith in this dark time was a positive sign for everyone else."

Sacraments give the grace they signify. The grace of the Sacrament of Matrimony perfects the couple's love and strengthens their indissoluble unity. In marriage, the husband and wife become a revelation of God and the source of God's grace for each other. This certainly happens in the joys

of marriage, especially in the unity of their sexual sharing in which they experience the gentleness, tenderness, fidelity, and creativity of God's love in a concrete and sensual way.

The sacramental grace of marriage is also experienced by married couples, like Jeff and Clare, in the typical everyday challenges and pains of life, but sometimes in the largeness of unspeakable hurts like the illness and loss of children.

RESEARCH AND REPORT

Choose one of the following topics and research relevant information to support taking one of the following positions:

- Married couples who follow the teachings of the encyclical *Humanae Vitae* have a happier and more satisfying marriage.

- There are several examples of married saints worthy of emulation.

- Because of Christ and the founding of the Church, women were given more esteem and value in married life.

- Divorced Catholics have served the Church well in ministry.

Write a five-hundred-word position paper supporting one of these positions. Cite specific evidence and examples to support your claims.

Christ Is the Source of Grace in Married Life

Jesus Christ is constantly present with a husband and wife in marriage. He loves them and is faithful to them as he wishes them to be for the other. The *Catechism of the Catholic Church* teaches:

Christ dwells with them, gives them the strength to take up their crosses and so follow him, to rise again after they have fallen, to forgive one another, to bear one another's burdens, to "be subject to one another out of reverence for Christ," and to love one another with supernatural, tender, and fruitful love. (*CCC*, 1642 quoting Eph 5:21)

It is in this journey of married life that the couple takes on this "supernatural" dimension for each other, for their children, and as a witness to the world. By recognizing and embracing the sacramental grace of marriage, they become a sign of Christ for others, the true meaning of a sacrament. Husbands and wives cooperate with and perfect the gift of sanctifying grace by participating in the other sacraments, especially the Eucharist, by praying, by constantly remembering the noble state of married life, and by reminding themselves that their lives witness Christ for the other and their life as a couple is a sign of Christ to the world.

The Fruits of Married Life

Matrimony is a sacrament at the service of communion; the self-giving of the husband to the wife and the wife to the husband helps to bring about their own salvation and the salvation of their children in Christ. It is in the joys of their love for one another and their family that Christ gives them a foretaste of Heaven. It makes perfect sense, then, that marriage only ends at the death of a spouse, the entrance for him or her into eternal life.

Jeff and Clare's son, Matthew, is a teenager now. He is completely blind and unable to walk.

Michael has lost most of his sight as well, as the disease slowly claims his life. The parents continue to feel the suffering of their children each day. But their daily lives have witnessed to some other fruits of married and family life even more dramatically.

There is the *tenderness* they share. Clare and Jeff are experts in massaging the boy's weakened muscles, strong hands that offer a loving touch.

Clare can't help remembering that she is the carrier of the Batten's gene. What could she have done to prevent their illness? Jeff reminds her, there was nothing she could have done. And in that moment she *forgives* herself.

Matthew and Michael skipped a lot of the sibling rivalry stuff and even the typical arguments between brothers. Because each knows what the other is going through, the *respect* they share for the other is often visible. They have been brothers and best friends.

"I promise to be true to you in good times and in bad. . . ." When she thinks of her life in whole, not in parts, Clare looks at it all as good: the beautiful gifts of her sons, and the love and *fidelity* she shares with Jeff. "Our married life has been hard, but we are still together and stronger as a couple than ever," she says.

The lawsuit against Jeff and Clare by the woman at the yard sale was dropped. Once she heard about the purpose of the sale and the condition of the children, she not only dropped the suit, she donated $100 to the Batten's Disease foundation. "We see the goodness in people all the time," said Jeff. "People have come to our aid in so many ways—they have been a model of *service* to us."

"It's been a two-way street," adds Clare. "I think our family has given back to the community, as well."

The fruit of married life is salvation.

study questions

1. What is sacramental grace?

2. How do husbands and wives take on a supernatural dimension for each other?

3. How do husbands and wives cooperate with and perfect the gift of sanctifying grace in their marriage?

4. What are some of the fruits of married life?

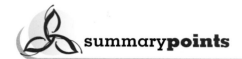

journaldiscussion

- What is a lesson about marriage that you learned from the story of Jeff, Clare, and their children?

- Describe a family that has been an inspiration to you because of their faith through a difficult situation.

summarypoints

Twists and Turns

- Catherine de Hueck Doherty was married twice, raised a son, and eventually founded an apostolate that served the poor.

- Catherine wrote about the way of happiness in married life in an article titled, "A Palace of Joy and Peace."

- Catherine de Hueck Doherty's cause for canonization was opened by the Church following her death in 1975.

Marriage Is a Lifelong Commitment

- The Christian marriage bond is perpetual and exclusive.

- There are several personal changes that affect marriage, including physical changes, emotional changes, and spiritual changes of one or both partners. The couple's commitment to their wedding vows helps them to remain loyal to one another in spite of any personal changes.

- Other transitions that may impact married life include career changes/job relocation, conflicts with children, the so-called "mid-life" crisis, and retirement.

- The sacramental graces of the Sacrament of Matrimony help married couples overcome the many challenges against the unity and indissolubility of their marriage.

Challenges to Marriage in American Culture

- The pluralism of American culture allows for many threats to marriage, including many anti-life practices and degradations of women.

- An even more serious threat to marriage is an individualistic attitude that encourages husbands and wives to make choices based on "what feels good" or "whatever is best for me."

- The most serious anti-life practice is the abortion of innocent children.

- Other anti-life practices have to do with permanent or temporary contraception and procreation that takes place without the conjugal act of the husband and wife.

- The predictions made by Pope Paul VI about the effects of the "contraceptive mentality" on society have been proven true.

- Marriage is also impacted negatively by several other offenses: adultery, incest, free union, and trial marriage. A more recent challenge is the proposal of a contractual union between two people of a homosexual orientation.

The Question of Divorce and Remarriage

- A valid marriage between baptized Catholics cannot be dissolved for any reason other than the death of a spouse.

- A divorce is a serious offense against God, the Church, and one's spouse.

- The gravity of divorce is made more serious when a person enters a new marriage outside of the Church.

- There are many variables in each divorce; for example, the culpability of the spouse who works to keep the marriage together is less than that of the one who did not.

- A civil divorce does not end a sacramental marriage. Divorced Catholics remain members of the Church in good standing.

- A decree of nullity determines, from the intentions of the man and woman on their wedding day, that no marriage took place.

◆ An annulment is a finding by the Church that at the time vows were exchanged, at least some element of a valid marriage was lacking.

◆ The Church remains caring of those who have been divorced and remarried, reminding them of God's grace of conversion and salvation.

✦ Sacramental Grace in Marriage

◆ The sacramental grace of Matrimony perfects the couple's love and strengthens their indissoluble unity.

◆ The sacramental grace helps couples overcome the challenges and pains of life.

◆ Fruits of married life and parenthood include tenderness, forgiveness, respect, fidelity, and service to others.

assignments applications

1. Read and report on the apostolate of Madonna House, founded by Catherine de Hueck Doherty. Also read the Restoration newspaper published by Madonna House. Write a letter to the paper commenting on an issue of social justice. See www.madonnahouse.org/index.html.

2. Interview five to ten married people. Ask each person to name four of the greatest challenges facing married couples in American society and culture today. List their examples in chart form. In an accompanying column, offer your comment on the challenges and/or a possible solution.

3. Write a hypothesis for why the divorce rate is high in the United States. Research several statistics about divorce in the United States and worldwide. Record the information and explain how it supports or refutes your original hypothesis.

4. Design a poster or chart that includes at least three Scripture passages that speak of the meaning of love.

5. Collect at least five wedding anniversary announcements (forty years and more) from the local newspaper. Paste them in a notebook or journal. Write a prayer for each couple based on some information about their lives that you gleaned from the article.

6. Research and report on the Roe v. Wade Supreme Court decision that led to the legalization of abortion in the United States. Summarize the dissenting opinion of Chief Justice William Rehnquist. See www.tourolaw.edu/patch/Roe/Rehnquist.asp.

7. Prepare a report that lists several of the physical side effects and possible risks of at least five forms of artificial birth control.

8. Interview a parish priest. Ask him to describe the annulment process in his parish and diocese. Write a report summarizing the information.

9. Make a novena on behalf of troubled marriages. Keep a daily journal recording your thoughts and special intentions. See page 332 of this book for more information about novenas.

10. Type "Pastoral Care of Divorced Catholics" into an Internet search engine. Read and summarize several different parish and diocesan programs of pastoral care. Write at least five unique ideas for aiding the healing of divorced Catholics and making them feel welcome again in the Church.

Notes

1. This quotation is from Restoration Madonna House, Inc., Combermere, Ontario, Canada (July–August 1994).

2. Cf., *Codex Iuris Canonici*, can. 1141, quoted in *CCC*, 1638.

3. Quoted from *Humanae Vitae*, 14.

4. These points were made by Archbishop Charles J. Chaput, OFM, Cap, of Denver in a Pastoral Letter, "The Truth and Meaning of Married Love" (July 22, 1998).

5. Quoted from *The Shepherd* 4:16.

6. Quoted from *Moralia*, 73, 1:PG, 31, 849–852.

7. Quotation and list are taken from *Familiaris Consortio*, 84.

8. Ibid.

Prayer
for the Vocation to Married Life

Allow at least thirty minutes for private prayer. Choose a quiet place where you can be alone and undistracted. Bring a journal and pen to help with your reflection.

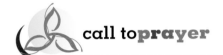

call to prayer

Pray in the following words or choose similar words of your own. After the prayer, pause in silence. Listen for God to speak to you in your silence.

Heavenly Father,

thank you for this time in your presence.

I have learned about the unbreakable and sacred bond of marriage.

Help me to begin to determine if I am called to married life.

If so, help protect me from the temptations against chastity.

Teach me to be a loyal friend.

Allow me to be relaxed as I form new friendships with people of the opposite sex.

Make me strong enough to keep the commitments you have entrusted to me now

so that I will be able to keep the life-long commitment of marriage

if I am called down that path.

And continue to offer your Holy Spirit to those married couples

who are dear to me: especially my parents, grandparents,

and others who have shared the graces of the Sacrament of Matrimony with me.

Remain with me always.

I make this prayer in the name of your Son, Jesus Christ, our Lord.

Amen.

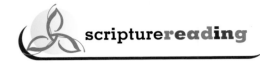

scripture reading

Slowly and carefully read the Scripture passage from 1 John 4:7–12. What is God's word saying to you about a possible vocation to married life?

A reading from the First Letter of John:

Beloved, let us love one another, because love is of God; everyone who loves is begotten by God and knows God. Whoever is without love does not know God, for God is love. In this way the love of God was revealed to us: God sent his only Son into the world so that we might have life through him. In this is love: not that we have loved God, but that he loved us and sent his Son as expiation for our sins. Beloved, if God so loved us, we also must love one another. No one has ever seen God. Yet, if we love one another, God remains in us, and his love is brought to perfection in us.

The Word of the Lord.
Thanks be to God.

reflection questions

Read through the entire list of questions. Then go back and choose one question to spend time with in greater detail. Listen to what God is saying to you. Write down your thoughts in a prayer journal. Choose another question and repeat the process. You can choose to do all or some of the questions. You can also form your own questions about marriage and write your responses to these as well.

- What elements of my friendship skills can I bring to a marriage?

- Can I put my career plans behind my marriage and family life?

- How do I imagine my future spouse?

- What would a typical weekday be like as a married person? weekend?

- How many children would I like to have?

- How would I fit in with my spouse's family? How would my spouse fit in with my family?

- What kind of parenting style will I have?

- How does married life seem fun and exciting?

- What will my wedding be like?

- If I could tell my future spouse anything right now, what would it be?

Prayer for My Future Spouse

End your time of reflection with a prayer for a potential future spouse. Use this prayer or your own words.

Holy God,

watch over my future spouse, if it is your will that I be married.
Protect my spouse from harm.
Keep my spouse chaste and pure as I promise the same.
Lead us to each other and instruct us in the ways of friendship.
As our love grows, let it be in your name.
I commend this prayer through the intercession of the Blessed Virgin Mary, our Mother,
and through Christ our Lord.

Amen.

unit**three**

✦ Always a Servant, Then a Priest

It would be the truth to say that Charles de Foucauld desired to serve others, especially the poor, before he ever desired to be a priest. In fact, Charles was disenfranchised from the Church and God altogether when, as a French soldier at war in Algeria, he became deeply attracted to the prayerfulness and hospitality of the Muslims living there. Charles decided to study Arabic and read the Koran and the Bible. He later made several peacekeeping and exploratory visits to Morocco and throughout the Saharan desert, wondering how the many resources of his homeland France might be shared with these poor people.

His admiration for the devotion of Muslims, his identification with the humble and poor lifestyle of the people of North Africa, and his ongoing desire to be in some way connected and of service to this people led Charles to reclaim the Catholic faith of his childhood and eventually give in to the requests of many that he be ordained a priest.

Charles de Foucauld was born in 1858 to an aristocratic family in Strasbourg, France. Both of his parents died when he was very young and left Charles and his sister a very large inheritance. Charles lived a lavish lifestyle. As an adult, he enjoyed the finest foods and champagne to the point that he became rather obese. In the 1880s, he entered the French army as an officer, though he resigned when his superiors requested that he not flaunt his relationship with his mistress at social functions where the wives of the other officers were not amused by this dalliance.

Rich and retired, Charles began to travel extensively throughout the oases of South Algeria and Tunisia and into Morocco. On one of these trips he had to pose as a Jew because Frenchmen were thought to be spies. Throughout his time in the desert, Charles met no other Christians, only Muslims or Jews. The faith that he had abandoned in childhood began to stir. He was moved whenever he saw a Muslim stop in the desert, unroll a rug, and bow in prayer to God. Likewise, the faithfulness of his Jewish companions was also impressive. Their faith certainly did not provide them with material comforts, Charles realized, but it did seem to provide them with a resolve that allowed them to face all kinds of suffering and persecution.

Briefly engaged to be married, Charles broke it off and returned to Paris. Not sure why, he began to pray on his knees for long hours each day at Saint Augustine's Church. He kept repeating what he called his "strange prayer": "My God, if you exist, make your presence known to me."

A priest at the Church suggested Charles make a good confession. It was at that moment that his life and heart were converted and he returned to the Church. The wheels of God's providence that were set in motion at that time would eventually lead Charles to give up his wealth, live a life of prayer, poverty, and solitude—mostly in the desert—and eventually become a priest. Charles later remembered the day he went to confession at Saint Augustine's: "My religious vocation dates from the same hour as my faith: God is so great."

Charles had a varied life of devotion to God and to ordinary people after that. He lived the life of a Trappist monk for a while, always requesting to be moved to poorer and poorer monasteries. In 1897 he moved to Nazareth and lived in the tool shed of the Poor Clare nuns while running errands for them in town.

Called to Service
through Holy Orders

Just before coming to Nazareth a tragedy occurred in the region. Nearly 150,000 Armenians were slaughtered by the Ottoman Turks. At that moment, Foucauld regretted not having been ordained a priest. He could have been there to minister to the Armenians in their suffering. Finally, in 1901, Charles returned to France where he was ordained.

For the next fifteen years, Father Charles lived in his beloved Morocco as a "hermit-missionary" in a tiny house of mud bricks and palm trunks. "I want to accustom everyone here—Christian, Muslim, Jew, pagan—to look on me as a brother to each one of them," he wrote.

In 1916, Charles de Foucauld was murdered by a band of traveling marauders during an uprising against the French government. Today several secular institutes and apostolic societies are active that follow Foucauld's instruction to serve others by living simply among the ordinary people, working at the same jobs the people of the area do, and living the Gospel by example. Charles de Foucauld was beatified on November 15, 2005.

Though late to be ordained, Charles de Foucauld's life reminds the Church what is essential about a vocation to priesthood: it is first and foremost a vocation from God to a life of service. The priest's life of service is undertaken in imitation of Jesus Christ, who offered his life in sacrifice for the salvation of the world. Christ is the one High Priest. His life of sacrificial service on behalf of others modeled what is essential for every priest.

Recall that those Catholics who have received Baptism and Confirmation are already made holy and are part of the common priesthood that shares in its own way in the one priesthood of Christ. Like Matrimony, the Sacrament of Holy Orders is a "sacrament at the service of communion." Those who are ordained receive a particular consecration in Christ's name to "feed the Church by the word and grace of God (*Lumen Gentium,* II)." It is this ministerial or hierarchical priesthood of bishops and priests that is the particular subject of Unit 3. The Unit will cover the historical and theological background of priesthood, the rite of Holy Orders, and some particular ministries of the bishop, priest, and deacon.

You likely have known some dedicated priests and are interested in knowing more about the special role they play in the Church. From your own experience, you are aware that their lives are rooted in sacrifice and service.

A Muslim friend of Charles de Fourcauld once said of him: "He has given his time to the Eternal." This statement certainly rings true in the lives of all who are ordained.

chapter**outline**

✦ The Scene in the Upper Room

At the Last Supper, Christ instituted the priesthood of the Church and established the line of apostolic succession.

✦ Sharing in Christ's Priesthood

All Christians participate in the one priesthood of Christ in either of two ways: by virtue of their Baptism into the common priesthood of the laity or in the ministerial priesthood as conferred in the Sacrament of Holy Orders.

✦ The Historical Development of Holy Orders

The structure of the ministerial priesthood emerged in the early Church, was reaffirmed at the Council of Trent, and is maintained today with renewed emphasis on the bishop's role in his diocese.

✦ A Definition of Holy Orders Today

Two degrees of priestly participation (episcopate and presbyterate) and one degree of service (diaconate) are conferred by the Sacrament of Holy Orders.

✦ Who Can Receive the Sacrament of Holy Orders

No one has the right to ordination; a man must be called to this special vocation by Christ.

chapter seven

Continuing the Work of the Apostles

"If I, therefore, the master and teacher, have washed your feet, you ought to wash one another's feet. I have given you a model to follow, so that as I have done for you, you should also do."

John 13:14–15

Jubilee Year

According to Jewish law, the Jubilee Year occurred every fiftieth year when all debts were removed and slaves freed. In Catholicism, the term is connected with a Holy Year in which the Pope grants special spiritual benefits to those who perform religious acts, including making a pilgrimage to Rome.

✦ The Scene in the Upper Room

Pope John Paul II made it his tradition to write a letter to the priests of the world each Holy Thursday. In his letter in the **Jubilee Year** 2000 the Pope meditated on the scene in the Upper Room, the place where Jesus shared his Last Supper with his Apostles, in these words:

> "It was night" . . . the hour of darkness, an hour of separation and of infinite sadness. Yet in the emotion-filled words of Christ the light of dawn already shines forth: "I will see you again and your hearts will rejoice, and no one will take your joy from you." (Jn 16:22)

We must never cease meditating on the mystery of that night. We should often return in spirit to this Upper Room where we priests especially can feel in a sense "at home." With regard to the Upper Room, it could be said of us what the Psalmist says of the peoples with regard to Jerusalem: "In the register of the peoples, the Lord will write: These were born here."[1]

Literally, the Upper Room was the place and the Last Supper was the event where Christ instituted the priesthood of the Church. He offered himself in the forms of bread and wine to his Apostles and said, "Do this in remembrance of me." This command may be the most observed in history. There is never a moment of the day or a place in the world where the Mass has not been celebrated countless times ever since.

In the Sacrament of Holy Orders, the priest receives the power to obey Christ's command and do what he did: to change ordinary bread and wine into Christ himself. Before

Views of the Upper Room today.

moving on in the text, reflect for a moment on how really *powerful* that gift is.

First, imagine being present in the same room with God-in-the-flesh, Jesus Christ.

Then, at the time he broke bread and shared cup, imagine witnessing what Saint Augustine described: "Christ held and carried himself in his own hands."

"Do this in memory of me." With these words the power of Christ and this event was passed directly to the Apostles who were present with him.

By the end of the first century the Church had expanded throughout the Roman Empire, to over one hundred dioceses. Each of these dioceses had a bishop who had received his power through the laying on of hands from one of the Apostles or from a bishop who had been ordained by one of them.

These bishops, in turn, laid hands on other bishops and the priests who would assist them.

The power of the Eucharist to this day comes directly from Christ through this **apostolic succession**.

At the Eucharist, Christ is among us, we celebrate his presence, and recall his love. At Eucharist, the priest exercises in a supreme degree the sacred office of his priesthood, "acting in the person of Christ and proclaiming his mystery" (*CCC*, 1566). At Eucharist, Christ's great sacrifice that redeemed the world is made present. The Eucharist strengthens and unites the entire Church. The power of the Eucharist is unsurpassed.

Without the priest, the Eucharist cannot take place. The previous sentence may be the most important one you will read in this unit on the Sacrament of Holy Orders. Two of the degrees of the apostolic ministry included in Holy Orders—the *episicopate* (bishops) and the *presbyterate* (priests)—share in the priesthood of Christ. The bishop and priest have other roles in the Church—including the preaching of the Gospel and governance of the Church—but none is more important than their role in celebrating the Eucharist.

In offering the Sacrifice of the Mass, the priest is able to exercise his sacred role in a supreme degree. Christ identifies himself so much with the priest that the priest is able

to say, "This is my body. This is my blood." The Holy Spirit, through the ministry of the priest, makes the saving acts of Christ present. Christ is truly present in the Eucharist through the role of the priest.

The Sacrament of Holy Orders is the Sacrament of Apostolic Ministry. Its purpose is to continue the work of the Apostles to the end of time. This chapter explains more of the distinction between the ministerial priesthood of bishops and priests and the

apostolic succession
The handing on of the Apostles' preaching and authority that occurred directly from the Apostles to the bishops through the laying on of hands.

common priesthood of the laity, tracing those differences to the intentions of Christ himself, the one, true priest. Also, the distinctions between the three orders are explained. Besides the episcopacy and presbyterate, the Sacrament of Holy Orders includes a third degree, the *dioconate*. Deacons help and assist bishops and priests in their ministries.

As you likely know, many parishes in the United States are without a priest. In 2005, the number of active diocesan priests was down over 40 percent from 1965.[2] This reality has been called a "priest shortage" and a "priest crisis." It certainly merits prayerful concern by all the Church, as the current number of parishes without a resident priest (almost 3,000 in 2003) is expected to continue to rise.

The Catholic Church is an apostolic Church. She was and remains built on the Apostles, the witnesses chosen and sent on mission by Christ himself. With the help of the Spirit, the Church keeps and hands on the teachings of the Apostles. And the Church continues to be taught, made holy, and guided by the successors of the Apostles—the bishops (assisted by the priests), in union with the Pope. This promise extends to the end of time. While the Church

---

PRAYER FOR PRIESTS AND BISHOPS

In the **Lectionary** instruction for the Holy Thursday Chrism Mass, the Mass the bishop of a diocese celebrates with his priests and at which all the sacred oils are blessed, there is the suggestion that in his homily the bishop "should urge the priests to be faithful in fulfilling their office in the Church and should invite them to renew publicly their priestly promises." After this renewal of promises, the bishop addresses the people in these words:

> My brothers and sisters,
> pray for your priests.
> Ask the Lord to bless them with the
>   fullness of his love,
> to help them be faithful ministers of
>   Christ the High Priest,
> so that they will be able to lead you
>   to him,
> the fountain of your salvation.

He also asks for prayers for himself:

> Pray also for me
> that despite my own unworthiness
> I may faithfully fulfill the office of
>   the apostle
> which Jesus Christ has entrusted to
>   me.
> Pray that I may become more like
> our High Priest and Good Shepherd,
> the teacher and servant of all,
> and so be a genuine sign
> of Christ's loving presence among
>   you.

The people respond to each, "Lord Jesus Christ, hear us and answer our prayer."

- Write your own prayer for priests and bishops.

- Write a prayer for an increase of vocations to the priesthood.

Lectionary

The book that contains the Scripture readings that have been chosen by the Church for public reading at Mass according to the liturgical calendar.

continues to pray for more men to be ordained, it is certain that because of its apostolic roots, it will forever be fulfilled.

journaldiscussion

- What do you find powerful about the scene in the Upper Room at the Last Supper?

- How do you understand the statement: "The Catholic Church is an apostolic Church"?

✦ Sharing in Christ's Priesthood

The first letter to Timothy contains what may have been a very primitive Christian creed:

> For there is one God,
> There is also one mediator between God and the human race,
> Christ Jesus, himself human, who gave himself as ransom for all. (1 Tm 2:5)

Christ, described in these words as the "one mediator between God and the human race," is the one high priest who can offer the perfect sacrifice. The priests of the Old Testament had offered animal sacrifices ceaselessly, but none of these had the power to effect our salvation. The bloody sacrifice of Christ on the cross is unique because it accomplished once and for all what the previous sacrifices failed to: our redemption. By virtue of Baptism, all Catholics are called to participate in the one priesthood of Christ. A focus of this section is to understand two ways that Catholics do this. The common

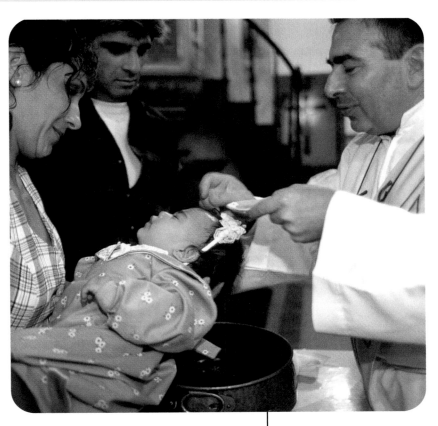

priesthood of the faithful is received at Baptism and deepened by Confirmation. The ministerial or hierarchical priesthood is received by bishops and priests through the Sacrament of Holy Orders.

Our share in the one priesthood of Christ was prefigured in the Old Testament. The entire nation of Israel had a priestly role through one tribe, the tribe of Aaron. In the instructions on priestly consecration, God said to Moses:

> Take the vestments and clothe Aaron with the tunic. . . . Put the miter on his head, the sacred diadem on the miter. Then take the anointing oil and anoint him with it, pouring it on his head. Bring forward his sons also and clothe them with the tunics, gird them with the sashes, and

redemption
God's saving action through Jesus Christ that saved people from sin and death.

tie the turbans on them. Thus shall the priesthood be theirs by perpetual law, and thus shall you ordain Aaron and his sons. (Ex 29:5–9)

Also, the book of Numbers describes an occasion when the Lord asked Moses to collect one staff from one prince of each of the twelve tribes and place them in the tent where the Commandments were kept. Aaron's staff sprouted flowers and even ripe almonds, prefiguring Christ's own body, which would miraculously bring forth the Baptism and Eucharist, signified by the water and blood that flowed from his side.

Aaron's tribe was the Levites. God chose the Levites to act as priests for the Israelite community. The Levites had a particular responsibility for the liturgical life of the community; and it was their job to act on behalf of the community in offering gifts and sacrifices to God. For example, if an Israelite man and son brought one of their prized sheep into the Temple grounds, they themselves would carry the sheep to a special place to cut the animal's throat and catch the animal's blood in a basin. When the sheep was dead, the father and son would carry it to the **altar of holocausts**, where a priest would meet them standing before a fire. The priest would take the blood from the basin and pour it around the altar. Then the priest would skin the animal and cut it into large pieces. Each part of the sheep, including its head and feet, would be placed on the coals and consumed by the fire.

Later in Israel's history, as the circumstances changed, priests took on other roles besides that of offering sacrifices. When the Israelites were in exile in Babylon, there were no sacrifices because they were exiled from the Temple. The priests emerged during this time as teachers and leaders. They led regular sessions of study and prayer. Also, it was the priests who rewrote and organized large portions of the Scriptures during the time of captivity. When the people were finally released and permitted to return to Jerusalem, the priests resumed their role of offering sacrifice, but continued on as leaders and teachers. The Israelite kings of that period were weak and ineffective and were typically nothing more than political puppets of the foreign government in charge. It was the priests to whom the people looked for moral, religious, and even political leadership.

altar of holocausts
In the Old Testament, a small mound of stones upon which the flesh of sacrificed animals could be burned. The word holocaust means "sacrifice."

The Common Priesthood Shares in the Priesthood of Christ

There was one Old Testament priest who explicitly prefigured Jesus Christ. His name was

Melchizedek, and he is identified in Genesis 14:18 as "king of Salem" and a "priest of God Most High" who brought the gifts of bread and wine to Abram prior to the establishment of the covenant with Abram and his renaming as Abraham.

In the New Testament, the letter to the Hebrews describes Jesus as a "high priest forever according to the order of Melchizedek" (Heb 6:20). By his sacrifice on the cross, a single offering, Jesus merited all the grace for the salvation of mankind. In Christ, we have a high priest who is compassionate and approachable. Hebrews also offers some other glimpses into how Jesus is the unique high priest:

- Jesus was called by God. He is the Son of God. "You are my son; this day I have begotten you" (Heb 5:5).

- Jesus is the perfect mediator because he is one of us, sharing our human weakness. "For we do not have a high priest who is unable to sympathize with our weaknesses, but one who has similarly been tested in every way, yet without sin" (Heb 4:15).

- Unlike the Jewish priests who offered sacrifices every day, Jesus had only to offer one, perfect sacrifice. "For by one offering he has made perfect forever those who are being consecrated" (Heb 10:14).

- Jewish priests offered the blood of animals; Jesus offered his own blood. "But when Christ came as high priest . . . he entered once for all into the sanctuary, not with the blood of goats and calves but with his own blood, thus obtaining eternal redemption" (Heb 9:11, 12).

- Jesus' sacrifice atoned for all sins, sanctified everyone, and established a New Covenant. "He is mediator of a new covenant: since a death has taken place for deliverance from transgressions under the first covenant, those who are called may receive the promised eternal inheritance" (Heb 9:15).

- Jewish priests entered the sanctuary and visited God alone; Jesus entered the sanctuary where God is and enabled us all to enter with him. "For Christ did not enter into a sanctuary made by human hands, a copy of the true one, but heaven itself, that he might now appear before God on our behalf" (Heb 9:24).

- Jesus now intercedes for us in Heaven. He is the eternal priest. "Just as it is appointed that human beings die once, and after this the judgment, so also Christ, offered once to take away the sins of many, will appear a second time, not to take away sin but to bring salvation to those who eagerly await him" (Heb 9:27–28).

Jesus Christ, the High Priest and mediator, is the head of the Body of Christ, the Church. Through the Sacraments of Baptism and Confirmation,

common priesthood

The priesthood of the faithful. Christ has made the Church a "kingdom of priests" who share in his priesthood through the Sacraments of Baptism and Confirmation.

Catholics become members of a priestly people. We not only become members of Christ's body, we become priests who share in the one priesthood of Christ and mediate or bring God's presence to others. This **common priesthood** is lived through the expression of the graces received at Baptism—"a life of faith, hope, and charity, a life according to the Spirit" (*CCC*, 1547). More specifically, we participate in the common priesthood and share in the priesthood of Christ when we:

- share our faith with others in our words and actions;

- participate in building up the Church and the community, especially in the service of the poor and less fortunate;

- join in the sacraments, especially the Eucharist;

- take up our cross and accept the suffering that comes our way.

As Saint Paul's letter to the Colossians advises: "And whatever you do, in word or in deed, do everything in the name of the Lord Jesus, giving thanks to God the Father through him" (Col 3:17).

Christ Is Made Present through the Ministerial Priesthood

Saint Thomas Aquinas wrote: "Only Christ is the true priest, the others being only his minister."[3] In the ordained minister (especially the bishop and the priest), it is Christ himself who is present to the Church. Through the Sacrament of Holy Orders, the priest acts in the person of Christ, teaching, sanctifying, and

"Go-betweens" for Christ and the World

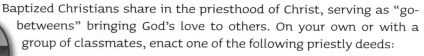

Baptized Christians share in the priesthood of Christ, serving as "go-betweens" bringing God's love to others. On your own or with a group of classmates, enact one of the following priestly deeds:

- *Share Christ's Message.* Organize a Scripture study during the lunch hour or after school. Study a Scripture passage with some friends. Discuss its meaning. Plan ways to put the passage into action.

- *Build Up the Community.* Bridge differences and hurt feelings within your school or peer group. Reconcile with anyone you have hurt and offer forgiveness to anyone who has hurt you. On a school-wide basis, discover peer groups or individuals in conflict. Reflect on ways to bring everyone together.

- *Serve Others.* Reflect on the servant leadership modeled by Christ. How can you serve others "as the least" rather than as someone in power? Determine several possibilities and then put one of the ideas into practice.

- *Worship.* Share in Christ's priesthood by offering your prayer and worship to God the Father. Let the Spirit pray through you. With a friend, attend a weekday Mass. After Mass, talk over the meaning of the Scripture readings. Think about ways you can put the readings into practice.

governing the people. Through bishops and priests, Christ's presence as head of the Church is made visible to the rest of the faithful, the common priesthood.

Jesus Christ is present in the bishop and his co-worker priests. It is through bishops and priests that Christ preaches the Word of God, administers the sacraments, evangelizes new members, and guides the Church toward eternal happiness. The ordained ministers are "servants of Christ and dispensers of the mysteries of God."[4] Again, recall how this ministerial priesthood differs from the common priesthood: whereas the laity are concerned with the unfolding of baptismal grace for their own life, the ministerial priesthood is at the service of the common priesthood. It is directed at the unfolding of the baptismal grace of all Christians. The ministerial priesthood is a *means* by which Christ unceasingly builds up and leads his Church. For this reason it is transmitted by its own sacrament, the Sacrament of Holy Orders (*CCC*, 1547).

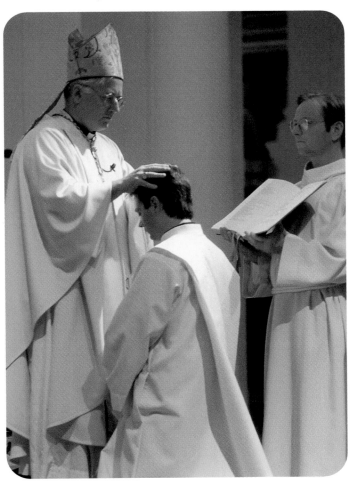

Through the Sacrament of Holy Orders, the Holy Spirit empowers men for the ministerial priesthood. The Sacrament confers on the man a sacred power, which is none other than the power of Christ. But as Christ exercised his power by making himself the least and servant of all, bishops and priests must do the same, taking up the instruction of Jesus himself from Mark 10:43–45.

The priest also acts in the name of the whole Church when presenting to God the prayer of the Church, especially the Eucharist. However, the priest does not offer the prayer as a delegate or representative of the community. Rather, the prayer and offering cannot be separated from the prayer and offering of Christ, who worships in and through the Church. The whole Church prays and offers itself "through him, with him, in him" in the unity of the Holy Spirit to God the Father. Because the priest is a representative of Christ, he is also a representative of the Church. When the priest consecrates the bread and wine at Eucharist, he does so in the person of Christ. Through the Sacrament of Holy Orders, the priest is configured to Christ at the very depth of his being.

study questions

1. Why is Christ alone the one high priest?

2. What is the difference between the sacrifices offered by the priests of the Old Testament and the sacrifice of Christ?

3. How did Aaron's staff prefigure Christ's body?

4. Which tribe was to act as priests for the Israelite community?

5. Besides offering sacrifices, what were some other roles priests took on in Israel's history?

6. Who was Melchizedek?

7. Name three ways the letter to the Hebrews describes Jesus as the unique high priest.

8. How do Catholics participate in the common priesthood and share in the priesthood of Christ?

9. How does the common priesthood differ from the ministerial priesthood?

10. How does the priest exercise the sacred power conferred on him in the Sacrament of Holy Orders?

pastors
From the word "shepherd," pastors, such as the Pope and bishops, care for the people using the model of Christ the Good Shepherd.

journal**discussion**

- Describe a time you sacrificed for another. Describe a time someone sacrificed on your behalf.

- Who is someone you know who models the servant leadership of Christ? How so?

◆ The Historical Development of Holy Orders

The ministerial priesthood is also called the hierarchical priesthood because by its very nature and at its founding it established an essential structure: the Church was made up of a flock and **pastors** who were appointed to care for them. The first pastors were the Apostles. The successors to the Apostles were the order of bishops who were chosen by the Apostles.

Like the Church itself, the ordained ministry is a product of apostolic succession. Jesus chose twelve *Apostles*, a word that means "one sent" to be his emissaries or ambassadors to the world. Through the Apostles, Christ continues his own mission: "As the Father has sent me, even so I send you" (Jn 20:21). And when the Apostles were welcomed in their ministry, those who received them were actually receiving Christ and God who sent him. As an ancient Church tradition expressed: "The Church from the Apostles, the Apostles from Christ, Christ from God."[5]

The number twelve is significant because it represents the twelve tribes of Israel and the universality of the Church. The Apostles were with Jesus throughout his life, hearing his teachings, witnessing his miracles, his Death, and his Resurrection. Note that Matthias, the Apostle who replaced Judas, had also been with Jesus since the start of his ministry and had witnessed the resurrected Lord (see Acts 1:21–26).

The ministry of the Apostles and the age of the Church really begins at Pentecost with the coming of the Holy Spirit. The gift of the Spirit gave the Apostles courage to preach the Gospel to the ends of the earth. The Apostles did indeed proclaim the Gospel. They forgave sins, healed the sick, and celebrated the Lord's Supper in the name of Jesus. The Apostles also guided the Christian communities and helped to settle any disputes that arose. In the first letter of Peter, on whom Jesus founded the Church, Peter writes that presbyters should care for the Church in imitation of Christ, the "chief Shepherd":

> So I exhort the presbyters among you, as a fellow presbyter and witness to the sufferings of Christ and one who has a share in the glory to be revealed: Tend the flock of God in your midst, [overseeing] not by constraint but willingly, as God would have it, not for shameful profit but eagerly. Do not lord it over those assigned to you, but be examples to the flock. And when the chief Shepherd is revealed, you will receive the unfading crown of glory. (1 Pt 5:1–4)

During the first century, a number of Christian churches necessarily began to meet without one of the Apostles present. Several false teachers emerged who used the name of Christ to do things that were very different from what Christ intended. The Apostles appointed helpers who fulfilled different ministries. Jewish Christian communities included the model of ministry used in Jewish synagogues with elders, prophets, and preachers. It was the early Gentile Christians who developed the more familiar structure with the *episcopos,* or bishop, who was to be the one chief administrator in each community. The bishop was responsible for overseeing the religious and moral life, for ensuring that those in need were cared for, and for safeguarding Church doctrine. As the local churches multiplied both in total number and in membership within each community, presbyters, or priests, were given the responsibility of pastoral care for these churches. Deacons aided the bishops and priests by ministering to the poor and widows, serving at Eucharist, and preaching God's word.

The Structure of the Ordained Ministry Emerges

The Church functions through the ministry of people with a variety of different gifts. This was true from the beginning. Saint Paul used the image of how each person's gifts function as part of the one body of Christ (see 1 Cor 12). Paul applied this image to the Church as a whole and to the ministry tasks of its members:

> Now you are Christ's body, and individually parts of it. Some people God has designated in the church to be first, apostles; second, prophets; third, teachers; then, mighty deeds; then gifts of healing, assistance, administration, and varieties of tongues. Are all apostles? Are all prophets? Are all teachers? Do all work mighty deeds? Do all have gifts of healing? Do all speak in tongues? Do all interpret? Strive eagerly for the greatest spiritual gifts. (1 Cor 12:20–31)

In all these cases, the gifts of the minister were for the benefit of building up Christ's body and not the glory of the individual having the gift. In the Scriptures, those appointed by the Apostles were marked through the external rite of the laying on of hands, which conferred a sacramental character. When Saint Timothy was made bishop, the influx of grace was attached to the laying on of hands. Timothy was told to "stir into flame the gift of God that you have through the imposition of my hands" (2 Tm 1:6).

Meanwhile a clear hierarchical structure in the Church arose at the beginning of the second century. During this time a bishop was chosen by the community after the apparent presence of the Holy Spirit was recognized within him. After his election, a bishop received the imposition of hands from another bishop. Saint Ignatius of Antioch emphasized the importance of the bishop. He decreed that only a bishop or his appointee could preside at Eucharist or baptize. Ignatius wrote:

> See that you all follow the bishop, even as Jesus Christ does the Father, and the presbytery as you would the apostles; and reverence the deacons, as being the institution of God. Let no man do anything connected with the Church without the bishop. Let that be deemed a proper Eucharist, which is [administered] either by the bishop, or by one to whom he has entrusted it. Wherever the bishop shall appear, there let the multitude [of the people] also be; even as, wherever Jesus Christ is, there is the Catholic Church.[6]

At this time, presbyters were ordained by the bishop, and other presbyters joined in the laying on of hands at the rite of ordination. Deacons were ordained by the bishop alone, and were ordained specifically to assist the bishop in his ministry. Acts of the Apostles lists the names of the first deacons, seven men, including Saint Stephen, the first martyr, who were designated to care for the poor. Once they were chosen, the community "presented these men to the apostles who prayed and laid hands on them" (Acts 6:6).

Saint Stephen

Events and Influences on the Priesthood

The edict of the emperor Constantine in 313 that led to the legalization of Christianity in the Roman Empire also had a profound effect on the priesthood. The edict conferred civil authority, status, and privilege on bishops and priests. The ordained came to be called the **clergy**, and divisions arose between them and the laity. The clergy

clergy

From a Latin word for "clerk," the clergy is distinguished from the laity and is made up of deacons, priests, and bishops.

were viewed to be devoted to the "higher things of the spirit" while lay people were concerned with the "lower things of the flesh."

Also, at this time the will of the people to choose and elect a bishop was no longer enough to guarantee a man would become a bishop; the approval of the state was also necessary, and the state paid his salary. Nevertheless, the Church Council of Chalcedon in 451 stated that priests were to be called by the people of a particular parish and ordained for work within that parish:

> No one, whether presbyter or deacon or anyone at all who belongs to the ecclesiastical order, is to be ordained without title, unless the one ordained is specially assigned to a city or village church or to a martyr's shrine or a monastery.[7]

Anyone who was ordained without being called by the parish was to have his ordination declared null and void, and the bishop who ordained him, not the state, was responsible for paying his salary.

From the sixth through twelfth centuries there were other significant influences on the life of the ordained. In the Middle Ages, priests took a role in the **feudal system** and were responsible for the collection of taxes in certain cases. Second, new rites of ordination were added in the Frankish churches. The bishop was anointed with holy chrism, presented with a **crosier** and ring, and enthroned. The ordination rite for priests was expanded with the anointing of the hands, the presentation of the gifts of bread and wine, and a second laying of hands for the absolution of sins. This German

influence on ordination represented the connection between a princely power for bishops and a local cultic power for priests.

The growing monastic life of the Middle Ages also had a great influence on the priesthood. Though most monks were not ordained, there was a need for priests in the monasteries. Some monks were ordained and

Depiction of an eleventh-century monk, archbishop, and priest.

many priests of that period did take on the religious habit, prayers, study, and strict discipline of monasticism, including celibacy. These practices led to the requirement of celibacy for

feudal system
A political and economic system of the Middle Ages that traded use of land for obedience to the owner of the land.

crosier
A crook-shaped staff carried by bishops to represent the bishop's pastoral or shepherding role.

the ordained at the Second Lateran Council in 1139. Prior to that time, priests (not bishops) were permitted to be married, though many priests already lived a single, celibate life.

Also during the Middle Ages, more and more priests were needed to celebrate Mass, so while the ordinations to the presbyterate increased, the order of the diaconate declined as an active ministry. The diaconate evolved to a step on the way to priesthood. A series of other minor orders for men on the way to priesthood were initiated: *porters*, who called the community to worship by ringing the bells; *lectors*, who read the Scripture readings at Mass (other than the Gospel); *exorcists,* who would assist the bishop and priest in driving out the evil spirits of the **catechumens** in preparation for Baptism; and *acolytes*, who served at Mass and at one time assisted the celebrant in the breaking of the eucharistic bread for distribution at communion. In 1972, Pope Paul VI cancelled the four minor orders and replaced them with the ministries of lector (reader) and acolyte, now celebrated as steps on the path to ordination.

Reaffirming Holy Orders

The Protestant reformers, among whom Martin Luther, a former Catholic priest, was most prominent, emphasized the role of the common priesthood and taught that there was no ministerial power received through the Sacrament of Holy Orders. The sixteenth century Council of Trent countered this teaching and reaffirmed that Holy Orders was one of the Seven Sacraments and that bishops and priests depend on the graces of the

Sacrament for their authority and power to celebrate Eucharist and forgive sins, not on a call from the Church. The Council of Trent did inspire several reforms in the Church, including the establishment of **seminaries** to train the candidates for priesthood. The teachings of Trent continue to influence Catholic belief and practice to this day.

The Second Vatican Council (1962–1965) emphasized two teachings regarding Holy Orders and the priesthood. First, it reaffirmed that the mission of the common priesthood is to live the baptismal calling to be priest, prophet, and servant of God's Kingdom. Second, it taught that the role of the ordained minister was to be of service to the common priesthood and to "unfold" the baptismal grace of all Christians. The ordained are called to facilitate the action of God's grace within the Church so that lay people may receive grace within the sacraments and then be able to share that grace with the world.

Another teaching of the Council surrounded the importance of the bishop; it reminded the Church that the fullness of the Sacrament of Holy Orders resides in the episcopate. Through ordination, bishops receive the mandate to sanctify, teach, and govern in the Church. Priests share with the bishops in the one priesthood and ministry of Christ.

Also, the Second Vatican Council restored the *permanent diaconate*, an order of service ministry open to both married and single men. Deacons continue to minister in their original roles of service to bishops and priests in pastoral duties like caring for the needs of the poor, catechetical ministries such as preparing catechumens for Baptism and candidates for Confirmation, and liturgical duties such as preaching at Mass, performing Baptisms, and witnessing marriages.

1. Why is the ministerial priesthood also called the hierarchical priesthood?

2. Why is the number twelve significant as a number of Apostles?

3. What were the responsibilities of the bishop in Church life during the first century?

4. How were bishops chosen in the second century?

5. What were the effects of the edict of Constantine and the legalization of Christianity on the priesthood?

6. What was the German influence on ordination in the Middle Ages?

7. How did the Church mandate for priestly celibacy arise?

8. Name and define the functions of the four minor orders.

9. How did the Council of Trent reaffirm the Church's understanding of Holy Orders?

10. What are two main teachings on Holy Orders emphasized by the Second Vatican Council?

Qualities of Leadership

Do you consider yourself a leader? In fact, if you are planning to apply for college, you will find out one of the most important criteria for admission is evidence of leadership skills. For example, most colleges today may give more credence to a person who organized and led a clothing drive for the poor over a person who simply donated a few clothing items and claimed himself or herself as a "clothing drive participant." For each of the leadership qualities below, rate yourself using the following scale: **3**=I strongly agree; **2**=I agree; **1**=I do not agree.

1. I am confident in meeting most new challenges.

2. I have a vision of where I should be going in my personal life, and where society, in general, should be heading.

3. I am willing to learn new things and am open to many possible solutions.

4. I can apply my previous experience and knowledge to new tasks.

5. I possess stamina and energy from the start to the finish of a task or project.

6. I work well with others and view myself as a collaborative leader.

7. I possess integrity, honesty, and moral character: I act on what is right.

8. I am an active and effective listener.

9. I understand and respect the nature of power.

10. I keep perspective. I understand that my place in life is as a child of God.

One responsibility of bishops, priests, and deacons is to build up and support the common priesthood of the People of God. This task requires leadership skills. Read the following passages from the Gospel of Matthew. Write what value of leadership Jesus is describing in each passage. Tell why this is a necessary value of leadership for a bishop, priest, or deacon.

- ✦ Matthew 5:13–16
- ✦ Matthew 6:31–34
- ✦ Matthew 10:7–10
- ✦ Matthew 18:15–20
- ✦ Matthew 20:20–28
- ✦ Matthew 26:26–29

primacy
The Pope, as successor of Saint Peter as Bishop of Rome, exercises highest authority as Vicar of Christ and shepherd of the whole Church.

Ecumenical Council
A worldwide official assembly of the bishops under the direction of the Pope. There have been twenty-one Ecumenical Councils. The first was the First Council of Nicaea (325). The most recent was the Second Vatican Council (1962–1965).

Saint Peter

journaldiscussion

- What does this phrase mean to you: "The Church from the Apostles, the Apostles from Christ, Christ from God"?

- What are some ways in your life that you show your devotion to "higher things of the spirit"?

✦ A Definition of Holy Orders Today

From the earliest days of the Church, its ministry has been ordered in different degrees by men who have been called bishops, priests, and deacons. Before beginning a discussion in this section of some of the traditional roles and ministries of the three degrees of Holy Orders, it is appropriate to first examine the role of the Supreme Pontiff, or Pope, in the hierarchical structure of the Church.

The hierarchy of the Church continues the ministry of Saint Peter and the Apostles. The Pope—from the Latin word for "papa" or "father"—is the successor of Peter. As the bishop of Rome—the place where Peter ministered and was martyred—the Pope has **primacy** of authority over the whole Church. This belief is based on Christ's own teaching in response to Peter identifying Jesus as the Messiah (see Mt 16:17–19).

The Pope and all the bishops form a single entity called the college of bishops. The bishops, in communion with one another and with the Pope, have the task of truthfully teaching the Word of God. They do this when they come together in an **Ecumenical Council**. The Pope's special role is to be a sign of unity when the bishops speak as one. He is the head. He speaks with the bishops as the voice of Christ alive in the Church. His role among them has been described as "first among equals." More information about the role of the Pope and the election process for a Pope is included in the Catholic Handbook for Faith, pages 314–315.

The Pope and other bishops participate in the priesthood of Christ through their ordination into the episcopacy, one of the two degrees of ministerial priesthood. The presbyterate is the other degree of ministerial participation in the priesthood of Christ. The diaconate is the third degree of ordination. Deacons are ordained to help and serve the priests and bishops. The two degrees of priestly participation and one degree of service are conferred by the Sacrament of Holy Orders. Saint Ignatius of Antioch wrote:

> Let everyone revere the deacons as Jesus Christ, the bishop as the image of the Father, and the presbyters as the senate of God and the assembly of the apostles. For without them one cannot speak of the Church.[8]

Episcopacy—The Bishop

The episcopate represents the fullness of the Sacrament of Holy Orders, the high priesthood, and the summit of sacred ministry. Like the Pope, a bishop is part of an unbroken succession of leadership that can be traced to the Apostles. The Apostles were given a special outpouring of the Holy Spirit by Christ, and, by the laying on of hands, passed on this special gift of the Spirit. This gift is now transmitted through the consecration of a new bishop at ordination.

The Second Vatican Council likewise taught that the fullness of the Sacrament of Holy Orders is conferred with the bishop's consecration. In the traditional language of the Church, this consecration ordains the bishop for the high priesthood, the summit of sacred ministry.

Today, a bishop is chosen by the Pope from among priests, often based on the recommendation of the bishop of the priest's home diocese, though even if selected for the episcopacy, the new bishop can be assigned to any diocese by the Vatican. Ordination to the episcopacy makes a bishop a member of the college of bishops. He is then empowered as a "true and authentic teacher of the faith." This membership also allows a bishop to be able to consecrate new bishops. In fact, several bishops participate in the ordination of new bishops to represent their **collegiality**. According to Church law, the ordination of a new bishop requires the approval of the Pope.

A bishop is assigned the pastoral care of his own church, a diocese. But at the same time, he bears responsibility with all of the bishops for the care of the entire universal Church.

There is great significance when a bishop celebrates the Eucharist because it is "an expression of the Church gathered around the altar" (*CCC*, 1561) as one who represents Christ, the High Priest and Good Shepherd.

collegiality
The participation of each of the worldwide bishops, with the Pope as their head, in a "college," which takes responsibility for both their local diocesan churches and the Church as a whole.

Presbyterate—The Priest

The presbyterate, or priesthood, is the second level of Holy Orders. The presbyterate is a subordinate degree to the episcopacy. Priests are ordained to be the coworkers of the bishop and to help him with the various tasks of his ministry.

Like the episcopacy, the priesthood is conferred with its own sacrament, apart from Baptism. Through the Sacrament of Holy Orders, priests are signed with a special character and configured to the priesthood of Christ so that they are able to act in the person of Christ.

Priests collaborate with the bishop by serving the People of God. The role of the priest can best be described as being the representative of the bishop in local parishes. Bishops are not able to be everywhere at once. In the parish, the priest is challenged with a diverse ministry to people of all ages, genders, races, and social classes. It is a challenging life. The parish becomes the priest's family as he takes a central and focused role in many of the significant events—both joyful and sorrowful—in the lives of his parishioners. Other priestly ministries are discussed in chapter 9.

Alter Christus

Father Theodore Hesburgh, C.S.C. (see also pages 160–161), was President of the University of Notre Dame for thirty-five years, retiring in 1987. In many ways, being president of a major university was only Father Ted's "day job." During those years and beyond, Father Ted has been an adviser to seven presidents of the United States. He served on fifteen presidential commissions and was a member of the Presidential Clemency Board after the Vietnam War, charged with reviewing thousands of clemency cases for those who avoided or resisted the military draft.

Father Ted has received over 120 honorary degrees, flown in a Mach 3.35 jet faster than the speed of sound, and said Mass all over the world, including Antarctica.

In spite of this varied and storied career, he said, "I have been asked, if only one word could be put on my tombstone, what would I choose? My answer was, 'Priest.'" In a testimony on priesthood, Father Ted reflected on the special contribution a priest can make to society:

> I believe it is simply to be an *alter Christus*, "another Christ." Jesus wants to be present to people everywhere, and one of the ways he can do that is through his priests. We can make him present first by delivering his message. To be effective, that message must be adapted to current times, made real for people to whom it would otherwise be just words. Jesus could do that in his day; he can't do it now. He needs someone to convey his message to people of every century in a form that has meaning. Second, the priest dispenses grace, officially through the sacraments, but often by just being there. Cardinal Emmanuel Suhard of Paris, one of my early heroes, had a wonderful expression, *l' apostolate de la presence*, "the apostolate of the presence," just being there.[9]

Fr. Theodore Hesburgh, C.S.C.

No matter the priest's specific type of ministry, he can only exercise it in obedience to the bishop; he is dependent on the bishop and has no authority apart from him. At ordination, the priest makes a promise of obedience to the bishop and receives a kiss of peace from the bishop at the end of the ordination liturgy. This kiss means that the bishop considers the priest his coworker, his son, his brother, and his friend, and that the priest owes him his love and obedience. Likewise, priests find friendship and brotherhood with other priests—a sacramental brotherhood—and in a special way with the priests of their own home diocese. This connection is represented in the Sacrament of Holy Orders when the priests from the diocese impose hands on the newly ordained after the bishop does the same.

As the Eucharist is the heart and summit of the Church's life, the eucharistic liturgy is likewise at the heart of the priest's life. To offer the Sacrifice of the Mass is the principal power of the presbyterate. At Eucharist, priests act in the person of Christ and unite the offerings of the faithful to the sacrifice of Christ, the one high priest. The priest draws strength for his entire priestly ministry from his role in the celebration of Eucharist.

In addition to their role at Eucharist, priests are also consecrated to preach the Gospel and to shepherd the faithful; they are proper ministers of the Sacraments of Baptism, Penance, and Anointing of the Sick and serve as the Church's witness at the Sacrament of Matrimony.

Diaconate—The Deacon

The diaconate is the third level—"a lower level of the hierarchy"[10]—of the Sacrament of Holy Orders. At ordination, only the bishop lays hands on the candidate, thus conveying the deacon's special attachment to the bishop in the tasks of service.

Deacons participate in the mission and grace of Christ in a way that marks them with a character that cannot be removed and that also configures them to Christ. The word deacon comes from the Greek word *diakonoi*, which translates as "servant" or "waiter." The call of Stephen and the other deacons in the Acts of the Apostles arose because the Apostles were spending too much of their time handling the distribution of goods to the needy rather than preaching the Gospel. The Apostles gathered together a large group of disciples and said, "It is not right for us to neglect the word of God to serve at table" (Acts 6:2).

Among the tasks of service for the bishop to which the deacons are assigned are assisting the bishops and priests at Mass, witnessing marriages, reading the Scripture and preaching the homily at Mass, presiding at funerals, and participating in various works of charity.

There are two types of deacons. There are those who are ordained to the diaconate as a step along the way to priesthood. These "transitional deacons" make promises of obedience and celibacy at the time of ordination. The permanent diaconate is the second type. This can be conferred on men of more mature age, both married and single. The permanent diaconate was restored at the Second Vatican Council by the Latin Church. The Eastern Church had always ordained men to serve as permanent deacons. Christ himself is the model of the diaconate. His entire ministry and vocation was devoted to service on behalf of others.

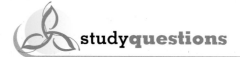

studyquestions

1. What does it mean to say that the Pope has primacy over the whole Church?

2. What is the Pope's role in the college of bishops?

3. How is a man chosen as a candidate for the episcopacy today?

4. What does a bishop's consecration empower him to do?

5. What is the significance of a bishop's celebrating the Eucharist?

6. Describe the role of the priest.

7. What is the promise a priest makes to the bishop at his ordination? What is the promise a bishop makes to the priest?

8. What is the principal source of power of the priesthood?

9. To what tasks are deacons assigned?

10. Name and explain the two types of deacons.

journaldiscussion

- Tell about a time you have participated in decision making in a collegial way.

- How can you practice "the apostolate of the presence" in bringing Christ to others?

✦ Who Can Receive the Sacrament of Holy Orders

Think ahead to your high school graduation. Let's say that you imagine yourself to be a pretty fair public speaker. You enjoy getting up before large groups of people and persuading them to your point of view, telling a few jokes, or making some very cogent points on a number of topics of interest. You decide you are the one to give your class's valedictorian address.

What would happen if you approached your school principal or dean in charge of determining the valedictorian and other speakers for graduation day? How would your demand be received? More than likely, you would be told that the right to choose the valedictorian belongs to the school, not you. The school officials might then list for you all of the established criteria for selecting the class valedictorian, i.e., leadership skills, grade point average, participation in school activities. Your desire to be valedictorian may or may not end right at that point. In fact, the principal may tell you, "Don't call us; we'll call you!"

Apply this analogy to the priesthood. Just because a person desires for himself to be a priest, does not mean one has a *right* to receive the Sacrament of Holy Orders. Rather, a person is first called to the priesthood by God. Next,

> Anyone who thinks he recognizes the signs of God's call to the ordained ministry must humbly submit his desire to the authority of the Church, who has the responsibility and right to call someone to receive orders. Like every grace this sacrament can only be *received* as an unmerited gift. (*CCC*, 1578)

To be considered a candidate for ordination, a man must be called to this special vocation by Christ. Therefore, ordination is not a right that

anyone can demand, but a privilege for those who have been called by God.

Why Only Men Can Be Priests

Pope John Paul II addressed the Catholic practice of ordaining only men to the priesthood in a 1995 Apostolic Letter to the Catholic bishops. The Pope, quoting Pope Paul VI, explained that there are very fundamental reasons why the Church holds that it is not admissible to ordain women to the priesthood. The reasons for this teaching form part of the Church's "deposit of faith," which it has received from Christ.

First, when Jesus chose the twelve Apostles to carry on his work, he only chose men. Christ made this choice in union with the will of God the Father: These men received from Christ very specific instructions regarding their mission and ministry: "He appointed twelve [whom he also named Apostles] that they might be with him

Jesus choosing the Apostles.

and he might send them forth to preach and to have the authority to drive out demons" (Mk 3:14–15). Christ chose the Apostles to have a role of leadership and as the foundation for his Church.

Likewise, when it was the turn of the twelve Apostles to pass on the mission they were given by Christ, they, too, chose only men to be their successors. See 1 Timothy 3:1–13, 2 Timothy 1:6, and Titus 1:5–9 for examples from Scripture in which the Apostles, including Saint Paul, chose men to be bishops or presbyters. Even when the Apostles had the chance to replace Judas, they did not replace him with a woman, though many women disciples, including the Blessed Virgin Mary, were often present with them in the time surrounding Pentecost.

That Mary herself did not receive the specific mission of the Apostles nor the call to ministerial priesthood is not only a sign that Christ intended only men to be ordained, but it also, according to Pope John Paul II, demonstrates clearly that the non-admission of women to priestly ordination cannot mean that women are of lesser dignity, nor can it be construed as discrimination against them. Rather, it is to be seen as the faithful observance of a plan to be ascribed to the wisdom of the Lord of the universe.[11]

Jesus went against the cultural norms of his day in his relationships with women. Jesus regularly interacted with a group of women and had several women disciples during a period and place in history in which women and men typically were not friends, especially in public. He taught women "at his feet." In his society, women were not usually allowed to learn directly from a rabbi at the synagogue or any other forum. The Gospels record that a group of women disciples were the first to attest to Jesus' Resurrection and were counted on to proclaim the Resurrection to others. Nevertheless, Jesus still did not count them among the twelve Apostles.

This deposit of faith is often questioned today when the fundamental equality and dignity of women is stressed. But the Church responds that the gift of a vocation to the priesthood for men can be compared to the vocation of motherhood for women. Like ordination, motherhood can only be received as an unmerited gift. A woman cannot will herself to be a mother. Also, as Holy Orders is a sacrament for the service of others, motherhood is not primarily for the benefit of the mother, but for the good of the child.

Finally, though they are not called to ordination, the presence and role of women in the life and mission of the Church remains invaluable. Women can hold many leadership positions in the Church. Many of the ministries that were once traditionally done exclusively by priests are done by the laity now and do not require ordination. Under the direction of the bishop and pastors, these ministries are now undertaken by lay people, both men and women.

The Gift of Celibacy and Other Spiritual Requirements for Priests

While the presence of married priests in the early history of the Church and in the Eastern Church still today shows that celibacy is not demanded of priests by the nature of the Sacrament of Holy Orders, it is also clear that a commitment to chastity or celibacy for the sake of the Kingdom of Heaven was recommended by Christ by his own example (he did not marry) and in his own words:

> Some are incapable of marriage because they were born so; some, because they were made so by others; some, because they have renounced marriage for the sake of the kingdom of heaven. Whoever can accept this ought to accept it. (Mt 19:12)

Also, Saint Paul in his letters expressed that remaining celibate for the sake of the kingdom was the preferred or superior state of life for those who were able to keep it:

> Indeed, I wish everyone to be as I am, but each has a particular gift from God, one of one kind and one of another. Now to the unmarried and to widows, I say: It is

a good thing for them to remain as they are, as I do. (1 Cor 7:7–8)

Celibacy for the ordained in the Catholic Church is a discipline, not a doctrine. While the practice of celibacy in the Latin Rite for priests dates from the time of Christ, it was not made mandatory for priests until the Second Lateran Council declared that any marriage entered into by a priest was to be considered invalid. Pope Paul VI reconfirmed the Church's mandatory requirement of celibacy for the priesthood with the reminder that it should be firmly linked to Church ministry and that the law of celibacy should support the priest in his "exclusive, definitive and total choice of the unique and supreme love of Christ."[12]

There are practical reasons that celibacy is a wonderful gift for the ordained and an enhancement of their ministry. For example:

- Jesus is the model for chastity for all people according to their particular states in life. The commitment of a priest to celibacy is in imitation of Christ who himself was celibate.

- Remaining celibate allows priests to more easily dedicate themselves to Christ and to the service of God. Celibacy frees a person from family obligations and therefore allows priests or bishops to give themselves totally to the Lord.

- By not marrying, a priest is a living sign of the future when there will be no marriage and when Christ will be the Church's only spouse.

- Jesus spoke of the requirements of discipleship along with the willingness to give up one's life for his sake and the sake of the Gospel. Forsaking the blessings of a spouse and a family is a dramatic example of a person's acceptance of the path of a disciple. Jesus said, "And everyone who has given up houses or brothers or sisters or father or mother or children or lands for the sake of my name will receive a hundred times more, and will inherit eternal life" (Mt 19:29).

The Eastern Churches have practiced a different discipline regarding married clergy for many centuries. Married men can be ordained priests and deacons, while bishops are chosen solely from among celibate men. There are also some married priests in the Latin Rite Church. Since the Second Vatican Council, exceptions have been made for some Anglican priests and other Protestant ministers who have later converted to Catholicism and wish to be priests in the Catholic Church. As noted previously, the Council also restored a permanent diaconate to which married men are ordained.

In union with the pledge to celibacy, a priest also makes a pledge to the spiritual gifts of humility and obedience and, particularly in the case of religious-order priests, voluntary poverty of worldly goods. More information about these spiritual requirements will be covered in chapter 9.

Celibacy in Other Religious Traditions

There are many variations on celibacy rules for priests and leaders in other Christian denominations and religious traditions. As mentioned, in the Eastern-Rite Catholic churches (which are in full communion with the Pope and the Roman Catholic Church), married men may be ordained deacons or priests, but may not be ordained bishops. Also, a man may not marry after he is ordained to any level of Holy Orders.

Anglican (Episcopalian) Churches allow married deacons, priests, and bishops. Some Anglican religious orders do require their priests to remain celibate.

Other Protestant denominations have no rules about celibacy or marriage for their clergy or ministers.

Jewish rabbis may marry. In some traditions of Buddhism, monks are required to remain celibate.

Research more about the connection between the practice of celibacy and religious life. Complete one of the following:

- Read and report on statements of early Church councils—the Council of Elvira (300–306) and the Council of Carthage (390)—on priestly celibacy.

- Research the stance on clerical celibacy in two or more Eastern Churches not in communion with the Roman Church (e.g., the Russian Church, the Coptic Church, the Armenian Church).

- Report on the actual circumstances of a Latin Rite priest who is married.

study questions

1. What does it mean to say that "no one has a right to receive the Sacrament of Holy Orders"?

2. What are the fundamental reasons that the Church ordains only men?

3. How is motherhood for women comparable to ordination for men?

4. What are practical reasons that celibacy is an enhancement to the ordained ministry?

5. How does the Eastern Church's tradition differ from the Latin Rite in regards to celibacy and the priesthood?

journal discussion

- What would you tell a young man who told you he wanted to be a priest?

- What are some ways that a celibate lifestyle can help a priest better serve the Church?

summary points

✦ The Scene in the Upper Room

✦ The Upper Room was the place and the Last Supper was the event where Christ instituted the priesthood.

✦ The priest exercises his sacred role in a supreme degree in the offering of Mass.

✦ The Sacrament of Holy Orders is the Sacrament of Apostolic Ministry.

✦ The Eucharist only comes to us to this day from Christ through apostolic succession.

✦ Sharing in Christ's Priesthood

✦ Jesus Christ is the one high priest who can offer the perfect sacrifice.

✦ By virtue of Baptism, all Catholics are called to participate in the one priesthood of Christ.

✦ Jesus Christ, the High Priest and mediator, is the head of the Body of Christ, the Church.

+ Through the ministerial priesthood, Christ's presence as head of the Church is made visible to the rest of the faithful, the common priesthood.

+ The Sacrament of Holy Orders empowers men for the ministerial priesthood.

+ The priest is configured to Christ at the very depth of his being.

The Historical Development of Holy Orders

+ Christ chose twelve Apostles. The successors to the Apostles were the order of bishops who were chosen by the Apostles.

+ From the earliest times, Apostles appointed helpers who fulfilled different ministries; these included bishops, priests, and deacons.

+ Those appointed by the Apostles were marked through the external rite of the laying on of hands that conferred a sacramental character.

+ The legalization of Christianity conferred civil authority, status, and privilege on bishops and priests.

+ Two significant influences impacted the priesthood in the Middle Ages: the priest's role in the feudal system and the example of the growing monastic life.

+ The Council of Trent reaffirmed the power and authority of the ministerial priesthood and the Sacrament of Holy Orders.

+ The Second Vatican Council emphasized the mission of the common priesthood and the importance of the bishop to sanctify, teach, and govern.

A Definition of the Three Holy Orders Today

+ As bishop of Rome, the Pope has primacy over the whole Church.

+ The episcopate represents the fullness of the Sacrament of Holy Orders, the high priesthood, and the summit of sacred ministry.

+ Episcopal ordination makes each bishop a member of the college of bishops.

+ A bishop, with the approval of the Pope, is able to consecrate new bishops.

+ The presbyterate, or priesthood, is the second level of Holy Orders.

+ Priests are ordained to be coworkers of the bishop and to be obedient to him.

+ Generally, the priest is a representative of the bishop in local parishes.

+ The diaconate is the third level of the Sacrament of Holy Orders.

+ Deacons do not share in the ministerial priesthood; rather, they are called to aid the bishop in tasks of service.

+ There are two types of deacons: transitional deacons, who are on the way to priestly ordination, and permanent deacons, who may be married men or single men of a mature age.

Who Can Receive the Sacrament of Holy Orders

+ No person has the *right* to receive the Sacrament of Holy Orders. Rather, a person is first called to priesthood by God.

+ Only men can be called to the priesthood. Jesus chose twelve male Apostles and did not call women to the ministerial priesthood.

+ Priests in the Roman Catholic Church observe the discipline of celibacy. This gift helps priests dedicate themselves more easily to Christ and the Church, to be a sign of the eternal kingdom, and to follow Christ's call to discipleship that asks for one to forsake the blessings of spouse and family.

1. Use a computer program that allows for charts and grids to make a comprehensive schedule of the weekend Masses at all the parishes within a ten-mile radius of where you live. Note any Masses with special features (e.g., language, teen-focus, etc.). Make copies and distribute the list to your classmates.

2. Graph statistics since 1965 on the number of priests, seminarians, parishes without a priest, ratio of priests to laity, and other relevant statistics. See the CARA website for more information: http://cara.georgetown.edu/bulletin/index.htm.

3. The Old Testament prophets reminded the people of the right interior disposition for offering sacrifices. Write a statement describing what each of these passages says about that disposition:

Jeremiah 6:19–20   Amos 5:21–27   Hosea 6:6

Apply each of these statements to your participation at Eucharist. Write a short essay describing the interior disposition you should bring to Mass.

4. Read Hebrews 4:14–8:6. Write a list of all of the ways this passage defines Jesus as the High Priest.

5. Research and report on the priesthood in the Middle Ages. Contrast the influence of the feudal system and monastic life on the role and ministry of priests during that period.

6. Use a diocesan directory to list the names of every bishop in the history of your diocese and the years he served.

7. Interview five priests. Ask each the same question: "What is at the heart of your life as a priest?" Record and share their answers.

8. Inquire in your parish about how to fulfill one of these ministries: a minister of Eucharist, a reader at Mass, or a sponsor for a catechumen. Take the proper steps to participate in one of these ministries. Write a report explaining the preparation that you went through.

9. What happened to each of the Apostles: Simon Peter, Andrew, James son of Zebedee, John, Philip, Bartholomew, Thomas, Matthew, James son of Alphaeus, Thaddeus, Simon the Cananean, and Matthias, who replaced Judas? Use information from the *Catholic Encyclopedia*, http://newadvent.com, to determine which local Church each Apostle served and how it is believed his life ended.

10. Choose and use any art form (e.g., drawing, painting, sculpture, film) to express the scene in the Upper Room on the night of the Last Supper when Jesus commissioned the Apostles as priests.

Notes

1. Quoted from Holy Thursday Letter of Pope John Paul II to His Priests, 2000.

2. According to The CARA Report, in 1965 there were 35,925 diocesan priests. In 2005 there were 28,375 diocesan priests.

3. Saint Thomas Aquinas, *Hebr.* 8, 4, quoted in *CCC*, 1545.

4. Quoted from *Lumen Gentium*, 22.

5. Tertullian, quoted from *De Praecr. Haer* XXI, 4.

6. Quoted from the *Letter to the Smyrnaeans*, Chapter 8.

7. Quoted from Canon 6 of the Council of Chalcedon.

8. Saint Ignatius of Antioch, *Ad Trall.* 3, 1: SCh 10, 96 quoted in *CCC*, 1554.

9. Quoted from *Extraordinary Lives: Thirty-Four Priests Tell Their Stories* by Francis P. Friedl and Rex Reynolds (Notre Dame, IN: Ave Maria Press, 1997).

10. Quoted from *Lumen Gentium*, 29.

11. Quoted from *Ordinatio Sacerdotalis*, 3.

12. Quoted from *Sacerdotalis caelibatus*, 14.

chapteroutline

chapter eight

The Sacrament of Holy Orders

Then he said to his disciples, "The harvest is abundant but the laborers are few; so ask the master of the harvest to send out laborers for his harvest."

Matthew 9:37–38

✦ Hearing God's Voice

When Abram was seventy-five years old, he heard God's voice. The Lord told Abram to leave his family, his father's house, and his home to go "to a land that I will show you." Abram—soon to be Abraham—"went as the Lord directed him" (Gn 12:1, 4).

Moses saw a "remarkable sight" in the desert, a bush that, though on fire, was not consumed. When he went nearer, God called out to Moses from the bush. Moses answered, "Here I am" (Ex 3:2–4).

Young Samuel was asleep when the Lord spoke to him in a dream. Samuel woke up Eli, the priest he was serving, several times saying, "Here I am. You called me." Finally Eli understood it was God who was calling to Samuel. He told Samuel that if God called him again, he should answer by saying, "Speak, Lord, for your servant is listening." Samuel did as he was told, and the Lord called him to his service as a prophet (1 Sm 3:1–19).

The Lord told Elijah to "Go outside and stand on the mountain before the Lord; the Lord will be passing by." Elijah did so and:

> A strong and heavy wind was rending the mountains and crushing rocks before the Lord—but the Lord was not in the wind. After the wind there was an earthquake—but the Lord was not in the earthquake. After the earthquake there was fire—but the Lord was not in the fire. After the fire there was a tiny whispering sound. When he heard this, Elijah hid his face in his cloak and went and stood at the entrance of the cave. (1 Kgs 19:11–13)

God's call to Elijah was not what he expected. But Elijah was able to recognize the Lord's voice.

In the New Testament, God's voice was heard loud and clear in the words of the Incarnate Son, Jesus Christ. Watching Simon and his brother Andrew cast their fishing nets into the sea, Jesus said to them, "Come after me, and I will make you fishers of men" (Mk 1:17). Though the charge was rather obscure—what did it mean to be "fishers of men"?—the two brothers left their fish, their boat, and their father to follow Jesus.

Perhaps God spoke the loudest of all to Saint Paul. On his way to Damascus to persecute more Christians, Paul was knocked to the ground as a flash of blinding lightning shone around him. Jesus' voice spoke to Paul telling him to "get up and go into the city and you will be told what you must do" (Acts 9:6).

There are two important messages to glean from these examples. First, from Abraham to Paul, the Scriptures are filled with occasions when God calls people to his service. Second, God calls people in countless different ways: in a command, in a dramatic natural sign, in a whisper, or even in a crushing knock to the ground.

God continues to call all Christians to his service and some men to his priestly service. Every ordained man today could likely tell of a specific occasion when he felt called to the priesthood. As in biblical times, the call comes in many different ways.

For example, in the first half of the twentieth century, the parish was the center of the everyday life for Catholics young and old. Priests were present in the schoolyard, in classrooms, in the neighborhood, as chaperones at CYO dances, and as coaches for athletic teams. Priests and the priestly life had charism and appeal to the young men who grew up in the parish. These young men naturally considered a vocation to the priesthood. But it still didn't hurt to be asked. Father Charles Gallagher, S.J., who was ordained in 1960, recalls a time growing up in Garrison, New York:

> When I was perhaps ten years old, I was walking down the street throwing a ball against the buildings. I passed an Irish cop twirling his stick. He looked at me and said, "Well now, you look like a nice boy. Have you ever thought of being a priest?" I said nothing, but from that time on I couldn't get the idea out of my head.[1]

Today, it still helps to be asked. This is one of the easier ways to discern God's call. But the ways that people ask a man to consider priesthood differ from the earlier era. Because of lower numbers of priests, a priest may not so often be present in the natural events of parish life. Also, mothers, neighbors, and teachers are not as likely to encourage their sons and other young men they know to the priesthood. In fact, many parents today discourage their sons' interest in the priesthood. It can be concluded that today, while God continues to call men to priesthood, there is a lack of fostering and hearing that call.

The Church is initiating many efforts to encourage vocations to the priesthood. For example, a high school sophomore, Patrick, told how he had thought of being a priest, but he wasn't sure what step to take next. He didn't know if his parents would be for this idea or not. Then a parish priest asked him to come to a "Project Andrew" dinner with other high school students who were thinking of the priesthood. He told his parents and was pleased to find out that they were "supportive, but not pushy."[2]

CYO
Letters that stand for Catholic Youth Organization. The CYO provides opportunities for young people to develop strong moral character, self-esteem, and leadership qualities through activities of a social, educational, recreational, and athletic nature.

In the Archdiocese of Los Angeles, a vocation program has begun that respects the anonymity of teenagers who might want to explore priesthood (or religious life). The program offers about one event per month with various kinds of activities. One of the most popular allows a boy to

shadow a priest for the day. All the teens meet at one site at 7 a.m. for prayer, then are assigned to a priest and his ministry. They return in the afternoon for Mass, food, and entertainment. To identify young men for this program, Cardinal Roger Mahony of Los Angeles asks each parish priest to identify two young men per year who might be candidates for the priesthood. Father Richard Martini, the diocesan vocation director, then follows up with phone calls and news of Project Andrew events, including a dinner with the Cardinal, who answers questions about his own vocation.

"God provides the music, but we're free to work out the dance steps," said Father Martini about the process of vocation discernment.[3] And, as in the past clear back to the time of Abraham, God's call to priestly service comes in many different ways and from many different sources.

VOCATION EFFORTS

Nearly every diocese and religious community with priests has a vocation director and staff in charge of encouraging men to explore their desire to be a priest. In 2005 the United States Conference of Catholic Bishops started its own national program called "Fishers of Men." The program is being implemented in four phases that will eventually include a Priestly Life and Vocations Summit that will allow priests to reflect on the opportunities they might have to invite other men into the priesthood.

In announcing the program, it was revealed that only about 30 percent of priests ever invite other men into the priesthood. The bishops hope that number will increase. "One of the most effective ways of encouraging a man to consider the priesthood is for a priest to invite him to do so," said Bishop Blase Cupich of Rapid City, South Dakota, the chairman of the USCCB's vocation's committee.

Do both of the following:

- Look up the vocations office of your diocese. Report on three initiatives they offer that are designed to encourage new candidates to the priesthood.

- Choose a religious community with priests. Examine the vocations area of their website. Report on how the community's efforts to encourage priest candidates differs from your diocese's efforts.

journal**discussion**

- How would your parents and family react if you were considering a vocation to the priesthood (or religious life)?

- Brainstorm a list of ways that God calls people to service.

✦ The Call to Priesthood

Everyone in the Church—male and female—has a role in helping a man to determine if God is calling him to the priesthood and decide whether or not he will accept the call. Father Robert Stec from the Diocese of Cleveland said that during his senior year in high school,

"no less than twenty-five people suggested that I be a priest." This invitation by his classmates led Stec to attend a weekend at the local seminary for those who might be interested in the priesthood. He added,

> I attended with the idea that I would dis-prove that I had a vocation, but in that weekend I knew that this is where I

needed to be—to listen, to hear, and to understand God's call. I prayed, "What is it, God, that you want me to do?" I listened and felt peacefulness in God's answer. Later, I kept being affirmed in this vocation choice.[4]

Personally, for the man involved, the call to the priesthood may be present from early in life, manifesting itself as a nagging but pleasant feeling that God is calling him to a different type of life. He may begin to think of himself as a leader. Or a teacher. He may recognize in himself the virtue of compassion for others and empathy for the larger problems of the world. In all cases, he may sense a deep connection with God and an attraction to the Gospel of Jesus Christ.

Besides other people telling him that he would make a good priest, here are some other signs that are a good way for a man to gauge a possible vocation to the priesthood. He may notice:

- His prayer life is getting better.

- He is attending Mass and the other sacraments more frequently.

- He is spending more time in Church and/or service-related activities.

- He is progressing beyond a generic idea of being a priest to imagining himself acting as one more concretely, that is, preaching, teaching, celebrating the sacraments.

- He finds himself fighting the thoughts of being a priest but not being able to get them out of his head.

- He may be presented with many other attractive options for career and relationships, but left wondering if he will regret it some day if he does not pursue the initial steps of a priestly vocation.

A person who recognizes these signs should begin some further discernment on the possibility of being a priest. Abandoning himself to God's providence and enacting a prayerful process as described in chapter 2 is one way to do this. The information that follows considers more specific ways a man could discern this calling.

Marriage and Holy Orders

Responding to the Call

In the words of Pope Benedict XVI, the first task of a priest "is to be a believer and to become one ever anew and ever more." To be a believer is to be someone who converses with God and lives

with God. This aspect of the priest's life is not exclusively his, of course. Lay people are believers and hear God's voice in other unique ways. This sets up "a mutual give-and-take in faith in which priests and lay people become mediators of the nearness of God for one another."[5]

A man who is discerning a call to the priesthood must also be, first, a believer. He must recognize

God's voice in his life and know how to listen to it. This was the pattern of the biblical figures (see pages 228–229) who heard God's voice and responded to it. Pope John Paul II reiterated:

> The history of every priestly vocation, indeed of every Christian vocation, is the history of an inexpressible dialogue between human beings, between the love of God who calls and the freedom of individuals who lovingly respond to him.[6]

The recounting of Jesus' call to his Apostles in the Gospel of Mark emphasizes the aspect of God's call followed by the freedom of human response: "He went up the mountain and summoned those whom he wanted and they came to him" (Mk 3:13). As Pope John Paul II pointed out: "On the one hand, we have the completely free decision of Jesus; on the other, the 'coming' of the Twelve, their 'following' of Jesus. Men today who experience the grace of God calling them to the priesthood are likewise free to come to Jesus or not."[7]

In these times, the road up the mountain remains a very steep climb. The commitment to celibacy remains a challenge. Recent scandals involving the clergy and sexual abuse have led some men to further question why they should want to be a priest. As several bishops have pointed out, there is never an easy time to be a priest, but any historical period is a great time to be a priest for those who truly have a calling. The great majority of priests live their vows faithfully. There are many good models for men considering the priesthood to emulate. The next era in the Church is one in which men who have even firmer faith and deeper belief than previous generations will be called to make the priesthood a true witness of Christ, the High Priest, and the Gospel.

The man's response to God's call can occur in several ways. Another way to think of the response is that the man is "testing out" the call to find out if it is truly in God's will. There are several ways for a man to facilitate and maintain dialogue with God involving the decision. Some ideas are:

- *Going to daily Mass.* At Mass, the man is nourished by God's word and by his Body and Blood in the Eucharist.

- *Setting aside regularly scheduled time for prayer.* This strategy may begin to follow the Church's official prayer, the **Liturgy of the Hours**, which the person prays at specific times during the day, focusing on daily readings from the Psalms and other Scripture.

- *Volunteering in some parish or campus ministry activity.* This may include outreach to the poor, teaching religious education, reading Scripture at Mass, taking communion to the sick, or sponsoring a catechumen. As this service continues, the person can discern levels of satisfaction and imagine themselves taking on a fuller role in these ministries.

- *Doing some research.* There are hundreds of websites on the Internet devoted to priestly vocations. Reading through information from his home diocesan website as well as websites from several religious communities with priests is another way to become familiar with the candidacy process as well as the lifestyle of a priest.

- *Speaking with a spiritual director.* A spiritual director is someone who accompanies another on the faith journey of life. A person considering priesthood should speak on a regular basis with a priest about his prayer life, personal reading list, and ways he is practicing the faith. In addition, the man should talk over the possibility of priesthood with family members and close friends who know him the best.

- *Trying out another career or interest that is appealing.* The thought of priesthood may be competing with another dream or goal a man had for life. Maybe he also has excellent skills in the areas of math and technology and is thinking about a career in computer sciences. If so, he might pursue a job or graduate school in this area to discover how passionate this desire is and whether the pull to priesthood remains strong. Also, it is important to remember that several ministries within priesthood allow a man to combine his other interests with them (e.g., as a teacher).

- *Participating in a discernment program.* Programs for men discerning a vocation in the priesthood may be formal or informal and are often sponsored by a

diocese, religious community, seminary, or parish. The program may include evenings of reflection, participating in a discussion group with other men discerning a vocation, or attending a weekend retreat.

- *Practicing the virtues.* Faith provides the content of a fruitful prayer life, hope gives the promise of reaching the goal of prayer, and loving others allows a person to respond to Christ's love for us by praying. It is in a prayer that a man receives direction to this life or another by God.

Liturgy of the Hours
The official daily prayer of the Church. It is also called the "Divine Office." It is a set of prayers for certain times of the day in response to Saint Paul's command to "pray without ceasing" (1 Thes 5:17).

religious superior
The head or leader of a religious community charged with cultivating in the members of the community a spirit of obedience to God's will, the Church, and the rules of the community as well as fostering a lifestyle of prayer, fraternal love, and commitment to minisrty.

As the dialogue between the man and God continues and he receives help deciphering the messages from his family, friends, parish community, and spiritual directors, he may feel ready to approach a vocation director from the diocese or religious community. The vocation director can help with these later stages of the discernment process as well as let the man know what shape his candidacy would take if he decided to make a formal application.

The duty for everyone—teenagers included—in encouraging priestly vocations is to continue to help restore a "Christian mentality" in every aspect of life: "More than ever, what is now needed is an evangelization which never tires of pointing to the true face of God the Father who calls each one of us in Jesus Christ. . . ."[8]

More Vocation Awareness

Develop a marketing and advertising campaign that emphasizes several appealing features about the lifestyle of priests. Prepare several posters with photos that represent the basic ways a priest serves. Arrange for a priest to prepare an audio or video presentation highlighting the theme and message of vocation awareness. Play the message school-wide or in each theology class. Include a way for students to recommend men at your school who would make good priest-candidates. Collect the names and arrange for their pastor or diocesan representative to contact them about doing further reflection and discernment on this vocation.

Applying for Candidacy

The discernment process for priesthood described in the previous section is mainly done in an "unofficial" manner. Once the man decides to make a formal inquiry and/or application to be a candidate for priesthood, he will undergo a series of interviews with a priest to determine both his sense of calling and whether or not he meets some candidacy requirements. Often this formal time of discernment is called the *aspirancy*, suggesting that the person is aspiring to know more about the priestly vocation. It will usually take place over four or five months and involve conversations between the man and a priest adviser.

Often the formal application process for candidacy for priesthood also includes submitting a written application along with several letters of recommendation and school transcripts. The man may also be asked to write an autobiographical statement that expresses his sense of calling and complete a full psychological evaluation. If the man is applying for diocesan priesthood, the bishop will likely request a formal, one-to-one interview with him at this time. In a religious order, several interviews may be required between the applicant and representatives of the community, including the **religious superior**.

To be accepted as a candidate for ordination, a person must be a mature male (generally between ages eighteen and forty years old) who has completed Christian initiation, who willingly and knowingly wishes to be ordained, and who has been accepted as a candidate by Church authorities. Other "qualifications" may include:

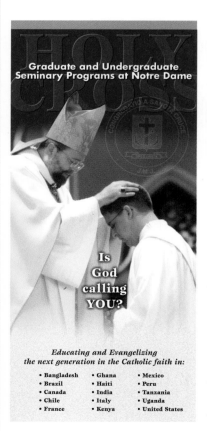

- a genuine love for the Catholic Church

- a minimum grade point average in high school and/or college

- freedom from psychological or medical conditions that would inhibit one from exercising a full life of ministry

- emotional maturity for one's age

- a record of service and/or liturgical ministry which indicates a serious interest in a life dedicated to these pursuits

- good social skills

- solid leadership qualities for exercising public ministry as evidenced through school and/or work experience

- freedom from all canonical impediments and other grounds for disqualification on moral or legal grounds, e.g., prior criminal record, personal legal obligations, or sexually inappropriate conduct

- a demonstrated ability to live the religious vows (poverty, chastity, and obedience) faithfully.

A prospective candidate for priesthood should also be willing to learn and grow in many new areas in life. He should have a respect for other people and an openness to other cultures and ethnic groups. In many dioceses in the United States, knowing and speaking Spanish is a requirement for ordination. Most importantly, the man should have a compelling desire to respond to Christ's call to have a closer relationship with him. In other words, he should have a great desire to be holy.

study questions

1. What are some signs to help a man determine if he might make a good priest?

2. What did Pope Benedict XVI say was the first task of a priest?

3. How does a man's discernment over a priestly vocation involve a dialogue with God?

The Issue of Homosexual Candidates for the Priesthood

In November 2005, the Vatican's Congregation for Catholic Education released an instruction discerning the suitability of candidates for the priesthood with homosexual orientations.

The instruction differentiated between men with "deep-seated homosexual tendencies" and those whose homosexual tendencies "were only the expression of a transitory problem." In the former case, men would not be considered suitable candidates for priesthood. In the latter, men who had "clearly overcome [the tendencies] at least three years before ordination to the diaconate" could be considered candidates for the priesthood.

The issue was commented on by many in and outside of the Church, pointing out rightly that there are many faithful, celibate priests with a homosexual orientation. The November 2005 Instruction, signed by Pope Benedict XVI, included a reminder of various Church teachings that distinguished between homosexual acts, which are sinful, and homosexual tendencies, which constitute a grave trial. The instruction stated: "Every sign of unjust discrimination in their regard should be avoided. They are called to fulfill God's will in their lives and to unite to the sacrifice of the Lord's cross the difficulties they may encounter" (2).

4. What are some ways a man can test out a vocation to the priesthood?

5. Define *aspirancy* as it relates to priesthood.

6. Describe the formal application process for candidacy to the priesthood.

7. What does the Church teach about homosexual candidates for the priesthood?

- How are priestly vocations the responsibility of the entire Church?

- How can the Church encourage more priestly vocations? List several practical suggestions.

✦ Preparing for Ordination

One of the last products of the Second Vatican Council was the "Decree on the Training of Priests," *Optatum totius*, released in October 1965. It provided a series of directives for priestly formation, stating in its first sentence that "animated by the spirit of Christ, this sacred synod is fully aware that the desired renewal of the whole Church depends to a great extent on the ministry of its priests."[9] Pope John Paul II echoed the words of the Council on the importance of priestly formation in his 1992 Apostolic Exhortation, *Pastores Dabo Vobis* "I Will Give You Shepherds," in which he outlined four crucial areas of formation.

The first area is *human formation*, "the basis of all priestly formation." All of the priest's ministry—the proclamation of the Scripture, the celebration of sacraments, the guiding of the Church to love—is done through the relation of the priest to individual human beings and to the community. For this reason, the priest needs to be formed so that his personality is a help, not a hindrance, to other people meeting Jesus Christ through him. Of special importance is the ability of the priest to relate well with others. He must develop himself so that he is affable, hospitable, sincere, prudent, generous, encouraging,

understanding, and forgiving. Part of this growth comes from living at a seminary with other men in brotherhood while completing the mundane but cooperative tasks of assisting with meals, doing laundry, along with more fun endeavors, including participating in athletics. Through his growth, he must come to a central

University of St. Thomas defensive tackle and seminarian Bob Kessler.

awareness of the role of love in human life. While learning for himself, he must share with others the encompassing nature of love and how love involves the entire person—physical, psychological, and spiritual.

Spiritual formation is a second crucial area of concentration for a candidate for ordination. Formation should be such that the candidate forms an intimate friendship with Jesus Christ. Jesus himself said to his Apostles, "I no longer call you slaves . . . I have called you friends, because I have told you everything I have heard from my Father" (Jn 15:15). Spiritual formation also centers on the priest learning to live the Paschal Mystery in his own life—the Passion,

Death, and Resurrection of Christ—so that he can teach the people he will minister to how to live it in their lives. Attention to this area of formation should also include developing the habit of prayerful and meditative reading of the Scripture called **lectio divina**. The priest should also cultivate a deep prayer life, including a renewed appreciation for the Eucharist, the high point of Christian prayer. Part of spiritual formation teaches the candidate how to embrace, love, and live celibacy so that he will live it for its true motives and use the gift to help him share a love for all people.

If you were asked to describe your working knowledge of what a man does in his years of preparation for ordination, you might be likely to answer "go to school" or "study." These answers would be correct and relate to a third area of necessary formation: *intellectual formation*. A candidate does spend years studying primarily theology, but also philosophy, which leads to a deeper understanding of what it means to be human. Theology itself focuses on understanding Sacred Scripture and Sacred Tradition as handed down by the Magisterium. It also has a pastoral focus, as it will be the priest's job to help the laity understand theology and the truth of Christ's teaching, especially when that truth is contradicted by modern culture. Finally a sound intellectual formation will help the priest evangelize, that is, share the Gospel of Christ in a clear manner with a multicultural world.

The fourth area of priestly formation outlined by Pope John Paul II is *pastoral formation*, which is the goal of the whole formation for candidates for the priesthood. Priests are to be formed in pastoral ministry so as to

make them shepherds of souls in imitation of Jesus Christ, the Good Shepherd. It was around the time of the Second Vatican Council that opportunities were made open to candidates to serve part of their formation in the parish where they would eventually return as an ordained deacon or priest. This practical pastoral experience in the form of an "internship" allows candidates to engage in many concrete examples of pastoral ministry: visiting the sick, caring for immigrants, and engaging in other charitable works prior to ordination.

All of these areas of priestly formation—human, spiritual, intellectual, and pastoral—take place in the context of seminary training where an additional area of formation takes place—the growth in fraternal love and communion among seminarians, which will eventually translate into the same type of love among brother priests.

lectio divina
A classical prayer practice that involves a prayerful reading of the Bible. It means "holy reading."

A PRAYER TO HEAR GOD'S CALL

The ancient practice of *lectio divina*—"holy reading"—involves focused meditation on the Scriptures. Choose one of the Scripture readings suggested below. Then follow the process of lectio divina as it is outlined. Reflect on the call to priesthood or religious life. Reflect on how God is calling you.

Scripture Suggestions

- Jeremiah 1:4–9 ("Before you were born I dedicated you.")

- 1 Corinthians 12:4–11 ("There are different kinds of spiritual gifts but the same Spirit.")

- John 21:15–19 ("Feed my lambs. Tend my sheep. Follow me.")

Process

1. Choose the Scripture passage you wish to pray.

2. Find a comfortable and quiet place. Choose a "prayer word" from the passage (see "centering prayer" on page 48). Recite the word to yourself. Stay silent for a few minutes.

3. Read the Scripture text slowly and carefully. Pay special attention to a phrase that seems to be speaking to you. Stay with that phrase for awhile.

4. Memorize the important phrase. Repeat it to yourself.

5. Speak to God about what he is saying to you. Listen for some images or memories that seem to provide an answer.

6. Return to a quiet time. Rest in God's presence.

Agents and Setting for Priestly Formation

The Church herself and the bishop are the first representatives in forming a man for the priesthood. Recall that the priest is formed first through his family, friends, and through the invitation of others to him that he might make a good priest. These people all act as visible representatives of Christ. It is the grace of Christ and

the gifts of the Holy Spirit that help to throw light on the man's vocation. Another early source for priestly formation, though less common today, is a minor seminary. In effect this is a boarding or commuter high school for boys that features a structured life with the regular high school subjects along with daily Mass, a program of cooperative athletics, and an emphasis on Latin. The purpose of a minor seminary is to prepare young men to enroll in a major seminary.

When a young man does become a candidate for priesthood, he typically meets with the bishop, the first representative of Christ, the High Priest, and a successor of the Apostles. It is the bishop's responsibility to bring one identity to the priests of his diocese and unite it with the priesthood and ministry of Christ. This responsibility begins when the candidates are in formation. The bishop not only personally interviews prospective candidates, he visits with them often in their preparation as a way of guiding their pastoral preparation. After all, they will eventually serve him in the diocese and the bishop should have a key role in their formation.

It is at the seminary—staffed by various people involved in formation—that the candidate spends most of his time in residence and training. A man has an opportunity to apply at a seminary of his choice, though if his plan is to be ordained a diocesan priest, he will usually apply to the bishop of his home diocese. If he feels called to religious life in addition to ordination, he will explore his vocation with the director and priest from a religious community with a **charism** that feels compatible with his life.

The major seminary is the primary setting for priestly formation. The entire formation program—encompassing the four areas described above—is aimed at "enabling students to be formed as true pastors of souls, following the example of our Lord Jesus Christ, teacher, priest, and shepherd."[10] Assuming the man enters the seminary with a Bachelor's degree including some courses in theology and philosophy, the seminary program of formation is usually four years in length, followed by a fifth supervised year of pastoral experience that usually takes place in a parish.

The first two years of the seminary program initiate the candidate into Christian community and the spiritual life. During this time he names his personal spiritual goals and develops a plan for achieving them. He receives help in a discernment process that will enable him to continue examining his readiness for the advanced levels of priestly formation. Courses may be taken in areas like sacraments, moral theology, systematic theology, Scripture, and language.

Often, the third year of the seminary program is a break from academic and theological study to allow for a focus on pastoral skills. This year of "internship" allows the candidate to be mentored by a pastor, live in a rectory, and learn the daily and weekly rhythms of parish life. The man then returns to the seminary for a final two years of study designed to make him accomplished in understanding core theological ideas and a program of formation meant to solidify a strong and committed spiritual life rooted in prayer, worship, celibacy, obedience, and service as he nears ordination.

Life in the Seminary

A seminary is essentially a house of prayer, study, and formation. Study makes up quite a bit of a seminarian's daily life; typically a seminarian takes twelve to fifteen hours of academic courses per semester, which translates to many hours of reading and participation.

During the week, a seminarian's day usually begins with morning prayer from the Liturgy of the Hours. He may have time for a leisurely breakfast with classmates in the seminary dining room before beginning a morning of classes.

Afternoons may be less structured with a chance for exercise and individual study. Probably at least once per week the candidates will attend a conference with the seminary rector or spiritual director with the ongoing theme related to the seminarians' progress toward ordination. There

charism
A special blessing of a religious community that helps to define its particular mission and spirituality.

may also be a weekly practicum exploring the various parts of the liturgy, including workshops that allow candidates to perfect their skills in writing and delivering homilies at Mass. Liturgy courses also allow the seminarians the opportunity to collaborate with faculty members in planning the various liturgical celebrations that will take place at the seminary.

The life of a seminarian includes many meetings. Each seminarian has a spiritual director with whom he meets regularly. Also, a faculty member is assigned as an adviser to a seminarian to monitor his progress in each of the areas of formation.

Attendance and participation at daily Mass is a requirement. Mass may take place early in the morning, at midday, or near supper, depending on the day. Most of the days the entire seminary may celebrate Eucharist together; sometimes separate classes of seminarians may plan and participate in Mass in smaller groups.

Saturdays in a seminary are usually "free days" in which the candidates can catch up with studies, socialize, or participate in other planned activities much like any college student might. However, attendance at Mass may still be required. Sundays are centered around Eucharist. Many seminaries allow the candidates to invite family and friends to the Sunday Eucharist and to share in a festive brunch to follow.

In the midst of this routine, the ongoing preparation for ordination and priesthood and the formation of the man as a priest continues. A proximate step toward priesthood is taken by a man when he is ordained a deacon. Usually, a transitional deacon spends six months to a year in this role before priestly ordination. Ordination to the diaconate is an important step because this is the time the man makes a promise to live a life of obedience, celibacy, and prayer for the Church.

Seminarians on College Campus

Religious communities usually sponsor their own seminaries. Some Catholic colleges that are operated by a religious order offer a college seminary program along with the regular academic program. For example, the Congregation of Holy Cross

at the University of Notre Dame allows those men considering priesthood to enter a program where they attend college at Notre Dame, participate fully in campus life, but live together with others who are considering priesthood. Those who have already graduated from college and are slightly older (twenty-two to thirty-five years old) may spend a year of discernment during which they would explore a religious vocation in more depth, as well as catch up on the theology and philosophy undergraduate courses they may have missed.

- Read about the Old College program for men considering a vocation to priesthood in the Congregation of the Holy Cross at http://vocation.nd.edu.

- Compare the Holy Cross vocation program with vocation programs of two other religious communities that operate Catholic colleges in the United States. Write a report summarizing each program.

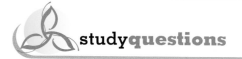

study questions

1. Why is human formation the "basis for all priestly formation"?

2. What does human formation entail?

3. What is *lectio divina*?

4. How does a candidate's intellectual formation also have a pastoral focus?

5. Why is pastoral formation the goal of all priestly formation?

6. Explain the difference between a minor seminary and a major seminary.

7. How might a religious order's seminary be unique?

8. Outline a typical five-year program at a major seminary.

9. What is the central part of a seminarian's day and week?

journal discussion

● If you could ask a seminarian three questions, what would they be?

● How can you apply the four areas of a seminarian's formation—human, spiritual, intellectual, and pastoral—to a program for your own life?

✦ Celebration of the Sacrament of Holy Orders

All three ordinations of the bishop, priest, and deacon follow the same movement and take place within the Eucharistic liturgy. Given the significance of the Sacrament of Holy Orders in the life of the Church, ordinations are scheduled for either Saturdays or Sundays in the diocesan cathedral so as many people as possible can attend and participate.

The essential rite of the Sacrament of Holy Orders for all three degrees consists in the bishop's imposition of hands on the head of the man to be ordained while reciting a prayer of consecration that asks God for an outpouring of the Holy Spirit and the specific gifts related to the ministry for which he is being ordained.

In the ordination for the priesthood, the candidate wears an **alb** and a deacon's stole at the beginning of the Mass. He takes the first place ahead of the other priests who will concelebrate the liturgy in the opening procession. A chair is reserved for him in the sanctuary so that all who attend have a complete view of the rites that will take place.

The initial rites of ordination begin after the Gospel. The bishop, wearing his miter, sits at his chair. The candidate is called forward and goes before the bishop, making a sign of reverence. A designated priest, often the rector of the seminary, testifies for the candidate to the bishop. The election of the man takes place and the bishop asks for the consent of all the people. He says:

> We rely on the help of the Lord God and our Savior Jesus Christ, and we choose this man, our brother, for priesthood in the presbyteral order.

alb
The long white linen robe worn by anyone who takes a leadership role at Mass. It is connected to the tradition of the newly baptized putting on the white robe of purity after they have received the Sacrament. Only the clergy may wear a stole over the alb.

The faithful give their consent by saying, "Thanks be to God." The bishop then offers his homily, in which he spells out the essential duties of the priesthood. He touches on some of the following duties:

- *Teaching.* The new priest is called to share the Word of God with others both with his own words and by his actions. He will communicate the doctrine he has studied in the seminary as nourishment for the People of God.

- *Sanctifying.* Through his role as minister of the sacraments, the priest will carry the sanctifying power of Christ. The bishop reminds the new priest that it is his responsibility to pray not only for the Church, but for the whole world. In the Mass, the priest is called to make every effort to die to sin and to live a new life in the Lord.

- *Shepherding.* Following the model of Christ, the Good Shepherd, the new priest will be subject to his bishop while seeking to unify the Church and bring the faithful to God the Father, through Christ and in the Holy Spirit.

After the homily, the candidate stands before the bishop and is questioned about his resolution to fulfill the duties of the priesthood, to celebrate the sacraments as they have been handed down by Christ, to preach the Gospel and teach the Catholic faith, and to unite himself more closely to Jesus, the High Priest. The candidate answers, "I am" or, "I am, with the help of God" to each question. Then the candidate goes to the bishop, kneels before him, places his joined hands between the hands of the bishop, and pledges his respect and obedience to the bishop.

Litany of the Saints
A prayer made up of various petitions addressed to the saints. It was first prescribed by Pope Saint Gregory the Great in the sixth century.

The initial rites of Holy Orders conclude with the candidate's lying prostrate on the floor of the sanctuary as a sign of his unworthiness and need

for God's help. The bishop kneels on a small folding kneeler as the cantors sing the **Litany of Saints**. The purpose of praying the litany is to allow for the whole Church—including the Church in Heaven—to pray for the candidate. At the end of the litany, the bishop stands and prays:

> Hear us, Lord our God,
> and pour out upon this
> servant of yours
> the blessing of the Holy
> Spirit
> and the grace and power of
> the priesthood.
> In your sight we offer this

man for ordination:
support him with your unfailing love.
We ask this through Christ our Lord.
Amen.

The candidate then stands, goes to the bishop, and kneels before him. The bishop lays his hands on the candidate's head in silence. Next all the priests who are concelebrating lay their hands on the candidate's head, as well. The laying on of hands is the essential rite of ordination. The bishop then sings or recites the prayer of consecration, concluding with these words:

Almighty Father,
grant to this servant of yours
the dignity of the priesthood.
Renew within him the Spirit
of holiness.
As a coworker with the order
of bishops
may he be faithful to the
ministry
that he receives from you,
Lord God,
and be to others a model of
right conduct.
May he be faithful in working with the order of bishops,
so that the words of the
Gospel may reach the ends of
the earth,
and the family of nations,
made one in Christ,
may become God's one, holy
people.
We ask this through our Lord
Jesus Christ, your Son,
who lives and reigns with
you and the Holy Spirit,
one God, forever and ever.
Amen.

Other Rites of Priestly Ordination

There are several additional rites which follow the consecration of the new priest. These rites express and complete the mystery that is accomplished in ordination. The assisting priests prepare the **stole** of the newly ordained priest and vest him in a **chasuble**. The man has worn the stole over his left shoulder after being ordained a deacon; as a priest, he wears it over both shoulders. The stole is worn as a sign of order and authority by priests and bishops at liturgies celebrated by them like Mass, the other sacraments, or exposition of the Blessed Sacrament. Administering the stole, the bishop may remind the priest of the comforting words of Jesus in calling disciples to himself:

Take my yoke upon you and learn from me, for I am meek and humble of heart; and you will find rest for yourselves. For my yoke is easy, and my burden light. (Mt 11:29–30)

Kneeling before the new priest, the bishop anoints his palms as a sign of the special anointing of the Holy Spirit.

The Mass continues and a deacon assists the bishop in receiving the gifts of the people. The deacon prepares the bread on a paten and the wine and water in the chalice for the offering of the Eucharist. These gifts are then brought to the bishop, who hands them to the new priest as a gift, saying:

Accept from the holy people of God the gifts to be offered to him.

stole
A long, narrow cloth that comes in the color of the liturgical season and is worn by the bishop, priest, or deacon. Stoles were originally worn by Jewish rabbis as a sign of their authority.

chasuble
The outer garment worn by the priest over the alb and stole. It is the same color as the stole and the liturgical season.

Know what you are doing, and imitate the mystery you celebrate: model your life on the mystery of the Lord's cross.

Before continuing with the Mass, the bishop stands and exchanges a sign of peace with the newly ordained priest. Then the liturgy of the Eucharist proceeds with the newly ordained priest, all the priests present, and the bishop concelebrating the Mass.

Holy Orders for Bishops and Deacons

As mentioned, the rite of Holy Orders for the other two degrees of the Sacrament follows the same form as for priests. Recall, too, that the fullness of the Sacrament of Holy Orders occurs in the ordination of bishops (see pages 214–215). Nevertheless, there are only slight differences for the rites in the three degrees, mainly involving the secondary rites. The essential rite of the laying on of hands while praying a solemn prayer remains the same for the ordination of bishops and deacons. However, only the principal bishop celebrating the liturgy and other participating bishops—not the concelebrating priests—lay hands on the bishop-elect's or the deacon candidates' heads.

A bishop-elect is presented by one of the priests of the diocese who asks for ordination on his behalf. The consecrating bishop asks the priest, "Have you a mandate from the Holy See?" Answering in the affirmative, the bishop asks that the **apostolic letter** be read to the congregation. The apostolic letter is usually sent to the man upon being nominated as bishop by the Pope. Such a letter was sent by Pope Benedict XVI to Father Philip Tartaglia, a priest in the diocese of Paisley, Scotland, nominating him as bishop. It read:

> Benedict, Bishop, Servant of the Servants of God, sends greetings and the Apostolic Blessing to his dear son, Philip Tartaglia of the clergy of Glasgow, until now rector of the Pontifical Scots College, Rome, Bishop Elect of Paisley. Since our Venerable Brother John Aloysius Mone has resigned from the office of governing the see of Paisley we have sought to nominate speedily a new Bishop and experienced pastor to that same See. Having diligently considered the matter, our mind turned to you, dear Son, whom we consider suitable to take up this task. You have distinguished yourself in the diligent exercise of your priesthood in the Archdiocese of Glasgow and in your wise administration of the Pontifical Scots College, Rome. Accordingly, by virtue of Our Apostolic Authority, on the advice of the Congregation for Bishops, we appoint you Bishop of the Diocese of Paisley and we grant you all the powers and faculties, and we also impose the obligations, which the sacred canons attach to this nomination. Having made the Oath of office and the profession of faith, you may then receive Episcopal Ordination according to the liturgical rites of the Church anywhere in the world, outside, however, of the city of Rome. At the same time

apostolic letter
A document issued by the Pope or Vatican for various appointments, approving religious congregations, designating basilicas, and the like.

we give you the task of suitably informing the flock of Paisley of this our decree in which we have entrusted you with this mission. By diligent preaching of the Gospel, the correct administration of the Sacraments, in association with the priests and lay faithful you are to increase the spiritual strength of the whole Church of Paisley. Given at Rome, at Saint Peter's, on the thirteenth day of September, in the year of Our Lord 2005, the First of Our Pontificate.[11]

A bishop is not presented a paten and chalice like a newly ordained priest. He is given the Book of Gospels as a sign of his apostolic mission to proclaim the Word of God. The new bishop is

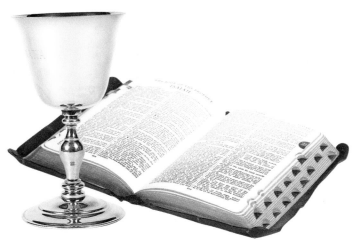

anointed with holy chrism, not on the hands like the helper priest, but on the head as a sign of the coming of the Holy Spirit, who makes the bishop's ministry fruitful. As gifts, the new bishop is also invested with a ring, miter, and pastoral staff, or crosier. The bishop's ring symbolizes his fidelity and authority. It remains a sign of reverence for Catholics to kiss the ring of a bishop as a sign of respect for his authority. The miter is a tall pointed hat with peaks in the front and back that the bishop wears while celebrating liturgy, though it is removed when he sings or leads the assembly in prayer, as in the Eucharistic prayer. The tradition of the miter traces back to the Old Testament when the high priests, including Aaron, wore headdresses that may have resembled turbans. The last gift to the new bishop is

his staff, symbolizing his role as Good Shepherd. The celebrating bishop says:

> Take this staff as a sign of your pastoral office:
> keep watch over the whole flock
> in which the Holy Spirit has appointed you
> to shepherd the Church of God.

At the ordination of a deacon, he is invested with a deacon's stole and dalmatic, the white outer garment he wears at liturgy. Kneeling before the bishop, the Book of Gospels is placed in the newly ordained deacon's hands while the bishop says:

> Receive the Gospel of Christ,
> whose herald you now are.
> Believe what you read,
> teach what you believe,
> and practice what you teach.

study questions

1. What is the essential rite of ordination?

2. Name and explain the three areas of duties for the priesthood touched on by the bishop at ordination.

3. What is symbolic about the priest's stole?

4. What are the symbolic meanings of the following gifts presented to a bishop at ordination: Book of Gospels, miter, ring, crosier?

5. How does the ordination of a deacon differ from that of a bishop and priest?

journal discussion

- What is the best advice you could offer to a new priest on his ordination day?

- What are some qualities a bishop needs to be a good leader?

A Priest's First Mass[12]

Described as a perfectionist, newly ordained Father James Farnan of the Diocese of Pittsburgh, had his first Mass at his home parish in Upper Saint Clair, Pennsylvania, planned to the smallest details. He didn't plan to start a fire on the altar. As he raised his arms to give the final blessing, his chasuble got caught on the altar cloth knocking over a candle and starting a fire. A nearby deacon doused the flames with water from a flower vase. The fire was out, but Father Farnan was also drenched. He gave the blessing all wet.

One of Father Farnan's friends, Father Leo Patalinghug, noted that "the fire and water represent the Holy Spirit, teaching him some humility. And that brings up a piece of advice I'd give to James: leave some room for God in the sanctuary."

Even with the dramatic ending, the day of Father James's Mass was very special, much like a wedding day is for a husband and wife. Nearly eight hundred friends and relatives filled the pews of Saint Louise de Marillac Church, including twenty priests who concelebrated the Mass.

The pastor from Father James's youth preached the homily. His seminary rector stood behind him and helped him when he briefly lost his place during the liturgy of the Eucharist. The priest who had supervised Father James's summers of field work while in the seminary and vested him with his first stole and chasuble at ordination was also there. So was the priest whose homily first inspired him to consider the priesthood and the other priest from whom he sought advice before entering the seminary. Several of his classmates from the North American College Seminary in Rome were also present.

"It's a brotherhood based on the blood of Christ, which is thicker than family blood," Father Patalinghug said. The brotherhood also included Archbishop Donald Wuerl, who had dined informally with all his seminarians several times over the years. "I would not call to orders a diocesan priest who I didn't know," Archbishop Wuerl said.

After the Mass, the guests stood in line for nearly an hour to receive Father James's blessing. There was also a table with many ordination gifts, for which he was grateful. Father James was also relieved not to come out of the seminary with much debt. After ordination, the diocese assumed payment of the loans he took for two years of undergraduate studies at Duquesne University, and it paid outright for four years of graduate school.

But there were some personal and family expenses involved in ordination. His family and friends chipped in to purchase his vestments and his most cherished gift, his chalice. Made of gold-plated silver, it was designed by Father James and handcrafted by an artisan in Rome. The engravings have special meaning for him. On one side are the signs for Saint Peter and Saint Paul, the patrons of the Church and his home diocese. On the other side is an image drawn from Fatima, where Mary appeared to three children. A renewed devotion to the rosary was instrumental in Father James's call to the priesthood. He left the chalice in Pope John Paul II's private chapel while he was in Rome so that the Pope became the first priest to use it. Archbishop Wuerl also celebrated with the chalice before Father James's ordination.

When Father James briefly lost his place in the Eucharistic prayer, the other priests behind him whispered a cue. He later let the congregation know that he had some help. "As I said to my driving instructor when I took my driving exam for the first time, 'Hey, I remembered all of the important stuff.'"

The Effects of the Sacrament of Holy Orders

The Sacrament of Holy Orders configures the man who receives it to Christ by a special grace of the Holy Spirit. It confers an "indelible spiritual character" or "sacred power" on the man that is granted once and for all, similar to the permanent character received in the Sacraments of Baptism and Confirmation. In Holy Orders, the permanent share is in Christ's triple office of priest, prophet, and king. The fullness of this sacred power is given in the consecration of a bishop.

In the bishop and his priest designate, it is Christ himself who is acting in the celebration of the sacraments. Through the bishop or priest, it is Christ who offers the Sacrifice of the Mass, Christ who baptizes, Christ who anoints the sick, Christ who witnesses marriages, and, in the case of bishops, Christ who ordains. Also, when the bishops offer a teaching or ruling to the Church, it is the Sacrament of Holy Orders that guarantees that he is acting as a representative of Christ himself. As the *Catechism of the Catholic Church* teaches:

> Through the ordained ministry, especially that of bishops and priests, the presence of Christ as head of the Church is made visible in the midst of the community of believers. (*CCC*, 1549)

It is important to stress again that it is not the person or personality of the bishop or priest that is a substitute for Christ, nor does even the way that he acts affect Christ's presence in the sacraments. "Since it is ultimately Christ who acts and effects salvation through the ordained minister, the unworthiness of the latter does not prevent Christ from acting" (*CCC*, 1584). This guarantee extends to the sacraments so that even a bishop's or priest's sinfulness can not impede the grace of the sacraments. However, many other sinful actions of a bishop or priest do leave negative marks on the Church. It is true that some men who are validly ordained can, for serious reasons, be discharged from the functions and obligations linked to ordination, including celebrating the sacraments, but he can never again be a layman in the strict sense because the character imprinted at ordination is truly permanent and forever.

The sacred power communicated by the Sacrament of Holy Orders is ultimately one that puts service before authority. When the Apostles James and John asked to be able to sit at Jesus' right and left hand when he came in glory, Jesus told them "You do not know what you are asking." What Jesus meant was that true power and authority was different from what they were seeking. True power and authority comes from being least, not great, and by serving the needs of others: "'Whoever wishes to be greatest among you will be your servant; whoever wishes to be first among you will be the slave of all,' Jesus told them" (Mk 10:43–44).

In his encyclical *Deus Caritas Est*, Pope Benedict XVI wrote of the responsibility of bishops to be the leaders in sharing God's charity to those most in need and to live the rule established in the early Church "to devote themselves to the teaching of the Apostles and to the communal life, to the breaking of the bread and to the prayers" (Acts 2:42):

> In the rite of episcopal ordination, prior to the act of consecration itself, the candidate must respond to several questions

which express the essential elements of his office and recall the duties of his future ministry. He promises expressly to be, in the Lord's name, welcoming and merciful to the poor and to all those in need of consolation and assistance.[13]

Graces of the Sacrament

In general, the grace of the Holy Spirit for bishops, priests, and deacons from the Sacrament of Holy Orders is a connection to Christ as priest, teacher, and pastor. However, the graces differ according to each of the three degrees of ordination.

For the bishop, the gift of the Spirit is first of all the grace of strength to govern the Church, to defend it, and to show a preferential love for the poor, sick, and needy. This grace leads him to proclaim the Gospel to all, to be the model for his people, and to identify himself with Christ, the redeemer at Eucharist, while not fearing himself to offer his life on behalf of his flock.

Victor Mundo, sixteen, holds a poster of with an image of Archbishop Oscar Romero in San Salvador.

Archbishop Oscar Romero of San Salvador was a living example of this grace. Consecrated archbishop in 1977 in the midst of social, political, and military turmoil in El Salvador, which included coups, countercoups, and fraudulent elections. Oscar Romero strongly aligned himself with the poor and with those who were being mistreated after he found himself saying Mass at the funeral of his friend, Father Rutilo Grande, a Jesuit priest who was assassinated as a result of his commitment to the poor and social justice. Romero began a series of weekly radio broadcasts in which he told of the recent violations of human rights and called the Church to serve "the God of life rather than the idols of death."

On March 23, 1980, Archbishop Romero appealed directly to the military: "We are your people. The peasants you kill are your own brothers and sisters. When you hear the voice of man commanding you to kill, remember instead the voice of God." The next day while saying Mass in the chapel of a hospital where he lived, a single shot rang out from the rear of the chapel and pierced his heart. He died within minutes.

Ordination confers on priests the grace to offer the Sacrifice of the Mass, to forgive sins in the Sacrament of Penance, and to prepare people for their eternal destiny by preaching the Gospel. Saint Paul described priests as "servants of Christ and stewards of the mysteries of God" (1 Cor 4:1). The priest's threefold mission and grace to teach, govern, and sanctify is received from the bishop, who holds these in fullness. In turn, priests share the grace of ordination with the faithful of the Church in the key moments of their lives. Father Stephen Rosetti explains:

> A diocesan priest, as one who lives among the people, is present in the very mundane parts of human life. He is a leaven in the society, calling the people to remember that Christ is living among and in them. But in the critical moments of people's lives, the births, weddings, sicknesses, reconciliations, and deaths, he is particularly sought out. By the power of Christ in the sacraments, the priest sanctifies these moments, joining the human and divine, fusing nature and grace.[14]

Deacons receive in sacramental ordination the graces of service in the liturgy, in sharing the Gospel, and in works of charity. These translate to various tasks, such as administering Baptism and witnessing weddings, reading the Scripture and preaching at Mass, and taking communion to the dying. Saint Polycarp offered this counsel to deacons: "Let them be merciful, and zealous, and let them walk according to the truth of the Lord, who became servant of all."[15]

Many saints and other Catholics have commented on the dignity and responsibility of those men who receive the graces of the Sacrament of Holy Orders, particularly of bishops and priests. Listed below are some of their words:

> Whenever Divine Goodness chooses a man for some particular service, God bestows upon him all gifts necessary for the man and his office and richly adorns him.
>
> **Saint Bernardine**
>
> If preachers and priests of God's word make so few conversions, it is because there is in them too much of human wisdom, and too little of divine fire.
>
> **Saint Teresa of Avila**
>
> The priest does not belong to himself, just as he does not belong to his family, or friends, or even to a particular country. His very thought, will, sentiments are not his; they belong to Christ, his Life.
>
> **Pope Pius XII**
>
> The priest continues the work of redemption on earth. . . . If we really understand the priest on earth, we would die not of fright but of love. . . . The priesthood is the love of the heart of Jesus.
>
> **Saint John Vianney**

As with all the sacraments, Holy Orders deepens the life of Jesus in the ordained man who is called to serve him. The Sacrament also gives the actual graces to provide the wisdom and fortitude to live as an ordained minister throughout life.

study questions

1. What is the "indelible spiritual character" a man receives in Holy Orders?

2. Explain why this statement is not true: "Through Holy Orders, a bishop or priest becomes a substitute for Christ."

3. Why can't the grace of the sacraments ever be impeded by the sins of the minister?

4. Cite a scriptural example that shows that a bishop or priest should put service before authority in exercising his sacred power.

5. In general, what is the grace of the Holy Spirit for bishops, priests, and deacons given in the Sacrament of Holy Orders?

6. What is the gift of the Holy Spirit specifically for a bishop?

7. What graces does ordination confer on priests?

8. Name some liturgical tasks taken on by deacons as a result of the graces of the Sacrament.

journal discussion

- How does knowing that it is Christ acting in the sacraments through the priest help you to explain the Sacraments of Eucharist and Penance to a non-Catholic friend?

- Whom do you know who exercises power through service, not authority? Explain how.

summary points

✦ Hearing God's Voice

✦ The Scriptures are filled with examples of God calling his people to service.

✦ God calls people in many different ways, including men to the priesthood.

+ One of the ways God calls men to priesthood is through the invitation of others in the faith community.

The Call to Priesthood

+ All Catholics are responsible to help a man to determine if he is being called by God to the priesthood and to help him decide whether or not to accept that call.

+ From an early age, a person may feel called to the priesthood.

+ There are several signs that help a man determine if he is being called to priesthood; for example, a man telling him he would be a good priest.

+ A man who is discerning a call to the priesthood must first be a believer who can recognize God's voice and know how to listen to it.

+ Among the ways a man tests his call to the priesthood are: going to daily Mass, praying regularly, volunteering in service work, participating in a discernment program, and many others.

+ After a time of personal discernment, a man makes a formal application to be a candidate for priesthood.

+ There are several qualifications for a man to be accepted as a candidate for either a diocesan or religious priest.

Preparing for Ordination

+ There are four main areas of priestly formation: human formation, spiritual formation, intellectual formation, and pastoral formation.

+ The Church itself and the bishop are the first representatives who help in forming a man for the priesthood.

+ The major seminary is the place for priestly formation.

+ Life in the seminary includes prayer, study, and formation.

Celebration of the Sacrament of Holy Orders

+ The ordination of bishop, priest, and deacon all follow the same movement and all take place during the Mass.

+ The essential rite of ordination is the laying on of hands by the bishop on the candidate while reciting a prayer of consecration.

+ Some of the duties of priestly ordination are shared by the bishop in his homily: teaching, sanctifying, and shepherding.

+ There are other secondary rites of ordination; for example a priest receives the gifts of bread and wine to help him model his life on the cross of Christ; the bishop receives the Book of Gospels as a sign of his mission to proclaim God's word, and deacons are given the Book of Gospels, as well, as a sign that they, too, will support the bishop by heralding God's word.

The Effects of the Sacrament of Holy Orders

+ Holy Orders confers an indelible spiritual character or sacred power on the man that lasts for a lifetime.

+ Holy Orders guarantees that Christ acts through the bishop and priest, especially in the sacraments.

+ Even if the minister is unworthy or sinful, this does not prevent Christ from acting in the sacraments.

+ The sacred power of Holy Orders is one of service over authority.

+ In general, the grace of the Holy Spirit that comes from ordination is a connection to Christ as priest, teacher, and pastor.

1. Read Jesus' description of the Good Shepherd in John 10:1–21. Using any mixed media, create an art project that depicts this passage while also incorporating modern images of the Good Shepherd.

2. Watch the classic motion picture *Going My Way* starring Bing Crosby as Father O'Malley. Write a review of the movie. What impression did it leave you about the life of a Catholic priest?

3. Interview three priests who were ordained in three different decades. Ask each to tell you the story of his call to the priesthood, his experience in the seminary, and his remembrances of his ordination. Write a report that compares the different experiences.

4. Choose a famous American priest or bishop and research and report on his life. For example: Archbishop John Carroll, Saint John Neumann, Archbishop John Ireland, Cardinal James Gibbons, Father Michael McGivney, Father Theodore Hesburgh, or Archbishop Fulton J. Sheen.

5. Attend a retreat or workshop sponsored by your diocese or a religious community that focuses on discerning a religious vocation. Bring home a copy of the program's schedule. Make copies for your classmates and share with them the details of the experience in an oral presentation.

6. Read the Second Vatican Council document *Optatum totius* ("Decree on the Training of Priests") at the Vatican website. There are seven main sections in the document. List the sections and write a summary paragraph for each section and an introductory paragraph explaining the subject and purpose of the document.

7. Design two favorite images that might appear on a chalice.

8. Make a chart listing data on minor seminaries in the United States. Include statistics like: the year founded, high enrollment, current enrollment, courses offered, number of alumni who were ordained, tuition, and other statistics of your choice.

9. Research and report on the Serra Club, a Catholic organization that encourages vocations to the priesthood. If possible, arrange for a representative of the Serra Club to speak to your class.

10. Inquire in your diocese about the discernment and training process for permanent deacons. Write a report detailing what you found out.

Notes

1. Quoted from *Extraordinary Lives* by Francis P. Friedl and Rex Reynolds (Notre Dame, IN: Ave Maria Press, 1997), p. 39.

2. Quoted from the Archdiocese of Washington website at www.adw.org/vocations/priest_today.asp.

3. Quoted from the article "In Los Angeles, Vocations Programs Flourish" by John Allen. See www.suxxb.org/vocations/articles/allen.htm.

4. Quoted from *Called to Love* by Kathleen Glavich, S.N.D. (Notre Dame IN: Ave Maria Press, 2000), p. 33.

5. Quoted from Cardinal Joseph Ratzinger, from *A New Song for the Lord*, tr. by Martha M. Matesich (New York: Crossroad Publishing, 1996) and quoted in the Magnificat for Holy Thursday, March 24, 2005.

6. Quoted from the Apostolic Exhortation *Pastores Dabo Vobis*, 36.

7. Ibid.

8. Ibid., 37.

9. Quoted from *Optatum totius*, par. 1.

10. Ibid., p. 4.

11. Quoted from the Paisley diocese website at www.paisleydiocese.org.uk/Apostolic%20Letter.htm.

12. This feature was adapted from the article "Rookie Priest: How A Priest Learns He's Not Alone" by Ann Rodgers-Melnick in the *Pittsburgh Post-Gazette* (July 4, 2000).

13. Quoted from *Deus Caritas Et*, 32.

14. Rossetti, Stephen J. *The Joy of Priesthood* (Notre Dame, IN: Ave Maria Press, 2005), p. 143.

15. Saint Polycarp, *Ad. Phil.* 5, 2 quoted from *Lumen Gentium*, 29.

chapter nine

The Ministry and Life of Bishops, Priests, and Deacons

After he had finished speaking, he said to Simon, "Put out into deep water and lower your nets for a catch." Simon said in reply, "Master, we have worked hard all night and have caught nothing, but at your command I will lower the nets." When they had done this, they caught a great number of fish and their nets were tearing.

Luke 5:4–6

✦ Renewing the Priesthood

Do you remember this important sentence from the beginning of chapter 7: *Without the priest, the Eucharist cannot take place?* This truly is an essential statement as the number of parishes without resident priests increases by the year and the faithful are either deprived of many opportunities to celebrate the Mass at their home parish or find their parish closed altogether as one way to address the problem.

This issue is a fundamental one not only for current Catholics but for all those people who have yet to hear the Gospel and know Christ's presence in the sacraments. The Catholic Church is a sacramental Church. Sacramental ministry is the essence of the Church: without Baptism there would be no membership, without the Sacrament of Penance there would be no reconciliation, and without the Eucharist we would not able to share in the saving events of Christ's Passion and Death.

Christ gave the Church its ministry as a means to provide grace through the sacraments, to give the Church authority and mission, and to guide all of its members to the eternal destiny of Heaven. The hierarchical structure and ministries provided by bishops and priests, as well as the service of charity offered by deacons, is necessary to maintain this structure. "No one can bestow grace on himself; it must be given and offered. This fact presupposes ministers of grace, authorized and empowered by Christ" (*CCC*, 875). The ministers of grace are the bishops and priests.

With the Holy Spirit's help and guidance, there is no danger that the Church will ever lose this structure of the hierarchical ministry. Nevertheless, the current shortage of priests in North America has led to challenges and struggles among both the faithful and the clergy, mostly in rural areas where priests often drive fifty miles or more to celebrate Mass, hear confessions, and anoint the sick. The priests who do this are sometimes retired from active ministry and are able to arrange to come to an area to make sure Sunday

Mass is celebrated. These priests often have a difficult time feeling a part of the community because they are not there during the week to experience the ups and downs of parish life.

Typically in these priestless parishes the Saturday vigil Mass is replaced by a communion service that consists of Scripture readings, hymns, a reflection on the reading led by a layperson, and distribution of previously consecrated communion hosts. An interesting study has shown that attendance for the communion services is nearly equal to that of the Sunday Mass. This points to what may seem a lesser "crisis," but what is really a more profound problem. Some Catholics who do not have the opportunity to participate in the celebration of the Eucharist on a regular basis are increasingly not understanding why this is important.

Statistics have shown that the priest shortage will get worse before it gets better. Each year more priests reach retirement age or die and are not being replaced in like numbers by newly ordained men. However, studies and surveys also point out some positive trends for the priesthood. Key findings of a study of the priests of the Archdiocese of Chicago at the start of this century revealed:

- Priests generally felt satisfied, skilled, and comfortable in their ministries.

- Priests' vocations stem from a desire to serve and a sense of God's call. Their motivation to serve in sacramental and pastoral ministry has grown over the years.

- Most priests in active ministry are pastors and would like to continue serving in some way even after they retire.

- Priests value the presence of lay ministers and deacons and enjoy flexibility in living arrangements and pastoral ministry.

- Priests affirm their relationship with the bishop and (arch) diocesan leadership.

- Priests most value their opportunity to serve in parishes.[1]

A renewed hope, vision, and spirit among priests nationwide seems to be more typical than not, even at a time when the priests' biggest concern is the heavy workload and the related issue of burnout. Another recent study by Father Stephen Rossetti found that 92.1 percent of the priests agreed with the statement, "Overall, I feel fulfilled ministering as a priest." A slightly higher percentage said "yes" to the statement "I am committed to the ministry of the Catholic Church."[2]

As the Church needs more priests to maintain its essential sacramental ministry, so does the world need more priests, as well, to act in the person of Christ. Global society is becoming more secular,

immoral, violent, environmentally at risk—the list of problems and challenges can be staggering. This is the attraction to men who might be considering priesthood: the opportunity to receive the graces of the Holy Spirit in ordination to allow them to act *in persona Christi Capitis*—in the person of Christ the Head.

In the name of Christ and on the basis of their Holy Orders, the bishop, priest, and deacon live a ministry and life like no other. The character of service of Holy Orders makes them "slaves of Christ" (1Cor 7:22) as they freely become servants to all. The collegial character of their ministry connects them through their bishop with Peter and the Apostles. And the personal character of ministry calls them to a life of holiness as they strive to attain the perfection Jesus called for: "So be perfect, just as your heavenly Father is perfect" (Mt 5:48).

This chapter looks at how the Church's hierarchical and sacramental ministry functions in the three degrees of Holy Orders: bishop, priest, and deacon. At the same time it will explore more about the ministries and lives typical to each. Finally, it will look at more of the challenges of the "vocation climate today" and offer some suggestions for increasing vocations to the priesthood and religious life.

Unique Ministries

The Center for Applied Research in the Apostolate (CARA) based at Georgetown offers survey information in several areas of Catholic life, including Church leadership and mission. Use the index of the CARA site (http://cara.georgetown.edu) to locate reports pertaining to Church ministry, especially pertaining to clergy. Write a three-page report that summarizes pertinent statistics related to the life and ministry of bishops or priests in the United States. Cite other sources besides CARA in your report.

archbishop
An honorary title for a bishop who heads a larger diocese or a diocese of special importance.

nuncio
An archbishop who acts as the official Vatican delegate for a country. He is also called the Apostolic Delegate.

journal**discussion**

- Besides a decrease in the opportunities for Mass and the other sacraments, what are other disadvantages faced by parishes without priests?

- Make a list of "the ten best things about being a priest." Share your list with a group of classmates. Incorporate your suggestions into one list that can be shared with all.

✦ The Role of the Bishop

The role of the bishop can be described by three main tasks: to teach, to sanctify, and to govern. These roles are also shared by his priests as coworkers. The ministry of bishops is collaborative in another way. Together with the college of bishops and united with the pope, bishops have a role of authority and decision-making in the universal Church. Bishops also have particular responsibilities in their own dioceses with emphasis on being a pastor for their local church.

Bishops are always chosen and appointed by the Pope. How does the Pope uncover the names of worthy candidates to be bishop? For example, in the United States the Church is divided into provinces that are made up of neighboring dioceses, each province under an **archbishop**. One of the tasks at a province meeting is for the bishops gathered to consider and promote names of priests who might be worthy candidates for the episcopacy. Some of the characteristics of worthiness may include:

- a good reputation
- irreproachable morality
- even-tempered and stable character
- loyal to the Pope and the Magisterium of the Church
- thorough knowledge of theology and canon law
- prayerful and pious
- an aptitude for governing.

The names of the candidates are voted on and, if accepted, passed on to the United States Conference of Catholic Bishops, which has a committee for the selection of bishops. The nominations are also forwarded to the **nuncio**, the Pope's representative in the United States. The nuncio may send a questionnaire that deals with more of the intellectual, spiritual, social, moral, and priestly characteristics hoped for in a bishop to those who have recommended someone for the episcopacy or to someone who is being asked to comment on a particular candidate for the episcopacy. Though not obliged to stay with the nominees on the list, in the great majority of cases, the nuncio will draw up the list of three names—a *terna*—that he sends to the Congregation for Bishops at the Vatican. This congregation eventually recommends a choice of bishop to the Pope at a Saturday audience. The Pope can take an active role at this point, especially if he personally knows the candidate. More typically, the Pope gives direction to the bishops, nuncio, and Congregation of Bishops to choose candidates with certain emphasis. For example, Pope John Paul II stressed that candidates should display fidelity to the

Magisterium along with exceptional pastoral skills.

Also, all bishops in the world are required to submit a report every five years on issues faced in their dioceses, including any difficulties the people face there. About the time that their report is submitted, the bishops of the nation or region make their visit *ad limina Apostolorum* ("to the thresholds of the Apostles") when they travel to Rome to pray before the tombs of Saint Peter and

Pope Benedict XVI prays at the tomb of St. Peter in the grottoes beneath St. Peter's Basilica, at the Vatican.

Saint Paul and to meet in person with the Pope. These visits help the Pope keep abreast of the state of the Church throughout the world.

Upon ordination to the episcopacy, a bishop becomes part of the college of bishops:

> This college, in so far as it is composed of many members, is the expression of the variety and universality of the people of God; and of the unity of the flock of Christ, in so far it is assembled under one head.[3]

The college of bishops has no authority on its own except in union with the Pope. The authority over the whole Church that the college exercises takes place in an Ecumenical Council. It is up to the Pope to convoke a council, preside over it, and confirm its decisions. The same authority of the college of bishops can take place without assembling bishops in one place, provided that it is the Pope who summons them to action and approves of any decision reached. This collegial unity is also represented in the way that individual bishops represent the teachings of the universal Church in their own dioceses.

The diocesan bishop is also called an *ordinary* or *local ordinary*. He is the pastoral and legal head and representative of his diocese. When the diocese is large in area or population or there is a special pastoral issue, such as many different spoken languages, there may be other bishops who assist the ordinary. These are known as *auxiliary bishops*. Sometimes a *coadjutor bishop* is appointed in a diocese. This is a bishop who is appointed with the right to succeed the ordinary when he retires, resigns, or dies. (The mandatory retirement age for an ordinary is seventy-five.)

There are three other titles related to the episcopacy that are important to mention:

- An *archbishop* is a bishop who governs a diocese that is usually greater in size or prestige than others. Archbishop is an honorary title. There is no further degree of Holy Orders to receive this title. An archbishop has no jurisdiction over a neighboring diocese.

- All bishops must have a diocese under their care. *Titular bishop* is the title given to auxiliary bishops or other bishops in administrative posts who are not ordinaries of their own dioceses so that they can be head of dioceses that once existed in countries surrounding the Mediterranean or in other areas of the world where there are not a great number of Christians.

- Among the college of bishops, the Church has traditionally given the title *cardinal* to certain bishops and archbishops, though to be named a cardinal does not require being either. These are usually archbishops of the largest dioceses in their countries. The word cardinal comes from the Latin *cardo* for "hinge," as cardinals were seen as a key administrative link in assisting the Pope. Cardinals have been called "Princes of the Church," and they have the exclusive role of electing a new Pope. However, cardinals who have reached eighty years of age cannot enter into the conclave and participate in the election. Cardinals are also titular bishops of outlying sees around Rome.

The Bishop as Teacher

The teaching office of the bishop is named as the first pastoral task of bishops by the *Catechism of the Catholic Church*. Bishops are called "heralds of faith" and "authentic teachers." They have been given the power to call all people to belief and to strengthen those who already have a living faith. Bishops teach the mystery of Jesus Christ in its entirety so that all people can find salvation in him and his Church. They also teach people how to pray and worship the Lord, thus leading them to eternal happiness.

Bishops teach on three levels within the Church. In his own diocese, the bishop teaches directly to his people and through his priests. This task is handled in several ways. First, the bishop regularly visits parishes in his diocese. He is often present for occasions like the dedication of a new church, the installation of a pastor, a special Lenten or Advent series in which he is the featured speaker, and usually once per year as the minister

Bishop Kenneth Angell, of the Diocese of Burlington, gets a hug following a Mass Wednesday, Sept. 12, 2001. Angell offered prayers not only for the thousands killed and injured in the New York and Washington, DC, terrorist attacks, but also for his brother David Angell and his wife, Lynn, who were killed when the American Airlines jet they were flying in from Boston to Los Angeles was hijacked and flown into one of the World Trade Center towers.

of the Sacrament of Confirmation. On each of these occasions, he uses the opportunity to initiate and promote dialogue with the people and offer clear teaching on matters of faith and morals. Some of this instruction may occur in his homily at Mass.

Secondly, the bishop teaches by supervising the training of catechists and setting a curriculum for religious instruction that is based on Scripture, Tradition, liturgy, and on the teaching authority and life in the Church. The bishop also has the responsibility to teach all the people of his diocese, not only Catholics. To fulfill this responsibility, he may write articles in the local newspaper or appear in interviews done by the local media offering the Gospel perspective on issues facing the community: perhaps the plight of local farm workers or the impending execution of a capital criminal.

Third, bishops also teach on a national level, working with a conference of bishops from their own country to address issues that impact the entire nation. The United States Conference of Catholic Bishops is one such organization. The group is made up of the entire body of bishops in the United States along with hundreds of support staff. It meets as a body two times per year. The USCCB has recently addressed several ethical life issues, family issues involving marriage and women in society, as well as social justice issues impacting both the United States and the world at large.

When collaborating collegially with other bishops and the Pope, bishops also teach on a worldwide level. This teaching office is the Magisterium, which is the official teaching authority of the Church. It is the task of the Magisterium to preserve the truth first taught by Christ and handed down through apostolic succession. This is done through the gift of **infallibility**. Guided by the Holy Spirit, the college of bishops, in union with the Pope, can exercise the gift of infallibility when teaching about or protecting Christ's Revelation on matters of faith or morality. As mentioned, an infallible teaching may be released by an Ecumenical Council or by individual bishops when they teach collectively and in union with the Pope.

The Pope himself can teach infallibly by virtue of the "chair of Saint Peter," where he sits as supreme teacher and pastor in the Church. The Pope teaches infallibly when he teaches as pastor of all the faithful, is proclaiming a definitive doctrine pertaining to faith or morals, and does so intending to use his full authority in an unchangeable decision. A Pope may offer several teachings about the faith that are without error, but only rarely does he offer infallible declarations of the faith. The most recent occurrence was Pope Pius XII's declaration in 1950 of the dogma of the Blessed Mother's Assumption into Heaven. Because Christ promised to remain with the Church through the Holy Spirit, Catholics owe their assent and obedience of faith to infallible statements of the Pope and bishops. In addition, Catholics also owe their religious assent (as distinct but linked to their assent of faith) to the non-infallible teachings of the Pope in a special way and to the non-infallible statements of the bishops that are in communion with the Pope.

infallibility
The charism or gift of the Church offered by Christ whereby it is protected from error in matters of faith and morals. This gift is most exclusively exercised by a Pope or an Ecumenical Council of bishops acting in union with him.

The Bishop as Priest

Bishops take up the task demanded by Christ: to help people achieve perfection. The bishop and his priests sanctify the Church by their prayer, by their work, by sharing the Word of God, and by celebrating the sacraments, with special focus on the Eucharist. The Eucharist is "the source and summit of Christian life," the center of the universal and local Church and the work of the Holy Trinity. The Eucharist contains the spiritual treasury of the Church, who is Christ himself. All of the other sacraments are directed to the Eucharist. The Sunday liturgy is the place and time when the community gathers to worship, pray, and come to know and live the Paschal Mystery more deeply. Likewise the Eucharist is at the heart of the ministry of the diocesan Church. Because of their reception of the fullness of Holy Orders, it is the "bishops who are the principal dispensers of the mysteries of God, and it is their function to control, promote and protect the entire liturgical life of the Church entrusted to them."[4]

The bishop must know his entire flock (diocese) as the Good Shepherd knows his sheep. The first letter of Peter describes this mission:

> Tend the flock of God in your midst, [overseeing] not by constraint but willingly, as God would have it, not for shameful profit but eagerly. Do not lord it over those assigned to you, but be examples to the flock. (1 Pt 5:2–3)

The bishop pays special attention to the spiritual, intellectual, and material needs of his priests. The bishop provides opportunities for the priest to continue his studies in theology and to take extended retreats to refresh himself spiritually. Likewise, the bishop is welcoming of the gifts and talents offered by the laity and makes sure that their rights and duties to take part in the building up of their personal lives and the life of the Church are respected. A survey of diocesan ministries reveals lay people taking leadership roles in such ministries as catechesis, communications, finance, Catholic schools, and family life.

Also, bishops exercise their role as priests by befriending those who don't share the Catholic faith, encouraging **ecumenism** as it is

---

ecumenism
The movement that seeks Christian unity and eventually the unity of all peoples throughout the world.

Bishop Daniel Buechlein escorts Mother Teresa on a visit to Memphis, Tennessee, in 1989.

understood by the Church. This task may play out both in local and national settings. For example, a bishop may participate in an inter-faith prayer service or conference with the minister of another religious denomination in his own diocese. On the national level, he may be assigned to a committee of bishops that looks for commonalities with other faiths as a way to promote an ecumenical spirit.

The bishop, priests, deacons, and laity are on a journey together—the journey to the perfection of eternal life. It is the bishop who is the focus of this journey, marking the way and making it holy.

The Bishop as Ruler

The governing office of the bishop is held in union with the Pope. Bishops govern the dioceses assigned to them through their words and actions. As in his relationship with the college of bishops, he interacts with the faithful of his diocese in dialogue and with compassion.

The bishop has several helpers in fulfilling his role of authority. His coworker priests are given the authority to act in his name in parishes. Like the bishop himself, a pastor of a parish promotes the spiritual welfare of the faithful by preaching, administering the sacraments, and exercising certain powers of supervision, as well as teaching and administering Church precepts. These powers are offered as a father for his children. Hence, priests are addressed by the title "Father."

The person with the most authority in the diocese after the bishop is the *vicar general*. A vicar general is a priest or auxiliary bishop who acts in place of the bishop throughout the diocese except in the areas that are reserved for the bishop alone. Each diocese is required to have a vicar general. This is helpful in large dioceses or in places where the bishop may be called to serve on committees or functions that affect the Church on a national or universal scale. Similarly, an *episcopal vicar* helps the bishop rule in certain predetermined areas of the diocese.

For example, an episcopal vicar may be assigned to a certain geographic region, or to supervise the religious orders of the diocese or other fraternal organizations like the Knights of Columbus.

In summary, "the faithful should be closely attached to the bishop as the Church is to Jesus Christ and as Jesus Christ is to the Father."[5]

study questions

1. What are the three main tasks of a bishop?

2. How are bishops chosen?

3. What are some characteristics of worthiness in a bishop candidate?

4. What is the difference between a bishop and an archbishop?

5. What happens at an *ad limina Apostolorum* visit?

6. How does the college of bishops act with authority?

7. Differentiate between a coadjutor bishop, auxiliary bishop, titular bishop, and cardinal.

8. Share an example of the way a bishop teaches on each level within the Church: universal, national, and local.

9. Define *infallibility*.

10. How does the bishop practice his sanctifying office?

11. Name two roles of people who help the bishop in his governing office.

journal discussion

- Name a priest that you think would make a good bishop. Explain why.

- Recall the occasion when you have had the closest contact with your local bishop.

The Bishop's Calendar

Besides the daily administrative tasks and meetings that take place at the cathedral, a bishop has a variety of special functions that allow him closer contact with the people of his diocese. Examine one bishop's recent monthly planner:

SUN	MON	TUE	WED	THUR	FRI	SAT
Lutheran/ Catholic Prayer Breakfast **1**	Final Exam for Conversational Spanish Class **2**	**3**	Presbyteral Council Meeting **4**	**5**	Diocesan Development Office Meeting **6**	Meeting with Caucus of Black Catholics **7**
Sacrament of Confirmation, Saint Bavo's Church **8**	Dinner at College Seminary **9**	Catholic College Student Retreat all day **10**	Meet with Office of Vicar for the Clergy **11**	Mass for Catholic Schools Week **12**	Ski Trip with Saint Stephen's Youth Group **13**	RCIA Class: Presentation on the Sacrament of Penance **14**
15	Diocesan Finance Council Meeting **16**	**17**	**18**	Mass for Diocesan High Schools at the City Arena **19**	Day off! **20**	**21**
Bishop's Administra-tive Advisory Council Meeting **22**	Celebrate My Sister and Brother-in-Law's Fortieth Wedding Anniversary Mass & Party **23**	Catechist Enrichment Day: Keynote and Celebrant for Mass **24**	Celebrate Mass at County Correctional Facility **25**	Tijuana Orphanage Fundraiser **26**	Sacrament of Confirmation, Saint Monica's Church **27**	**28**
29	**30**					

✦ The Role of the Priest

In the Sacrament of Holy Orders, priests are consecrated to share in the bishop's ministry and serve the Church in three basic ways:

● The priest preaches the Gospel.

● The priest celebrates divine worship.

● The priest provides pastoral governance.

In fulfilling these roles in the Spirit of Christ, priests grow in their own holiness and build up the laity so they can live lives of faith, hope, and charity and, like the priest, reach for perfection.

The first task for a priest is to preach the Word of God. This order is logical because the other two tasks—worship and governance—cannot take place until people have heard the message of the Gospel and come to believe it. When Jesus commissioned the ministry of his Apostles he described the same order:

> "Go into the whole world and proclaim the Gospel to every creature. Whoever believes and is baptized will be saved; whoever does not believe will be condemned." (Mk 16:15–16)

Faith is awakened first by the preaching of the Word to people both within and outside of the Church. This is done in several different ways, in both words and actions. By leading exemplary lives, priests model the Gospel for others. In areas of the world where there are many non-Christians, it is often the *practice* of the Gospel—for example, attending to the physical needs of the people—that first attracts people to the person and message of Christ. In Western nations, priests are able to preach the Gospel by applying it to contemporary conditions that affect the entire community: e.g., offering shelter to immigrants in a parish facility or walking with others in a pro-life march. Specifically within the Church, the preaching of the Gospel does involve the use of the spoken word, especially during the liturgy when the priest proclaims the Gospel reading and connects it to the lives of the people in his homily.

The celebration of the Eucharist and the other sacraments is at the center of the priest's ministry. At Mass, the priest teaches the faithful to share in the offering Christ made of his life and in turn make an offering of their own lives to God the Father. He instructs the people to ask the Church for forgiveness of their sins in the Sacrament of Penance. The priest helps the faithful to develop their own prayer life as he deepens his own. The priest prays the daily Divine Office or Liturgy of the Hours in the name of the whole Church and *in fact* for the whole world. As part of his task of leading worship, the priest is responsible for the décor of the church where Mass is celebrated, making sure that it is "in good taste and a worthy place for prayer and sacred ceremonial."[6]

Priests care for the Church as pastoral ministers, fulfilling their share in support of the bishops in governing the Church. The priest is typically known for carrying out his role of pastor in a parish. At ordination, diocesan priests, also called "secular priests," promise their obedience to the bishop where they will serve. The service of priests is modeled in the role of Christ, who taught that people should live not only for themselves but for others. It is the responsibility of priests to help the faithful to reach Christian maturity. The pastor's care is directed to all, but toward some with unique needs he must act in a more particular way. Priests are instructed to provide special care to:

- the poor and weaker ones of society
- young people
- married couples and parents
- the consecrated religious men and women
- the sick and the dying.

It is through taking on the daily tasks of the priesthood—their whole ministry which is in union with the bishop and other priests—that the priest remains on the course for perfection of life:

Since every priest in his own way assumes the person of Christ he is endowed with a special grace. By this grace the priest, through his service of the people committed to his care and all the people of God, is able the better to pursue the perfection of Christ, whose place he takes.[7]

While it is possible for God's grace to unfold through unworthy priests, it is in priests who have chosen the path of holiness through the guidance of the Holy Spirit who reap the most

benefits both for themselves and those whom they serve. Although most diocesan priests are responsible for a parish, where they teach the people, guide them in making moral decisions, and call forth their gifts, the scope of the priest's mission really encompasses the universal Church.

Life of a Parish Priest

"The diocesan priest is someone who lives with the people and each becomes a part of the other's life."[8] By the diocesan priest's very calling, Father Stephen Rossetti continues, the diocesan priest is bound to a particular geographic area and called to live among a particular group of people. In doing so, he is not just a physical presence in a parish, but he is also emotionally and spiritually connected to the people. A parish priest is present in the daily lives of his parishioners, sharing both the joys and sadness that accompany everyday life. In his role as parish priest, he is privy to the deeper and often hidden stories of both kinds of experiences.

A diocesan priest pledges obedience to his bishop and works to support his bishop's ministry. Part of this promise involves being obliged to accept assignments at the bishop's service. While most bishops have a personnel board or council made up of about seven priests to help them determine the priest's assignments, the bishop ultimately has responsibility for all appointments. For newly ordained priests, he takes special care to assign them to a parish where they are more likely to work well with the current pastor. Though the shortage of priests does often demand it, it remains rare for a newly ordained priest to be installed as a pastor of a parish right after ordination. Parish pastors generally have more input about where they will be assigned; for example, in some dioceses they are able to apply confidentially to be pastor at a specific parish. Other bishops may have a predetermined time period for rotating pastors—perhaps something in the neighborhood of twelve years.

Some parishes are always considered "more desirable" than others, but for different reasons. For example, one priest may prefer an assignment in a parish with an upper-middle class socioeconomic base because he knows that the parish's ministries—including the outreach to the poor—will be more easily funded than in other parishes, and he will be able to spend more time in the roles of preaching the Gospel, celebrating the sacraments, and counseling people. However, another priest may prefer a parish with a poorer economic base because of his preference for living and working directly with people who have great needs.

Certainly the small parish at Ars, France, was not considered the most desirable of assignments when it was given to newly ordained Father Jean-Baptiste-Marie Vianney in 1818. The village had only forty houses, but four taverns. It was a farming community where people worked on Sunday and didn't often go to church.

Father John Vianney made himself at home in Ars. He regularly visited the people in their homes and helped them in difficult times. When one of the taverns went out of business, Father John helped the owner raise money to buy his own farm. Then he tore the tavern down. The townspeople noticed some other things about their new priest. He seemed to spend most of the night in prayer. He gave away all of his clothing and much of the furniture in the **rectory** to the poor and ate only two potatoes per day, explaining "some devils can only be cast out by prayer and fasting."

But what Father John Vianney became best known for in Ars and well beyond was the advice and counsel he offered people who came to him for confession. During the last ten years of his life, he spent from sixteen to eighteen hours per day in

the confessional. In 1855, over 20,000 pilgrims came to Ars for Father John to hear their confession. He would hear up to three hundred confessions per day, sometimes being able to tell what sins were being withheld by the penitent. John Vianney's life was his parish. He said of his parishioners at Ars:

Saint John Vianney

My God, grant me the conversion of my parish. I am willing to suffer all my life whatsoever it may please you to lay upon me. Yes, even for a hundred years I am prepared to endure the sharpest pains; only let my people be converted.[9]

Parish priests today are under the patronage of Saint John Vianney. He was canonized in 1925. The ministry of the parish priest depends somewhat on the priest's personal interests and skills, but will in any case demand much time preparing for and

rectory
The house in which a pastor and other parish priests live.

celebrating the sacraments. One of the most crucial responsibilities a priest has for teaching the people is his Sunday homily. The priest prays about this reflection on the theme of the Scripture readings with special attention to the Gospel message during the week leading up to Sunday. His words connect not only the theme of the Scripture, but also must relate it to events in the parish and in the worldwide Church. To be able to effectively do this, part of each day is set aside for personal prayer.

Visiting the sick, visiting people in their homes, visiting children in a parish school or religious education program, and working with various parish committees and neighborhood organizations are all part of a priest's daily ministry. He also helps to prepare catechumens for the sacraments and couples for marriage. He may counsel several couples who are having difficulties in their marriage. A required focus of ministry for all priests is paying special attention to the needs of the poor. When John Vianney was pastor in Ars in the years after the French Revolution, there were many young orphan girls wandering the streets as prostitutes. To combat this problem, Father John founded an orphanage across the road from the parish church. He would spend the noon hour at the orphanage offering catechetical instruction to the girls. Today, all Catholic parishes have formal and informal outreach to the poor. The pastor is often the one overseeing these efforts, and he participates in them in a personal way, as well.

The life of a parish priest is not an easy one. But it is rewarding, with most of the tangible benefits coming from his proximity to the Eucharist and other sacraments, the emphasis on personal prayer, and his special connection with the parishioners. Father Rossetti writes:

> A consistent support and challenge for priests comes from the people of God. Their presence is an important way in which God is manifested to us. As we personally connect with the people whom we serve, we are affirmed, supported, challenged, and "stretched."[10]

Other Priestly Ministries and Callings

Not all priests are parish priests. Even with the shortage of priests, a diocesan priest may take on a different primary ministry. For example, he may be a spiritual director, prison chaplain, hospital chaplain, school principal, college or high school teacher, diocesan administrator, author, retreat director, vicar general, director of reli-

gious education, or even a full-time student. When doing these special ministries, a diocesan priest will most often still live "in residence" at a parish. On the weekends and at other times when he is free, he will be asked to assist at the parish by celebrating Mass and the other sacraments and perhaps by sharing in a parish-based ministry.

As previously alluded, not all priests are diocesan priests. Some religious communities are "clerical," meaning that they include priests. A religious priest takes vows of poverty, chastity, and obedience and follows the charism of his community. His obedience is both to his religious superior and to the bishop of his diocese. With the great need for priests, many religious priests have been called on to "share in the care of souls and in the practice of apostolic works under the authority of bishops" just as the diocesan clergy.[11] Many religious communities—for example, the Jesuits, Franciscans, and Holy Cross—sponsor and staff parishes. For example, in South Bend, Indiana, the home of its provincial headquarters and the University of Notre Dame, which it sponsors, the Congregation of Holy Cross founded several parishes and still maintains seven with Holy Cross priests serving as pastors.

Holy Cross priests gather on the steps of the Main Building at the University of Notre Dame.

In most cases, religious priests do not serve in a parish. Their ministries are more varied and they are not bound to one diocese. A young man gauging whether or not he is more suited to be a religious priest or a diocesan priest must examine two main issues in his discernment. The first involves discerning the call to priesthood. This would involve a process similar to the one described on pages 231–235. To then determine between diocesan priesthood and religious priesthood, he must consider questions like these:

- Do you prefer living and serving the people in a well-defined area (a diocese)?

- Are you drawn to parish ministry?

- Do you feel called to live in a community of men who share the same ideals, commitment, and mission?

- Are you attracted to the possibility of a wide variety of ministries?

In general, answering affirmatively to the first two questions would indicate an attraction to the diocesan priesthood. "Yes" answers to the last two questions might indicate a preference for being a member of a religious community. Father Warren Sazama, S.J., vocation director for Wisconsin-province Jesuits, compared diocesan priests to "general practitioners" and religious priests to "specialists." "As in medicine, the Church needs both," Sazama wrote.[12]

Determining *which* religious community to apply to would involve further discernment. The particular charism or spirit of the community would be one point of reference. The charism is typically drawn from the vision of the community's founder. For example, the founder of the Society of Jesus, or Jesuits, was Saint Ignatius Loyola. His commitment to the apostolate of education and his development of what has become known as **Ignatian spirituality** make up a great part of the charism of the Jesuits.

Also, religious communities are differentiated among those that are engaged in active ministry (like the Jesuits or the Holy Cross) versus

Ignatian spirituality
Following the example of Saint Ignatius, Ignatian spirituality centers on the imitation of Christ—focusing on those priorities that constitute his mind, heart, values, priorities, and loves.

those that are cloistered, contemplative, and monastic. These terms are similar and may be used to refer to the same religious community. *Cloistered* refers to communities where the members live in an enclosed space, not accessible to outsiders, and who do not go outside the area without permission. *Contemplative* religious usually do not engage in active ministries; rather, they live in seclusion and devote themselves to prayer and meditation. Contemplatives may support their communities by farming, creating art-

work, baking, or typesetting. *Monasticism* refers to persons living in seclusion from the world and living under the vows of poverty, chastity, and obedience. Most of the members of these types of communities are religious brothers, not priests. However, some priests in each monastery are needed to help fulfill the sacramental needs of all the members.

The formation process for religious priests incorporates both studies and training specific to preparing for the priesthood along with initiation

A Priest and a Dream

The University of Notre Dame is well-known for its famous Fighting Irish football team. But fewer know that the college in Northern Indiana began as the dream of priests of a fledgling religious order from France and with the cooperation of their bishop who lived hundreds of miles away.

The dream began when Father Basil Moreau, the founder of the Congregation of the Holy Cross, chose a young priest, Father Edward Sorin, to lead a group of six religious brothers to the frontier of Southern Indiana to set up a mission and, hopefully, to be granted permission to build a college. The bishop in Indiana agreed to the offer with some stipulations. The land was in a remote area 250 miles away. The Holy Cross Fathers could have the land if they could build a college within two years. If not, the land would revert back to the bishop.

In the winter of 1842, Father Sorin and the brothers arrived in the Northern Indiana woods with only $300 and twenty-four months to build a college. The mission was successful, and the bishop granted the land for Notre Dame to the Holy Cross. But the challenge was not over. In 1879, a fire broke out on campus and destroyed the main building, which housed all of the student records, most of the classrooms, the library, dining hall, and dorms—not to mention a dome with a statue of the Blessed Virgin that was on top of the roof.

In his 2005 inauguration address as the University's seventeenth president, Father John I.

Jenkins, C.S.C., told how Father Sorin persevered in keeping the dream alive:

> Father Sorin walked through the ruins, felt the devastation of the community, and signaled to everyone to enter the Church, where he stood on the altar steps and spoke.

> "I came here as a young man and dreamed of building a great university in honor of Our Lady," he said. "But I built it too small, and she had to burn it to the ground to make the point. So, tomorrow, as soon as the bricks cool, we will rebuild it, bigger and better than ever." Later that same day, the students saw Father Sorin, then sixty-five years old, stepping slowly through the ruins of his life's work, bent slightly forward, pushing a wheelbarrow full of bricks, getting ready to rebuild.

> Three hundred laborers worked sixteen hours a day to rebuild the main building in time for classes that fall. They rebuilt it from the ground up, and when they got to the top, and came to the place where the dome had been, they built one taller and wider than the one before, and this time—for the first time—they covered it with gold.[13]

Write an essay that tells about:

● A dream you have for your own life.

● A plan you have for accomplishing your dream.

● How God is part of your dream and plan.

into the religious community. Because of this dual track, preparation for religious priesthood usually takes longer than the preparation for diocesan priesthood. A man will usually take final vows into the religious community before being ordained, though in the Jesuits, the final vows may come three or more years after the man is ordained. The Jesuits have a long formation process. From the time a man first enters the community to the day of ordination is about eleven years.

Some religious communities are *active contemplatives*, meaning they mix an apostolate outside of the community with a devotion to prayer. Also, most communities have a combination of apostolates. The Congregation of the Holy Cross is devoted not only to parish ministry, but to education, work with orphans, publishing, and missionary work in places like Bangladesh, Ghana, Kenya, Tanzania, and Uganda, to name a few.

studyquestions

1. How did Saint John Vianney ingratiate himself with the people at Ars?

2. How does a priest plan for his homily?

3. What are some other typical ministries of a priest at a parish?

4. Why might a priest be "in residence" at a parish?

5. What is the difference between a diocesan priest and a parish priest?

6. Define *apostolate* related to the role of a priest.

7. Why might formation and training take longer for a religious priest than a diocesan priest?

8. Why are most members of cloistered, contemplative, or monastic orders brothers and not priests?

journaldiscussion

● Describe a parish priest you know who has woven his life well within the entire faith community.

● How would you define a "desirable parish"?

● Create a list of pluses and minuses for both diocesan and religious priesthood.

✦ The Role of the Permanent Deacon

The very heart of the diaconate is service. The deacon serves at liturgy and is also in service to the needs of the entire Church and world. His service in charity encompasses many ministries and is multifaceted. In an address to permanent deacons of the United States, Pope John Paul II explained:

The charity is both love of God and love of neighbor. . . . Certainly today's world is not lacking opportunities for such a ministry, whether in the form of the simplest acts of charity or the most heroic witness to the radical demands of the Gospel. All around us many of our brothers and sisters live in either spiritual or material poverty or both. . . . In the midst of the human condition, it is a great source of satisfaction to learn that so many permanent deacons in the United States are involved in direct service to the needy: to the ill, the abused and battered, the young and old, the dying and bereaved, the dead, the blind, and disabled, those who have known sufferings in their marriage, the homeless, victims of substance abuse, prisoners, refugees, street people, the rural poor, victims of racial and ethnic discrimination, and many others. As Christ tells us, "as often as you did it for one of my least brothers, you did it for me."[14]

In liturgy, the deacon serves as minister of the Word of God and at the altar. The Second Vatican Council, in restoring the permanent diaconate, established several functions and roles the deacon can perform in liturgy. A deacon may be the ordinary minister of Baptism. A deacon is also able to officiate at the Sacrament of Matrimony. While he is not able to celebrate a funeral Mass, a deacon can conduct funerals apart from Mass and burial services at the grave site. A deacon may also be the minister of **benediction**,

benediction
The rite in which Jesus is exposed to the adoration of the faithful in the Blessed Sacrament contained in a monstrance. It is not so much the priest who blesses the people in this rite, but Jesus himself.

including offering the people a blessing with the host in its monstrance. At Mass, a deacon assists around the altar, bringing the offerings of bread and wine to the priest from the faithful. Through his ordination and connection with the bishop, a deacon is able to read the Gospel and preach a homily. Sharing the Word of God in this manner is one of the deacon's primary roles.

The restoration of the permanent diaconate and the number of permanent deacons (nearly 15,000 in the United States) has been an asset to the Church as priestly ordinations decreased during the same time period since the end of the Second Vatican Council. The stories of men who have accepted the calling to the diaconate, undergone training, and been ordained are varied and significant. Consider the following four:

- Deacon Bernie Ouellette of the Edmonton Diocese in Canada felt called to the diaconate in 1994 after reading an article on deacons in the Knights of Columbus magazine. "I spoke to my spiritual adviser and he told me 'You should go to see your bishop and tell him to make you a deacon,'" Ouellette explained.

  In his home parish, Deacon Bernie trains lay ministers, coordinates the catechumenate, visits schools, hospitals, and the elderly in the nursing home, and assists priests at Mass. Married to Audrey, who encouraged and supported him through his formation and in his ministry, Deacon Bernie supports himself and his family as an accountant. Married deacons are not paid.[15]

- Deacon Terry Collins of Chicago was ordained to the diaconate in 2003. Terry was nearing fifty years old and had three decades experience as a high school and college basketball coach when he felt called to the priesthood. The archbishop and spiritual advisers suggested the diaconate where he would be able to continue to coach and teach, ministries very compatible with the service ministry of the diaconate.

  Besides coaching, Deacon Terry worked with the youth group and preached at Mass at an urban Chicago parish. Single at the time of ordination, Deacon Terry will remain celibate since "a man who has already received the Sacrament of Holy Orders can no longer marry" (CCC, 1580).

- The vocation to the diaconate for Deacon Ron Searles is a true partnership between him and his wife, Eileen. Ordained for the Diocese of Joliet, Deacon Ron works with abused and neglected children as a volunteer in the county court system in addition to his various parish ministries. His focus on helping children arises from his own family life: he and Eileen have four grown children and have on a number of occasions taken into their home unwed pregnant girls who need shelter and support as they ready to give birth.

  Speaking of sharing his life and ministry with his wife, Deacon Ron said, "We have the best of both worlds. We share our growing love for the Lord and each other. We minister together whenever possible, sharing our individual gifts as well as our witness of love."[16]

- A class of 1961 graduate of Notre Dame, Deacon Greg Gehred and his wife raised six children, all Notre Dame graduates themselves. A doctor with a general practice in Fort Atkinson, Wisconsin, Deacon Greg was ordained for Saint Joseph's Parish in 2004. Besides his parish ministries, which include a regular schedule of preaching, he maintains a free clinic in the area where he provides medical support to those without insurance.

The life and ministry of the permanent diaconate continues to evolve in the generation following its reinstitution. The call to service—both in the Church and in society—is its basic mission. Pope John Paul II explained what is expected of permanent deacons:

As Christians we must not be ashamed to speak of the qualities of a servant to which all believers must aspire, and especially deacons, whose ordination rite describes them as "servants of all." A deacon must be known for fidelity, integrity, and obedience, and so it is that fidelity to

Pope John Paul II

Christ, moral integrity, and obedience to the bishop must mark your lives, as the ordination rite makes clear.[17]

Call and Formation to the Diaconate

The brief vignettes above describing the lives and ministries of current deacons introduce some basic requirements for the permanent diaconate.

For example, single men who are ordained to the permanent diaconate, like Deacon Terry, must make a promise to be celibate. Married men who apply for candidacy to the diaconate must be in a stable marriage. Listed below is a more complete list of requirements:

- *Status.* The diaconate is open to mature Roman Catholic males, married or single, firm in work and career, and of sound moral character, possessing a mature faith, and having a strong inclination for service. Maturity typically involves an age requirement. A deacon should usually be at least age thirty-five at the time of ordination and not more than sixty. Deacons—married or single—who work full-time in a secular profession are expected to support themselves and their families financially.

- *Family.* If the candidate is married, he must be in a stable marriage for at least five to ten years and have the consent and support of his wife. His children must be at an age that they will not be impacted greatly by the special time commitments of their father's ministries. Also, he should understand that he is not allowed to remarry if his spouse should die.

- *Natural Gifts.* The man should demonstrate the potential to develop the ministerial skills of relating to people, speaking well, and being a spiritual leader.

- *Spirituality.* He should be committed to a life of prayer and willing to make personal sacrifices to be a consecrated sign of God's love for others in his vocation to serve.

- *Education.* In some dioceses, at least two years of college or its academic equivalent is required. In others, the man may have to have completed high school and be capable of doing college work.

- *Service and Involvement.* The man should have some previous experience of active apostolic involvement in leadership and service both in the Church and in his community.

While the call to the diaconate will arise from the parish—a pastor may recommend a man from his

parish for the diaconate—whenever a man is ordained, he is to serve the diocesan Church. When the bishop lays hands on the candidate, it signifies the "deacon's special attachment to the bishop in the tasks of his "**diakonia**" (*CCC*, 1569). The bishop will assign the deacon to ministries where there are the greatest needs. Usually this is in a parish (but maybe not the man's home parish), where the deacon will be assigned under the direct supervision of the pastor.

The formation process leading to ordination is similar to priestly formation in that it involves four important areas: human, spiritual, intellectual, and pastoral. Generally formation will take about five years. It requires a commitment of time; for example, about two full Saturdays per month for most of the year. It also involves a significant commitment of "spirit." A candidate for the diaconate must remain spiritually engaged in the process during the time he is away from the classes or meetings. A spirit of service and prayer must permeate his entire life, including at work and with friends and family.

A candidate program, sponsored by a diocese, may resemble the following structure: ministry formation, aspirancy, and candidacy.

Ministry formation may serve as a prerequisite step for candidacy and last for about three years. Ministry formation takes place in programs intended to train and form both men and women for several lay ministries in a diocese. For potential deacons, focused attention is given to the academic, spiritual, and pastoral requirements for the diaconate. The program may include classes, one-to-one meetings with advisers and spiritual directors, writing papers, making retreats, and engaging in ongoing theological reflections. At the completion of ministry formation, a man may make formal application to candidacy for ordination.

Recall that aspirancy refers to a person "aspiring to know more about" something, in this case, the diaconate. In this context, aspirancy usually is a year-long period with more focused discernment in which the candidate prayerfully determines whether or not he wants to seek the graces and responsibility that come with the Sacrament of Holy Orders. Courses on preaching, liturgical practice, canon law, and the theology of Holy Orders may take place. Regular meetings with a mentor deacon and his wife will also help in the discernment process for a candidate and his own wife.

A candidacy year precedes ordination. Formal training including more advanced courses in homiletics, canon law, and liturgy, along with selected courses in theology and an introduction to philosophy, will continue. Regular meetings with a spiritual director and the mentor deacon also continue. During the final year, the candidates participate in at least one day of recollection. A five-day canonical retreat is required by Church law at the end of the formation time.

As with ordination to the episcopacy and presbyterate, ordination for a deacon is on a Sunday in the diocesan cathedral with encouragement for as many of the faithful who can come to attend and participate.

diakonia
A Greek word that literally means "service."

The Permanent Diaconate: A Unique Opportunity

The order of the permanent diaconate was instituted in the early Church by the Apostles following a need for assistants. Seven men—Stephen, Philip, Prochorus, Nicanor, Timon, Parmenas, and Nicholas of Antoich—were chosen and presented to the Apostles, "who prayed and laid hands on them" (Acts 6:6). The ministry of these original seven deacons broadened beyond the distribution of food and the waiting of tables to the preaching of the Gospel. Stephen was the first Christian martyr, stoned to death for his defense of the faith.

The permanent diaconate continued before waning in about the third century, when the diaconate was maintained almost exclusively as a transition to priesthood. During the time of World War II, Catholic men imprisoned in Nazi camps came together for prayer and support. After their release they continued to meet in groups offering their service and stewardship to the Church. Pope Pius XII recognized what came to be called "the Deacon's Circle" and encouraged dioceses around the world to initiate similar apostolates. These groups were the precursor of the modern diaconate, restored by a majority vote of the Second Vatican Council on October 30, 1963.

While honoring the gift of celibacy as a special gift for the benefit of the Church, the Council allowed for the diaconate to be conferred on "mature married men." The decision allows for an explicit union of the Sacraments of Holy Orders and Matrimony, and the life and ministries unique to each. Married deacons and their wives are called to give a clear witness to the holiness of marriage and family life to the world. Pope John Paul II reiterated this when he said of a deacon and his wife:

> By facing in a spirit of faith the challenges of married life and the demands of daily living, they strengthen the family life not only of the Church community but of the whole of society. They also

show how the obligations of family, work, and ministry can be harmonized in the service of the Church's mission. Deacons and their wives and children can be a great encouragement to all others who are working to promote family life.[18]

The restoration of the permanent diaconate "constitutes an important enrichment for the Church's mission" (*CCC*, 1571). The permanent imprint or character of Holy Orders configures the deacon to Christ and makes him the servant of all.

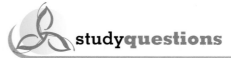

study questions

1. What are the two main areas of a deacon's service?

2. What are some ways that a deacon is able to serve at liturgy?

3. Who is eligible to be a candidate for the diaconate?

4. Describe each of the areas of a candidate program for the diaconate: ministry formation, aspirancy, and candidacy.

5. What is the scriptural foundation of the diaconate?

6. How did the permanent diaconate re-emerge prior to the Second Vatican Council?

7. What is the unique opportunity for a married deacon and his wife?

journal discussion

- What are some service opportunities in your community that you have done or to which you are attracted?

- Imagine your father was a deacon. What kind of responsibility would that bring for you?

✦ The Rewards of Holy Orders

Whom do you think of when you hear someone described with the words "radical" or "countercultural"? If you lived in the 1960s, you might associate the descriptions with an old-fashioned "hippie," that is, someone who dropped out of the mainstream of society to protest the Vietnam War or left to work overseas in the Peace Corps. Or, to update

a bit, today you may associate radical and countercultural with something as simple as one of your classmates or peers wearing alternative clothing or style of hair. In a few years, you may hear of friends who graduate from college, acquire a beat-up car, and explore the country or even another continent for months at a time with little more than the clothes on their back and a few basic supplies.

That is radical! And countercultural, too, as the more frequently chosen path for young people today goes something like this:

- Graduate from high school.
- Go to a four-year college.
- Specialize in an academic major in an area that is more likely to lead to a high-paying career.
- Graduate from college.
- Attend graduate or pre-professional school.
- Begin that high-paying career!

What about associating the terms *radical* and *countercultural* with the priesthood and religious life? Would you find that to be an accurate comparison? Certainly, in a global society tied to consumerism, it is radical to trade the desire for more income for a desire for companionship with the poor and needy. And, with free unions and open sexual behaviors continuing to press more and more extremes of immorality, the idea of making a promise to live chastely and celibately is certainly countercultural. Perhaps a vow of obedience is the most radical idea associated with priesthood and religious life. Today's Western society holds as most sacred the freedom to choose one's lifestyle and values. Obedience to any person or principle does not jive with this view.

In the famous words of the poet Robert Frost:

> Two roads diverged in a wood, and I—
> I took the one less traveled by,
> And that has made all the difference.[19]

The vocations of priesthood and religious life are a road less traveled. They are a radical departure from typical career and vocational choices. In an increasingly secular world, it is a countercultural and dramatic sign of discipleship in Jesus Christ. For the Catholic Church, besides being essential for the hierarchical and sacramental ministry, the life of a priest is one that is meaningful, satisfying, and never boring. God has never stopped calling a significant number of men to this vocation. It is the task of today's Church to pray and encourage these men to accept this call.

In one of his last public statements, Pope John Paul II prayed for vocations and encouraged young people to reflect on the same challenge Jesus gave to Peter:

HELPING TO INCREASE VOCATIONS

During the fifteen years that Father James Gould was vocation director for the Diocese of Arlington, this diocese of only sixty-five parishes in northern Virginia produced an average of eight new priests per year. By the year 2000, the average age of priests in the diocese was forty-two, nearly twenty years below the national average. Father Gould's goal during those years was to look for ten new priesthood candidates per year. A few of the years he fell short of the goal, but in one year Arlington had twenty-two men enter the seminary. In this one diocese, there is not a priest shortage.

Father Gould outlined a simple formula for success:

- "Unswerving allegiance to the Pope and magisterial teaching;

- perpetual adoration of the Blessed Sacrament in parishes, with an emphasis on praying for vocations;

- and the strong effort by a significant number of diocesan priests who extend themselves to help young men remain open to the Lord's will in their lives."[21]

This formula has been shared with other vocation directors and dioceses, and the potential for success is strong. How might they work in your parish and diocese? What are some other ways that you can help promote vocations to the priesthood? Read through the list of ideas below. Choose at least one of the ideas or come up with one on your own. Develop a plan to work with others to implement this idea at your school or parish.

Perpetual Adoration. Arrange for a schedule of continuous prayer for vocations before the Blessed Sacrament at a school chapel or at your parish. Collect names of people willing to sign up for fifteen minute or half hour blocks of time. Make this a regular event.

Publicize Special Vocation Events. Highlight special events during occasions like National Vocation Awareness Week, World Day for Consecrated Life, or World Day of Prayer for Vocations. Also take note of special events offered particularly in your own diocese. Volunteer to distribute flyers or other promotional material to people at your school or parish. Invite your peers to these events. Offer to be part of the program or to help with hospitality or clerical work.

Witness Talk. Broach the topic of vocations to the priesthood at a youth group meeting or at a campus ministry event. Speak personally about how you are discerning your own vocational call. Arrange for a priest or seminarian to speak about his own calling.

Seminary Visit. Call a local seminary and arrange for a group of classmates to come to the seminary to hear a presentation by the vocation director and seminarians, and perhaps tour the campus as well.

Website Links. Create a set of links to vocation websites in your own diocese and beyond and include them on your personal homepage. Or, write about the importance of vocational efforts on a blog. Include links to relevant vocation sites there, as well.

Jesus says to Peter: "*Duc in altum*—Put out into deep water" (Lk 5:4). Peter and the first companions trusted Christ's words and cast their nets.

Dear adolescents and young people, it is to you in a particular way that I renew the invitation of Christ to "put out into the deep." You find yourselves having to make important decisions for the future.

Dear young men and women! Trust Christ; listen attentively to his teachings, fix your eyes on his face, persevere in listening to his Word. Allow Him to focus your search and your aspirations, all your ideals and desires of heart.

Do not forget that today too there is a need of holy priests, of persons wholly consecrated to the service of God![20]

- Is there someone you know who has chosen a radical or countercultural lifestyle? Describe the person and the lifestyle.

- How do you imagine your commitment to discipleship in Jesus Christ for the future? Rate it on a scale of 1 to 10 with 10 being "extremely committed." Explain why you chose the number you did and how this level of commitment will translate to your everyday life.

✦ Renewing the Priesthood

- The hierarchical structure and ministries of bishop, priest, and deacon are essential to maintain the Church's sacramental structure.

- The priest shortage in the United States is expected to get worse before it improves.

- Key statistics show that priests today generally are happy and feel valued by their bishop and parishioners.

- The attraction to the priesthood is the opportunity to act in the person of Christ the Head.

✦ The Role of the Bishop

- The three main tasks of the bishop are to teach, to sanctify, and to govern.

- Bishops have a role of authority and decision-making both in the universal Church and in their own local dioceses.

- The nuncio—the Pope's representative—is responsible for making the final nominations of bishop candidates to the Congregation of Bishops at the Vatican.

- Upon ordination, a bishop becomes a member of the college of bishops.

- The diocesan bishop is called the ordinary or local ordinary.

- A bishop's first pastoral task is to teach; when collaborating with other bishops and the Pope, bishops help to preserve the truth of Christ and the Church.

- Bishops are the principal dispensers of the sacraments.

- Bishops govern their dioceses with the help of their priests and in relation with the college of bishops.

✦ The Role of the Priest

- Priests share in the bishop's ministry and serve the Church by preaching the Gospel, celebrating the sacraments, and offering pastoral governance.

- A diocesan priest, also called a "secular priest," promises his obedience to the bishop in the diocese where he will serve.

- Priests act in the person of Christ and are endowed with a special grace through the Sacrament of Holy Orders.

- Most diocesan priests serve the bishop by being his representative in parishes.

- Parish priests are under the patronage of Saint John Vianney.

- A priest who is part of a religious community is called a "religious priest."

- Choosing a religious order involves further discernment on the charism of the community along with discernment on whether or not to seek ordination.

The Role of the Permanent Deacon

- A deacon is ordained to serve both at liturgy and for the needs of the entire Church and world.

- The permanent diaconate was a part of the Church from her earliest times and restored at the Second Vatican Council.

- At liturgy, a deacon serves both as minister of the word and at the altar.

- Requirements for the diaconate include status (mature married or single men), family life, natural gifts, spirituality, education, and service and involvement.

- The formation process for the diaconate involves the same four areas as priestly formation: human, spiritual, intellectual, and pastoral development.

- The opportunity for married men to be ordained deacons allows for a unique union between the Sacraments of Holy Orders and Matrimony.

The Rewards of Holy Orders

- Accepting a call to the priesthood goes against the norms of secular society.

- The life of a priest is meaningful, satisfying, and never boring.

- The entire Church is responsible for praying and working for an increase in priestly vocations.

assignments applications

1. Research the meaning of the coat of arms of your bishop or of any Pope in history. Create artwork depicting the image and write a brief report that explains its symbolism. Or, develop an album of the coats of arms of five recent Popes or five recent bishops of your diocese.

2. Read about the Notre Dame Vision program designed to encourage teenagers to explore vocational choices at www.nd.edu/~ndvi/index2.html. Answer the following questions after you spend some time discerning a possible calling:

- When do I feel most myself?

- Is there something someone told me that I would be good at?

- What is my greatest desire?

- Do I have the gifts to do this thing I dream of?

- What would I do if it didn't matter what anyone else would think?

3. Design a vocation poster for religious communities. List on the poster at least five different communities with a quotation that highlights the charism of each community.

4. Read and summarize some of the qualities and duties of a deacon in the early Church from the following passages:

- 1 Timothy 3:8–13

- Acts 6:1–4

- Acts 7

- Acts 8:4–13

5. Do an Internet search for the papal document *Sacrum Diacontus Ordinem* by Pope Paul VI that reinstated the permanent diaconate. Write five questions and answers based on information

gleaned from the document. Then work with a group of two other students who have also written five questions and answers from the document. Take turns quizzing each other on the material using the questions and answers each of you has written.

6. Write a letter (not an e-mail) to one of the bishops in the United States (see www.usccb.org/dioceses.shtml) requesting information about their personal call to the priesthood; strategies for increasing priestly vocations in their diocese; and what they find most meaningful about their ministry. Share your e-mail address. Ask the bishop to respond by e-mail or letter. Write a summary of his response.

7. Read a short biography on Saint John Vianney. With some classmates, develop a role play or skit that details an element from his life (e.g., his devotion to prayer, his dealings with townspeople who did not go to Sunday Mass, or his skills as a confessor). Practice and present the skit to the class.

8. Research and report on the specific efforts to increase vocations to the priesthood of the Sierra Club and Knights of Columbus. Enact one of their suggestions. Write about what you did.

9. Read and report on the Jesuit missionaries in the United States including the life and death of the North American Martyrs.

10. Search for copies of your bishop's daily calendar. Write a summary sentence for each event classifying it by what type of ministry it seems to entail: for example, council meeting/governance, Sacrament of Confirmation/liturgical; prison visit/pastoral.

Notes

1. From the Center for Applied Research in the Apostolate study (Georgetown University, Spring 2000).

2. Rossetti, Stephen J. *The Joy of Priesthood* (Notre Dame, IN: Ave Maria Press, 2005), p. 26.

3. Quoted from *Lumen Gentium*, 22.

4. Quoted from *Christus Dominus*, 15.

5. Quoted from *Lumen Gentium*, 2.

6. Quoted from *Presbyterorum Ordinis*, 7.

7. Ibid., 12.

8. Rossetti, p. 135.

9. Quoted from www.ignatius.com/magazines/hprweb/cihak.htm.

10. Rossetti, p. 137.

11. Cited from *Presbyterorum Ordinis*, 33.

12. Quoted from www.jesuitswisprov.org.

13. Quoted from http://newsinfo.nd.edu/content.cfm?topicid=13502.

14. Quoted from Papal Address to the Permanent Deacons, Detroit, Michigan, September 19, 1987.

15. Quoted from "Deacon Bernie Ouellette: Deacon's role is to serve the world," *Western Catholic Reporter* (February 6, 2006).

16. Quoted from the Diocese of Joliet Vocation website at www.vocations.com.

17. Quoted from Papal Address to the Permanent Deacons, Detroit, Michigan, September 19, 1987

18. Ibid.

19. Quoted from "The Road Not Taken" from *The Poetry of Robert Frost*, edited by Edward Connery (New York: Holt, Rinehart and Winston, 1969).

20. Quoted from "Message of his Holiness Pope John Paul II for the 42nd World Day of Prayer for Vocations," April 17, 2005.

21. Quoted from "The Four Marks of a Vocation: The Vocations Drought that Need not Be" by Michaell S. Rose, *New Oxford Review* (November 2003).

22. Quoted from Message of his Holiness Pope John Paul II for the 42nd World Day of Prayer for Vocations April 17, 2005.

Prayer

for the Vocation to Holy Orders

Contemplation is an expression of prayer that is a "*gaze of faith, fixed on Jesus.*" You look at him and he looks at you (see *CCC*, 2709–2719). Arrange to sit before the Blessed Sacrament in contemplation. Find a quiet place where you can sit alone. Begin by closing your eyes and centering yourself on Christ. Repeat a mantra of your choice. For example, "Jesus, be with me," or "Come, Holy Spirit," or "Jesus."

call to prayer

Pray in the following words or choose similar words of your own. After the prayer, pause in silence. Listen for God to speak to you in the stillness.

Compassionate Lord,
Through the gift of your Apostles and their successors I have come to know you.
In the word of truth and life proclaimed in your Gospel.
In the sacred gift of your Body and Blood in Eucharist.
In your presence in the foundation and strength of your Church.

I pray for my bishop, who has this local Church in his care.
With him, help me to remember all people who live near me,
especially the poor, sick, and homeless of our area.
I pray for all priests, especially those who have educated and refined my own faith. (*Pause to remember priests who have been influential in your life by name.*)

I pray for those devoted to your service through acts of love,

including those men consecrated for service as deacons
in the Sacrament of Holy Orders.
Help me to model my own charity on their example.

I pray for the Church throughout the world and its firm foundation and structure.

I pray for our Pope. May he guide the world under the inspiration of your Holy Spirit.

Be with me Lord.
Be with our Church.
Never abandon us.
Stay with us forever.
I ask this in your name.

Amen.

scripture reading

Slowly and prayerfully read the following Scripture passage from Hebrews 4:12–16. When you are finished, bring your needs and the special needs of the Church for more priestly vocations to Christ, the High Priest.

A reading from the Letter to the Hebrews:

> Indeed, the word of God is living and effective, sharper than any two-edged sword, penetrating even between soul and spirit, joints and marrow, and able to discern reflections and thoughts of the heart. No creature is concealed from him, but everything is naked and exposed to the eyes of him to whom we must render an account.

> Therefore, since we have a great high priest who has passed through the heavens,

Jesus, the Son of God, let us hold fast to our confession. For we do not have a high priest who is unable to sympathize with our weaknesses, but one who has similarly been tested in every way, yet without sin. So let us confidently approach the throne of grace to receive mercy and to find grace for timely help.

The Word of the Lord.

Thanks be to God.

quietreflection

Pray for bishops, priests, and deacons throughout the world. Use some of the following images to help fuel your reflection. Think of individual bishops, priests, and deacons whom you know. Pray for them by name.

+ A bishop working to find common ground in an ecumenical effort with our separated brothers and sisters in other Christian denominations.

+ A bishop discerning ways to keep the parishes of his diocese active and flourishing.

+ A priest discerning new ways to apply God's word to the lives of the people.

+ A priest consecrating the bread and wine into the Body and Blood of Christ.

+ A deacon bringing compassion to the dying and soon after praying at the grave of the deceased.

+ A deacon blessing his own wife and family in his ministry as they join to offer blessing on the entire Church.

✦ Prayer for Vocations

In Pope John Paul II's final prayer for vocations, he prayed the following words. Recite this prayer thoughtfully as you pray for your own personal vocation and for an increase in vocations to the priesthood and religious life:

Jesus, Son of God,
in whom the fullness of the Divinity dwells,
You call all the baptized to "put out into the deep,"
taking the path that leads to holiness.
Waken in the hearts of young people the desire
to be witnesses in the world of today
to the power of your love.
Fill them with your Spirit of fortitude and prudence,
so that they may be able to discover the full truth
about themselves and their own vocation.
Our Savior,
sent by the Father to reveal His merciful love,
give to your Church the gift
of young people who are ready to put out into the
    deep,
to be the sign among their brothers
of Your presence which renews and saves.
Holy Virgin, Mother of the Redeemer,
sure guide on the way towards God and towards
    neighbor,
You who pondered his word in the depth of your
    heart,
sustain with your motherly intercession
our families and our ecclesial communities,
so that they may help adolescents and young people
to answer generously the call of the Lord.
Amen.[22]

unit**four**

✦ Desiring Happiness

I t's easy to understand that everyone wants to be happy. The more difficult proposition is to define just what happiness is. Many people spend a lifetime trying to find out. For some, it is an exercise in futility. Think about some of the things people today search after in the name of happiness: wealth, power, and fame are considered items of great good and venerated by many. They accompany a slew of "if only" statements that end with things like "I will never complain again," or "I will be completely satisfied," or "I will be as happy as can be." For example:

- If only I get the lead in this play . . .

- If only this person will ask me out . . .

- If only I am accepted at my first-choice college . . .

Answering God's Call

- If only my parents got along better . . .
- If only I could hit the super lottery . . .
- If only I had the latest foreign sports car . . .

These desires, even if achieved, are in vain. Even the mega-millionaire hasn't found nirvana based on his bank account. If you don't believe it, consider the countless stories of actual lottery winners who find that the newfound money actually brings more heartache than happiness. Mack Metcalf and his estranged wife Virginia Mirida shared a 34 million dollar lottery payout.[1] Mack bought an estate in southern Kentucky with horses and vintage cars. Virginia bought a Mercedes and a mansion overlooking the Ohio River.

Then the bad luck came. Metcalf's first wife sued him for 31,000 dollars in child support. A former girlfriend stole half a million dollars from him while he was drunk. Mirida's boyfriend died of a drug overdose in her home, and her brother began to harass her. Just three years after the payout, Mack Metcalf died at age forty-five of complications from alcoholism. Virginia Mirida's decomposing body was found in her bed on the day before Thanksgiving 2005.

Money did not bring happiness to this couple. Similar stories ending in darkness can be told of people who sought notoriety or power in the hopes of finding lasting and perfect happiness.

The human desire for happiness is God-given. He has placed the desire for happiness in our hearts in order to draw us to him, the only one who can fulfill it. Saint Augustine said that we can only be happy when our hearts are finally at rest in God. Saint Thomas Aquinas likewise understood that "God alone satisfies."

Recall that the goal of our human existence is the beatitude to which God calls us. This is the goal for each person individually and for the Church as a whole—people who have accepted the promise and live from it in faith (see *CCC*, 1719).

This form of true happiness is described in several ways in the New Testament: as the coming of the Kingdom of God, as seeing God, as entering into the joy of the Lord, as entering into God's rest.

Ultimately, this beatitude or happiness will only come to fruition when we reach the eternal reward of Heaven. But even on earth we are called to the vocation of the Christian beatitude. We are called to know, to love, and to serve God so that we can be with him in paradise.

This calling begins now. It is not something to put off until "after college" or "when I am married" or "if I decide to do something dramatic like seek the priesthood or religious life." You are called to holiness and the life of God now as a Catholic, as a teenager, as a lay person. What you will be later you don't know. What you are called to be now is a person in tune with God's will for your life while examining and reflecting on ways he is calling you to love and serve him in the future.

Unit 4—Answering God's Call—is a reminder that right in this moment you are called to the fullness of Christian life and the perfection of God's love. You are called today to beatitude.

---

1. Reported in "Lottery Gold Turns to Brass" by James Dao, *New York Times,* December 8, 2005.

chapter**outline**

✦ Role Model

Mary is the model of the Christian's ultimate vocation to eternal life.

✦ Your Vocation Now

It is the responsibility of the laity to bring Christ to the secular world.

✦ Seeking Perfection

Practicing the virtues and seeking the way of the cross are ways to achieve the Christian Beatitude.

✦ Life Everlasting

Our belief in eternal life should affect all aspects of daily living.

chapter ten

The Fullness of Christian Life

Beloved, we are God's children now; what we shall be has not yet been revealed. We do know that when it is revealed we shall be like him, for we shall see him as he is. Everyone who has this hope based on him makes himself pure, as he is pure.

1 John 3:2–3

✦ Role Model

Your vocation exists in the *present* tense. In Baptism, you have been given grace to respond to God's call to become his children and to share his divine nature. That is something that is happening now—not when you finish college, or start a family, or achieve success in a career. Those mileposts may never come in God's plan for your life. But his grace to share in the intimacy of his life in the Trinity is given at Baptism.

Ultimately, your vocation is to eternal life. This is a "supernatural" vocation because it is beyond the powers of any person to know or reach without God. He alone takes the initiative to reveal himself and give himself to you. The life and tasks of some of the specific human vocations—including marriage and the priesthood—will be obsolete in Heaven. For example, when Jesus was asked to address which of seven deceased brothers would be husband to a widowed woman in Heaven, he said:

> You are misled because you do not know the scriptures of the power of God. At the resurrection they neither marry nor are given in marriage but are like the angels in heaven. (Mt 22:29–30)

The vocation to eternity is now. It must take precedence over any other desires or wishes you have for your life. It is a calling for which you must listen. You must be ready to place all of your other goals behind it whenever and wherever God gives you the grace to recognize that he is with you and that he is calling you to eternity. When Saint Joan of Arc was asked if she knew whether she was in God's grace, she replied: "If I am not, may it please God to put me in it; if I am, may it please God to keep me there." Saint Joseph

Cafasso said, "I have been made for Heaven and Heaven for me." The primary human task is to keep on the lookout for God's grace and to keep the focus of Heaven always in mind.

Mary of Nazareth is the role model *par excellence* for this kind of living. As a teenage Jewish girl, like many others of her day, she was engaged to marry a local man. It was then that God interrupted her life with other plans. It was a monumental message and a call that she was free to accept or reject: "Behold, you will conceive in your womb and bear a son, and you shall name him Jesus" (Lk 1:31). Mary said, "Behold, I am the handmaid of the Lord. May it be done to me according to your word" (Lk 1:38).

This openness to God's unexpected grace had drastic and unprecedented effects. First, Mary was now an unmarried, pregnant teen. She risked the shunning by her betrothed, Joseph, her family, and townspeople. But she did not waver in her acceptance of God's will for her life. She shared her good news with her cousin Elizabeth. The faithful Joseph welcomed her into his home. She bore a Son and raised him in a Jewish home. When he began his teaching ministry, Mary supported him. When he was unfairly arrested, tried, and hung on a cross to die, Mary was there.

The effect of Mary's openness to God's grace was that Jesus, conceived solely by the power of the Holy Spirit, was born. Saint Irenaeus later said of her acceptance, "Being obedient she became the cause of salvation for herself and the whole human race."

We need God's grace to be able to accept God's grace. God touches our hearts and moves us with "a longing for truth and goodness that only he can satisfy" (*CCC*, 2002). It is the promises and rewards of Heaven that keep us focused on this ultimate vocation.

Listening to Voices

Jeanne la Pucelle—more commonly known as Joan of Arc—grew up on a forty-acre farm in the little village of Domremy, which had remained loyal to the king of France in the midst of the Hundred Years War with the English. She was born in 1412.

Around the age of thirteen, she began to hear voices and see visions of angels and saints. She recognized the saints individually as Saint Michael, Saint Margaret, and Saint Catherine, along with some others. While she rarely discussed the details of these visions, later at her trial she told her accusers: "I saw them with these very eyes, as well as I see you." What the voices of the saints told her was that it would be her role to free France from its enemies.

In his essay about Joan, American author Mark Twain described what happened next:

> She went to the veteran Commandant of Vaucouleurs and demanded an escort of soldiers, saying she must march to the help of the King of France, since she was commissioned of God to win back his lost kingdom for him and set the crown upon his head. The Commandant said, "What, you? You are only a child." And he advised that she be taken back to her village and have her ears boxed. But she said she must obey God, and would come again, and again, and yet again, and finally she would get the soldiers. She said truly. In time he yielded, after months of delay and refusal, and gave her the soldiers; and took off his sword and gave her that, and said, "Go—and let come what may." She made her long and perilous journey through the enemy's country, and spoke with the King, and convinced him. Then she was summoned before the University of Poitiers to prove that she was commissioned of God and not of Satan, and daily during three weeks she sat before that learned congress unafraid, and capably answered their deep questions out of her ignorant but able head and her simple and honest heart; and again she won her case, and with it the wondering admiration of all that august company.

> And now, aged seventeen, she was made Commander-in-Chief, with a prince of the royal house and the veteran generals of France for subordinates; and at the head of the first army she had ever seen, she marched to Orleans, carried the commanding fortresses of the enemy by storm in three desperate assaults, and in ten days raised a siege which had defied the might of France for seven months.[1]

Eventually, jealousy among the French army and the lack of support from King Charles of France led to Joan's capture by the English. She was tried for witchcraft. One of the most "serious" charges leveled against her was that she put on men's clothes (which she wore while in battle). Her accusers said the voices she heard were the devil's. She was convicted and ordered to be burned at the stake on May 30, 1431. She confessed her sins and asked for communion. She held a cross as she suffered the torturous death, crying out the name of Jesus. Joan's ashes were scattered in the river so that her followers could not venerate them around a shrine. Just a few short years later her cause for sainthood was introduced. She was canonized in 1920 by Pope Benedict XV. She is the patron saint of France.

Do at least one of the following:

- Report on and draw samples of the clothing and armor Joan of Arc may have worn in battle. Also report on the banner that she carried into battle. At her trial she described a banner "of which the field was strewn with lilies."

- Develop a chronological timeline of key events in the life of Saint Joan of Arc.

- With a group of classmates, enact part or all of one of the trials of Joan of Arc. See www.stjoancenter.com/Trials/.

- Search for quotations attributed to Saint Joan of Arc. Use at least five quotations as the basis to write five original prayers.

- How do you hear the voice of God?

- What do you think keeps people from focusing on their eternal destiny as a primary vocation?

✦ Your Vocation Now

Being a part of the laity is not something you will grow into at a later time. By your Baptism, you are included in the laity—that is, membership of all the faithful except those in Holy Orders or in a consecrated religious community approved by the Church—right now. And, according to this state in life, you are called to share in the priestly, prophetic, and kingly office of Christ by carrying it out in specific ways in the world. For you, this includes the defined world of your age and peer group, your school, your community, and also the larger global society.

By definition, a lay person is out in the secular world. As a teenager, you likely belong to many organizations and associate with peers who are not Catholic. Think about the jobs you and your peers have. These are businesses that do not have a Catholic or Christian focus (e.g., fast food restaurant, clothing retailer). You also play sports on teams or in leagues with people of many different religions or no religion at all. You live in a community where you interact with people of all kinds both unofficially (e.g., at the grocery store, in traffic) and officially (e.g., by your voting record, use of the public library). In each of these places, a lay person is "called by God to contribute to the sanctification of the world from within, like leaven, in the spirit to the Gospel, by fulfilling their own particular duties."[2]

There are two ways that the laity live their vocation: as individuals and through an organized apostolate. In either case, the intention is to influence institutions, the social conditions, and the general mentality of secular society. The methods employed both as individuals and groups are through words and action.

One example of an apostolate dedicated to encouraging lay people to make a difference in the world is the Christophers. Founded in 1945 by a Maryknoll priest, Father James Keller, who believed that each person has a special task in life that belongs to no one else, the Christophers primarily use the media to reach people of all faiths with the Gospel message and its motto: "It's better to light one candle than to curse the darkness." An equal part of the apostolate counts on lay people to share the Christophers' message in their families, neighborhoods, and workplaces. Father Keller explained the message:

> Each of us has, by the grace of God, the power to change the world for the better. Every act of care and concern for others has a ripple effect, touching many lives. The love to which we are called by the gospel extends not only to our neighbors, but to all who live on God's Good Earth—today and in time to come. So, go

into the marketplace, into a job of your own choosing, without fanfare or flag-waving. Where there is hate, bring in love; where there is darkness, carry light. In other words, be a Christbearer, or Christopher.[3]

Individually, there are countless stories of teenagers who consciously share their Christian faith with others. The "making a difference" section of the Catholic website disciplesnow.com tells several stories, including that of Megan, a varsity golf team member from Oklahoma who volunteers two mornings per week to teach inner-city children how to play golf. Megan points out that golf is a way to help children develop confidence, patience, determination, and self-esteem. Representing her Catholic youth group is also a visible model of her faith to the children she teaches, her peers, and the rest of the community.

In the next sections, consideration is paid to ways that people growing into young adulthood can participate more fully in Christ's office of priest, prophet, and king.

The Christophers

Read more about the Christophers at their website, www.christophers.org. Check out the "Contests for Students" portion of the site and choose one of the suggestions (e.g., essay or poster contest) to complete. Turn in a copy of your contest entry to your teacher. Report on the results of the contest when available.

Participation in the Priestly Office of Christ

Recall that the priestly mission of Christ was to offer himself in a perfect sacrifice through his Death on a cross, winning salvation for all who believe in him. Baptism gives a person a share in the common priesthood of all believers. Lay people participate in the priestly mission of Christ by patiently bearing and offering all of their work, prayer, service, and even hardships in the name of the Holy Spirit to God the Father through Jesus Christ.

"Offering up" is a traditional practice in which a person makes a conscious effort in prayer to accept the hardships and suffering he or she experiences and offer them to God as a way to participate in the redemptive suffering of Christ. How can you "offer up" part of your life to God? Consider the following ways:

- Though you would rather stay home, work, and hang out with your friends, you agree to go on one last family vacation before you move away to college.

- You spend a few minutes chatting with your older, widowed neighbor even though you might be late meeting up with your friends.

- An ACL tear has wiped out your fall sports season. You work as hard as you can in rehabilitation in order to be able to play again by the next summer.

The most fitting place to offer these events of life is at Eucharist, where the offerings of the local Church are united in one prayer with the universal Church. There are some specific liturgical

functions lay people may take on if there are not lectors or acolytes present, namely, to be a minister of the word and to distribute communion at Mass.

Participation in the Prophetic Office of Christ

Jesus is the "great prophet" who proclaimed the Kingdom of God by both his life and words. The laity are called to share in this prophetic office until Christ comes again. Much of this witness takes place through a person's participation in family and social life. Because of this responsibility, everyone—young or old—must acquire a deeper knowledge of their faith and fuller possession of the gift of wisdom. Saint Thomas Aquinas

Saint Thomas Aquinas

wrote: "To teach in order to lead others to faith is the task of every preacher and of each believer."[4]

A way that lay people fulfill the prophetic mission is by **evangelization**. This is accomplished by setting an example of Christian living but also by being willing to speak out

for Christ whenever it is necessary. For example:

- You are taking a weekend visit to a college to which you might apply and you make sure to allow time to go to Sunday Mass.

- You make it known among your peers that you plan to save sex for marriage and connect the decision to your faith in Christ and belief in Church teaching.

- When a friend is suffering, you offer consolation by sharing stories and parables from the Gospel. Likewise, when a friend is joyful, you remind him or her to offer thanksgiving to God.

Participation in the prophetic office of Christ can also lead to several related careers. With the proper training and formation, lay people can be catechists, theologians, and writers. In each of these callings, a lay person is able to evangelize to a broader base of both Christians and non-Christians.

Participation in the Kingly Office of Christ

By freely accepting his Death on the cross, Christ lived out his mission to be servant of all. Recall the climax in the Gospel of Mark when Jesus told his disciples he "did not come to be served but to serve and to give his life as a ransom for many" (Mk 10:45). Service on behalf of others is the type of kingdom Jesus' proclaimed and lived.

Lay people work on behalf of Christ's kingdom by helping to improve the secular institutions and conditions that are often an occasion for sinfulness. On a large scale, this may mean

evangelization
To bring the good news of Jesus to others.

protesting against companies that underpay their workers or petitioning against corporations that violate environmental standards. Of course the first task in this duty is for the individual to work to avoid sinfulness in his or her own life before taking on the sinfulness of others.

High school and college-age students are involved in many of these efforts of righteousness and social justice. Think about these possible actions for your own life:

● You regularly confess your sins in the Sacrament of Penance.

● You find out that a fast food chain commissioned by your school for lunch underpays the farm workers who pick the lettuce for its sandwiches, and you lead a boycott among students.

● You help to welcome students at your school for whom English is a second language by

tutoring them in study halls and by encouraging their participation in extracurricular activities and social groups.

Lay people also have the right and responsibility to participate in the structure and governance of the Church. They may be asked to participate on parish or diocesan councils, finance committees, and tribunals. In many parishes, there are teen representatives on several committees and on the parish council itself. Lay people are also encouraged and sometimes have the duty to speak with their pastor about their religious views and their needs and desires, while always being willing to listen to him and accept his wisdom and counsel.

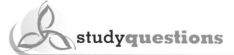

study questions

1. What is the duty of a lay person out in the world?

2. What are two ways that the laity live their vocation?

3. What is the mission of the Christophers?

4. Define and give an example of "offering up" something for Christ.

5. Define *evangelization* related to the prophetic office of Christ.

6. What is required of the kingly mission of a Christian before he or she takes on sinful occasions in secular institutions?

journal discussion

● What are some ways that teens you know participate in the priestly, prophetic, and kingly offices of Christ?

● What are some ways that you have or are planning to participate in these offices?

✦ Seeking Perfection

Every Christian, no matter his or her state in life—clergy, consecrated religious, or laity—is called to a full life of holiness and love. This is the perfection that Jesus demands of us: "be perfect, just as your heavenly Father is perfect" (Mt 5:48).

virtues
Good habits that enable us to live a moral life.

One of the ways to seek perfection is to practice the **virtues**. Saint Gregory of Nyssa wrote: "The goal of a virtuous life is to become like God."[5] The four cardinal virtues are prudence, justice, courage, and temperance. These virtues are especially applicable as you face temptations and look for ways to make good choices entering young adulthood.

Prudence equates with common sense and wisdom. A prudent person seems to have a plan for life and rarely deviates from the plan in any given situation. Think of a high school senior who has been awarded an athletic scholarship to college or an appointment to a military academy. He is not likely to do anything in the last semesters of high school that would jeopardize the years of hard work and planning that earned him that recognition. You are already on a course leading to a career and vocation, even if you do not know what it specifically will be. It is easier to recognize the paths that deviate from the course (e.g., alcohol use, promiscuity, illegal behaviors). The gift of prudence keeps a person moving forward while making good and moral decisions.

Justice has to do with fairness. You can't achieve happiness or perfection *and* leave everyone else behind. Justice recognizes the rights of others and considers how a person's own personal interests fit in with the rest of society. Truly successful people remain devoted to sharing goodness

and meeting the needs of all people. The virtue of justice also requires that a person obey God, his laws, and his providence. You may hear of "successful" business people who reach the top of their profession while stepping on the toes of others and making many enemies along the way. Or, you may witness men or women who hurt each other emotionally and spiritually as they move from one relationship to the next without being honest and caring. On the other hand, the just person always treats others with respect—be it the entry level employee at the company or the soon-to-be ex-boyfriend or ex-girlfriend.

Fortitude is another word for courage. It strengthens a person to avoid moral temptations and "enables one to conquer fear, even fear of death, and to face trials and persecutions" (*CCC*, 1808). As you become independent from your parents, this virtue will help you to live by the Christian values they instilled in you. There are also many life and death situations in the

forefront of your generation. Consider the decision faced by unmarried women who face pregnancy. Also, you may personally have to take a position on terrorism, national defense, and the rationale of fighting war in other countries. The gift of fortitude can help you to make courageous and Christian choices in these life-threatening areas.

Temperance moderates a person's attractions to pleasures and helps to balance the way we use created goods. This virtue helps to temper the desire for pleasures like food, alcohol, drugs, and sex by practicing acts of self-denial. This virtue helps us to surrender not only pleasures that are sinful, but also pleasures that are good and acceptable out of love for God and imitation of Christ, who gave up his life for our sakes.

The cardinal virtues are acquired by prayer and great effort. In other words, together with God, a person can learn to perfect and practice these virtues. These human virtues have their roots in the theological virtues—faith, hope, and charity (love)—which are not gained by human efforts. These are infused into our souls by God in order to make us capable of choosing goodness over sin, right from wrong.

Perfection by Way of the Cross

Saint Ignatius Loyola once said "If God causes you to suffer much, it is a sign that he has great designs for you." The *Catechism of the Catholic Church* teaches, "The way of perfection passes by way of the Cross" (*CCC*, 2015).

Our lives are patterned on the Paschal Mystery—Christ's saving actions through his Passion, Death, Resurrection, and Ascension. Through Christ's Death, our death was destroyed, and through his Resurrection, our life will be restored. In the liturgy, especially the Eucharist, we celebrate the Paschal Mystery by which we are saved.

Not only that, our lifetimes are a series of "little deaths" and "little resurrections" that prepare us for our eventual physical death and rising to the perfection of eternal life.

Some of the occasions of little deaths come to us by surprise: a chronic illness or serious injury that disables us, the unexpected death of a relative or friend, or the disappointment of losing a job or not getting accepted to a favorite college.

Other little deaths appear at transitional times in our lives. For example, accompanying the excitement and achievement of high school graduation comes the melancholy feeling of ending a life as you know it. Perhaps never again will you live full-time in your bedroom. Now only rarely will you see your parents and your siblings. When you do come home, even if it is for the entire summer, in some ways you will feel like a visitor.

Finally, there are some **mortifications** or penances that we seek out on our own in order to unite ourselves more closely with the cross of Christ. One of the most common times Catholics do this is during the season of Lent when they "give up" certain pleasures like sweets or television as an offering and a way to unite more closely with Christ's suffering. There are many other occasions where we deliberately choose the harder road. Think of the beginning jogger whose goal it is to run a marathon. Now imagine the many days, weeks, and months the person will have to put in of trying to get in shape and eventually working up to run over twenty-six miles without stopping. Or, consider the B-plus student who never wavers in the goal to attend medical school, even though an A average is a prerequisite. Working to meet either of these types of goals, when accompanied by prayer and an offering of the suffering to God are examples of participating in the way of the cross.

By the same token, life is also filled with glimpses of the perfection and pure joy that await us in Heaven. The graduating senior will soon move into the college dorm. Within a short time, new friends are made. An array of interesting classes fills the days. And,

mortifications
Ways to discipline the body and appetites by self-denial.

the person realizes that a new, perhaps better, way of relating with his or her parents and siblings is beginning, too. Though they see each other less, the relationship seems more honest and mature. The person has experienced a "little resurrection."

The progression to the peace and joy of the Beatitudes is a gradual and arduous one. The person who begins the journey may be much different than the one who ends it. For example, consider the eighteen-year-old woman who:

- entered college as an education major planning to teach first grade,
- worked in the college tech center and found out she liked computer programming,
- switched to a computer science major, completed grad school, and
- ended up teaching after all—at a junior college.

Or, the twenty-year-old man whose girlfriend talked him into going on a week-long service trip to an Indian reservation where he:

- helped put a new roof on a school,
- observed poverty like he had never seen before,

- returned home and began to go to daily Mass, and
- eventually inquired of his parish priest about how to apply to the seminary.

Jesus said to his disciples:

"Whoever wishes to come after me must deny himself, take up his cross, and follow me. For whoever wishes to save his life will lose it, but whoever loses his life for my sake will find it." (Mt 16:24–25)

The way of perfection, like the cross, is not a straight path. There are many questions, disappointments, and pains along the way. The glimpses of perfection and the understanding of other Christians will be our reward for the good works we do. The help of God's grace allows us to persevere.

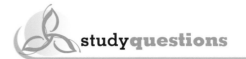

study questions

1. Name the four cardinal virtues.
2. How is prudence associated with wisdom?
3. Define *justice*.
4. What is another word for fortitude?
5. What is the benefit of temperance?
6. How does a person acquire the cardinal virtues?
7. What is the Paschal Mystery?
8. What does the Paschal Mystery have to do with a Christian seeking perfection?

journal discussion

- Describe a personal plan for achieving Christian perfection.
- Tell about a "little death" and "little resurrection" that you have experienced.

✦ Life Everlasting

You are nearing the end of this course and the end of your high school years. But as the Apostles' Creed reminds us, life itself is everlasting. It has no end. When you let this credal statement sink in, it can have profound effects. A person whose primary desire is to live forever in eternity will have different priorities than a person who only lives for life on earth. Think about what would really matter if you were on your death-bed:

- How many rooms in your mansion or how much room you made in your life for prayer?

- How many college degrees you amassed or to what degree you made time for the poor and needy?

- How many five-star restaurants you dined in or how many Sundays you shared in the banquet of Holy Eucharist?

- How many times you were able to do just what you wanted or how often you did God's will?

As Jesus said, "What profit would there be for one to gain the whole world and forfeit his life? Or what can one give in exchange for his life?" (Mt 16:26).

Any and all Christian vocations must prepare you for your death as one united to the Death of Christ. Human death is the entrance into everlasting life. In fact, in Baptism we have already "died with Christ"; our physical death merely completes our incorporation into his act of redemption. Thus, we should desire a good death and should be ready for death every day. While your life expectancy remains long, you certainly are aware of peers or other people your age who have died or were seriously injured due to an unexpected illness or accident. You may know of people like:

- Matt, eighteen, who was killed instantly when a drunk driver plowed through a busy intersection and struck the passenger side of the car in which he was riding.

- Ping, seventeen, who survived for nearly a year in a coma after falling off a ladder while taking down the family's Christmas lights.

- Sara, sixteen, who crashed her ATV and severed her spine causing permanent paralysis.

- Olivia, eighteen, who was diagnosed with non-Hodgkin's lymphoma six weeks before her high school graduation. The prognosis remains cautiously optimistic for survival.

Preparing for a good death is an exercise in faith. With faith, a Christian can legitimately long for death. Saint Teresa of Avila wrote, "I want to see

Next Steps for Planning Your Vocation

While you are not ready to make a commitment to permanent vocations of marriage, Holy Orders, or consecrated religious life, you should be continuing an ongoing discernment process of your Christian vocation while imagining yourself in one of the permanent vocations.

This section lists several resources designed to provide more information in the following areas:

- Catholic colleges in the United States

- Teen-focused retreats

- Catholic seminaries in the United States

- Committed service efforts

- Religious ministries guide

God, and in order to see him, I must die." Blessed Junipero Serra said, "A happy death, of all the things of life is our principal concern. For if we attain that, it matters little if we lose all the rest. But if we do not attain that, nothing else will be of any value."

The following subsections examine more closely what Catholics believe about life after death.

The End of Human Life

Death ends human life and also the known chance either to accept or reject God's grace offered in Christ. While the New Testament does speak of a judgment that will happen at the Second Coming of Christ, there are also many examples that show that a person is rewarded immediately at

the time of death based on his or her works of faith. Consider the parable of the rich man and Lazarus in Luke 16:19–31. The poor man Lazarus only longed for the scraps off the table of the rich man, but food and aid never came. When Lazarus died "he was carried away by angels to the bosom of Abraham" (Lk 16:22). However, when the rich man died he was left to be tormented in his sins. When he called out for help, Abraham, the father of the Jewish faith, answered:

> "My child, remember that you received what was good during your lifetime while Lazarus likewise received what was bad; but now he is comforted here, whereas you are tormented. Moreover, between us and you a great chasm is established to prevent anyone from crossing who might wish to go from our side to yours or from your side to ours." (Lk 16:25–26)

Also, recall Jesus' conversation with the good thief who was hanging next to Jesus to die. The man had faith in Christ: "Jesus, remember me when you come into your kingdom." Jesus replied by telling him, "Amen, I say to you, today you will be with me in Paradise" (Lk 23:42–43).

At the very moment of death, each person receives a **particular judgment** that is related to his or her life in Christ. Depending on that life, a person will enter Heaven—immediately or after purification (**purgatory**)—or immediately to hell, which is everlasting damnation.

particular judgment
God's judgment immediately after death on whether we should go to Purgatory, Heaven, or hell.

purgatory
Purification after death for those who die in God's friendship, yet still need to be purified to attain holiness before entering Heaven.

Last Judgment
The event that will take place at the end of time when Jesus comes to fully establish the Kingdom of God, bring final victory over evil, and judge the living and the dead.

If we live a good life and our actions are rooted in love of God and neighbor, there is nothing to fear about our particular judgment. God is full of loving compassion. His judgment is for us, not against us. Jesus said:

> Amen, amen, I say to you, whoever hears my word and believes in the one who sent me has eternal life and will not come to condemnation, but has passed from death to life. (Jn 5:24)

A general or **Last Judgment** will take place at the end of time. When that happens, God's saving plan will be clear to everyone who has ever lived. Christ will fully reveal each person's true relationship with God, the good one has done or not done in life, along with the results.

Prayer for a Good Death

Saint Thomas More died a martyr's death in 1535. His death was ordered by King Henry VIII because he refused to take an oath that declared Henry the head of the English church. In his letter to his daughter Meg, Thomas prayed these words for a good death:

Good Lord,
give me the grace so to spend my life,
that when the day of my death shall come,
though I may feel pain in my body,
I may feel comfort in soul;
and with faithful hope in thy mercy,
in due love towards thee
and charity towards the world,
I may, through thy grace,
part hence into thy glory.

● Write a prayer for your own "good death" while focusing on how you plan to spend your life doing God's will.

Heaven Is the Goal

Single, married, priest, or religious, the goal for each person is to spend eternity in Heaven. Everyone has some ideas of what Heaven is like. Saint Thérèse of Lisieux wrote, "God's gaze, his ravishing smile. This is my Heaven." The *Catechism of the Catholic Church* defines Heaven as "the ultimate end and fulfillment of the deepest human longings, the state of supreme, definitive happiness" (*CCC*, 1024). In Heaven, we will be in communion with the Holy Trinity, the Virgin Mary, the angels, and all the saints. To live in Heaven is to be with Christ.

In practical terms, in Heaven, time and space will have no effect on us. We will be reunited with family members and friends who have died

before us in God's grace and friendship. We will never be burdened with sickness, disease, pain, and suffering again. Heaven is our goal during this life. That is why we live our lives with death united in Christ in mind. Saint Thérèse said of her death, "I am not dying; I am entering life." Only through dying can we enter the fullness of God's Kingdom. That is Heaven.

A classic rock song described the budding love between a man and a woman and the excitement of this initial time in the relationship like this: "It's only the beginning. It's only just the start."[6] We can think of our love and life with God in the same way. Our time on earth is "only the beginning. It's only just the start."

With God's grace, you have many more days on earth to find and live your life's calling.

And, with the same grace, you have the infinite and vast heavenly kingdom to contemplate in this life and to enjoy forever in the next.

study questions

1. When does a Christian "die with Christ"?

2. Define: *particular judgment*, *Last Judgment*, and *purgatory*.

3. What evidence is there from Scripture of a particular judgment?

4. How does the *Catechism* define Heaven?

journal discussion

- Where does your goal to reach Heaven rate among the other goals for your life?

- How do you think of Heaven?

- On a scale of 1–10 (10 being the highest), rate the degree of your belief in everlasting life.

Next Steps for Planning Your Vocation

While you are not ready to make a committment to permanent vocations of marriage, Holy Orders, or consecrated religious life, you should be continuing an ongoing discernment process of your Christian vocation while imagining yourself in one of the permanent vocations.

The section lists several resources designed to provide more information in the following areas:

- Catholic colleges in the United States
- Committed service efforts
- Teen-focused retreats
- Religious ministries guide
- Catholic seminaries in the United States

Catholic Colleges in the United States

There are over two hundred Catholic colleges in the United States. They have undergraduate enrollments of all sizes—from under 1,000 students to over 20,000 students. They are also located in every region of the country, in urban, suburban, and rural areas. Some Catholic universities also have renowned medical and law schools and offer several other professional and graduate degrees. Besides these basic facts, there are some other reasons for you to consider attending a Catholic college. For example:

- *Community environment.* At a Catholic college you won't be treated like a number. You will meet new friends of many different racial, religious, and socio-economic backgrounds. You will be supported by caring professors and staff.

- *Moral environment.* Don't be fooled; students at Catholic colleges are not perfect and make their share of immoral choices. However, the policies of the institution itself should be geared to promote Christian morality (e.g., speaking out for the right to life for everyone, from the unborn to the aged and infirmed).

- *Global environment.* One of the marks of the Church is that it is catholic or universal. The first universities were Catholic and connected to monasteries. There are Catholics and Catholic colleges worldwide and many of the Catholic colleges in the United States have excellent study abroad programs. Also, courses are taught from a global perspective where solidarity with the entire human race—especially the poor—is stressed.

- *Faith environment.* Whether it is a crucifix in a classroom, a priest or religious serving as a rector in a dorm, a required theology course, or the celebration of the sacraments on campus, a Catholic college offers the opportunity to continue to practice the faith you first learned in your family and will want to practice in your own life and family in the future.

Father Bernie O'Connor, OSFS, a Catholic college president, wrote that preparing students for life is the number one reason for a student to attend a Catholic college. He added: "We know what makes a successful marriage, we know what is required for a happy and productive career, we know what it takes to care for children, we know about the struggles of the elderly, the sick, the disabled, the forgotten."

The National Catholic College Admission Association provides information for prospective students and their families at www.catholiccollegesonline.org.

If you are not able to attend a Catholic college, most public colleges sponsor a Newman Club, named after John Henry Cardinal Newman who was raised in the Anglican Church of the early nineteenth century before converting to Catholicism at the age of forty-two. In the past, it was rare for Catholics to attend non-Catholic colleges. The first Newman Club was sponsored at the University of Pennsylvania in 1883, insisting that its members not become "clannish or narrow in a religious sense." This motivation continues today as Newman Clubs have an interfaith focus while including celebration of the sacraments, RCIA classes, and catechetical studies more specifically for their Catholic members.

Committed Service Efforts

As part of a high school curriculum or parish project, you may have committed yourself to hours and work of Christian service. Typical efforts usually involve either focused work in your own community or a project where you travel to an area in need and spend a week or two helping to do physical repairs on houses, schools, or churches. If you have not participated in a committed service effort to this point in high school, it is a wise choice to begin to now.

Mother Teresa of Calcutta offered this advice about service: "Just begin, one, one, one," she said. "Begin at home by saying something good to someone in your family. Begin by helping someone in need in your community, at work, or at school. Begin by making whatever you do something beautiful for God."[7]

Catholic Charities USA is the largest private network of social service organizations in the United States working to support families, reduce poverty, and build communities. There are local chapters of Catholic Charities in each Catholic diocese. Explore the volunteer opportunities offered in your diocese through Catholic Charities at www.catholic charitiesinfo.org/states/. You may find a chance to volunteer in a food bank, as a senior citizen's companion, a mentor to a young student, or to assist in relief for a natural disaster in your area or even in another part of the country.

In the future, when you are of college age, there are several "summer immersion" volunteer opportunities that encourage participation in a focused area of service. These programs usually include time for community building, reflection and prayer, and education before, during, and after the actual experience. The programs may take place in the United States or in another country. For example, one Catholic college offered a program in which students worked with local agencies in the poverty-stricken Appalachian region as well as another program in Ghana in which students trained youth in computer skills.

After college, many new graduates choose to do a year of service prior to beginning their careers. Often, this year affords the opportunity to discern a future path clearly not only in career but also in vocation. For example, the largest Catholic volunteer agency is the Jesuit Volunteer Corps. Volunteers are assigned to various places and tasks, including working with the elderly, teaching in impoverished schools, and ministering to people with AIDS. The volunteers live in community with each other, making time for prayer and learning to model simple living. A similar and growing program is the Holy Cross Associates. One of the features of this program is a weekly "community night" in which dinner, an activity, and prayer are led and shared by the Associates themselves.

For more information see the Jesuit Volunteer Corps website at www.jesuitvolunteers.org/ and the Holy Cross Associates website at http://holycross associates.nd.edu.

Teen-Focused Retreats

You may have also been on one or more retreats. As the term indicates, the experience is meant to allow you to "retreat" from your daily cares, concerns, and responsibilities to take up a focused faith-filled experience that includes many of these elements: an opportunity for a deepening of prayer, a sense of belonging with fellow retreatants, interaction with adult Catholics of other ages (usually the retreat leaders), informal celebrations of the sacraments, especially Penance and Eucharist, and an increased awareness of and desire to make an adult-level faith commitment.

Teens Encounter Christ is a Catholic movement of spirituality that focuses on the Paschal Mystery. Founded in Lansing, Michigan, following the Second

Vatican Council in 1965, the purpose of the retreat is to encourage older teens and young adults to come to know Christ in a personal way and to make a heart-felt decision to follow him. The retreat is usually held over three days and includes songs, music, witness talks, and celebration of the sacraments. It is available on a regular basis in most dioceses.

Other popular outreach programs that you may consider attending, first as participant and perhaps later as a leader, are those sponsored by National Evangelization Teams (NET). NET is based in Saint Paul, Minnesota, but sends out "teams" of young adults (usually between eighteen and thirty years old) after a period of training to dioceses across the country. Once at their destination, the teams meet with a contact person there and are told specifically how the diocese would like them to minister to their youth. Some dioceses have NET work in a Catholic high school for a week, visiting a different class each day. Others sponsor youth rallies. Many have retreats scheduled at several different parishes. Usually a team will stay in a diocese for two to five weeks. Sometimes team members stay at a rectory or parish center. Mostly they stay with host families.

Look for an opportunity to participate in a retreat sponsored by your parish, school, or elsewhere in your diocese. Use the time away to reflect on your high school experience, your life with your family, and ways you will be able to take the lessons learned to a future vocation.

Religious Ministries Guide

The Catholic News Publishing Company annually releases *A Guide to Religious Ministries for Catholic Men and Women*. More information along with other online resources are listed at www.religiousministries.com. Links include information on colleges, seminaries, diocesan vocation offices, retreat houses, and more. There are several other tools for discerning a religious vocation listed in the guide, including a selection on some common apostolic works or ministries performed by priests, brothers, and sisters. Some of the most common ministries include parish work, social work, health care, home missions, campus ministry, child care, foreign missions, chaplaincies, religious education, counseling, education, communications, spiritual direction, and inner-city work.

If you have an interest in one or more of these ministries, explore more at the website above or through your local diocesan vocation office.

Catholic Seminaries in the United States

Catholic seminaries are places where students prepare humanly, spiritually, academically, and pastorally for the priesthood. Seminaries prepare men for both the diocesan and religious-order priesthood. There are over seventy-five seminaries in the United States in twenty-five states. There are six seminaries in the state of New York. There is a seminary in North Dakota, Cardinal Muench Seminary, that was founded in 1966.

If you are discerning the possibility of a vocation to the priesthood, explore the history and programs at several seminaries in the United States while also speaking with a parish priest and diocesan or religious community vocation director.

One link for Catholic seminaries in the United States websites is http://consortium.villanova.edu/statements/seminaries.htm.

As mentioned in Unit 2, there are several parish and diocesan programs for marriage preparation that you can seek out once you have become engaged and are planning your wedding. As to meeting a potential spouse, one of the best ways is to study, work, and socialize where good people like yourself are more likely to meet.

 summary**points**

✦ Role Model

- ✦ The Christian vocation is in the present.

- ✦ Ultimately the Christian vocation is to eternal life.

- ✦ Mary is the perfect role model for a Christian vocation.

✦ Your Vocation Now

- ✦ The laity live their vocation in two ways: as individuals or through an organized apostolate.

- ✦ The vocation of the laity is to share in the priestly, prophetic, and kingly office of Christ in the world.

- ✦ A way to participate in the priestly office is to offer up hardships and sufferings to God.

- ✦ Lay people fulfill the prophetic mission through evangelization.

- ✦ A primary way lay people work on behalf of the kingly office of Christ is by helping to improve the conditions in the secular institutions of which they are a part.

✦ Seeking Perfection

- ✦ Every Christian is called to a full life of holiness and love.

- ✦ A way to seek perfection is to practice the virtues, especially the four cardinal virtues of temperance, prudence, justice, and courage.

- ✦ The way of perfection passes through the cross of Christ.

- ✦ The progression to the peace and joy of the Beatitudes is a gradual and arduous one.

✦ Life Everlasting

- ✦ A Christian's belief in eternal life should affect all aspects of his or her life on earth.

- ✦ We should prepare for a good and holy death.

- ✦ At the moment of our death we will be judged based on our life in Christ.

- ✦ A general or Last Judgment will take place at the end of time when God's saving plan will be clear to everyone who has ever lived.

- ✦ In Heaven we will be in communion with the Holy Trinity, Mary, the angels, and all the saints, living with Christ.

assignments applications

Your final assignment for this course is to write a five-hundred-word essay that you could use as part of a college application. In lieu of face-to-face interviews, most colleges ask prospective students to write an essay that introduces the "real you" and allows the admissions staff to get a glimpse of your personality, sense of humor, and motivations, as well as your dreams and goals for life.

For this essay, follow the format listed below with one additional focus: refer to the discernment you have begun regarding your life's vocation and incorporate how a Catholic lifestyle that may include the vocations of marriage, Holy Orders, religious life, or committed single life fit into your plans.

Your completed essay has a dual purpose. Not only will it serve as the final assignment for this course, but you should also be able to re-craft it as an essay you can use when applying to one or more colleges making only minor revisions. Here are some more tips for writing:

- Be genuine. Don't write something you think your teacher or an admissions officer wants to read. Write something that describes the real you.

- Look deeper. Reflect on the heart of your life. Be soulful.

- Incorporate some of your uniqueness into your writing. Remember you are trying to communicate to the reader who you really are.

- Have fun. This isn't a typical term paper or theme. Let the writing flow.

✦ Prayer to Do God's Will

God created me
　to do him some definite service;
　　he has committed some work to me
　　　which he has not committed to another.
　　I have my mission—
　　　I may never know it in this life,
　　　　but I shall be told it in the next. . . .
　　　Therefore, I will trust him. . . .
　　　If I am in sickness,
　　　　my sickness may serve him;
　　　in perplexity,
　　　　my perplexity may serve him;
　　if I am in sorrow,
　　　my sorrow may serve him. . . .
　　He does nothing in vain;
　he may prolong my life,
　he may shorten it,
　he knows what he is about.

　　　　　　—John Henry Cardinal Newman

Notes

1. Quoted from www.catholic
   forum.com/saintS/stjo5003.htm.

2. *Lumen Gentium*, 31.

3. From the Christophers' website at www. christophers.org/andyou.html.

4. Saint Thomas Aquinas, *STH*. III, 71, 4 *ad* 3.

5. Saint Gregory of Nyssa, *De beatitudinibus*, 1: PG 44, 1200D.

6. The song quoted from is "Beginnings" by Chicago.

7. Quoted from *Words to Love By* by Mother Teresa (Notre Dame, IN: Ave Maria Press, 1983).

appendix

A. Beliefs

From the beginning, the Church expressed and handed on its faith in a brief formula accessible to all. These professions of faith are called "creeds" because their first word in Latin, "credo," means "I believe." The following creeds have special importance in the Church. The Apostles' Creed is a summary of the Apostles' faith. The Nicene Creed developed from the Councils of Nicaea and Constantinople and remain in common between the Churches of both the East and West.

Apostles' Creed

I believe in God,
the Father almighty,
Creator of heaven and earth,
and in Jesus Christ, his only Son, our Lord,
who was conceived by the Holy Spirit,
born of the Virgin Mary,
suffered under Pontius Pilate,
was crucified, died and was buried;
he descended into hell;
on the third day he rose again from the dead;
he ascended into heaven,
and is seated at the right hand of God the Father
    almighty;
from there he will come to judge the living and the
    dead.

I believe in the Holy Spirit,
the holy catholic Church,
the communion of saints,
the forgiveness of sins,
the resurrection of the body,
and life everlasting. Amen.

Nicene Creed

I believe in one God,
the Father almighty,
maker of heaven and earth,
of all things visible and invisible.

I believe in one Lord Jesus Christ,
the Only Begotten Son of God,
born of the Father before all ages.
God from God, Light from Light,
true God from true God,
begotten, not made, consubstantial with the Father;
through him all things were made.
For us men and for our salvation
he came down from heaven,
and by the Holy Spirit was incarnate of the Virgin
    Mary,
and became man.

For our sake he was crucified under Pontius Pilate,
he suffered death and was buried,
and rose again on the third day
in accordance with the Scriptures.
He ascended into heaven
and is seated at the right hand of the Father.
He will come again in glory
to judge the living and the dead
and his kingdom will have no end.

I believe in the Holy Spirit, the Lord, the giver of life,
who proceeds from the Father and the Son,
who with the Father and the Son is adored and glorified,
who has spoken through the prophets.

I believe in one, holy, catholic, and apostolic Church.
I confess one Baptism for the forgiveness of sins
and I look forward to the resurrection of the dead
and the life of the world to come. Amen.

Catholic Handbook for Faith

B. Faith in God: Father, Son, and Holy Spirit

Our profession of faith begins with God, for God is the First and the Last, the beginning and end of everything.

Attributes of God

Saint Thomas Aquinas named nine attributes that tell us some things about God's nature. They are:

1. *God is eternal.* He has no beginning and no end. Or, to put it another way, God always was, always is, and always will be.

2. *God is unique.* God is the designer of a one and only world. Even the people he creates are one of a kind.

3. *God is infinite and omnipotent.* This reminds us of a lesson we learned early in life: God sees everything. There are no limits to God. Omnipotence is a word that refers to God's supreme power and authority over all of creation.

4. *God is omnipresent.* God is not limited to space. He is everywhere. You can never be away from God.

5. *God contains all things.* All of creation is under God's care and jurisdiction.

6. *God is immutable.* God does not evolve. God does not change. God is the same God now as he always was and always will be.

7. *God is pure spirit.* Though God has been described with human attributes, God is not a material creation. God's image cannot be made. God is a pure Spirit who cannot be divided into parts. God is simple, but complex.

8. *God is alive.* We believe in a living God, a God who acts in the lives of people. Most concretely, Jesus Christ, the Son of God, assumed human nature in order to accomplish our salvation in it.

9. *God is holy.* God is pure goodness. God is pure love.

The Holy Trinity

The Trinity is the mystery of one God in three Persons—Father, Son, and Holy Spirit. It is the central mystery of the Catholic faith. This mystery is impossible for human minds to understand. Some of the Church dogmas, or beliefs, can help:

- *The Trinity is One.* There are not three Gods, but one God in three Persons. Each one of them—Father, Son, and Holy Spirit—is God whole and entire.

- *The three Persons are distinct from one another.* For example, the Father is not the Son, nor is the Son the Holy Spirit. Rather, the Father is eternally in relation to the Son, the Son is begotten of the Father, and the Holy Spirit proceeds from the Father and the Son.

- *The divine Persons are related to one another.* Though they are related to one another, the three Persons have one nature or substance.

Saint John Damascus used two analogies to describe the doctrine of the Blessed Trinity.

The Father is a sun with the Son as rays and the Holy Spirit as heat.

Read the *Catechism of the Catholic Church* (232–267) on the Holy Trinity.

God the Father

Calling God "Father" indicates two main things: that God creates and has authority over everything and, at the same time, cares for his creation as a loving parent. Jesus revealed that God is Father in this previously unheard of sense:

> He is Father not only in being Creator; he is eternally Father in relation to his Son, who is eternally Son only in relation to the Father: "No one knows the Son except the Father, and no one knows the Father except the Son and anyone to whom the Son chooses to reveal him." (CCC, 240 quoting Mt 11:27)

Think of the Father as a root, of the Son as a branch, and of the Spirit as a fruit, for the substance of these is one.

God the Son

Jesus is inseparably true God and true man. He is truly the Son of God who, without ceasing to be God and Lord, became a man and our brother. The Council of Chalcedon (451) addressed this doctrine in what has come to be known as "The Symbol of Chalcedon":

> Following therefore the holy Fathers, we unanimously teach to confess one and the same Son, our Lord Jesus Christ, the same perfect in divinity and perfect in humanity, the same truly God and truly man composed of rational soul and body, the same one in being (*homoousios*) with the Father as to the divinity and one in being with us as to the humanity, like unto us in all things but sin (cf. Heb 4:15). The same was begotten from the Father before the ages as to the divinity and in the later days for us and our salvation was born as to his humanity from Mary the Virgin Mother of God.
>
> We confess that one and the same Lord Jesus Christ, the only-begotten Son, must be acknowledged in two natures, without confusion or change, without division or separation. The distinction between the natures was never abolished by their union but rather the character proper to each of the two natures was preserved as they came together in one person (*prosôpon*) and one hypostasis. He is not split or divided into two persons, but he is one and the same only-begotten, God the Word, the Lord Jesus Christ, as formerly the prophets and later Jesus Christ himself have taught us about him and as has been handed down to us by the Symbol of the Fathers.

God the Holy Spirit

The Holy Spirit is the last of the Persons of the Holy Trinity to be revealed. Saint Gregory of Nazianzus explained the progression of divine Revelation:

The Old Testament proclaimed the Father clearly, but the Son more obscurely. The New Testament revealed the Son and gave us a glimpse of the divinity of the Spirit. Now the Spirit dwells among us and grants us a clearer vision of himself. It was not prudent, when the divinity of the Father had not yet been confessed, to proclaim the Son openly and, when the divinity of the Son was not yet admitted, to add the Holy Spirit as an extra burden, to speak somewhat daringly. . . . By advancing and progressing "from glory to glory," the light of the Trinity will shine in ever more brilliant rays.

C. Deposit of Faith

"Deposit of faith" refers to both Sacred Scripture and Sacred Tradition handed on from the time of the Apostles, from which the Church draws all that it proposes is revealed by God.

Canon of the Bible

Listed below are the categories and books of the Old Testament and New Testament:

The Old Testament

The Pentateuch

Genesis	Gn
Exodus	Ex
Leviticus	Lv
Numbers	Nm
Deuteronomy	Dt

The Historical Books

Joshua	Jos
Judges	Jgs
Ruth	Ru
1 Samuel	1 Sm
2 Samuel	2 Sm
1 Kings	1 Kgs
2 Kings	2 Kgs
1 Chronicles	1 Chr
2 Chronicles	2 Chr
Ezra	Ezr
Nehemiah	Neh
Tobit	Tb
Judith	Jdt
Esther	Est
1 Maccabees	1 Mc
2 Maccabees	2 Mc

The Wisdom Books

Job	Jb
Psalms	Ps(s)
Proverbs	Prv
Ecclesiastes	Eccl
Song of Songs	Sg
Wisdom	Wis
Sirach	Sir

The Prophetic Books

Isaiah	Is
Jeremiah	Jer
Lamentations	Lam
Baruch	Bar
Ezekiel	Ez
Daniel	Dn
Hosea	Hos
Joel	Jl
Amos	Am
Obadiah	Ob
Jonah	Jon
Micah	Mi
Nahum	Na
Habakkuk	Hb
Zephaniah	Zep
Haggai	Hg
Zechariah	Zec
Malachi	Mal

The New Testament

The Gospels

Matthew	Mt
Mark	Mk
Luke	Lk
John	Jn
Acts of the Apostles	Acts

The New Testament Letters

Romans	Rom
1 Corinthians	1 Cor
2 Corinthians	2 Cor
Galatians	Gal
Ephesians	Eph
Philippians	Phil
Colossians	Col
1 Thessalonians	1 Thes
2 Thessalonians	2 Thes
1 Timothy	1 Tm
2 Timothy	2 Tm
Titus	Ti
Philemon	Phlm
Hebrews	Heb

The Catholic Letters

James	Jas
1 Peter	1 Pt
2 Peter	2 Pt
1 John	1 Jn
2 John	2 Jn
3 John	3 Jn
Jude	Jude
Revelation	Rv

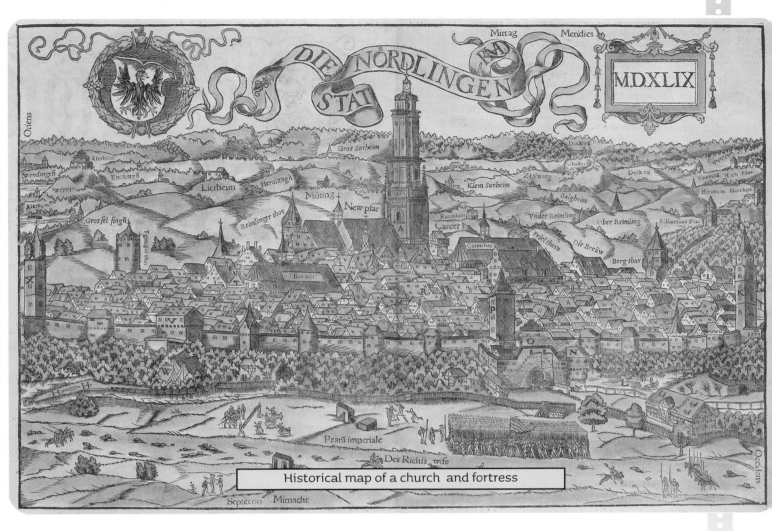

Historical map of a church and fortress

Relationship Between Scripture and Tradition

The Church does not derive the revealed truths of God from the holy Scriptures alone. Sacred Tradition hands on God's word, first given to the Apostles by the Lord and the Holy Spirit, to the successors of the Apostles (the bishops and the Pope). Enlightened by the Holy Spirit, these successors faithfully preserve, explain, and spread it to the ends of the earth. The Second Vatican Council fathers explained the relationship between Sacred Scripture and Sacred Tradition:

It is clear therefore that, in the supremely wise arrangement of God, sacred Tradition, Sacred Scripture, and the Magisterium of the Church are so connected and associated that one of them cannot stand without the others. Working together, each in its own way, under the action of the one Holy Spirit, they all contribute effectively to the salvation of souls. (*Dei Verbum*, 10)

D. Church

The Church is the Body of Christ, that is, the community of God's people who profess faith in the risen Lord Jesus and love and serve others under the guidance of the Holy Spirit. The Roman Catholic Church is guided by the Pope and his bishops.

Timeline of Church History

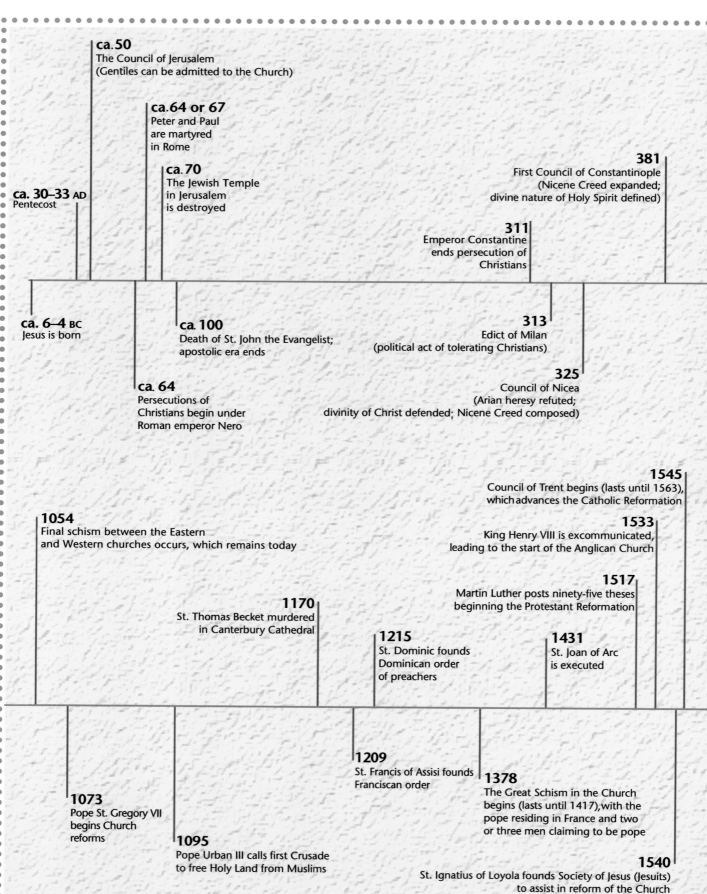

ca.50
The Council of Jerusalem
(Gentiles can be admitted to the Church)

ca.64 or 67
Peter and Paul
are martyred
in Rome

ca.70
The Jewish Temple
in Jerusalem
is destroyed

381
First Council of Constantinople
(Nicene Creed expanded;
divine nature of Holy Spirit defined)

311
Emperor Constantine
ends persecution of
Christians

ca. 30–33 AD
Pentecost

ca. 6–4 BC
Jesus is born

ca. 100
Death of St. John the Evangelist;
apostolic era ends

313
Edict of Milan
(political act of tolerating Christians)

ca. 64
Persecutions of
Christians begin under
Roman emperor Nero

325
Council of Nicea
(Arian heresy refuted;
divinity of Christ defended; Nicene Creed composed)

1545
Council of Trent begins (lasts until 1563),
which advances the Catholic Reformation

1533
King Henry VIII is excommunicated,
leading to the start of the Anglican Church

1517
Martin Luther posts ninety-five theses
beginning the Protestant Reformation

1054
Final schism between the Eastern
and Western churches occurs, which remains today

1170
St. Thomas Becket murdered
in Canterbury Cathedral

1215
St. Dominic founds
Dominican order
of preachers

1431
St. Joan of Arc
is executed

1209
St. Francis of Assisi founds
Franciscan order

1378
The Great Schism in the Church
begins (lasts until 1417), with the
pope residing in France and two
or three men claiming to be pope

1073
Pope St. Gregory VII
begins Church
reforms

1095
Pope Urban III calls first Crusade
to free Holy Land from Muslims

1540
St. Ignatius of Loyola founds Society of Jesus (Jesuits)
to assist in reform of the Church

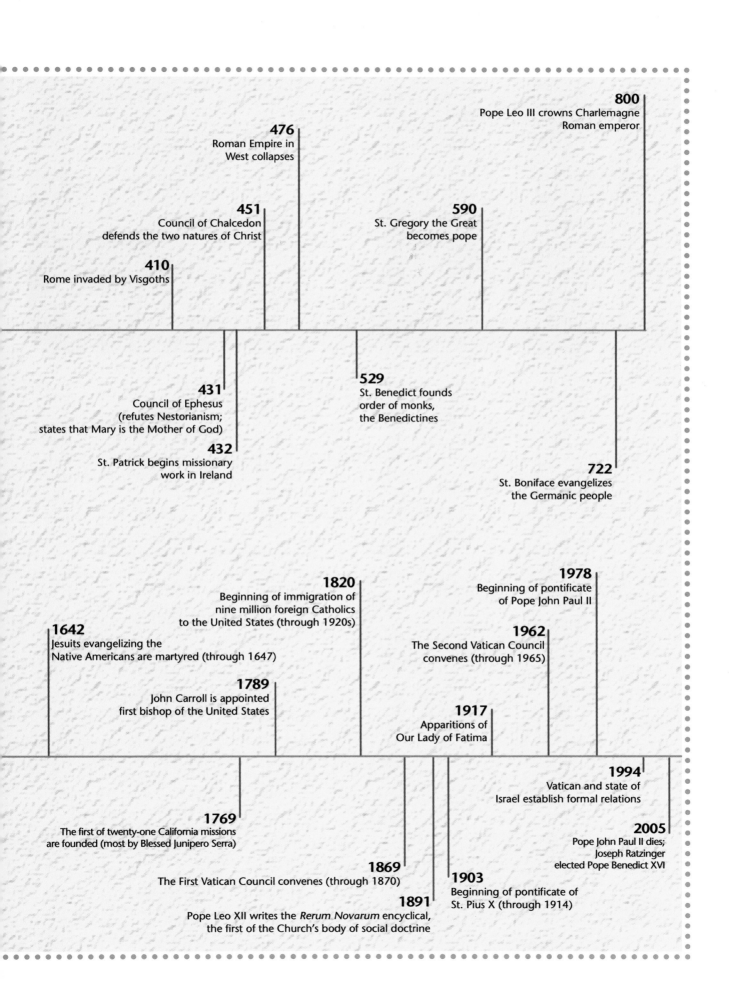

800
Pope Leo III crowns Charlemagne
Roman emperor

476
Roman Empire in
West collapses

451
Council of Chalcedon
defends the two natures of Christ

590
St. Gregory the Great
becomes pope

410
Rome invaded by Visgoths

431
Council of Ephesus
(refutes Nestorianism;
states that Mary is the Mother of God)

529
St. Benedict founds
order of monks,
the Benedictines

432
St. Patrick begins missionary
work in Ireland

722
St. Boniface evangelizes
the Germanic people

1820
Beginning of immigration of
nine million foreign Catholics
to the United States (through 1920s)

1978
Beginning of pontificate
of Pope John Paul II

1642
Jesuits evangelizing the
Native Americans are martyred (through 1647)

1962
The Second Vatican Council
convenes (through 1965)

1789
John Carroll is appointed
first bishop of the United States

1917
Apparitions of
Our Lady of Fatima

1994
Vatican and state of
Israel establish formal relations

1769
The first of twenty-one California missions
are founded (most by Blessed Junipero Serra)

2005
Pope John Paul II dies;
Joseph Ratzinger
elected Pope Benedict XVI

1869
The First Vatican Council convenes (through 1870)

1903
Beginning of pontificate of
St. Pius X (through 1914)

1891
Pope Leo XII writes the *Rerum Novarum* encyclical,
the first of the Church's body of social doctrine

Marks of the Church

- *The Church is one.* The Church remains one because of its source: the unity in the Trinity of the Father, Son, and Spirit in one God. The Church's unity can never be broken and lost because this foundation is itself unbreakable.

- *The Church is holy.* The Church is holy because Jesus, the founder of the Church, is holy and he joined the Church to himself as his body and gave the Church the gift of the Holy Spirit. Together, Christ and the Church make up the "whole Christ" (*Christus totus* in Latin).

- *The Church is catholic.* The Church is catholic ("universal" or "for everyone") in two ways. First, it is Catholic because Christ is present in the Church in the fullness of his body, with the fullness of the means of salvation, the fullness of faith, sacraments, and the ordained ministry that comes from the Apostles. The Church is also catholic because it takes its message of salvation to all people.

- *The Church is apostolic.* The Church's apostolic mission comes from Jesus: "Go, therefore, and make disciples of all nations" (Mt 28:19). The Church remains apostolic because it still teaches the same things the Apostles taught. Also, the Church is led by leaders who are successors to the Apostles and who help to guide us until Jesus returns.

The Pope

The bishop of Rome has carried the title "Pope" since the ninth century. Pope means "papa" or "father." Saint Peter was the first bishop of Rome and, hence, the first Pope. He was commissioned directly by Jesus:

> And so I say to you, you are Peter, and upon this rock I will build my church, and the gates of the netherworld shall not prevail against it. I will give you the keys to the kingdom of heaven. Whatever you bind on earth shall be bound in heaven; and whatever you loose on earth shall be loosed in heaven. (Mt 16:18–19)

Because Peter was the first bishop of Rome, the succeeding bishops of Rome have had primacy in the Church. The entire succession of Popes since Saint Peter can be traced directly to the Apostle.

The Pope is in communion with the bishops of the world as part of the Magisterium, which is the Church's teaching authority. The Pope can also define doctrine in faith or morals for the Church. When he does so, he is infallible and cannot be in error.

The Pope is elected by the College of Cardinals by a two-thirds plus one majority vote in secret balloting. Cardinals under the age of eighty are eligible to vote. If the necessary majority is not achieved, the ballots are burned in a small stove inside the counsel chambers along with straw that makes dark smoke. The sign of dark smoke announces to the crowds waiting outside Saint Peter's Basilica that a new Pope has not been chosen. When a new Pope has been voted in with the necessary majority, the ballots are burned without the straw producing white smoke, signifying the election of a Pope.

Recent Popes

Since 1900 and into the pontificate of Pope Benedict XVI, there have been ten Popes. Pope John Paul II was the first non-Italian Pope since Dutchman Pope Adrian VI (1522–1523). The Popes since the beginning of the twentieth century through Benedict XVI with their original names, place of origin, and years as Pope are as follows:

Pope Leo XIII
> (Giocchino Pecci): Carpineto, Italy, February 20 1878–July 20, 1903.

Pope Saint Pius X
> (Giuseppe Sarto): Riese, Italy, August 4, 1903–1914.

Pope Benedict XV
> (Giacomo della Chiesa): Genoa, Italy, September 3, 1914–January 22, 1922.

Pope Pius XI
> (Achille Ratti): Desio, Italy, February 6, 1922–February 10, 1939.

Pope Pius XII
> (Eugenio Pacelli): Rome, Italy, March 2, 1939–October 9, 1958.

Pope John XXIII
> (Angelo Giuseppe Roncalli), Sotto il Monte, Italy, October 28, 1958–June 3, 1963.

Pope Paul VI
> (Giovanni Battista Montini): Concessio, Italy, June 21, 1963–August 6, 1978.

Pope John Paul I
> (Albino Luciani): Forno di Canale, Italy, August 26, 1978–September 28, 1978.

Pope John Paul II
> (Karol Wojtyla): Wadowice, Poland, October 16, 1978–April 2, 2005.

Pope Benedict XVI
> (Joseph Ratzinger): Marktl am Inn, Germany, April 19, 2005–

Pope Benedict XVI

Fathers of the Church

Church Fathers, or Fathers of the Church, is a traditional title that was given to theologians of the first eight centuries whose teachings made a lasting mark on the Church. The Church Fathers developed a significant amount of doctrine that has great authority in the Church. The Church Fathers are identified by the language they wrote in, as either Latin Fathers (West) or Greek Fathers (East). Among the greatest Fathers of the Church are:

Latin Fathers

Saint Ambrose
Saint Augustine
Saint Jerome
Saint Gregory the Great

Greek Fathers

Saint John Chrysostom
Saint Basil the Great
Saint Gregory of Nazianzen
Saint Athanasius

Doctors of the Church

The Doctors of the Church are men and women honored by the Church for their writings, preaching, and holiness. Originally the Doctors of the Church were considered to be Church Fathers Augustine, Ambrose, Jerome, and Gregory the Great, but others were added over the centuries. Saint Teresa of Avila was the first woman Doctor (1970). Saint Catherine of Siena was named a Doctor of the Church the same year. The list of Doctors of the Church:

Name	Life Span
Saint Athanasius	296–373
Saint Ephraem the Syrian	306–373
Saint Hilary of Poitiers	315–367
Saint Cyril of Jerusalem	315–386
Saint Gregory of Nazianzus	325–389
Saint Basil the Great	329–379
Saint Ambrose	339–397
Saint John Chrysostom	347–407
Saint Jerome	347–419
Saint Augustine	354–430
Saint Cyril of Alexandria	376–444
Saint Peter Chrysologous	400–450
Saint Leo the Great	400–461
Saint Gregory the Great	540–604
Saint Isidore of Seville	560–636
Saint John of Damascus	645–749
Saint Bede the Venerable	672–735
Saint Peter Damian	1007–1072
Saint Anselm	1033–1109
Saint Bernard of Clairvaux	1090–1153
Saint Anthony of Padua	1195–1231
Saint Albert the Great	1206–1280
Saint Bonaventure	1221–1274
Saint Thomas Aquinas	1226–1274
Saint Teresa of Avila	1515–1582
Saint Catherine of Siena	1347–1380
Saint Peter Canisius	1521–1597
Saint John of the Cross	1542–1591
Saint Robert Bellarmine	1542–1621
Saint Lawrence of Brindisi	1559–1619
Saint Francis de Sales	1567–1622
Saint Alphonsus Ligouri	1696–1787
Saint Thérèse of Lisieux	1873–1897

Designation

1568 by Pius V

1920 by Benedict XV

1851 by Pius IX

1882 by Leo XIII

1568 by Pius V

1568 by Pius V

1295 by Boniface VIII

1568 by Pius V

1295 by Boniface XIII

1295 by Boniface XIII

1882 by Leo XIII

1729 by Benedict XIII

1754 by Benedict XIV

1295 by Boniface XIII

1722 by Innocent XIII

1890 by Leo XIII

1899 by Leo XIII

1828 by Leo XII

1720 by Clement XI

1830 by Pius VIII

1946 by Pius XII

1931 by Pius XI

1588 by Sixtus V

1567 by Pius V

1970 by Paul VI

1970 by Paul VI

1925 by Pius XI

1926 by Pius XI

1931 by Pius XI

1959 by John XXIII

1871 by Pius IX

1871 by Pius IX

1997 by John Paul II

Ecumenical Councils

An Ecumenical Council is a worldwide assembly of bishops under direction of the Pope. There have been twenty-one Ecumenical Councils, the most recent being the Second Vatican Council (1962–1965). A complete list of the Church's Ecumenical Councils with the years each met are as follows:

Nicaea I	325
Constantinople I	381
Ephesus	431
Chalcedon	451
Constantinople II	553
Constantinople III	680–681
Nicaea II	787
Constantinople IV	869–870
Lateran I	1123
Lateran II	1139
Lateran III	1179
Lateran IV	1215
Lyons I	1245
Lyons II	1274
Vienne	1311–1312
Constance	1414–1418
Florence	1431–1445
Lateran V	1512–1517
Trent	1545–1563
Vatican Council I	1869–1870
Vatican Council II	1962–1965

Catholic Colleges in the United States by Regions

The following list of colleges is taken from information provided by Catholic dioceses in the United States.

West

Chaminade University of Honolulu, Honolulu, HI
www.chaminade.edu

College of Santa Fe, Santa Fe, CA
www.csf.edu

Dominican University of California, San Rafael, CA
www.dominican.edu

Don Bosco Technical Institute, Rosemead, CA
www.boscotech.edu

Gonzaga University, Spokane, WA
www.gonzaga.edu

Heritage University, Toppenish, WA
www.heritage.edu

Holy Names College, Oakland, CA
www.hnc.edu

Loyola Marymount University, Los Angeles, CA
www.lmu.edu

Marylhurst University, Marylhurst, OR
www.marylhurst.edu

Marymount College, Rancho Palos Verdes, CA
www.marymountpv.edu

Mount Saint Mary's College, Los Angeles, CA
www.msmc.la.edu

Notre Dame de Namur University, Belmont, CA
www.ndnu.edu

Queen of the Holy Rosary College, Fremont, CA
www.msjdominicans.org

Saint Martin's College, Lacey, WA
www.stmartin.edu

Santa Clara University, Santa Clara, CA
www.scu.edu

Seattle University, Seattle, WA
www.seattleu.edu

St. Mary's College, Moraga, CA
www.stmarys-ca.edu

Thomas Aquinas College, Santa Paula, CA
www.thomasaquinas.edu

University of Portland, Portland, OR
www.up.edu

University of Sacramento, Sacramento, CA
www.universityofsacramento.org

University of San Diego, San Diego, CA
www.sandiego.edu

University of San Francisco, San Francisco, CA
www.usfca.edu

Mountain

Carroll College, Helena, MT
www.carroll.edu

Regis University, Denver, CO
www.regis.edu

University of Great Falls, Great Falls, MT
www.ugf.edu

Southwest

Our Lady of the Lake University, San Antonio, TX
www.ollusa.edu

St. Gregory's University, Shawnee, OK
www.stgregorys.edu

St. Mary's University of San Antonio,
San Antonio, TX
www.stmarytx.edu

The College of St. Thomas More, Fort Worth, TX
www.cstm.edu

University of Dallas, Irving, TX
www.udallas.edu

University of St. Thomas, Houston, TX
www.stthom.edu

University of the Incarnate Word, San Antonio, TX
www.uiw.edu

Southeast

Barry University, Miami, FL
www.barry.edu

Belmont Abbey College, Belmont, NC
www.belmontabbeycollege.edu

Saint Leo University, Saint Leo, FL
www.saintleo.edu

St. Thomas University, Miami Gardens, FL
www.stu.edu

South

Aquinas College, Nashville, TN
www.aquinas-tn.edu

Bellarmine University, Louisville, KY
www.bellarmine.edu

Brescia University, Owensboro, KY
www.brescia.edu

Christian Brothers University, Memphis, TN
www.cbu.edu

Loyola University New Orleans, New Orleans, LA
www.loyno.edu

Our Lady of Holy Cross College, New Orleans, LA
www.olhcc.edu

Spalding University, Louisville, KY
www.spalding.edu

Spring Hill College, Mobile, AL
www.shc.edu

St. Catharine College, St. Catharine, KY
www.sccky.edu

Thomas More College, Covington, KY
www.thomasmore.edu

Xavier University of Louisiana, New Orleans, LA
www.xula.edu

Midwest

Alverno College, Milwaukee, WI
www.alverno.edu

Ancilla Domini College, Donaldson, IN
www.ancilla.edu

Aquinas College, Grand Rapids, MI
www.aquinas.edu

Ave Maria College, Ypsilanti, MI
www.avemaria.edu

Avila University, Kansas City, MO
www.avila.edu

Benedictine College, Atchison, KS
www.benedictine.edu

Benedictine University, Lisle, IL
www.ben.edu

Briar Cliff University, Sioux City, IA
www.briarcliff.edu

Calumet College of St. Joseph, Whiting, IN
www.ccsj.edu

Cardinal Stritch University, Milwaukee, WI
www.stritch.edu

Chatfield College, Saint Martin, OH
www.chatfield.edu

Clarke College, Dubuque, IA
www.clarke.edu

College of Mount St. Joseph, Cincinnati, OH
www.msj.edu

College of Saint Benedict, St. Joseph, MN
www.csbsju.edu

College of St. Catherine, St. Paul, MN
www.stkate.edu

College of St. Mary, Omaha, NE
www.csm.edu

College of St. Scholastica, Duluth, MN
www.css.edu

Creighton University, Omaha, NE
www.creighton.edu

De Paul Universtiy, Chicago, IL
www.depaul.edu

Dominican University, River Forest, IL
www.dom.edu

Donnelly College, Kansas City, KS
www.donnelly.edu

Edgewood College, Madison, WI
www.edgewood.edu

Fontbonne University, St. Louis, MO
www.fontbonne.edu

Franciscan University of Steubenville,
    Steubenville, OH
www.franciscan.edu

Holy Cross College, Notre Dame, IN
www.hcc-nd.edu

John Carroll University, University Heights, OH
www.jcu.edu

Lewis University, Romeoville, IL
www.lewisu.edu

Lourdes College, Sylvania, OH
www.lourdes.edu

Loyola University-Chicago, Chicago, IL
www.luc.edu

Madonna Universtiy, Livonia, MI
www.madonna.edu

Marian College of Fond du Lac, Fond Du Lac, WI
www.mariancollege.edu

Marian College, Indianapolis, IN
www.marian.edu

Marquette University, Milwaukee, WI
www.marquette.edu

Marygrove College, Detroit, MI
www.marygrove.edu

Mercy College of Health Sciences, Des Moines, IA
www.mchs.edu

Mercy College of Northwest Ohio, Toledo, OH
www.mercycollege.edu

Mount Marty College, Yankton, SD
www.mtmc.edu

Mount Mary College, Milwaukee, WI
www.mtmary.edu

Newman University, Wichita, KS
www.newmanu.edu

Notre Dame College, Cleveland, OH
www.notredamecollege.edu

Ohio Dominican University, Columbus, OH
www.ohiodominican.edu

Presentation College, Aberdeen, SD
www.presentation.edu

Rockhurst University, Kansas City, MO
www.rockhurst.edu

Saint Joseph's College, Rensselaer, IN
www.saintjoe.edu

Saint Louis University, St. Louis, MO
www.slu.edu

Saint Mary's College, Notre Dame, IN
www.saintmarys.edu

Saint Mary's University of Minnesota, Winona, MN
www.smumn.edu

Saint Mary-of-the-Woods College, Saint Mary-of-
    the-Woods, IN
www.bishopchatard.org

Saint Xavier University, Chicago, IL
www.sxu.edu

Siena Heights University, Adrian, MI
www.sienahts.edu

Silver Lake College of the Holy Family,
    Manitowoc, WI
www.sl.edu

St. Ambrose University, Davenport, IA
www.sau.edu

St. John's University, Collegeville, MN
www.csbsju.edu

St. Norbert College, De Pere, WI
www.snc.edu

The Franciscan University of the Prairies, Clinton, IA
www.tfu.edu

The University of Dayton, Dayton, OH
www.udayton.edu

University of Detroit Mercy, Detroit, MI
www.udmercy.edu

University of Notre Dame Du Lac, Notre Dame, IN
www.nd.edu

University of Saint Francis, Fort Wayne, IN
www.sf.edu

University of Saint Francis, Joliet, IL
www.stfrancis.edu

University of Saint Mary, Leavenworth, KS
www.st.mary.edu

University of St. Thomas, St. Paul, MN
www.stthomas.edu

Ursuline College, Cleveland, OH
www.ursuline.edu

Viterbo University, La Crosse, WI
www.viterbo.edu

Walsh University, North Canton, OH
www.walsh.edu

Xavier University, Cincinnati, OH
www.xu.edu

Middle Atlantic

Assumption College for Sisters, Mendham, NJ
www.acscollegeforsisters.org

Cabrini College, Radnor, PA
www.cabrini.edu

Caldwell College, Caldwell, NJ
www.caldwell.edu

Canisius College, Buffalo, NY
www.canisius.edu

Carlow University, Pittsburgh, PA
www.carlow.edu

Catholic University of America, Washington, DC
www.cua.edu

Chestnut Hill College, Philadelphia, PA
www.chc.edu

College Misericordia, Dallas, PA
www.misericordia.edu

College of Mount Saint Vincent, New York, NY
www.mountsaintvincent.edu

College of Saint Elizabeth, Morristown, NJ
www.cse.edu

D'Youville College, Buffalo, NY
www.dyc.edu

Dominican College, Orangeburg, NY
www.dc.edu

Duquesne University of the Holy Spirit,
   Pittsburgh, PA
www.duq.edu

Felician College, Lodi, NJ
www.felician.edu

Fordham University, Bronx, NY
www.fordham.edu

Gannon University, Erie, PA
www.gannon.edu

Georgetown University, Washington, DC
www.georgetown.edu

Georgian Court University, Lakewood, NJ
www.georgian.edu

Gwynedd-Mercy College, Gwynedd Valley, PA
www.gmc.edu

Hilbert College, Hamburg, NY
www.hilbert.edu

Holy Family University, Philadelphia, PA
www.holyfamily.edu

Immaculata University, Immaculata, PA
www.immaculata.edu

Iona College, New Rochelle, NY
www.iona.edu

Kings College, Wilkes-Barre, PA
www.kings.edu

La Roche College, Pittsburgh, PA
www.laroche.edu

LaSalle University, Philadelphia, PA
www.lasalle.edu

Le Moyne College, Syracuse, NY
www.lemoyne.edu

Manhattan College, Bronx, NY
www.manhattan.edu

Marymount College of Fordham, Tarrytown, NY
www.marymt.edu

Marymount Manhattan College, New York, NY
www.mmm.edu

Marywood University, Scranton, PA
www.marywood.edu

Mercyhurst College, Erie, PA
www.mercyhurst.edu

Molloy College, Rockville Centre, NY
www.molloy.edu

Mount Saint Mary College, Newburgh, NY
www.msmc.edu

Neumann College, Aston, PA
www.neumann.edu

New York Medical College, Valhalla, NY
www.nymc.edu

Niagara University, Niagara University, NY
www.niagara.edu

Quincy University, Quincy, IL
www.quincy.edu

Rosemont College of the Holy Child Jesus,
    Rosemont, PA
www.rosemont.edu

Saint Peter's College, Jersey City, NJ
www.spc.edu

Saint Vincent College, Latrobe, PA
www.stvincent.edu

Seton Hall University, South Orange, NJ
www.shu.edu

Seton Hill University, Greensburg, PA
www.setonhill.edu

St. Bonaventure University, St. Bonaventure, NY
www.sbu.edu

St. John's University, Staten Island, NY
www.stjohns.edu

St. Joseph's College, Patchogue, NY
www.sjcny.edu

St. Joseph's University, Philadelphia, PA
www.sju.edu

St. Thomas Aquinas College, Sparkill, NY
www.stac.edu

The College of New Rochelle, New Rochelle, NY
www.cnr.edu

The University of Scranton, Scranton, PA
www.scranton.edu

Trinity College, Washington, DC
www.trinitydc.edu

Trocaire College, Buffalo, NY
www.trocaire.edu

Villa Maria College of Buffalo, Buffalo, NY
www.villa.edu

Villanova University, Villanova, PA
www.villanova.edu

Wheeling Jesuit University, Wheeling, WV
www.wju.edu

New England

Albertus Magnus College, New Haven, CT
www.albertus.edu

Anna Maria College, Paxton, MA
www.annamaria.edu

Assumption College, Worcester, MA
www.assumption.edu

Boston College, Chestnut Hill, MA
www.bc.edu

College of Our Lady of the Elms, Chicopee, MA
www.elms.edu

College of St. Joseph in Vermont, Rutland, VT
www.csj.edu

College of the Holy Cross, Worcester, MA
www.holycross.edu

Fairfield University, Fairfield CT
www.fairfield.edu

Holy Cross Fathers Religious, North Easton, MA
www.holycrosscsc.org

Magdalen College, Warner, NH
www.magdalen.edu

Providence College, Providence, RI
www.providence.edu

Rivier College, Nashua, NH
www.rivier.edu

Saint Anselm College, Manchester, NH
www.anselm.edu

Saint Joseph College, West Hartford, CT
www.sjc.edu

Saint Joseph's College, Standish, ME
www.sjcme.edu

Salve Regina University, Newport, RI
www.salve.edu

Saint Michael's College, Colchester, VT
www.smcvt.edu

Stonehill College, North Easton, MA
www.stonehill.edu

The Thomas More College of Liberal Arts,
Merrimack, NH
www.thomasmorecollege.edu

Seminaries in the United States

A recent list of Catholic seminaries in the United States follows by state:

California

Saint John's Seminary, Camarillo
Saint Patrick Seminary, Menlo Park

Colorado

Archdiocesan Redemptoris Mater Missionary Seminary, Archdiocese of Denver
Saint John Vianney Theological Seminary, Denver

Connecticut

Holy Apostles College and Seminary, Cronwell
Marian Friary of Our Lady of Guadalupe, Griswold
Saint John Fisher Seminary, Stamford

District of Columbia

Dominican House of Studies, Washington, DC
National Seminary of the Catholic University of America, Washington, DC
Washington Theological Union, Washington, DC

Florida

Our Lady of Perpetual Help Retreat and Spirituality Center, Venice
Saint John Vianney College Seminary, Miami
Saint Vincent de Paul Regional Seminary, Boyton Beach

Illinois

Archbishop Quigley Preparatory Seminary, Chicago
Catholic Theological Union, Chicago
Immaculate Heart of Mary Novitiate, Missionary Oblates of Mary Immaculate, Godfrey
Mundelein Seminary in University of Saint Mary of the Lake, Chicago
Quigley Preparatory Seminary, Chicago
Saint Joseph College Seminary, Chicago

Indiana

Moreau Seminary at the University of Notre Dame, Notre Dame
Saint Meinrad Archabbey and Seminary, Saint Meinrad

Iowa

Divine Word College Seminary, Epworth
Saint Ambrose Seminary, Diocese of Davenport

Louisiana

Josephite House of Studies, New Orleans
Notre Dame Seminary, New Orleans
Saint Joseph Abbey and Seminary, Saint Benedict
Saint Joseph Seminary College, Saint Benedict

Maryland

Holy Family Seminary, Silver Spring
Mount Saint Mary's College and Seminary, Emmitsburg
Saint Mary's Seminary & University, Baltimore

Massachusetts

Blessed John XXIII National Seminary, Weston
Saint John's Seminary, Brighton

Michigan

Sacred Heart Major Seminary, Detroit

Minnesota

Immaculate Heart of Mary Seminary, Winona
Loyola—A Spiritual Renewal Resource, Saint Paul
Saint Benedict's Monastery, Sisters of the Order of Saint Benedict, Saint Joseph
Saint John Vianney College Seminary, Saint Paul
Saint John's School of Theology and Seminary, Collegeville

Missouri

Aquinas Institute of Theology, Saint Louis
Conception Seminary College, Conception
Kenrick-Glennon Seminary, Archdiocese of Saint Louis
Saint Dominic Priory, Order of Preachers, Saint Louis

Nebraska

Saint Gregory the Great Seminary, Seward

New Jersey

Immaculate Conception Seminary, Seton Hall University, South Orange
"Redemptoris Mater" Archdiocesan Missionary Seminary, Archdiocese of Newark
Saint Michael House of Formation, Ramsey

New York

Cathedral Preparatory Seminary, Elmhurst
Cathedral Seminary Residence of the Immaculate Conception, Brooklyn
Saint Joseph's Seminary, Yonkers
Saint Joseph's Seminary, Dunwoodie
Seminary of the Immaculate Conception, Huntington
Wadhams Hall, Ogdensburg

North Dakota

Cardinal Muench Seminary, Fargo

Ohio

Borromeo College Seminary, Diocese of Cleveland
Mount Saint Mary Seminary, Cincinnati
Pontifical College Josephinum, Columbus
Saint Mary Seminary and Graduate School of Theology, Cleveland

Oregon

Mount Angel Seminary, Saint Benedict

Pennsylvania

Saint Charles Borromeo Seminary, Wynnewood
Saint Vincent Seminary, Latrobe

Texas

Assumption Seminary, San Antonio
Holy Trinity Seminary, Dallas
Moreau House, The Congregation of Holy Cross, Austin
Oblates School of Theology, San Antonio
Saint Charles Borromeo Seminary, El Paso
Saint Mary's Seminary at the University of Saint Thomas, Houston

Washington

Bishop White Seminary, Spokane

Wisconsin

Casa San Antonio, Archdiocese of Milwaukee
Sacred Heart School of Theology, Hales Corner
Saint Francis Seminary, Saint Francis
Saint Lawrence Seminary, Mount Calvary

E. Morality

Morality refers to the goodness or evil of human actions. Listed below are several helps the Church offers for making good and moral decisions.

The Ten Commandments

The Ten Commandments are a main source for Christian morality. The Ten Commandments were revealed by God to Moses. Jesus himself acknowledged them. He told the rich young man, "If you wish to enter into life, keep the commandments" (Mt 19:17). Since the time of Saint Augustine (fourth century), the Ten Commandments have been used as a source for teaching baptismal candidates.

I.	I, the Lord, am your God: you shall not have other gods besides me.
II.	You shall not take the name of the Lord, your God, in vain.
III.	Remember to keep holy the sabbath day.
IV.	Honor your father and your mother.
V.	You shall not kill.
VI.	You shall not commit adultery.
VII.	You shall not steal.
VIII.	You shall not bear false witness against your neighbor.
IX.	You shall not covet your neighbor's wife.
X.	You shall not covet your neighbor's goods.

The Beatitudes

The word *beatitude* means "happiness." Jesus preached the Beatitudes in his Sermon on the Mount. They are:

Blessed are the poor in spirit, for theirs is the kingdom of God.

Blessed are they who mourn, for they will be comforted.

Blessed are the meek, for they will inherit the land.

Blessed are they who hunger and thirst for righteousness, for they will be satisfied.

Blessed are the merciful, for they will be shown mercy.

Blessed are the clean of heart, for they will see God.

Blessed are the peacemakers, for they will be called children of God.

Blessed are they who are persecuted for the sake of righteousness, for theirs is the kingdom of heaven.

Blessed are you when men revile you and persecute you

and utter all kinds of evil against you falsely on my account.

Rejoice and be glad,

for your reward is great in heaven.

Cardinal Virtues

Virtues—habits that help in leading a moral life—that are acquired by human effort are known as moral or human virtues. Four of these are the cardinal virtues as they form the hinge that connect all the others. They are:

- Prudence
- Fortitude
- Justice
- Temperance

Theological Virtues

The theological virtues are the foundation for moral life. They are related directly to God.

- Faith
- Hope
- Love

Corporal (Bodily) Works of Mercy

1. Feed the hungry.
2. Give drink to the thirsty.
3. Clothe the naked.
4. Visit the imprisoned.
5. Shelter the homeless.
6. Visit the sick.
7. Bury the dead.

Spiritual Works of Mercy

1. Counsel the doubtful.
2. Instruct the ignorant.
3. Admonish sinners.
4. Comfort the afflicted.
5. Forgive offenses.
6. Bear wrongs patiently.
7. Pray for the living and the dead.

Precepts of the Church

1. You shall attend Mass on Sundays and on holy days of obligation and rest from servile labor.
2. You shall confess your sins at least once a year.
3. You shall receive the Sacrament of Eucharist at least during the Easter season.
4. You shall observe the days of fasting and abstinence established by the Church.
5. You shall help to provide for the needs of the Church.

Catholic Social Teaching: Major Themes

The 1998 document Sharing Catholic Social Teaching: Challenges and Directions—Reflections of the U.S. Catholic Bishops *highlighted seven principles of the Church's social teaching. They are:*

1. Life and dignity of the human person
2. Call to family, community, and participation
3. Rights and responsibilities
4. Option for the poor and vulnerable
5. The dignity of work and the rights of workers
6. Solidarity
7. God's care for creation

F. Liturgy and Sacraments

The sacraments and the Divine Office constitute the Church's liturgy. The Mass is the most important liturgical celebration.

Church Year

The cycle of seasons and feasts that Catholics celebrate is called the Church Year or Liturgical Year. The Church Year is divided into five main parts: Advent, Christmas, Lent, Easter, and Ordinary Time.

Holy Days of Obligation in the United States

1.	Immaculate Conception of Mary	December 8
2.	Christmas	December 25
3.	Solemnity of Mary, Mother of God	January 1
4.	Ascension of the Lord	Forty days after Easter
5.	Assumption of Mary	August 15
6.	All Saints Day	November 1

The Liturgy of the Hours

The Liturgy of the Hours is part of the official, public prayer of the Church. Along with the celebration of the sacraments, the recitation of the Liturgy of the Hours, or Divine Office, allows for constant praise and thanksgiving to God throughout the day and night.

The Liturgy of the Hours consists of five major divisions:

1. Office of Readings
2. Morning Prayer (Matins)
3. Midday Prayer
4. Evening Prayer (Vespers)
5. Night Prayer (Compline)

Scriptural prayer, especially the Psalms, is at the heart of the Liturgy of the Hours. Each day follows a separate pattern of prayer with themes closely tied in with the liturgical year and feasts of the saints.

The Liturgy of the Hours is traditionally recited by priests and professed religious on behalf of the entire Church. In previous years, lay people prayed the Angelus, a shortened version of the Liturgy of the Hours three times a day: in the morning before work, at the midday lunch break, and in the evening as work lets out (see page 334). The ringing of bells signified these prayer times.

More recently, many lay people have taken to praying the entire long form of the Liturgy of the Hours. Parishes, too, sometimes celebrate Morning Prayer or Evening Prayer.

The Seven Sacraments

1. Baptism

2. Confirmation

3. Eucharist

4. Penance (Reconciliation)

5. Anointing of the Sick

6. Holy Orders

7. Matrimony

Order of the Mass

There are two main parts of the Mass, the Liturgy of the Word and the Liturgy of the Eucharist. The complete order of Mass:

The Introductory Rites

The Entrance
Greeting of the Altar and of the People
    Gathered
The Act of Penitence
The *Kyrie Eleison*
The *Gloria*
The Collect (Opening Prayer)

The Liturgy of the Word

Silence
The Biblical Readings (the reading of the
    Gospel is the high point of theLiturgy of the
    Word)
The Responsorial Pslam
The Homily
The Profession of Faith (Creed)
The Prayer of the Faithful

The Liturgy of the Eucharist

The Preparation of the Gifts
The Prayer over the Offerings
The Eucharistic Prayer
The Communion Rite
The Lord's Prayer
The Rite of Peace
The Fraction (Breaking of the Bread)
Communion
Prayer after Communion

The Concluding Rites

Communion Regulations

To receive Holy Communion properly, a person must be in the state of grace (free from mortal sin), have the right intention (only for the purpose of pleasing God), and observe the communion fast.

The fast means that a person may not eat anything or drink any liquid (other than water) one hour before the reception of communion. There are exceptions made to this fast only for the sick and aged.

How to Go to Confession

Catholics are obligated to confess mortal sins (serious sins that result in the loss of sanctifying grace) in the Sacrament of Penance at least once a year or before receiving Holy Communion, which requires a state of grace. Although we are not required to confess venial sins (sins that weaken but do not destroy our relationship with God), doing so helps us grow in the spiritual life. Following is a process for celebrating the Sacrament of Penance:

1. Spend some time examining your conscience. Consider your actions and attitudes in each area of your life (e.g., faith, family, school/work, social life, relationships). Ask yourself, "Is this area of my life pleasing to God? What needs to be reconciled with God? With others? With myself?"

2. Sincerely tell God that you are sorry for your sins. Ask God for forgiveness and for the grace you will need to change what needs changing in your life. Promise God that you will try to live according to his will for you.

3. Approach the area for confession. Wait an appropriate distance until it is your turn.

4. Make the Sign of the Cross with the priest. He may say: "May God, who has enlightened every heart, help you to know your sins and trust his mercy." You reply: "Amen."

5. Confess your sins to the priest. Simply and directly talk to him about the areas of sinfulness in your life that need God's healing touch.

6. The priest will ask you to pray an act of contrition. Pray an Act of Contrition you have committed to memory (see page 335). Or, saying something in your own words, like: "Dear God, I am sorry for my sins. I ask for your forgiveness and I promise to do better in the future."

7. The priest will talk to you about your life, encourage you to be more faithful to God in the future, and help you decide what to do to make up for your sins—your penance.

8. The priest will then extend his hands over your head and pray the Church's official prayer of absolution:

   "God, the Father of mercies, through the death and resurrection of his Son, has reconciled the world to himself and sent the Holy Spirit among us for the forgiveness of sins; through the ministry of the Church may God give you pardon and peace, and I absolve you from your sins in the name of the Father, and of the Son, and of the Holy Spirit."

   You respond: "Amen."

9. The priest will wish you peace. Thank him and leave.

10. Go to a quiet place in church and pray your prayer of penance. Then spend some time quietly thanking God for the gift of forgiveness.

G. Mary and the Saints

The doctrine of the communion of saints flows from our belief that we Christians are closely united as one family in the Spirit of Jesus Christ. Mary is the Queen of the Saints. Her role in the Church flows from an inseparable union with her Son.

Mother of God

Mary, the mother of Jesus, is the closest human to cooperate with her Son's work of redemption. For this reason, the Church holds her in a special place. Of her many titles, the most significant is that she is the Mother of God.

The Church teaches several truths about Mary.

First, she was conceived immaculately. This means from the very first moment of her existence she was without sin and "full of grace." This belief is called the Immaculate Conception. The Feast of the Immaculate Conception is celebrated on December 8.

Second, Mary was ever-virgin. She was a virgin before, in, and after the birth of Jesus. As his mother, she cared for him in infancy and raised him to adulthood with the help of her husband, Joseph. She witnessed Jesus' preaching and ministry, was at the foot of his cross at his crucifixion, and present with the Apostles as they awaited the coming of the Holy Spirit at Pentecost.

Third, at the time of her death, Mary was assumed body and soul into heaven. This dogma was proclaimed as a matter of faith by Pope Pius XII in 1950. The Feast of the Assumption is celebrated on August 15.

The Church has always been devoted to the Blessed Virgin. This devotion is different than that given to God—Father, Son, and Holy Spirit. Rather, the Church is devoted to Mary as her first disciple, the Queen of all Saints, and her own Mother. Quoting the fathers of the Second Vatican Council:

> In the meantime the Mother of Jesus, in the glory which she possesses in body and soul in heaven, is the image and the beginning of the Church as it is to be perfected in the world to come. Likewise she shines forth on earth, until the day of the Lord shall come, a sign of certain hope and comfort to the pilgrim People of God. (*Lumen Gentium*, 68)

Marian Feasts Throughout the Year

January 1	Solemnity of Mary, Mother of God
March 25	Annunciation of the Lord
May 31	Visitation
August 15	Assumption
August 22	Queenship of Mary
September 8	Birth of Mary
September 15	Our Lady of Sorrows
October 7	Our Lady of the Rosary
November 21	Presentation of Mary
December 8	Immaculate Conception
December 12	Our Lady of Guadalupe

Canonization of Saints

Saints are those who are in glory with God in Heaven. *Canonization* refers to a solemn declaration by the Pope that a person who either died a martyr or who lived an exemplary Christian life is in Heaven and may be honored and imitated by all Christians.

The canonization process first involves a process of beatification that includes a thorough investigation of the person's life, and certification of miracles that can be attributed to the candidate's intercession.

The first official canonization of the universal Church on record was Saint Ulrich of Augsburg by Pope John XV in 993.

Some non-Catholics criticize Catholics for "praying to saints." Catholics *honor* saints for their holy lives but we do not pray to them as if they were God. We ask the saints to pray with us and for us as part of the Church in glory. We can ask them to do this because we know that their lives have been spent in close communion with God. We also ask the saints for their friendship so that we can follow the example they have left for us.

H. Devotions

Catholics have also expressed their piety around the Church's sacramental life through practices like the veneration of relics, visits to churches, pilgrimages, processions, the Stations of the Cross, religious dances, the rosary, medals, and many more. This section lists some popular Catholic devotions.

The Rosary

Joyful Mysteries

1. The Annunciation
2. The Visitation
3. The Nativity
4. The Presentation in the Temple
5. The Finding of Jesus in the Temple

Mysteries of Light

1. Jesus' Baptism in the Jordan River
2. Jesus' Self-manifestation at the Wedding of Cana
3. The Proclamation of the Kingdom of God and Jesus' Call to Conversion
4. The Transfiguration
5. The Institution of the Eucharist at the Last Supper

Sorrowful Mysteries

1. The Agony in the Garden
2. The Scourging at the Pillar
3. The Crowning with Thorns
4. The Carrying of the Cross
5. The Crucifixion

Glorious Mysteries

1. The Resurrection
2. The Ascension
3. The Descent of the Holy Spirit
4. The Assumption of Mary
5. The Crowning of Mary as the Queen of Heaven and Earth

How to Pray the Rosary

Opening

1. Begin on the crucifix and pray the Apostles' Creed.
2. On the first bead, pray the Our Father.
3. On the next three beads, pray the Hail Mary. (Some people meditate on the virtues of faith, hope, and charity on these beads.)
4. On the fifth bead, pray the Glory Be.

The Body

Each decade (set of ten beads) is organized as follows:

1. On the larger bead that comes before each set of ten, announce the mystery to be prayed (see above) and pray one Our Father.
2. On each of the ten smaller beads, pray one Hail Mary while meditating on the mystery.
3. Pray one Glory Be at the end of the decade. (There is no bead for the Glory Be.)

Conclusion

Pray the following prayer at the end of the rosary:

Hail, Holy Queen (see pages 333–334)

Stations of the Cross

The Stations of the Cross are a devotion and also a sacramental. (A sacramental is a sacred object, blessing, or devotion.) The Stations of the Cross are individual pictures or symbols hung on the interior walls of most Catholic churches depicting fourteen steps along Jesus' way to the cross. Praying the stations means meditating on each of the following scenes:

1. *Jesus is condemned to death.*
2. *Jesus takes up his cross.*
3. *Jesus falls the first time.*
4. *Jesus meets his mother.*
5. *Simon of Cyrene helps Jesus carry his cross.*
6. *Veronica wipes the face of Jesus.*

7.   Jesus falls the second time.

8.   Jesus consoles the women of Jerusalem.

9.   Jesus falls the third time.

10. Jesus is stripped of his garments.

11. Jesus is nailed to the cross.

12. Jesus dies on the cross.

13. Jesus is taken down from the cross.

14. Jesus is laid in the tomb.

Some churches also include a fifteenth station, the resurrection of the Lord.

Novenas

The novena consists of the recitation of certain prayers over a period of nine days. The symbolism of nine days refers to the time Mary and the Apostles spent in prayer between Jesus' Ascension into Heaven and Pentecost.

Many novenas are dedicated to Mary or to a saint with the faith and hope that she or he will intercede for the one making the novena. Novenas to Saint Jude, Saint Anthony, Our Lady of Perpetual Help, and Our Lady of Lourdes remain popular in the Church today.

The Divine Praises

These praises are traditionally recited after the benediction of the Blessed Sacrament.

Blessed be God.
Blessed be his holy name.
Blessed be Jesus Christ, true God and true man.
Blessed be the name of Jesus.
Blessed be his most Sacred Heart.
Blessed be his most Precious Blood.
Blessed be Jesus in the most holy sacrament of the altar.
Blessed be the Holy Spirit, the Paraclete.
Blessed be the great Mother of God, Mary most holy.

Blessed be her holy and Immaculate Conception.
Blessed be her glorious Assumption.
Blessed be the name of Mary, Virgin and Mother.
Blessed be Saint Joseph, her most chaste spouse.
Blessed be God in his angels and in his saints.

I. Prayers

Some common Catholic prayers are listed below. The Latin translation for three of the prayers is included. Latin is the official language of the Church. There are several occasions when you might pray in Latin; for example, at a World Youth Day when you are with young people who speak many different languages.

Sign of the Cross

In the name of the Father,
and of the Son,
and of the Holy Spirit.
Amen.

In nómine
    Patris,
et Filii,
et Spíritus
    Sancti.
Amen.

Our Father

Our Father
who art in heaven,
hallowed be thy name.
Thy kingdom come;
thy will be done on earth as it is in heaven.
Give us this day our daily bread
and forgive us our trespasses
as we forgive those who trespass against us.
And lead us not into temptation,
but deliver us from evil.
Amen.

Pater Noster qui es in caelis:
sanctificétur Nomen Tuum;
advéniat Regnum Tuum;
fiat volúntas Tua,
sicut in caelo, et in terra.
Panem nostrum
cotidiánum da nobis hódie;
et dimítte nobis débita nostra,
sicut et nos
dimíttimus debitóribus nostris;
Et ne nos inducas in tentatiónem,
sed libera nos a Malo.
Amen.

Glory Be

Glory be to the Father
and to the Son
and to the Holy Spirit,
as it was in the beginning,
is now,
and ever shall be,
world without end. Amen.

Glória Patri
et Filio
et Spiritui Sancto.
Sicut erat in princípio,
et nunc et semper,
et in sae-cula saeculórum.
Amen.

Hail Mary

Hail Mary, full of grace,
the Lord is with thee.
Blessed art thou among women
and blessed is the fruit of thy womb, Jesus.
Holy Mary, Mother of God,
pray for us sinners now
and at the hour of our death. Amen.

Ave, María, grátia plena,
Dóminus tecum.
Benedicta tu in muliéribus,
et benedíctus fructus ventris
tui, Iesus.
Sancta María, Mater Dei,
ora pro nobis peccatóribus
nunc et in hora mortis nostrae.
Amen.

Memorare

Remember, O most gracious Virgin Mary,
that never was it known
that anyone who fled to your protection,
implored your help,
or sought your intercession was left unaided.
Inspired by this confidence,
I fly unto you,
O virgin of virgins, my mother,
To you I come, before you I stand,
sinful and sorrowful.
O Mother of the Word Incarnate,
despise not my petitions,
but in your mercy hear and answer me. Amen.

Hail, Holy Queen

Hail, holy Queen, Mother of Mercy,
our life, our sweetness and our hope!
To you do we cry,
poor banished children of Eve;
to you do we send up our sighs,

mourning and weeping in this valley of tears.
Turn then, O most gracious advocate,
your eyes of mercy toward us,
and after this exile,
show us the blessed fruit of your womb, Jesus.
O clement, O loving, O sweet Virgin Mary.
V.   Pray for us, O holy Mother of God.
R.   that we may be made worthy of the promises
     of Christ. Amen.

The Angelus

V.   The angel spoke God's message to Mary.
R.   And she conceived by the Holy Spirit.

Hail Mary . . .

V.   Behold the handmaid of the Lord.
R.   May it be done unto me according to your
     word.

Hail Mary . . .

V.   And the Word was made flesh.
R.   And dwelled among us.

Hail Mary . . .

V.   Pray for us, O holy Mother of God.
R.   That we may be made worthy of the promises
     of Christ.

Let us pray: We beseech you, O Lord, to pour out
your grace into our hearts. By the message of an
angel we have learned of the Incarnation of Christ,
your Son; lead us by his Passion and Cross to the
glory of the resurrection. Through the same Christ
our Lord. Amen.

Regina Caeli

*Q*ueen of heaven, rejoice, alleluia.
The Son you merited to bear, alleluia,
has risen as he said, alleluia.
Pray to God for us, alleluia.

V. Rejoice and be glad, O Virgin Mary, alleluia.
R. For the Lord has truly risen, alleluia.

Let us pray.

God of life, you have given joy to the world by the
Resurrection of your son, our Lord Jesus Christ.
Through the prayers of his Mother, the Virgin Mary,
bring us to the happiness of eternal life. We ask this
through Christ our Lord. Amen.

Grace at Meals

Before Meals

*B*less us, O Lord,
and these your gifts,
which we are about to receive from your bounty,
through Christ our Lord. Amen.

After Meals

*W*e give you thanks, almighty God,
for these and all the gifts
which we have received
from your goodness
through Christ our Lord. Amen.

Guardian Angel Prayer

Angel of God, my guardian dear,
to whom God's love commits me here,
ever this day be at my side,
to light and guard, to rule and guide. Amen.

Prayer for the Faithful Departed

V. Eternal rest grant unto them, O Lord.

R. And let perpetual light shine upon them.

V. May their souls and the souls of all the faithful departed,
    through the mercy of God, rest in peace.

R. Amen.

Morning Offering

O Jesus, through the Immaculate Heart of Mary, I offer you my prayers, works, joys, and sufferings of this day in union with the Holy Sacrifice of the Mass throughout the world. I offer them for all the intentions of your Sacred Heart: the salvation of souls, reparation for sin, the reunion of all Christians. I offer them for the intentions of our bishops and all members of the apostleship of prayer and in particular for those recommended by your Holy Father this month. Amen.

Act of Faith

O God,
I firmly believe all the truths that you have revealed
and that you teach us through your Church,
for you are truth itself
and can neither deceive nor be deceived.
Amen.

Act of Hope

O God,
I hope with complete trust that you will give me,
through the merits of Jesus Christ, all necessary grace in this world
and everlasting life in the world to come,
for this is what you have promised
and you always keep your promises.
Amen.

Act of Love

O my God, I love you above all things, with my whole heart and soul, because you are all good and worthy of all my love. I love my neighbor as myself for the love of you. I forgive all who have injured me, and I ask pardon of all whom I have injured. Amen.

Act of Contrition

O my God, I am heartily sorry for having offending Thee, and I detest all my sins because of thy just punishments, but most of all because they offend Thee, my God, who art all good and deserving of all my love. I firmly resolve with the help of Thy grace to sin no more and to avoid the near occasion of sin. Amen.

glossary

alb—The long white linen robe worn by anyone who takes a leadership role at Mass. It is connected to the tradition of the newly baptized putting on the white robe of purity after they have received the Sacrament. Only the clergy may wear a stole over the alb.

altar of holocausts—In the Old Testament, a small mound of stones upon which the flesh of sacrificed animals could be burned. The word holocaust means "sacrifice."

annulment—The Church's declaration that a sacramental marriage was invalid, that it never existed in the first place.

apostolate—An association of men and women committed to discerning ways to apply the Gospel to everyday life.

apostolic letter—A document issued by the Pope or Vatican for various appointments, approving religious congregations, designating basilicas, and the like.

apostolic succession—The handing on of the Apostles' preaching and authority that occurred directly from the Apostles to the bishops through the laying on of hands.

archbishop—An honorary title for a bishop who heads a larger diocese or a diocese of special importance.

benediction—The rite in which Jesus is exposed to the adoration of the faithful in the Blessed Sacrament contained in a monstrance. It is not so much the priest who blesses the people in this rite, but Jesus himself.

career—A chosen occupation that is more likely to express one's talents than a job.

catechesis—The process of religious instruction and formation in the Christian faith.

catechumen—An unbaptized person who is undergoing instruction and formation in preparation for reception of the Sacraments of Initiation.

centering prayer—A method of prayer which readies us to receive the gift of God's presence by quieting our spirit to allow God to rest within.

charism—A special blessing of a religious community that helps to define its particular mission and spirituality.

chastity—The virtue by which a person integrates his or her sexuality into his or her whole self, body, and spirit, according to the vocation or state in life.

chasuble—The outer garment worn by the priest over the alb and stole. It is the same color as the stole and the liturgical season.

Church—The Church is the community of people who profess faith in Jesus Christ and who are guided by the Holy Spirit. The Roman Catholic Church is guided by the Pope and his bishops. The Apostles' Creed describes the Church as one, holy, catholic, and apostolic.

civil divorce—The dissolution of the marriage contract by the legal system.

clergy—From a Latin word for "clerk," the clergy is distinguished from the laity and is made up of deacons, priests, and bishops.

coitus—A term for sexual intercourse between a man and a woman.

collegiality—The participation of each of the worldwide bishops, with the Pope as their head, in a "college," which takes responsibility for both their local diocesan churches and the Church as a whole.

common priesthood—The priesthood of the faithful. Christ has made the Church a "kingdom of priests" who share in his priesthood through the Sacraments of Baptism and Confirmation.

conjugal love—The total love between a husband and wife that encompasses their entire being, body and soul.

continence—Partial or complete abstinence from sexual activity.

contraception—A method of preventing pregnancy that is intended to alter or avoid the body's natural state of fertility. Examples include condoms, the pill, and the intra-uterine device. The Church condemns the use of any artificial contraception.

covenant—A sacred and unbreakable agreement between human beings or between God and a human being that involves mutual commitments. The New Covenant is made in the name of Jesus Christ and it brings salvation to the world.

crosier—A crook-shaped staff carried by bishops to represent the bishop's pastoral or shepherding role.

CYO—Letters that stand for Catholic Youth Organization. The CYO provides opportunities for young people to develop strong moral character, self-esteem, and leadership qualities through activities of a social, educational, recreational, and athletic nature.

diakonia—A Greek word that literally means "service."

direct abortion—The deliberate and intentional killing of unborn human life by means of medical or surgical procedures.

discipleship—From the word "learner," the undertaking of learning and following Jesus Christ.

discipline—A process of training that is expected to produce an acceptable pattern of behavior as well as improved mental and social character.

divine providence—God's interest and action in guiding his creation to perfection.

divinized—In the Christian sense, sharing or partaking the nature of God.

dogmas—Central truths of Revelation that Catholics are obliged to believe.

domestic church—The "domestic church" is a name for the family, the Church in miniature.

dowry—Money or property brought to the bride's family by her husband at their marriage, or money or property given by the bride's family to the husband.

Ecumenical Council—A worldwide official assembly of the bishops under the direction of the Pope. There have been twenty-one Ecumenical Councils. The first was the First Council of Nicaea (325). The most recent was the Second Vatican Council (1962–1965).

ecumenism—The movement that seeks Christian unity and eventually the unity of all peoples throughout the world.

efficacious—Something that embodies the reality it represents.

eremitic life—The life of a hermit; a person who chooses the eremitic life most often lives alone and devotes himself or herself to developing a deep intimacy with Christ through silence, prayer, and penance.

evangelical counsels—Virtues needed to achieve perfection in Christian life: poverty, chastity, and obedience.

evangelization—To bring the good news of Jesus to others.

excommunication—A severe Church penalty resulting from serious crimes against the Catholic religion, imposed by Church authorities or incurred as a direct result of the commission of an offense.

exploitation—Using another person or group for selfish purposes, including for sexual gratification.

faith—One of the theological virtues. Faith is an acknowledgment of and allegiance to God.

feudal system—A political and economic system of the Middle Ages that traded use of land for obedience to the owner of the land.

fiancée—Meaning "to trust," a fiancée is a woman to whom a man is engaged to be married. The man engaged to the woman is called the fiancé.

filial love—Typically, this is the type of love that children have for their parents or siblings or friends have for each other.

free will—God's gift that allows us to shape our own lives and direct ourselves to the goodness God intends.

grace—The supernatural gift of God's friendship and life. Grace allows us to respond to God and share in his nature and eternal life.

Holy Family—The family of Joseph, Mary, and Jesus in which Jesus was raised and lived until he began his public ministry.

Ignatian spirituality—Following the example of Saint Ignatius, Ignatian spirituality centers on the imitation of Christ—focusing on those priorities that constitute his mind, heart, values, priorities, and loves.

impediments—External circumstances or facts that prevent a sacramental or legal marriage from taking place.

Incarnation—The taking on of human nature by God's Son.

infallibility—The charism or gift of the Church offered by Christ whereby it is protected from error in matters of faith and morals. This gift is most exclusively exercised by a Pope or an Ecumenical Council of bishops acting in union with him.

Jubilee Year—According to Jewish law, the Jubilee Year ocured every fiftieth year when all debts were removed and slaves freed. In Catholicism, the term is connected with a Holy Year in which the Pope grants special spiritual benefits to those who perform religious acts, including making a pilgrimage to Rome.

laity—All of the baptized faithful except those who have received the Sacrament of Holy Orders.

Last Judgment—The event that will take place at the end of time when Jesus comes to fully establish the Kingdom of God, bring final victory over evil, and judge the living and the dead.

lectio divina—A classical prayer practice that involves a prayerful reading of the Bible. It means "holy reading."

Lectionary—The book that contains the Scripture readings that have been chosen by the Church for public reading at Mass according to the liturgical calendar.

Litany of the Saints—A prayer made up of various petitions addressed to the saints. It was first prescribed by Pope Saint Gregory the Great in the sixth century.

Liturgy of the Hours—The official daily prayer of the Church. It is also called the "Divine Office." It is a set of prayers for certain times of the day in response to Saint Paul's command to "pray without ceasing" (1 Thes 5:17).

Magisterium—The teaching office of the Church. It was given by Jesus to Peter and the other Apostles and extends it to the Pope and the bishops.

marriage banns—Announcements of a couple's intention to be married printed in a parish bulletin for the three weekends preceding the marriage.

marriage tribunal—A staff of diocesan representatives of the bishop who have received special education and instruction to represent the Church in proceedings for marriage cases.

martyrdom—Giving one's life for one's faith. A martyr is willing to die in support of the Christian faith and doctrine.

messianic secret—A motif in the Gospel of Mark in which the recognition of the identity of Jesus as the Son of God is suppressed.

moral relativism—The belief that the standards of right and wrong are arbitrary or transitory, determined by the individual or culture.

mortifications—Ways to discipline the body and appetites by self-denial.

mystery—In a religious sense, a truth that is incomprehensible to reason and knowable only through God's Revelation.

Natural Family Planning—NFP is the Church-approved method for planning and spacing the birth of children in marriage.

nuncio—An archbishop who acts as the official Vatican delegate for a country. He is also called the Apostolic Delegate.

nuptial blessing—Nuptial is a Latin-derived word that means wedding. The nuptial blessing is intended for the bride and the marriage covenant. It takes place after the couple gives their consent to be married.

Original Sin—The first sin of Adam and Eve, in which they disobeyed the Commandment of God, choosing to follow their own will rather than God's will. The effects of Original Sin have been shared with humanity ever since.

ovulation—The time in a woman's fertile cycle when an egg is released from her ovary.

particular judgment—God's judgment immediately after death on whether we go to Purgatory, Heaven, or hell.

Paschal Mystery—The way our salvation is made known through the Life, Death, Resurrection, and Ascension of Jesus Christ. The Paschal Mystery is made present in the sacraments, especially the Eucharist.

pastors—From the word "shepherd," pastors such as the Pope and bishops care for the people using the model of Christ the Good Shepherd.

pluralism—A condition in which several distinct ethnic, religious, or cultural groups are present and tolerated within a society.

primacy—The Pope, as successor of St. Peter as Bishop of Rome, exercises highest authority as Vicar of Christ and shepherd of the whole Church.

purgatory—Purification after death for those who die in God's friendship, yet still need to be purified to attain holiness before entering Heaven.

rectory—The house in which a pastor and other parish priests live.

redemption—God's saving action through Jesus Christ that saved people from sin and death.

religious novices—Women or men who have entered a religious order but have yet to take their final vows.

religious superior—The head or leader of a religious community charged with cultivating in the members of the community a spirit of obedience to God's will, the Church, and the rules of the community as well as fostering a lifestyle of prayer, fraternal love, and commitment to ministry.

Sacraments at the Service of Communion—The Sacraments of Holy Orders and Matrimony, which, unlike the sacraments of initiation, are directed towards the salvation of others. "They confer a particular mission in the Church and serve to build up the People of God" (CCC, 1534).

sanctification—A word that means holiness or blessing. To sanctify means to consecrate or set apart for sacred use.

sees—The official seats, or centers of authority, of the office of a bishop.

seminarians—Men who attend a seminary or school focusing on theology in training and formation for the life of a priest.

seminaries—The place where the training of candidates for the priesthood takes place. The Council of Trent instructed the bishops in each diocese to set up a seminary college to train men for the priesthood.

sexual fidelity—The faithfulness of a husband and wife to each other and their marriage vows.

stole—A long, narrow cloth that comes in the color of the liturgical season and is worn by the bishop, priest, or deacon. Stoles were originally worn by Jewish rabbis as a sign of their authority.

surrogate mother—A woman who carries another woman's child by pre-arrangement or by legal contract.

temperance—The cardinal moral virtue that moderates the attraction of pleasure and provides balance in the use of created goods.

third-order Franciscan—Founded by Saint Francis of Assisi, the third order is comprised of people who are committed to living the Franciscan rule while out in the world.

virtues—Good habits that enable us to live a moral life.

vocation director—A contact person for a religious order or for a diocesan office dedicated to answering questions of inquirers and encouraging vocations.

index